MASS
COMMUNICATION

MASS
COMMUNICATION
an introduction

John R. Bittner

*The University of North Carolina
at Chapel Hill*

PRENTICE-HALL, INC.
ENGLEWOOD CLIFFS, NEW JERSEY 07632

Library of Congress Cataloging in Publication Data

Bittner, John R (date)
   Mass communication, an introduction.

   (Prentice-Hall series in speech communication)
   Includes bibliographies and index.
   1. Mass media.   I. Title.
P90.B515   1980   301.16'1   79-26615
ISBN 0-13-559278-X

© 1980, 1977 by Prentice-Hall, Inc., Englewood Cliffs, N.J. 07632

PRINTED IN THE UNITED STATES OF AMERICA

10   9   8   7   6   5   4   3

Prentice-Hall International, Inc., London
Prentice-Hall of Australia Pty. Limited, Sydney
Prentice-Hall of Canada, Ltd., Toronto
Prentice-Hall of India Private Limited, New Delhi
Prentice-Hall of Japan, Inc., Tokyo
Prentice-Hall of Southeast Asia Pte. Ltd., Singapore
Whitehall Books Limited, Wellington, New Zealand

for Denise

Contents

Preface, xix

1

WHAT IS MASS COMMUNICATION?   1

The Evolution of Mass Communication, 1
Beginnings of language, 2
Functional requirements of society, 2
Print technology, 2
New distribution systems, 2
Electronic communication, 6
Distinguishing among Types of Communication, 7
Intrapersonal communication, 8
Interpersonal communication, 9
Mass communication, 10
Characteristics of Mass Communication, 10
The gatekeeper concept, 10
Delayed feedback, 11
The Social Context of Mass Communication, 13
Changing Definitions: Specialized Audiences, Specialized Media, 13
Media and media systems, 13
Media and the postindustrial state, 15
Summary, 16
Opportunities for Further Learning, 17

2

NEWSPAPERS   18

Characteristics of a Newspaper, 19
An International Beginning, 19
   The posted bulletins, 19
   European foundations of the modern press, 20
   The English heritage, 21
Newspapering in Early America, 22
   Early colonial newspapers, 22
   The John Peter Zenger case, 24
   Surviving the revolution, 25
   The telegraph and instant news, 25
   The Atlantic cable: A link with Europe, 25
   The penny press, 26
The Minority Press, 28
   The black press, 28
   The American Indian press, 29
Women in Journalism, 31
The War between the States, 32
Reconstruction and Westward Expansion, 34
Yellow Journalism, 36
Newspapers and Newsgathering: The Twentieth Century, 38
The Changing Industry, 40
   Economic indicators, 41
   Newsprint: Cost and supply, 43
   Living with labor and new technology, 44
   Newspaper advertising, 45
The Electronic Newsroom, 46
   From hot to cold type, 46
   Goodbye to typewriters? 47
   Computer technology in advertising and distribution, 49
   Teletext, 49
Expanding Enterprises, 49
   Newspaper chains, 49
   Diversified holdings, 51
   Pros and cons of the media conglomerate, 51
Summary, 53
Opportunities for Further Learning, 54

3

MAGAZINES   56

Finding an Audience, 56
Prosperity and Transition, 57
Decline of Mass Circulation Magazines, 57
Reintroducing Familiar Publications, 58
Modern Magazine Publishing: The Specialized Audience, 61
   Special editions, 62
   Regional editions, 64
   International editions, 64
   New target audiences: New publications, 64
Characteristics and Types of Magazines, 67

Marketing Magazines, 71
    The audience and the advertiser, 71
    Magazine reader loyalty, 72
    Economic considerations, 73
Summary, 76
Opportunities for Further Learning, 77

4

BOOK PUBLISHING   78
Beginnings of Book Publishing, 79
Publishing and "Binding" in Colonial America, 82
Mass Textbook Publishing, 84
The Dime Novels, 85
Mass Market Paperback Book Publishing, 85
    Distributing paperbacks, 86
    Promoting paperbacks, 88
New Formats, 88
    Personalized books, 89
    Fotonovels, 89
Issues in the Book Publishing Industry, 90
    Distribution, printing, paper, 90
    New ventures: New income, 90
Regional Publishing, 92
Future Management Decisions, 92
Summary, 93
Opportunities for Further Learning, 94

5

RADIO   95
The Birth of Wireless: Marconi, 96
Improving Wireless, 98
    Fleming and de Forest, 98
    Voice broadcasting, 98
Radio Comes of Age, 99
    The early stations, 99
    Competition and cross licensing, 101
    WEAF: Beginnings of commercial radio, 102
Network Radio, 103
    NBC, 103
    ABC, 103
    CBS, 104
    Mutual, 105
    National Public Radio, 106
    The role of radio networks, 106
FM Radio, 107
Programming, 108
    Becoming a mass medium, 108
    The medium becomes specialized, 110
    Educational radio, 111

Impact of Radio, 112
    Radio's acceptance and potential, 112
    Radio's future perspective, 114
Summary, 116
Opportunities for Further Learning, 116

6

TELEVISION   117

Early Development, 117
    Nipkow's scanning disc, 117
    Zworykin and Farnsworth, 118
    Experimental programming succeeds, 120
    Color, the freeze, and UHF, 120
    Developments in television technology: Beyond the iconoscope, 121
Trends in Television Programming, 122
    The golden era, 122
    1960s: Politics and space, 122
    The 1970s, 124
Consumer Pressure and Self-Regulation, 126
    Pressure on government and industry, 126
    The NAB codes, 127
    Code enforcement, 127
Television Journalism, 128
    Surviving the red scares, 128
    TV news and technology: Microwave and ENG, 129
Public Broadcasting, 131
    Early stations and NET, 132
    The First Carnegie Commission and CPB, 134
    The Public Broadcasting Act and CPB, 134
    The Public Broadcasting Service—PBS, 135
    Affiliates, organizations, and licensees, 136
    Carnegie Commission II, 136
Television's Impact and Future, 136
Summary, 139
Opportunities for Further Learning, 140

7

PHOTOGRAPHY AND PHOTOJOURNALISM   141

Camera Obscura, 141
A Permanent Image, 142
    Niepce and Daguerre, 143
    Improving the photosensitive plate, 144
    George Eastman, 144
Early Illustrated Reporting, 146
    Sketch artists and illustrated newspapers, 146
    Illustrating westward expansion, 147
Photography Makes an Impact, 149
    Mathew Brady, 149
    The invention of the halftone, 150
The Tabloids, 152

Magazines and Documentary Photography, 154
  Life and Look, 154
  Still photography as documentary, 156
The Future, 157
Summary, 157
Opportunities for Further Learning, 158

8

MOTION PICTURES 159

Toward Reproducing Motion, 159
  Images and sequence, 160
  Edison's contributions, 160
  Projection: The Lumière Brothers, 160
  Expanding the story line: Méliès and Porter, 162
D. W. Griffith and the Silent Era, 164
  The technique, 164
  "The Birth of a Nation," and "Intolerance," 165
Silent Comedy: Sennett and Chaplin, 167
Laurel and Hardy, Keaton, and Lloyd, 169
Other Stars, Producers, Directors, 170
  Pickford and Fairbanks, 171
  Ince, DeMille, von Stroheim, 171
Lavish Sets, Lavish Scenery, 172
The International Influence, 170
  Germany and "The Cabinet of Dr. Caligari," 173
  Russia and "Potemkin," 174
  France and "Un Chien Andalou," 175
  "The Passion of Joan of Arc," 175
The Arrival of Sound, 176
  Technology, 177
  Restraint on creativity, 177
  Transition: Actors and directors, 178
Hollywood: The 1930s to World War II, 180
  Animation: The work of Walt Disney, 180
  The stars, 182
  The directors, 183
  "Gone with the Wind," and "Citizen Kane," 185
Film through the 50s: Changes and Trends, 187
  Transition to television, 187
  Spectaculars, 189
  Other solutions, 189
The Modern Era: Financial Transition, 190
  Big bank financing, 190
  Low budgets and big profits, 192
Accent on Youth, 193
Directors Leave their Mark, 194
Drawing Cards: Violence and Sex, 196
Emerging Black Films and Black Stars, 197
New Epics, 197
1980s: The Cartoon as Feature Film, 199
Summary, 200
Opportunities for Further Learning, 201

9

THE RECORDING INDUSTRY   203

Scope of the Recording Industry, 203
Prerecording Era: Broadsides and Sheet Music, 204
Beginnings of Acoustical Recording, 207
    The phonograph: Edison and Cros, 207
    The graphophone: Bell and Tainter, 210
    The gramophone: Berliner and Johnson, 212
The Electrical Era, 215
    John P. Maxfield and electrical recording, 215
    Rise and fall of depression profits, 216
    Battle of the speeds, 217
Tape, Television, and Stereo, 218
The Recording Artist: A Rising Identity, 218
Rock and Roll, 219
Disco, 222
    The dance beat, 222
    The stars, 222
    New role for the disc jockey, 223
Making a Hit Record, 223
    Demo and master recording sessions, 223
    Promoting the record, 225
    The charts, 225
Understanding Charts and Playlists, 227
    Billboard, 227
    Playlists, 228
    Syndicated charts and playlists, 228
Economic Issues, 228
    Promotion costs, 229
    Distribution, 230
    Pirating, 230
Summary, 231
Opportunities for Further Learning, 231

10

ADVERTISING AND PUBLIC RELATIONS   233

The Functioning of Ad Agencies, 233
    Talent, 234
    Research, 234
    Distribution, 235
    Monitoring feedback, 236
Economics of Ad Agencies, 239
    Ad agency income, 240
    Public relations, 241
    Future costs of making impressions, 241
    The agency's position, 243
Types of Advertising, 243
    Standard advertising, 243
    Public service advertising, 243
    Social responsibility advertising, 244
    Counter-advertising, 245

Corrective advertising, 247
Advocacy advertising, 248
Image advertising, 249
Advertising Appeals, 249
Value appeals, 249
Appeals to basic needs, 253
Our Perceptions of Advertising, 255
Public Relations, 256
Philosophy of public relations, 256
The publicity function, 257
Summary, 258
Opportunities for Further Learning, 259

11

MASS MEDIA NEWS   261

The Gatekeeper Chain, 261
The Gatekeeper Group, 263
News Diffusion, 265
Source and Media Credibility, 266
Forces Affecting News Selection, 267
Economics, 267
Legal restrictions, 268
Deadlines, 268
Personal and professional ethics, 269
Competition, 271
News value, 272
The news hole, 272
Attention factors, 273
Peer group pressure, 273
Reacting to feedback, 274
Processing News Under Crisis Conditions, 274
Summary, 276
Opportunities for Further Learning, 276

12

MEDIA DELIVERY SYSTEMS: CABLE, SATELLITES, AND COMPUTERS   278

Cable, 278
Components of a cable system, 281
Uses and issues, 283
Policy concerns affecting cable, 283
Regulating Cable, 285
Regulatory conflicts, 286
State control of cable, 286
Satellites, 287
Sputnik through SYNCOM, 287
COMSAT and INTELSAT, 291
Domestic satellite systems: Westar and Satcom, 291
Political Issues and Control of Satellites, 292
Legalities and cultural integrity, 292
International law, 292

Computer Technology, 293
   Operation and application, 294
   Transition to computer technology, 296
Summary, 297
Opportunities for Further Learning, 298

13

WIRE SERVICES, SYNDICATES, AND NETWORKS   299

The Wire Service Concept, 299
   In the beginning: AP and Reuters, 300
   Reuters pigeon service, 300
   Dissension in the AP ranks, 300
   John Vandercook and United Press, 301
Using a Wire Service, 302
   Backgrounding stories, 303
   Audio services, 303
   Pictures wires, 304
   Video feeds, 304
The Bureau's Role in Gathering News, 304
   Reporters, photographers, and technicians, 304
   Covering major events, 305
The Subscriber's Role in Gathering News, 306
Specialized Wire Services, 306
Wire Services and New Technology, 307
   Access to stories, 307
   Increased channel capacity, 308
Feature Syndicates, 308
Syndicated Comics, 309
   The readership, 310
   Panel cartoons, 310
Early Syndicate Development, 310
   Hearst and King Features, 311
   John Dille and Buck Rogers, 311
Scope of Syndicates: Golf to Gall Bladers, 311
Syndicated Broadcast Programming, 312
How Networks Operate, 313
Networks and Other Businesses, 314
The Network-Affiliate Relationship, 316
   Commercial networks, 316
   Public broadcasting, 317
Regional, Informal, and Sales Networks, 318
Summary, 319
Opportunities for Further Learning, 320

14

REGULATORY CONTROL OF MASS COMMUNICATION   321

A Model of Control, 321
Early Radio Legislation, 323
   The Wireless Ship Act of 1910, 323
   Radio Act of 1912, 324

Radio Act of 1927, 324
The Communications Act of 1934, 325
The Federal Communications Commission, 326
Organizational structure and effectiveness, 326
Policing the industry, 327
Complaints to the FCC, 328
Input to FCC rulemaking, 329
Section 315, 330
Pros and cons of access, 330
Exempting news programming, 331
The Fairness Doctrine, 332
The Fairness Doctrine is issued, 332
The 1974 report, 333
Reconsidering the Fairness Doctrine: 1976, 333
Ups and Downs of the Rewrite Issue, 333
Copyright, 334
National Telecommunication and Information Administration, 335
Advertising and the FTC, 337
Criticism and compliance, 340
Celebrity endorsements, 340
International Telecommunication Union, 341
Summary, 341
Opportunities for Further Learning, 342

15

LEGAL ISSUES AND THE WORKING PRESS   344

Four Theories of the Press, 344
Authoritarian theory, 344
Libertarian theory, 347
Social responsibility theory, 349
Soviet-Communist theory, 350
Freedom of the Press: The Constitution, 352
Reporters' Shield Laws, 354
Freedom of Information Laws, 356
Cameras in the Courtroom, 357
Television and Legislative Proceedings, 360
Gag Rules, 361
Scope of gag rules, 362
The judicial dilemma, 362
Voluntary cooperation, 363
Rights of the Student Press, 364
Libel and Slander, 365
Definition, 365
Avoiding libel, 365
Libel per quod, libel per se, 366
Defense against libel, 366
Invasion of Privacy, 367
Search and Seizure, 368
Alternative Controls: The National News Council, 368
Summary, 369
Opportunities for Further Learning, 371

16

AUDIENCE AND EFFECTS OF MASS COMMUNICATION   372

Audience Demographics, 372
Audience Psychographics, 373
Researching the Audience and Effects: Some Pitfalls, 374
    Methodology and theory, 374
    Experimental vs. survey methodologies, 375
Early Approaches to Understanding Effects: The Bullet Theory, 376
Revising the Bullet Theory, 376
    Subgroups, 376
    Opinion leaders and the two-step flow, 377
    Interpersonal influence, 377
Understanding Reaction to Media Messages, 378
    Individual differences approach, 378
    Categories approach, 379
    Social relationships approach, 379
Selective Exposure, Perception, Retention, 380
The Functional Use of Media, 380
    Film: Highbrow, middlebrow, lowbrow, postbrow, 381
    Stephenson's play theory, 381
    Uses and gratifications, 382
    Agenda-setting function, 384
    The broad context of functional use, 384
Socialization, 385
    Stages in studying effects of socialization, 386
    Studying the results, 386
Violence on Television, 388
    The Surgeon General's report, 388
    Effects of televised violence: The role of learning theory, 389
    Effects of portrayal on aggressive behavior, 390
Diffusion of Innovations, 391
Summary, 392
Opportunities for Further Learning, 392

17

MEDIA ETHICS AND SOCIAL ISSUES   394

Ethics and the Press, 394
    Specific cases, 395
    Public response, 396
Ethics and Decision Making, 397
Press Codes, 399
    The Society of Professional Journalists, Sigma Delta Chi, 399
    Radio/Television News Directors Association, 400
    American Society of Newspaper Editors, 400
    Code enforcement, 401
Censorship, 401
Media as "Big Brother," 403.
Media's Portrayal of Women, 404
    Women in television, 405
    Women in the print media, 406
    Ms., Miss, or Mrs., 406

Media and the Elderly, 407
    Media portrayal of the elderly, 407
    Special features and functional uses, 409
Mass Media Past, Present, and Future: McLuhan's Perspectives, 409
    The ages of technological determinism, 410
    Media hot and cold, 411
    Criticism of McLuhan, 412
    McLuhan and the future, 412
Summary, 414
Opportunities for Further Learning, 415

GLOSSARY 417

NOTES 425

INDEX 431

Preface

A completely revised edition of Mass Communication awaits the reader of this second edition.

Like the earlier edition, the book is designed primarily for use in introductory courses in mass communication and courses studying mass media in society. The book is designed for those who aspire to be responsible consumers of mass media or practicing professionals.

The aim is to help students understand the full impact of mass media. Human beings respond to many aspects of their environment. As far as mass communication is concerned, we must keep in mind that exposure to one message on one medium is not sufficient to explain human behavior. For this reason, this book examines the many different mass media—newspapers, magazines, radio, television, film, books, the recording industry—and their relationship to one another and to society.

In addition, the book examines advertising and public relations, photography and photojournalism, mass media news, media delivery systems such as satellites and computers, wire services, syndicates and research services, regulatory control of mass communication, legal issues and the working press, the audience and effects of mass communication and media ethics and social issues. "Opportunities for Further Learning" entice the student to dig deeper into the subject. A comprehensive Instructor's Manual accompanies the text.

ACKNOWLEDGMENTS

I am especially grateful to the many people who adopted the earlier edition and provided feedback for this revision. The acceptance of the first edition exceeded the highest expectations of myself and the publisher, and it is with deep and humble gratitude that a sincere thank you is expressed.

Many people—more than can be mentioned here—have in some way played a part in the development of this second edition.

Few authors could ask for the support of a professional organization the caliber of Prentice-Hall, Inc. Editors such as John Busch and Brian Walker kept constant attention to detail with the help of Jean Wachter. Barbara Christenberry continues to receive unmeasurable debts of gratitude. Working with Bruce Kennan's staff means working with the best in the business. Other tremendously important personnel include: Larry Barker, Colette Conboy, Beverly Fulton, Karen Thompson, Denise Moderack, Shelia Whiting, Patricia Daly, Jeanne Hoeting, Cathie Mahar, Judy Mortell, Robert Thoresen, Tom Kubiak, Christine Beranek, Bill Kestle, Betsy Perry, Ted Arnold, Bob Molitar, Susan Weeg, Willis Bilderback, Rita Vale, Jim Panther, David Fleenor, Michael Sutton, John Davis Jr., Anne Smith, Terry Brennan, Dale Brown, John Paul Jones, David Pallai, Jo Ellen Sesker, John Allison, Martin Tenney, and Cindy Jennings Meurer.

Robert J. Kibler's encouragement as a friend, colleague, and teacher are very deeply missed.

At DePauw University, a library staff welcomes any challenge that confronts them, including the author's request for obscure documents located in foreign libraries.

Eric Bernsee again provided immeasurable help. Charles Jones adds enthusiasm for writing, as does John Jakes.

Elinor Ziegelman and Midge Cook kept an office running smoothly and trifles from interfering with progress.

Serving with equal distinction as a wife, lover, friend, and corporate vice president means no one deserves more credit than Denise.

MASS
COMMUNICATION

What Is
Mass Communication?

What is mass communication? It is the deadline of the investigative journalist, the creative artistry of documentaries, the bustle of a network newsroom, the whir of a computer, the hit record capturing the imagination of millions, the radio disc jockey setting the pace of a morning show, and the advertising executive planning a campaign. It is radio, research, recordings, resonators, and ratings. It is television, talent, telephones, and tabloids. It is satellites, storyboards, systems, and segues. It is all these things and many more. It *is* dynamic and exciting, but it is *not* new. Let us go back for a moment to the dawn of civilization—more than two and a half milllion years ago.

THE EVOLUTION OF MASS COMMUNICATION

If you will, try to imagine our prehistoric ancestors emerging from their caves and reacting to their environment. Archeologists, who refer to this era as the Ramapithecus age, tell us that cave people possessed the basic senses of sight, hearing, touch, smell, and taste. Genetically different from creatures of the twentieth century, they resembled apes more than humans. However, as their brains and central nervous systems began slowly to evolve, later generations gradually acquired the basic tools for communication. They began to distinguish between pleasurable and unpleasurable experiences. More refined perception and a more sophisticated brain and central nervous system developed simultaneously and aided in satisfying basic needs—light to see, air to breathe, food to eat, water to drink, sleep to strengthen, and shelter to protect them from the environment. By the year 300,000 B.C., their nervous systems and brain, as well as their genetic features began to resemble those of present humans.

beginnings of language

Two hundred thousand years later, an embryonic language began to develop. Before this time, people communicated mostly through touch. Anthropologists are still debating whether this language developed through learning or instinct. Nevertheless, genetic evolution had now been joined by language evolution. By about 7000 B.C., Homo sapiens had evolved genetically to their present form, and the ability to communicate had gained another medium, *pictographics*. These wall etchings inside caves and temples remain vivid picture messages that depict the life and religious beliefs of these first humans. In the period from 3000 to 2000 B.C., these etchings became highly stylized, and the first symbols came into existence. Primitive alphabets, sometimes consisting of more than 600 characters, marked the beginning of recorded history. Mankind was now able to

Figure 1-1 Early forms of communication were pictographs— etchings or drawings made on caves, trees, or animal skins. This one represents an Indian war song. Translated, it reads, "I am rising to seek the war-path. The earth and the sky are before me. I walk by day and by night And the evening star is my guide." (Source: W. L. Hubbard, ed., *History of American Music*. London: Irving Squire, 1908)

record sociocultural events, attitudes, values, and habits, and to trace the development of moral codes (Figure 1-1).

functional requirements of society

Society's survival and growth depended on a number of things, among them a *system of communication* through which people could exchange symbols and thus propagate learning at a much accelerated rate; a *system of production* to create goods and services both for their needs and for barter and exchange; *systems of defense* to protect their domain against intruders; a method of *member replacement* sufficient to counteract disease and other elements of member destruction; and a method of *social control* to maintain order in the society. In the following centuries, each of these functional requirements was, and is still, fulfilled by ever more sophisticated and efficient systems, especially in communication.

As civilization continued to expand, interpersonal communication was used cross-culturally. Relay runners would carry messages to distant places and different people. However learning about people living in different ways still was very slow, mostly determined by how fast a messenger could run or ride. In some cases, the messages took months and even years to reach their destination.

print technology

In the fifteenth century, human ingenuity created a major breakthrough in technology—the invention of movable type—and introduced it to the European continent. People now could produce and send messages much faster. From this point on, breakthroughs in communication technology mushroomed. The facility with which people now could record knowledge made possible a much more rapid exchange of information.

Two important developments followed the invention of movable type. First, the use of a *paper-making machine* (Figure 1-2) in the eighteenth century made it possible to mass produce and cut paper in specific sizes, reducing the cost of production. The second was the *application of steam to the printing press.* Steam power, the first alternative to human labor, made possible true mass production of printed material. Sources of power, improved printing presses (Figure 1-3) and improved paper manufacturing processes developed continuously during the nineteenth century. Such devices as cylinder-fed paper rolls and type cylinders continued the advancement of printing. Mechanical typesetting machines also become part of the printing process. With the aid of larger and faster presses, newspapers could print editions with as many as a dozen pages.

new distribution systems

Three other nineteenth-century inventions further aided the ability to communicate. First, the development of *major transportation systems* permitted large

Figure 1-2 A paper mill showing the paper-making process—from dipping the screen into a vat of paper pulp to new sheets being stacked and readied for pressing. (From *DIDEROT* and courtesy: *The Printer in 18th-Century Williamsburg.* Williamsburg, Va.: Colonial Williamsburg, 1955)

Figure 1-3 Early mechanical press used in small print shops of the nineteenth and twentieth century.

quantities of newspapers to be carried to people residing outside the major cities. Railroads became the key to this network and distribution system. Second, just as railroads began to prosper, *the telegraph* (Figure 1-4) was invented, permitting people to communicate over long distances with considerable speed. By means of the mechanical transmission of short and long sounds—dots and dashes— representing the letters of the alphabet, a skillful telegraph operator could easily send or receive twenty words per minute. However, only those centers equipped with telegraph lines could receive messages. Newspapers used the telegraph to communicate bulletins, and when the Atlantic Cable was completed, news of commercial and political events could be exchanged between the United States and England via Newfoundland. By the late nineteenth century, a network of telegraph lines had developed over the United States.

The third major development of the nineteenth century, the device that enabled people to send voices over the wires, soon supplanted the telegraph signal because of its immediacy of communication. Although the *telephone* helped people to communicate with each other on a one-to-one basis over long distances, its impact was minor compared to that of the next technological revolution that loomed on the horizon.

Figure 1-4 Samuel F. B. Morse's first telegraph. The needle protruding from the horizontal bar caused a perforation in a paper tape permitting a "coded" record of the message. (Smithsonian Institution Photo No. 14593-B)

electronic communication

Just as the twentieth century dawned, a system was perfected by which electromagnetic impulses could be sent through the air without wires, carrying voice transmission over long distances. This new invention was to become known as radio. Low-cost receivers were developed which could be purchased by almost everyone for a few dollars, enabling them to listen to mass-produced messages

Figure 1-5 The NASA Voyager spacecrafts carried television to the planet Jupiter and beyond. Electronic data pictures were relayed to home television screens and gave scientists a new close-up look at Jupiter's surface. Space voyages permitted similar television close-ups as well as landings on the Moon and Mars. (NASA)

from thousands of transmitters located all over the world. Societies and cultures were within an instant of communicating with each other, and a news event on one side of the world could be transmitted almost simultaneously to any other point in the world. For the first time in civilization, people had a medium of mass communication that just a century before had belonged to the world of science fiction.

In the same century, the ability to capture moving visual images with the camera was perfected. People also discovered ways of capturing movement as well as sound on film to produce the motion picture and the electronic system called videotape. Scientists, in deciding how these motion pictures could be transmitted over wires and subsequently without wires, created a new medium called television. In much the same way that steam aided the printing presses, jet propulsion took television to the galaxies and beyond (Figure 1-5). Using computers in mass communication systems has aided in the transmission, monitoring, and logical development of information.

But let us stop for a moment. Have we answered our question of what mass communication is? We have, partially.

We have learned it includes such entities as newspapers, radio, and television, what we call the *mass media*. But we still need to distinguish it from two other types of communication—*intra*personal and *inter*personal communication.

DISTINGUISHING AMONG TYPES OF COMMUNICATION

One of the best ways to distinguish among different types of communication is to use a *communication model*. This *pictorial representation of the communication process* contains the basic components of communication. Figure 1-6 shows the relationship among the parts of the model: sender, medium, message, receiver, feedback, and noise. With this model in mind, let's begin by discussing *intra*personal communication.

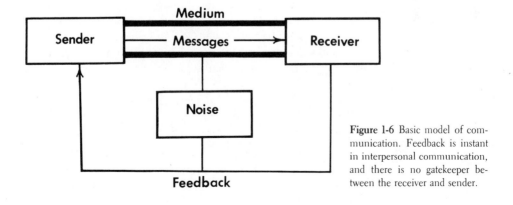

Figure 1-6 Basic model of communication. Feedback is instant in interpersonal communication, and there is no gatekeeper between the receiver and sender.

We can assume that, even before history recorded such things, early humans used their senses to help them understand their world. If they looked into a clear midday sky, light and heat touched their eyes and were communicated to their brain via the central nervous system. If they felt cool rain on a hot day, this pleasant feeling also was communicated to the central nervous system. Cold winter air probably initiated an avoidance reaction. Our prehistoric subjects thus began to perceive, judge, and act accordingly. Perhaps the next time the temperature was hot and it began to rain, they went outside the cave and cooled off. When it was cold, they built a fire. The process of sunlight entering the eye and communicating brightness to the central nervous system, the tactile sense organs communicating the feeling of cold air, the thought processes of deciding whether to brave the cold or build a fire, stay inside or walk in the rain—all were the result of communication taking place *within* the individual. This is the electrochemical action of the body taking part in the process of *intrapersonal communication—communication within ourselves.*

Intrapersonal communication is the basis of all other forms of human communication. Without an effective system of intrapersonal communication, an organism is unable to function in its environment, that is, to be open to external forms of communication. Ideally, this communication system allows one to make decisions based on information received through the senses. For instance, when you watch television, your eyes and ears receive information and communicate it to your brain. If what you see and hear is pleasurable and/or interesting, your intrapersonal communication system indicates that, and you attend to it. If you do not like it, your brain sends a message to your muscles which results in a decision to change stations or to push the "off" button.

Just as the electronic components in your television set prohibit more than one station from being received at a time, your central nervous system also sorts out the different stimuli so that you can concentrate on one immediate thought—which station to watch. Perhaps the telephone rings just as you begin to think about changing stations. Instead of answering the phone, your central nervous system may give priority to the television message, and you may continue to pay attention to that. However, if you had been anxiously awaiting a call from a close friend, then your central nervous system will probably give the telephone message priority, and you will answer its ring. The entire process requires intrapersonal communication. Now imagine the phone rings, and just as you get up to answer it, the doorbell rings. You stop. You cannot decide whether to answer the door or the telephone. You just stand there. The doorbell has interfered with your intrapersonal communication processes. Or perhaps just as you get up to answer the phone, you drop back in your chair with a splitting headache. Again, you cannot concentrate. The headache also has interfered with your process of intrapersonal communication.

Applying our example of watching television to the components of our basic model of communication (Figure 1-6), we can see that your eyes and ears become the *senders* or transmitters of electrochemical impulses (*messages*) through a *medium* of communication, which in this case was your central nervous system. Your brain becomes the *receiver* of these impulses which transmits additional electrochemical impulses in the form of *feedback* to muscles, producing such physical activity as changing stations or answering the telephone. We also saw interference to successful intrapersonal communication. The doorbell produced external *noise* which interfered with this process. You also experienced internal noise in the form of a headache. The headache and doorbell interrupted the normal flow of electrochemical impulses, thus adding new factors to your decision-making task and temporarily distorting the process of intrapersonal communication.

interpersonal communication

With the crude beginnings of language, the process of *interpersonal communication*—communication in a face-to-face situation—bridged the gap from the concrete to the abstract. It became possible to communicate about persons or things not directly in view. If we apply our basic model to interpersonal communication, a typical situation might be as follows: You (sender) may speak (medium) words (message) to a friend (receiver) across the room, and the friend replies with an approval (feedback). While you are speaking and while your friend is reacting, intrapersonal communication also is taking place. When the two of you are talking, if a baseball (noise) comes flying through the window, it will disrupt both the process of intrapersonal communication and that of interpersonal communication. Perhaps one of you uses a cliché or a phrase which the other person does not understand; then, *semantic noise* interferes with the communication process. The possibility of semantic noise is one reason why a basic rule of journalism is to avoid using clichés.

For example, put yourself in the position of the television reporter from Idaho who visited New York to be interviewed for a job with a major television network. During the interview, the reporter commented how after a hard day on the job, he would literally "come apart at the seams" before sitting down for dinner. The network executive conducting the interview jotted down in her notes that the reporter "can't withstand pressure, becomes mentally deranged, and goes berserk before dinner!" To the Idaho reporter, "coming apart at the seams" simply meant totally relaxing before eating dinner. Obviously, the reporter did not get the job. Semantic noise obstructed the process of interpersonal communication and consequently the job interview.

Every day we use interpersonal communication. However, the number of people we can reach with our ideas is limited if this is the only means of communication available to us. To understand the full potential of our communication processes, we need to look beyond interpersonal communication to the process of mass communication.

mass communication

To understand mass communication as a process distinct from interpersonal and intrapersonal communication, imagine that you are attending a party where a politician is mingling and conversing with guests. About an hour later, the party ends and you join a few thousand people in an auditorium to hear the politician deliver a major address. Stop and ask yourself whether mass communication was taking place either at the party or in the auditorium where a large number of persons was present. The answer is *no*. For mass communication to exist, we need an intermediate transmitter of information, a *mass medium* such as newspapers, magazines, film, radio, television, books, or combinations of these. The politician who delivered a major address without the aid of the mass media would be forfeiting his chance to reach thousands, even millions of persons not physically present. Essentially, then, *mass communication is messages communicated through a mass medium to a large number of people.* For further clarification, we shall use the word "mass" to refer to a large body of persons. Although by definition we have answered our question of what mass communication is, we need to examine more closely the specific characteristics of the process.

CHARACTERISTICS OF MASS COMMUNICATION

The process of mass communication requires additional persons, most often complex societal organizations and institutions, to carry messages from the speaker to the audience. Returning to our simplified examples, sitting next to you in the auditorium is a reporter who hears the politician's speech, writes a story about it, and delivers it to the local newspaper that publishes it the next morning. In this example, relay people aid in carrying the speaker's remarks beyond the auditorium to the reading public. The reporter who wrote the speech, the newspaper editor who edited the reporter's remarks, the typesetter, and the printer all helped relay this information through a medium of mass communication. Both the individuals (termed "relay people") and the organizations are called *gatekeepers.*

the gatekeeper concept

The term gatekeeper first was employed by the Austrian psychologist Kurt Lewin who used it to refer to individuals or groups of persons who govern "the travels of news items in the communication channel." We will expand Lewin's definition and define gatekeeper as *any person or formally organized group directly involved in relaying or transferring information from one individual to another through a mass medium.* A gatekeeper can be a film producer who cuts a scene from the original script, a propaganda artist who prepares leaflets to be dropped from an airplane, the engineer at the local control center for cable television, or any other individual in the processing or control of messages disseminated through mass media to the public.

We can readily see that such an individual has the ability to *limit* information we receive from the mass media. A magazine editor may "kill" or eliminate a feature story judged to be of little interest or importance to the magazine's readers. A reporter may edit a story about the work of a congressional committee or a meeting of Parliament by deleting parts of the story he or she feels may be irrelevant. On the other hand, a gatekeeper also can *expand* information to the public by supplying facts, attitudes, or viewpoints his or her audience would not usually receive. The reporter who covers the congressional hearing or reports on Parliament's deliberations increases the total amount of information we receive—in this case, in absentia—from our environment. The reporter also may *reorganize or reinterpret* the information we, the public, receive. Facts may be rearranged or a new slant may be given to the story of the politician's speech. This is not always the case, but it can happen.

Thus, it is important to remember that there are three functions of the gatekeeper: (1) to *limit* the information we receive by editing this information before it is disseminated to us; (2) to *expand* the amount of information we receive by increasing our informational environment; and (3) to *reorganize* or *reinterpret* the information.

delayed feedback

Returning to our example of the politician, perhaps the next day after reading about the speech in the local newspaper, an angry constituent writes a letter to the editor of the newspaper criticizing the politican's stand on an issue. Another constituent, somewhat more upset, decides to write directly to the politician. A lobbyist who heard the speech on radio may personally approach the politician and express approval of the speech. Each example is a form of *delayed feedback*, which differs from the immediate feedback the politician received from the members of the live audience. In the auditorium, for example, reporters could ask questions about certain ideas they did not understand. The politician could, in turn, clear up any misunderstandings or project new messages for further thought. The difference between the reporters' responses and those of the constituents and the lobbyist may be accounted for by the time delay.

Delayed feedback is not unique to the mass communication situation. It can occur on an intrapersonal level, as when one is temporarily baffled by an optical illusion. It also occurs often on the interpersonal level when one person temporarily refrains from commenting about another's remark or suggestion. However, since delayed feedback will in many cases result from the mass communication situation, we shall use it as one of our distinguishing characteristics. Adding the concepts of the gatekeeper and delayed feedback to our basic model of communication gives us the model of mass communication illustrated in Figure 1-7.

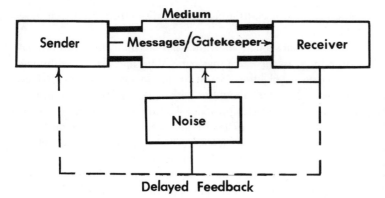

Figure 1-7 Model of mass communication. Feedback is delayed in mass communication, since the sender and receiver are not in the physical presence of each other. Also, a gatekeeper "processes" the message and events. Noise, both semantic and physical, can occur at many places and at different settings in both interpersonal and mass communication.

As noise can interfere with interpersonal and intrapersonal communication, so can it disrupt the process of mass communication. The politician may have had a headache and have difficulty concentrating (intrapersonal communication). The air conditioner may have been too loud for the reporter to hear everything the politician was saying (interpersonal communication). The printing press at the newspaper may have failed, creating blurred pages and making it difficult to read the story (mass communication). Figure 1-8 shows the politician's speech broken down into the various components of our communication model. Keep in mind that the components present in intrapersonal and interpersonal communication also are part of mass communication. Note, for instance, that in the case of the receiver, for there to be a "public" to receive mass communication, there also has to be a "reporter" to receive interpersonal communication and a "brain" to receive intrapersonal communication. All three components are part of the process of human communication.

	Intrapersonal	Interpersonal	Mass
Sender	Sense Organs	Politician	Politician
Receiver	Brain	Reporter	Public
Messages	Electro-Chemical Impulses	Language	Language
Medium	Central Nervous System	Voice	Newspaper
Feedback	Electro-Chemical Impulses	Questions	Letters
Noise	Headache	Breaking Glass	Blurred Printing

Figure 1-8 Components of the communication process applied to our example of the politician's speech. Keep in mind that the communication process differs from situation to situation, and that communication models are but pictorial representations of this process which can be altered by different settings.

THE SOCIAL CONTEXT OF MASS COMMUNICATION

Up to this point, our model of mass communication has been primarily concerned with how we send and receive messages. But forces also affect the messages themselves, in addition to how consumers react to these messages. Specifically, these forces consist of society's social groups and systems.

Mass communication does not operate in a social vacuum as a machine does. When a computer receives a message, for instance, it will provide an answer based on that original message. If the computer is functioning properly, the same answer will appear every time we send it the identical message. Now contrast this process with what occurs in mass communication. Imagine that you, a consumer of mass media, read the newspaper story about the politician's speech. After you talked with your family, friends, and co-workers about it, you decided to write a letter to the politician. It is thus possible that three social groups—your family, friends, and co-workers—affected your reaction to the speech.

Now imagine that you are the newspaper reporter responsible for writing about the speech. Social groups also will affect your reporting of the story to the public. Perhaps you are a member of a union that goes on strike just as you return to your office to write the story. Perhaps you belong to a journalism association with a code of reporting ethics to which you personally adhere. The code states that you cannot accept gifts as part of your job as a reporter. Your morning mail brings an invitation from a major oil company to be their guest on a flight to Kuwait for an on-the-spot story about oil exploration. You are faced with accepting the free trip and doing the story or rejecting the free trip and permitting other media in your city to obtain the story. You obviously are faced with a dilemma attributable at least in part to the influence various social groups have on you.

CHANGING DEFINITIONS: SPECIALIZED AUDIENCES, SPECIALIZED MEDIA

Because mass media are such an important part of our lives, we tend to think of media audiences as being total populations or mass national audiences. Although to some degree this is correct, we also should understand that today the *mass audience* is becoming a *specialized audience*. Similarly, many *mass media* are also very *specialized media*.

media and media systems

Although a magazine publisher may want to reach as many readers as possible, another publisher may want to reach only specific readers. For example, if you published *City Woman* (Figure 1-9) magazine, you would want to concentrate

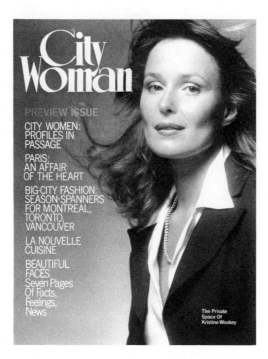

Figure 1-9 Typical of a contemporary specialized medium are magazines such as *City Woman*, which is directed toward a specific audience—the woman living and/or working in a metropolitan area. (COMAC COMMUNICATIONS LIMITED)

your efforts on reaching professional women who lived or worked in the city. Moreover, your advertisers would not be interested in paying high rates to reach an audience that had no interest in buying their products, and you would not want to spend the additional money to print the magazine for these disinterested readers. This is just one example of how mass communication is a process not only designed to reach a mass audience but also a highly specialized one.

Radio presents another example of specialization. When radio's golden age began, it was truly a mass medium. Today that has changed; it has become a specialized medium. What was once predominantly network programming directed at mass audiences is now local programming directed at specialized audiences. The radio network programming over ABC, NBC, CBS, and MBS also has diversified. ABC has broken up into four different demographic networks. Mutual Broadcasting System, besides its standard programming, has added the Mutual Information Network and the Mutual Black Network. There even has been an outcropping of state radio networks directed at audiences in specific geographical regions.

Television also appeals to diversified audiences. Cable television, for instance, can provide as many as forty or more separate channels with different types of programming for different viewers. Besides the major network programs, special broadcasts can be produced by local colleges and universities, corporate programs can be used to train employees, and still other presentations can include citizen discussion groups talking about community issues. No longer does television simply aim at the "masses."

Consider newspapers. Although the large metropolitan dailies still mainly serve mass audiences, new computer technology permits many to reach specific audiences with area edition inserts and refined distribution systems. Smaller suburban newspapers, edited for communities adjacent to the metropolis, attribute their success to news of interest to their own particular community.

Wire services also have gone the way of the other media. At the turn of the century, the United States was served primarily by two wire services, Associated Press and United Press. In a sense, they were directed at the mass national audience through their subscribing newspapers. Today, however, although the two major wire services still function, numerous specialized wire services have come into existence. Some deal exclusively with weather information and news of prime importance to agricultural regions. Others, directed at the business audience, deal with stocks and commodities. Grain farmers, chicken farmers, and people in the lumber business have specialized wire services. Even AP and UPI have become specialized. They now offer both print and broadcast wires for subscribers in addition to audio services and special services to cable television operators.

Look at the recording industry. Back when the early television program *The Hit Parade* was popular, the ten songs performed each week were accorded a "mass" national audience. Today, a similar program would have a hard time finding an audience large enough to justify its staying on the air. For there now are top-forty charts, top country and western charts, top classical charts, top easy listening charts, and many more.

media and the postindustrial society

Richard Maisel has theorized that industrial society eventually necessitates the creation of specialized media. He contends that our present "postindustrial" society results in the growth of service industries, which are "great consumers of specialized media." He states, "The needs and tastes of specialized groups can only be satisfied by a form of specialized communication designed for a homogeneous audience."[1]

Although Maisel may seem to be referring to the industrial consumption of media, his concept applies just as well to many facets of nonindustrial consumption of media—for example, the entertainment function of media. Even the radio commercials that inform us of vital "services" in our postindustrial society are directed to local audiences.

Although it may at first seem that the growth of specialized media conflicts with the truly mass media, this is not necessarily the case. We now, however, have the *choice* of attending to the older, more generalized mass appeal media or to the newer specialized media. The future of mass communication in the very broad sense is still open to speculation. Our society is centuries old; yet with the exception of books and newspapers, we are mere infants in our experience with mass media. What effect the growth of specialized media will have on society is open to further study.

SUMMARY

Mass communication evolved from the fundamental process of human communication—people exchanging messages through verbal and written symbols. Technology increased the efficiency of mass communication until today the process sends messages around the world and into space.

We defined mass communication as messages communicated through a mass medium to a large number of people. We also learned how to distinguish mass communication from other types of communication by examining the components of human communication as represented in a communication model. These components include senders, receivers, messages, and medium of communication. Two additional components are feedback and noise. There is feedback when a receiver reacts to a message. Noise is anything that interferes with the communication process.

Mass communication is one of three basic types of human communication, the other two being intrapersonal and interpersonal communication. Intrapersonal communication is communication within ourselves, electrochemical impulses sent from the sense organs of sight, sound, touch, smell, and taste through the central nervous system to the brain. The brain, in turn, generates electrochemical impulses that activate the muscular system. Interpersonal communication is communication in a face-to-face situation. It contains the same basic components of the communication model as does intrapersonal communication.

Mass communication differs from both intrapersonal and interpersonal communication in that it requires a mass medium, such as television or newspapers. It also necessitates the presence of gatekeeper(s), people, and/or systems that control and process the information before it is disseminated to the public. In addition, mass communication almost always has delayed feedback rather than the immediate feedback present on the other two levels of communication. Mass communication also operates within a complex social context. Messages are affected by the attitudes of the various gatekeepers, and audience response, in turn is affected by social context. How we react to mass media is partially self-determined, however. To some extent we choose to associate with specific social groups, friends, neighbors, co-workers, and members of professional, religious, and political organizations. The people and groups we associate with influence how we respond to messages received through the mass media.

Mass communication increasingly is becoming a process designed to reach specialized audiences through specialized media. Virtually every medium is in some way directed toward specialized audiences. Researcher Richard Maisel views this changing definition of mass as a natural function of our postindustrial society.

OPPORTUNITIES FOR FURTHER LEARNING

AUSTIN-LETT, GENELLE, AND JANET SRAGUE, *Talk to Yourself: Experiencing Intrapersonal Communication.* New York: Houghton Mifflin Company, 1976.

DE LOZIER, WAYNE M., *The Matketing Communications Process.* New York: McGraw-Hill Book Comapny, 1976.

DEL POLITO, CAROLYN M., *Intrapersonal Communication.* Menlo Park, Calif.; Cummings Publishing Company, 1977.

GUMPERT, GARY, AND ROBERT CATHCART, *Inter/Media: Interpersonal Communication in a Media World.* New York: Oxford University Press, 1979.

HANNEMAN, GERHARD J., AND WILLIAM J. MCEWEN, *Communication and Behavior.* Reading, Mass.: Addison-Wesley Publishing Co., Inc., 1975.

LASWELL, HAROLD D., DANIEL LERNER, AND HANS SPEIER, eds., *Propaganda and Communication in World History, Vol. 1: The Symbolic Instrument in Early Times.* Honolulu: University of Hawaii Press, 1979.

MCCOMBS, MAXWELL E. AND LEE B. BECKER, *Using Mass Communication Theory.* Englewood Cliffs, N.J.: Prentice-Hall, Inc., 1979.

MORTENSEN, C. DAVID, ed., *Basic Readings in Communication Theory.* New York: Harper & Row, Pub., 1978.

POOL, ITHIEL DE SOLA, *Handbook of Communication.* Chicago: Rand McNally & Company, 1973.

2

Newspapers

Newspapers are an economic and social phenomenon of our society. They are a major force in forming public opinion the world over and thus mightily affect national and international efforts toward economic progress and global understanding. Specialty newspapers exist for elementary school students, major financial dailies appeal to the commerce tycoons of the world, tabloids dress the newsstands of city transportation hubs, and popular underground publications appear and disappear at the change of a trend or movement. Newspaper stories have turned ordinary men and women into heroes and have removed world leaders from power. Huge presses spew out hundreds of pages in a single edition, and modern transportation and communication systems can put that same edition on a breakfast table 3,000 miles away. Today, the newspaper industry has become one of the largest in the world. It employs hundreds of thousands of people, from managing editors, to investigative reporters, to carriers. It has survived wars, economic collapse, and social destruction, yet remains essentially the same type of medium that it was centuries ago—pages of print communicating information to readers.

Before beginning our discussion of early newspapers, we should stop and define what a true newspaper is.

CHARACTERISTICS OF A NEWSPAPER

In 1928, a German scholar, Otto Groth, developed a set of five standards which modern scholars generally hold as acceptable criteria for determining a true newspaper.[1] Groth's first standard was that a newspaper must be *published periodically* at intervals not less than once a week. Second, *mechanical reproduction* must be employed. Early Roman and Chinese publications would not qualify here. Third, anyone who can pay the price of admission must have *access to the publication*. In other words, it must be available to everyone, not just a chosen few. No organization can have an exclusive right to read or obtain the publication. Groth also defined the content of the publication. It must *vary in content* and include everything of public interest to everyone, not merely to small, select groups. Finally, publication must be *timely* with some *continuity of organization*.

Keep Groth's definitions in mind as we read about early newspapers, since the true beginnings of the press are found in many publications that may not meet Groth's standards. Yet his standards remain important to our study as a point of reference that historians use to refer to the newspapers' true impact on our society.

AN INTERNATIONAL BEGINNING

Scholars have never quite agreed on what could be considered the first true newspaper. This is partly because they could not reach a consensus on how to define the beginnings of the press.

the posted bulletins

In Italy, messengers disseminated mass news as early as 59 B.C. with the publication of daily events bulletins called *Acta Diurna*. They were posted in a public place for all to read and were kept on file as an official record of historical events (Figure 2-1). There are indications that the bulletin may have been copied and reproduced by hand for distribution to other countries by messenger and ship. Obviously, the ability of the publication to transmit messages to a mass audience was minimal based on today's standards. The number of "subscribers" were the number of persons who happened to read the poster.

The Romans also developed a system of news dissemination in which a "reader" would announce the day's news events at a given time and place, and those wishing to hear him would be charged admission. You would have paid one Italian *gazetta* to hear the news. Such contemporary newspapers as the *Sydney Gazette* of Australia and our own *Georgia Gazette* and *Colorado Springs Gazette* among many others, trace their name to this ancient custom. No one

Figure 2-1 Early distribution of news occurred through the posting of "bulletins" on the sides of buildings in public places, where passers-by could read about the events of the day. (John W. Houck, *Outdoor Advertising: History and Regulation.* Notre Dame, Ind.: University of Notre Dame Press, 1969)

country can claim the foundation of the modern press. The earliest *forerunner* of the modern newspaper can, however, be credited to the Chinese. A publication resembling a court journal appeared about A.D. 500, entitled *Tsing Pao*. The publication began in Peking and remained in publication into the twentieth century.

European foundations of the modern press

As the technological advances of printing made their way across Europe, newspapers cropped up frequently in almost all areas. Certain political atmospheres helped and in some cases hindered the development of the press, but for the most part it flourished. Figure 2-2 is a representative sampling depicting the international origins of the modern newspaper. We can see that the seventeenth century was deluged with this medium. During this period, the press flourished in England, the Scandinavian countries, France, Germany, and the United States. The turmoil of the Thirty Years' War during the first half of the seventeenth century contributed to the development of journalism in Europe mostly by providing a background against which many different issues could be aired. In general, the war did more to liberate journalism than to hinder it.

The first newspaper published in Germany was founded in 1609 by Egenolph Emmel, a bookseller, who started a weekly in Frankfurt in 1615. A competing Frankfurt newspaper published in 1617 by Johann von den Birghden

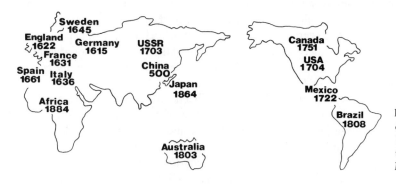

Figure 2-2 International origins of the modern newspaper. The United States' date, 1704, refers to the beginning of the *Boston News-Letter*.

led to the first legislation over a newspaper monopoly. Von den Birghden asserted in a lawsuit brought by Emmel that as postmaster, von den Birghden had an exclusive right to publish a newspaper. Similar controversies did not in any way discourage entrepreneurs from entering the business, however, as is indicated by the fact that in 1633 there were no fewer than sixteen newspapers in Germany.

the English heritage

In England, the press developed under the authoritarian atmosphere of the early seventeenth century. A product of the Tudor system designed to "license" official government printers, a free press was virtually nonexistent. In fact, some whose fever for free expression became too much to hold back found themselves at the end of a hangman's noose. William Caxton had established the first English printing press in 1476, but not until 1621 did "sheets" of news begin to appear sporadically across the English countryside. Called *corantos*, they still were not true newspapers by today's criteria. They usually skirted the restrictions against a free press by publishing news from outside the country.

The Thirty Years War is credited for the flourishing of the early English press. During that period, from 1618 until 1648, news of the war became both popular and profitable.

The voices calling for a free press were growing more strident. Most noted among these was the poet John Milton. Milton had been educated at Cambridge and had traveled widely in Europe, meeting many of the noted politicians, artists, and church leaders of his time. He had become disenchanted with the church's ritualism, and this had germinated similar feelings against government's control over its people. In his famous *Areopagitica*, Milton stated: "and though all the winds of doctrine were to let loose to play upon the earth, so Truth be in the field, we do injuriously by licensing and prohibiting to misdoubt her strength. Let her and Falsehood grapple: who ever knew Truth put to worse, in a free and open encounter?"

The licensing to which Milton was referring was an order issued one year earlier, in 1643, making the government-approved stationers' company responsible for putting its official stamp on anything printed in England. The company also had the right to search and seize publications which did not have its approval. Milton's argument for a free press became the foundation for arguments used by Thomas Jefferson in colonial times and even for contemporary lawyers championing the rights of the First Amendment.

In 1694, the licensing of the press finally ended in England. The powers of Parliament were beginning to conflict with those of the Crown and with rivaling factions competing for the same constituency, and none wanted its views muzzled. This freedom of expression increased the thirst for news, and eight years later, in 1702, the *Daily Courant* became the first, although not continuous, newspaper published in the English language. But between the edicts of the 1640s and the end of licensing, those most affected by both church and state already had ventured to a new world called America.

NEWSPAPERING IN EARLY AMERICA

If you had been among the first colonists in America, publishing a newspaper would not have been one of your priorities. There are a number of obvious reasons why not, even though skilled printers were among the first people to arrive from England. Basic needs of survival had to be met first: forests had to be cleared, fields plowed, houses built, and crops harvested. Second, news of international events arrived regularly via ships from London. In addition, you would have had little need for news about your own government, because that scarcely existed. Fourth, the closely knit geographical location of the New England communities facilitated news dissemination through interpersonal communication. Town meetings thus became the colonists' primary means of communication. Based on today's standards, early America was a closed society.

early colonial newspapers

The first attempt at a newspaper in the colonies was one started by the English printer Benjamin Harris.[2] Harris had been banished from England for operating the modern equivalent of an underground newspaper. Coming to Boston, he published in 1690 an edition of a newsletter entitled *Publick Occurrences, Both Forreign and Domestick* (Figure 2-3). In the publication, he made the mistake of taking a stance not favorable to the Indians in the area. The government of Massachusetts, one of whose primary aims was to win the favor of the Indians, did not appreciate Harris' ill-timed and undiplomatic remarks. As a result, Harris' publication was promptly confiscated, but the government gave him a subsidy to continue printing. He accepted. This may seem a rather cowardly act by today's journalistic standards, but the seriousness of Harris' financial position dictated a practical response. According to Groth's standards, Harris' publication

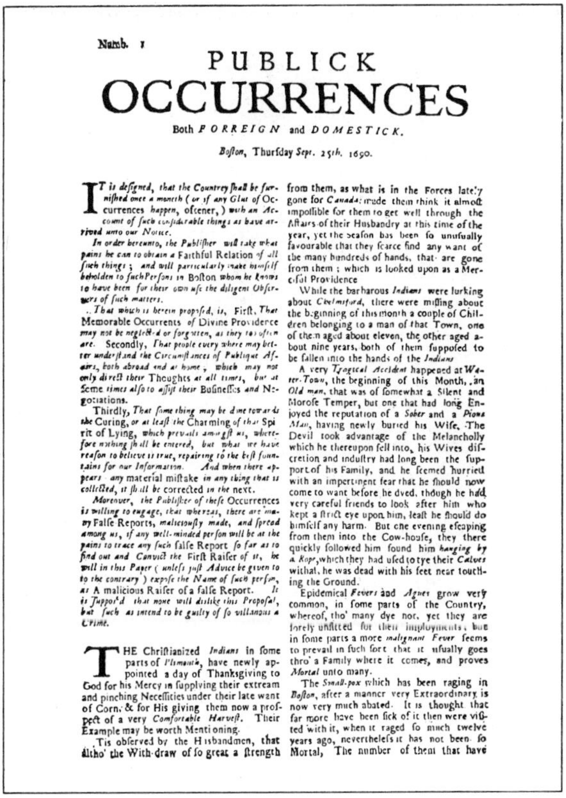

Numb. 1

PUBLICK

OCCURRENCES

Both *FORREIGN* and *DOMESTICK*.

Boston, Thursday *Sept.* 25th. 1690.

IT *is designed, that the Countrey shall be furnished once a moneth (or if any Glut of* Occurrences *happen*, oftener,) *with an Account of such considerable things as have arrived unto our Notice.*

In order hereunto, the Publisher will take what pains he can to obtain a Faithful Relation *of all such things; and will particularly make himself beholden to such Persons in* Boston *whom he knows to have been for their own use the diligent Observers of such matters.*

That which is herein proposed, is, First, *That* Memorable Occurrents *of* Divine Providence *may not be neglected or forgotten, as they too often are.* Secondly, *That people every where may better understand the Circumstances of Publique Affairs, both abroad and at home; which may not only direct their* Thoughts *at all times, but at* Some *times also to assist their* Businesses *and* Negotiations.

Thirdly, *That some thing may be done towards the* Curing, *or at least the* Charming *of that* Spirit of Lying, *which prevails amongst us, wherefore nothing shall be entered, but what we have reason to believe is true, repairing to the best fountains for our Information. And when there appears* any material mistake *in any thing that is collected, it shall be* corrected *in the* next.

Moreover, the Publisher of these Occurrences *is willing to engage, that whereas, there are many* False Reports, *maliciously made, and spread among us, if any well-minded person will be at the pains to trace any such* false Report *so far as to find out and Convict the* First Raiser *of it, he will in this Paper (unless just Advice be given to the contrary) expose the Name of such person, as* A malicious Raiser of a false Report. *It is suppos'd that none will dislike this Proposal, but such as intend to be guilty of so villanous a Crime.*

THE Christianized *Indians* in some parts of *Plimouth*, have newly appointed a day of Thanksgiving to God for his Mercy in supplying their extream and pinching Necessities under their late want of Corn, & for His giving them now a prospect of a very *Comfortable Harvest.* Their Example may be worth Mentioning.

Tis observed by the Husbandmen, that altho' the With-draw of so great a strength from them, as what is in the Forces lately gone for *Canada*; made them think it almost impossible for them to get well through the Affairs of their Husbandry at this time of the year, yet the season has been so unusually favourable that they scarce find any want of the many hundreds of hands, that are gone from them; which is looked upon as a Merciful Providence

While the barbarous *Indians* were lurking about *Chelmsford*, there were missing about the beginning of this month a couple of Children belonging to a man of that Town, one of them aged about eleven, the other aged about nine years, both of them supposed to be fallen into the hands of the *Indians*

A very *Tragical Accident* happened at *Water-Town*, the beginning of this Month, an *Old man*, that was of somewhat a Silent and Morose Temper, but one that had long Enjoyed the reputation of a *Sober* and a *Pious Man*, having newly buried his Wife, The Devil took advantage of the Melancholly which he thereupon fell into, his Wives discretion and industry had long been the support of his Family, and he seemed hurried with an impertinent fear that he should now come to want before he dyed, though he had very careful friends to look after him who kept a strict eye upon him, least he should do himself any harm. But one evening escaping from them into the Cow-house, they there quickly followed him found him *hanging by a Rope*, which they had used to tye their *Calves* withal, he was dead with his feet near touching the Ground.

Epidemical *Fevers* and *Agues* grow very common, in some parts of the Country, whereof, tho' many dye not, yet they are sorely unfitted for their imployments; but in some parts a more *malignant Fever* seems to prevail in such sort that it usually goes thro' a Family where it comes, and proves *Mortal* unto many.

The *Small-pox* which has been raging in *Boston*, after a manner very Extraordinary is now very much abated. It is thought that far more have been sick of it then were visited with it, when it raged so much twelve years ago, nevertheless it has not been so Mortal, The number of them that have

Figure 2-3 Newspaper published by Benjamin Harris in 1690.

would not have been considered a true newspaper since it appeared only once before its publisher returned to England. The first publication to meet all of the standards of a true newspaper made its appearance fourteen years later.

In 1704, postmaster John Campbell joined with printer Bartholomew Green to publish a newspaper called the *Boston News-Letter.* Campbell had several advantages, including a postmaster's free use of the mails. He also had been appointed by the Crown and reported directly to the governor of Massachusetts, and when he ran into financial trouble, a government subsidy was waiting. The *News-Letter* received competition from the *New England Courant* published by James Franklin, the older brother of Benjamin Franklin. The *Courant* distinguished itself as being independent from the publishing enterprises approved by the Crown's governors and carried forth numerous editorial crusades against both church and state. Samuel Keimer started the *Pennsylvania Gazette* (Figure 2-4) which was later managed by Benjamin Franklin. William Parks founded both the *Maryland Gazette* and the *Virginia Gazette.* The latter proved especially important because of Virginia's influence on American inde-

Figure 2-4 *The Pennsylvania Gazette.*

pendence and because the paper was published in Williamsburg, the capital of the Virginia colony.

the John Peter Zenger case

In 1733, there was a landmark case concerning freedom of the press. It involved John Peter Zenger, an immigrant from Germany who had been a colleague of William Bradford, a printer in the New York colony. Bradford's newspaper, the *New York Weekly Journal,* mostly expressed the government line. Upon Zenger's assumption of ownership, the tone of the paper, specifically that of the December 3, 1733 issue, became critical of the colonial government. Almost a year latter, Zenger was arrested and in 1735 was brought to trial for *seditious libel,* publishing false and defamatory statements against the government. The famous Philadelphia lawyer Andrew Hamilton defended him in one of the classic cases of American journalism. Hamilton argued that the jury had the right to determine (1) whether or not Zenger printed the paper, and (2) whether or not the material was in fact libelous. Hamilton fully admitted that Zenger had published the paper and the criticism of the governor. However, he also argued that the material was true and therefore could not be libelous. As the jury had the right to determine whether or not the material was true, it therefore had the right to determine whether or not Zenger had committed libel. The prosecutor in the case took the position that, though the jury could determine whether Zenger had in fact published the paper, it remained the judge's prerogative to determine whether the material was indeed libelous. When Hamilton argued that the jury had the right to *both* decisions, he won its favor; a not guilty verdict established, at least in principle, the freedom to criticize public officials.

surviving the revolution

With the American Revolution, the press became noticeably more political. Strife between the colonies and the Crown was bound to be aired in a press that reflected the colonists' deep mistrust of the political control they had fled. The Crown's attempt to place controls on the press also was a natural reaction. Newspapers, the stalwart of information during the Revolution, quenched the people's thirst for information during a time of crisis. Thus, despite all the economic tribulations of war, 75 percent of the newspapers that commenced production during the Revolution still were in existence at its conclusion. Those that survived were healthier for the experience. The war had made them more aware of their responsibility in a free society, and their content had become much more than just a regurgitation of commerce and government news. The press was on its way to becoming a true political force that would later join the ranks of the executive, legislative, and judicial branches of government as America's *fourth estate*. Although not the most objective press by modern standards, these newspapers were nevertheless the training ground for several notable persons who raised the prestige of the early colonial printer to that of publisher and editor.

the telegraph and instant news

During the nineteenth century, technology significantly aided the newspaper industry. In 1844, Samuel Morse invented the telegraph, and news now could be transmitted rapidly over long distances to major cities and rural communities. No longer did important information have to wait for ship, pony express, or stagecoach that sometimes took weeks and months to reach its destination The era of the "bulletin" meant that news could be reported on the same day (Figure 2-5) that it occurred. Consider your reaction if you had been used to receiving news from distant places weeks and months after it happened, when suddenly you could be in touch with events the day they occurred. Certainly your awareness and desire for information would increase. The desire for "instant" news often resulted in the common practice of newspapers' preceding their headlines by the word TELEGRAPHIC (Figure 2-6).

the Atlantic cable: a link with Europe

Along with an improved domestic relay system, another development, the Atlantic Cable, provided the international link for news coverage. Completed in 1866,

Figure 2-5 The telegraph and news of war were powerful ingredients to interest readers in the newspaper. In many communities, the arrival of the newspaper was a major event. A painting by Richard Caton Woodville graphically captured this excitement and showed the reading of news about the Mexican War (1846–1848).

the Atlantic Cable prompted predictions that the European mails would become little more than waste paper. "The profound discussions of the old world press will pass un-read." stated the *New York Times*. Although plagued with periodic breakdowns, the cable provided the first direct link between the United States and Europe and helped disseminate news of international events both in the United States and abroad. The American student of economics and politics could open the *New York Times* and read news of British commerce and the activities of Parliament. The student in England could check the latest edition of the *Times of London* to learn the actions of Congress and the going price of cotton. Clearly, the newspaper had become an international organ.

the penny press

Although the press was becoming well accepted, its appeal still was limited to society's elite. Written in dense prose and dealing with what often were complex political issues, the average American found little interest in these "statesmen" newspapers. All this began to change in the 1830s with the introduction of a new style of journalism and a new style of newspaper. Small newspapers with a lighter style, stressing not political issues but the crime, sex, and gossip of the day, sold for one cent. The new publications ushered in the era of the *penny press* which, although the price has increased, still sees its brand of journalism alive in certain contemporary tabloids.

The earliest penny press, the *New York Sun*, began in 1833 out of the desperation of an all but bankrupt printer named Benjamin H. Day. Day quickly left the impoverished ranks and, with news of immediate interest, achieved almost overnight success. The *Sun* was quickly copied by similar ventures, including one in 1835 by another hard-pressed editor named James Gordon Bennett. Bennett founded the *New York Morning Herald* which became eminently successful, even though it experienced a 100 percent price increase. Philadelphia with its *Public Ledger* and Baltimore with its *Sun* also joined the ranks of successful penny newspapers.

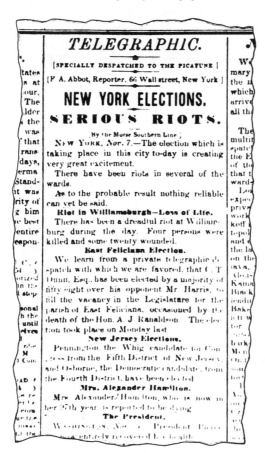

Figure 2-6 The telegraph signalled a new interest in news and even headlined columns of some mid-nineteenth century papers.

What the penny press managed to do was increase newspaper circulation to all-time highs, which meant that advertisers started paying attention to these penny newspapers, even if the social elite found them abhorrent. The penny press also was distributed on sidewalks, not through subscriptions. Bought wholesale by vendors, they were peddled on the streets by hucksters. Along with the cry of the newspaper vendor came bigger headlines, all designed to attract the attention of the readers.

The penny press, in content, did not vanish from the scene. It convinced many nineteenth-century publishers that the penny press's style of reporting, and its content based more on features and a variety of news rather than merely on political and business news, could be a powerful and profitale voice.

THE MINORITY PRESS

The history of American newspapers is dotted with publications directed to specialized audiences, specifically racial minorities. Today, we can find newspapers published in many different languages appealing to the various ethnic populations of the United States and Canada. Two early newspapers that stand out in history belonged to the black and American Indian populations.

the black press

The first black newspaper is dated March 16, 1827. *Freedom's Journal* (Figure 2-7) was edited by the Reverend Samuel Cornish and John Russwurm. The newspaper began publication in the politically restrictive atmosphere of New York City in the late 1820s. Slavery had been partially abolished by a new law that was to take effect on July 4 1827, but it applied only to those over forty. White slave owners were prohibited from transporting slaves outside New York state, but that had not stopped the practice. The right to vote, which had belonged to free blacks in both the North and the South, was beginning to be withdrawn by new state laws, and there were no newspapers to plead the cause of the black people. In fact, some of the newspapers were even making vile attacks on blacks. The time was ripe for a newspaper directed to and published by blacks.

The first issue had a four-page, four-column format. The headlines, small and brief, read "To Our Patrons," "Common Schools in New York," and "The Effects of Slavery," among others. The newspaper told its readers: "We wish to plead our own cause. Too long have others spoken for us. Too long has the publick been deceived by misrepresentations, in things which concern us dearly, though in the estimation of some mere trifles." Carrying news of foreign countries of special interest to blacks, the first issue had news of Haiti and Sierre Leone as well as the "Memoirs of Captain Paul Cuffee," who led a trading ship staffed by free blacks. *Freedom's Journal* went on to clash openly with other

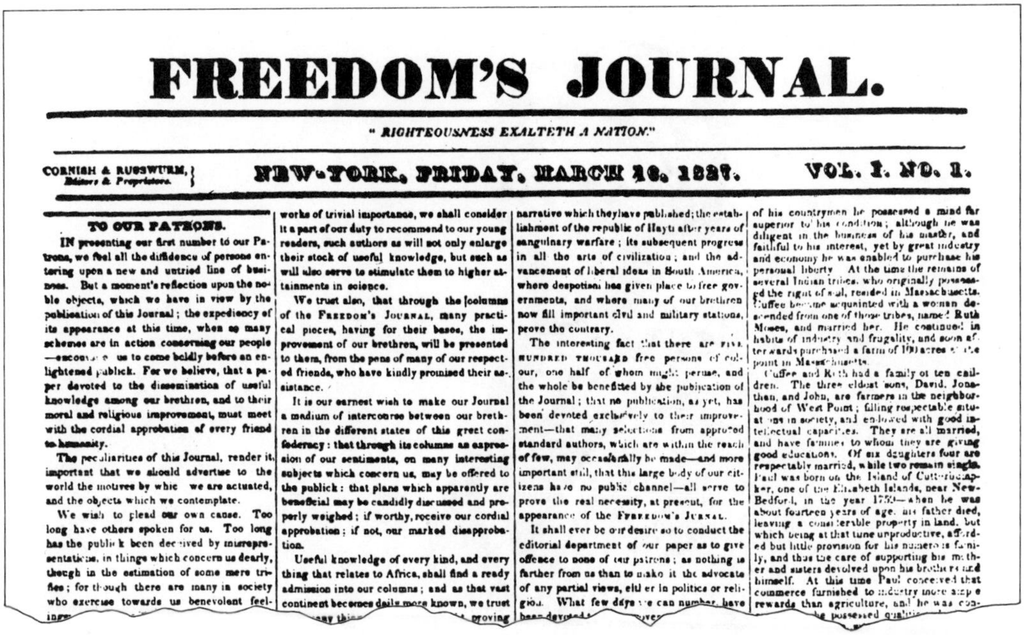

FREEDOM'S JOURNAL.

"RIGHTEOUSNESS EXALTETH A NATION."

CORNISH & RUSSWURM, Editors & Proprietors. | NEW-YORK, FRIDAY, MARCH 16, 1827. | VOL. I. NO. 1.

TO OUR PATRONS.

IN presenting our first number to our Patrons, we feel all the diffidence of persons entering upon a new and untried line of business. But a moment's reflection upon the noble objects, which we have in view by the publication of this Journal; the expediency of its appearance at this time, when so many schemes are in action concerning our people—encourage us to come boldly before an enlightened publick. For we believe, that a paper devoted to the dissemination of useful knowledge among our brethren, and to their moral and religious improvement, must meet with the cordial approbation of every friend to humanity.

The peculiarities of this Journal, render it important that we should advertise to the world the motives by which we are actuated, and the objects which we contemplate.

We wish to plead our own cause. Too long have others spoken for us. Too long has the publick been deceived by misrepresentations, in things which concern us dearly, though in the estimation of some mere trifles; for though there are many in society who exercise towards us benevolent feelings

[...] works of trivial importance, we shall consider it a part of our duty to recommend to our young readers, such authors as will not only enlarge their stock of useful knowledge, but such as will also serve to stimulate them to higher attainments in science.

We trust also, that through the columns of the FREEDOM'S JOURNAL, many practical pieces, having for their bases, the improvement of our brethren, will be presented to them, from the pens of many of our respected friends, who have kindly promised their assistance.

It is our earnest wish to make our Journal a medium of intercourse between our brethren in the different states of this great confederacy: that through its columns an expression of our sentiments, on many interesting subjects which concern us, may be offered to the publick: that plans which apparently are beneficial may be candidly discussed and properly weighed; if worthy, receive our cordial approbation; if not, our marked disapprobation.

Useful knowledge of every kind, and every thing that relates to Africa, shall find a ready admission into our columns; and as that vast continent becomes daily more known, we trust [...] proving

[...] narrative which they have published; the establishment of the republic of Hayti after years of sanguinary warfare; its subsequent progress in all the arts of civilization; and the advancement of liberal ideas in South America, where despotism has given place to free governments, and where many of our brethren now fill important civil and military stations, prove the contrary.

The interesting fact that there are FIVE HUNDRED THOUSAND free persons of colour, one half of whom might peruse, and the whole be benefitted by the publication of the Journal; that no publication, as yet, has been devoted exclusively to their improvement—that many selections from approved standard authors, which are within the reach of few, may occasionally be made—and more important still, that this large body of our citizens have no public channel—all serve to prove the real necessity, at present, for the appearance of the FREEDOM'S JOURNAL.

It shall ever be our desire so to conduct the editorial department of our paper as to give offence to none of our patrons; as nothing is farther from us than to make it the advocate of any partial views, either in politics or religion. What few days we can number, have been devoted [...]

[...] of his countrymen he possessed a mind far superior to his condition; although he was diligent in the business of his master, and faithful to his interest, yet by great industry and economy he was enabled to purchase his personal liberty. At the time the remains of several Indian tribes, who originally possessed the right of soil, resided in Massachusetts. Cuffee became acquainted with a woman descended from one of those tribes, named Ruth Moses, and married her. He continued in habits of industry and frugality, and soon afterwards purchased a farm of 100 acres at the point in Massachusetts.

Cuffee and Ruth had a family of ten children. The three eldest sons, David, Jonathan, and John, are farmers in the neighbourhood of West Point; filling respectable situations in society, and endowed with good intellectual capacities. They are all married, and have families to whom they are giving good educations. Of six daughters four are respectably married, while two remain single. Paul was born on the Island of Cutterhunker, one of the Elizabeth Islands, near New-Bedford, in the year 1759—when he was about fourteen years of age, his father died, leaving a considerable property in land, but which being at that time unproductive, afforded but little provision for his numerous family, and thus the care of supporting his mother and sisters devolved upon his brothers and himself. At this time Paul conceived that commerce furnished to industry more ample rewards than agriculture, and he was con[...] he possessed qualiti[...]

Figure 2-7 Freedom's Journal, published in 1827 in New York City.

newspapers of the day. Russwurm remained with the paper for only about a year. When he left, Cornish continued the publication under another name, *Rights for All.*

the American Indian press

At about the same time *Freedom's Journal* was championing its cause, another minority, the American Indians, was the object of similar oppression. In Georgia, the government was trying to move the Cherokees out of the South and into the Midwest to free southern lands for farming. An Indian named Sequoyah (Figure 2-8), a Cherokee, was laboring amid skepticism from the tribe to try to develop a code of symbols that would permit the Indians to communicate as the white people did, in written prose. He worked on this for almost twelve years. Finally, in a special demonstration for the tribal elders, Sequoyah watched as his sons demonstrated the new Cherokee alphabet of eighty-six symbols. Immediately, the rather speedy transition to literacy began to take place, and special arrangements were made to obtain a printing press capable of printing the new alphabet. The first Indian newspaper, the *Cherokee Phoenix* (Figure 2-9), was published on February 21, 1828 by a mixed-blood tribe member named Elias Boudinot. White printers friendly to the Indian cause were hired to print the

Figure 2-8 More than anyone in the Indian nation, "Se-Quo-Yah" was responsible for developing an alphabet (Cherokee Tribe) and introducing the first newspaper, *The Cherokee Phoenix* (Figure 2-9), for Indians. (The Library of Congress)

newspaper. Written in both Cherokee and English, the first issue of the newspaper had four pages.

Although the crusade to force the Indians from their land continued, the militia moved in approximately ten years later and drove the Cherokees westward. In what became known as the Trial of Tears, the Indians gradually settled in Oklahoma territory. Accounts of what happened to both Sequoyah and Boudinot are conflicting. Sequoyah fell out of favor with the tribe over his views on the western emigration. History records that he either crossed the border into Mexico or was labeled a traitor by the tribe and had his ears cropped and his forehead branded. Boudinot, whose favor with the tribe was equally perilous after the move West, is reported to have suffered a brutal death at the hands of his political tribal opponents.

WOMEN IN JOURNALISM

While the black and the Indian press were playing important journalistic roles during the early nineteenth century, women also were beginning to enter the profession and make their mark. Both as reporters and publishers, women carried not only the issues of the country but also those of their own cause to the readers. In 1831, sixty-one year-old Anne Royall founded a publication entitled *Paul Pry*. Another newspaper under Royall, called *The Huntress*, followed this example and bannered the cause of equal rights for Indians and immigrants. By 1850, the Washington press corps was beginning to accept women in its ranks. Jane Grey Swisshelm paved the way by entering the Senate press gallery on April 17, 1850.

At about this time, Ida Minerva Tarbell (Figure 2-10) was born in 1857 in Erie County, Pennsylvania. Educated at Allegheny College in Pennsylvania, she came from one of the old American oil families who made their fortunes from the Pennsylvania oil fields. By the turn of the century, Tarbell was writing for such major magazines as *McClure's*, and she was turning the oil industry's heads, and much of the journalism profession's as well, with her investigative reporting and her stories about big business.

Figure 2-9 First issue of *The Cherokee Phoenix* printed in both Cherokee and English.

Figure 2-10 Ida Tarbell, early journalist and author who wrote about the industrial life of Western Pennsylvania. (Allegheny College Archives)

Another famous woman reporter of the late nineteenth century was Elizabeth Cochrane Seaman. Under the pen name Nellie Bly (Figure 2-11), she became famous for her escapades in the interest of her employer, *The New York World.* Some of these escapades included being admitted to a New York insane asylum so that readers could have a firsthand report of the care of the mentally ill and being arrested so that she could report how police treated women prisoners. But the feat which gave Bly her greatest reputation was her around-the-world trip that beat the time described in Jules Verne's famous novel, *Around the World in Eighty Days.* By every conceivable means of transportation, including ships and hand carts, she made the trip in just over seventy-two days. Her career started at the age of eighteen with the *Pittsburgh Dispatch,* and she died in 1922.

Ida Tarbell, Nellie Bly, Jane Grey Swisshelm, and Anne Royall are just a few of the many women who contributed to journalism. From colonial printers to today's newspaper executives in charge of some of the largest and most influential papers in the world, women have been and continue to be tremendously important to the newspaper industry.

THE WAR BETWEEN THE STATES

The mood of the country was much different during the War Between the States than it was during the Revolution. The country was fractured in the middle, not unified from the center. The War was a trying time for editors and readers alike. The entire philsophy upon which the War was fought gave editors a variety of choices. The foremost one was choosing between two presidents—Abraham Lincoln and Jefferson Davis. In addition, within almost any readership could be found opponents to any war effort, significant in number and vocal in presence. Or, as in the border states, sympathy toward both sides could be equally strong. Thus, while their newspapers carried local news of this local War being fought by local troops, editors could choose among supporting two different armies, two different presidents, and three different causes—the North, the South, and the Union.

Many newspapers distinguished themselves for their war coverage. As wars had in the past, the War created an almost insatiable thirst for news. Newspapers such as the *Cincinnati Gazette*, the *Richmond Enquirer*, the *New York Herald*, the *New Orleans Picayune*, the *Memphis Appeal*, the *Savannah Republican*, and the *Charleston Courier*, were life lines of information to troops in the field, families, and businesspeople. Papers such as Horace Greeley's *Tribune* carried persuasive editorials. Correspondents such as Peter W. Alexander at Gettysburg and Antietam, B. S. Osbon at Fort Sumter, Whitelaw Reid at Shiloh, and Lawrence A. Gobright at Lincoln's death became historical by-lines. Newspapers

Figure 2-11 A world traveler and journalist, Nellie Bly achieved fame for, among other things, her around-the-world reporting assignment for *The New York World*.

also were life lines of information for the enemy, and a war correspondent's publicity of impending military campaigns tipped off more than one officer. The result was the nation's first experience with government censorship of the press during wartime. Unfortunately, the ability of the telegraph to speed news thousands of miles in a day suddenly became a liability for the press. With generals putting pressure on the government, some newspapers were temporarily suspended. Although war news still continued to flow, the prepublicity of military maneuvers came to a halt.

The War also changed the style of American journalism. The demands of battlefield dispatches, the unreliable transmission systems that could be cut off at any moment, all bred a new breed of writer. The concise lead and the headline formats became the standard, and that style continues today in both print and broadcast news.

RECONSTRUCTION AND WESTWARD EXPANSION

With the War Between the States behind it, the United States moved toward a new union, western expansion, and the industrial revolution. With all three traveled the newspapers.

The West also spawned its share of great journalists and editorial writers. Harvey W. Scott (Figure 2-12) of the Portland *Oregonian* was such an

Figure 2-12 Harvey Scott of the *Oregonian*. (The *Oregonian-Oregon Journal*)

Figure 2-13 Joseph Pulitzer, from
a portrait by John Singer Sargent.
(Photo by D. Bulick)

editorialist. The *Oregonian* had been founded in 1850, but it was not until the full effect of the western movement was felt that Scott's editorials began to be taken seriously east of the Mississippi River. He saw the industrial revolution from a viewpoint both touched by eastern technology yet tempered by the great expanses of the Northwest and its close proximity to the lumber industry. Perhaps through Scott's eyes, unfilled with the crowded populations of the East and the factories of New England, came some of the most intelligent writing of the day. Other early newspapers famous in the West included the *Sacramento Union* started in 1851, Salt Lake City's *Desert News* in 1850, and the *Dallas News* in 1885.

In the Midwest and South, newspapers made the transition from the Civil War to an industrial economy. Many began their publishing ventures in the fresh atmosphere of economic recovery. In Milwaukee, the *Journal* was founded in 1882 with its famous publisher, Lucius W. Nieman. Under Nieman's guidance, the newspaper became a respected voice, both nationally and internationally. Nieman later helped advance journalism education by establishing the Nieman Fellowships at Harvard University.

In St. Louis another publisher was making his mark, Joseph Pulitzer (Figure 2-13). He later had the Pulitzer Prizes in journalism named after him. Born in Hungary in 1847, Pulitzer came to America and worked on some German-language newspapers. After serving a term as a state officer in Missouri, he

Figure 2-14 Henry W. Grady. (*The Atlanta Journal-The Atlanta Constitution*)

managed to buy the *St. Louis Dispatch* at a bankruptcy auction. It became the *Post-Dispatch* and, although filled with its share of sensationalized reporting in its infancy, matured into a respected daily. Pulitzer broadened his journalism base in 1883 by buying the *New York World*.

In Kentucky, Henry Watterson of the *Louisville Journal-Courier* exerted a major influence on Civil War reconstruction. A border state, Kentucky felt the pressures of both the North and the South. Watterson, who became editor of the *Journal-Courier* in 1868, called for a united nation and garnered respect from both sides. Farther south, Henry W. Grady (Figure 2-14) in 1880 assumed the managing editor's position of the *Atlanta Constitution*. He increased the staff of the newspaper and strengthened the editorial page, bringing it up to a par with the Louisville *Journal-Courier*.

YELLOW JOURNALISM

The penny press not only proved that "light" news sold at an inexpensive price could be highly successful, it also laid the groundwork for an era of journalism that was to arise some forty years later. The star participants were Joseph Pulitzer, who published the *New York World*, and William Randolph Hearst (Figure

2-15), who in 1887 became the editor of the *San Francisco Examiner.* Hearst's association with the newspaper business came from his father, who was more an aspiring politician than a journalist and had originally acquired the *Examiner* for political purposes. William Randolph Hearst ventured East to Harvard where he gained fame more for his pranks than for his studies and was eventually expelled. He did manage to acquire newspaper experience on Pulitzer's *World,* and when he returned to San Francisco, took the lessons of sensationalism from the penny press and applied them to big-city journalism. With bold, eye-gripping headlines and various escapades to generate or report the news, Hearst's *Examiner* began to climb in circulation. The result? It doubled—then tripled—both circulation and profits.

But San Francisco was not the only place Hearst set out to tame. He had studied the ways of his old boss Pulitzer and had watched the new technology and somewhat sensational journalism already practiced by the Boston newspapers. Now, his lessons, already learned and proved workable in San Francisco, were about to be brought to New York to do battle with Pulitzer. Hearst used *Examiner* money to buy the faltering *New York Morning Journal.* He then "purchased" most of the good newspaper talent in New York City. The result was a steady climb in the *Morning Journal's* circulation as Hearst splashed more and more sensational headlines. Pulitzer himself could not even match the brazen Hearst.

Figure 2-15 William Randolph Hearst.

When Hearst hired away one of Pulitzer's top illustrators, Richard F. Outcault, it was the beginning of a battle that left an imprint on journalism that remains today. Outcault had drawn a cartoon about life in New York's crowded tenements that featured a child cartoon character. The extremely popular "kid" appeared in a yellow dress and became known as "the Yellow Kid." When Outcault came to the *Morning Journal*, the kid came too, almost. She also stayed behind to be drawn by George B. Luks of Pulitzer's newspaper. Appearing in the promotional literature of both newspapers, the "circulation war" was in full force, and a new title had been given to this era of sensational, competitive, and in many ways irresponsible journalism—*yellow journalism*.

It remained as a way of selling newspapers well into the 1900s and still can be seen today. National scandal sheets use the technique as common practice. Characterized by large headlines and sensational reporting, yellow journalism is credited by some with starting the Spanish-American War when it sensationalized the sinking of the warship *Maine* in 1898. Hearst and his empire became the subject of a famous movie, *Citizen Kane*, and most responsible journalists would rather the era of yellow journalism were banished to the archives.

NEWSPAPERS AND NEWSGATHERING: THE TWENTIETH CENTURY

The presence of professional organizations and the subsequent criticism of the press that began to appear in other media, namely magazines, began to temper the sensational "yellow" reporting. World War I arrived, and there was enough action to report without emphasizing the crime-sex-sin syndrome that splashed earlier front pages. World War I also prompted, as wars always do, a new public desire for news, and newspapers began to rely heavily on syndicated news services. Today, such services as United Press International, Associated Press, and Reuters are right hands to newspapers, which rely on them not only for national and international news but also for high-speed data networks and photographs.

Typical of the wire services that have evolved through the twentieth century is United Press International. UPI was born as the brain child of an aggressive newspaper executive named John Vandercook of the E. W. Scripps (Figure 2-16) newspapers. Scripps had been operating news services for his own newspapers when Vandercook convinced him of the wisdom of merging his news services with the Publishers Press Association to form the United Press Associations. Vandercook died a year later, and the United Press operations came under the directorship of Roy W. Howard (Figure 2-17). World War I brought the United Press into its own with the establishment of foreign bureaus serving both American and foreign newspapers. Roy Howard left United Press in 1920 and became an executive in the Scripps newspapers. United Press continued its expansion and pioneered such services as a broadcast news wire and the United Press Audio Service in 1956. In 1958, the service merged with the International

E.W. Scripps

Figure 2-16

Roy Howard

Figure 2-17 (Courtesy: Scripps-Howard and Jack Shannon)

News Service to become United Press International. It currently provides news pictures, a television news service, a cable television news service, and is pioneering efforts in high-speed news transmission.

Roy Howard, meanwhile, continued to move up the ranks of the Scripps newspapers—newspapers that were in many ways indicative of the style of journalism that evolved from the industrial revolution. A large class of factory workers had emerged from this revolution as a powerful but disorganized political force in America. E. W. Scripps, like many other publishers of his time, exercised a strong *personal* editorial influence on the American labor movement and called for the organization of the working class. Scripps took newspapers, some of them the outgrowth of the penny press, and began to direct their content to the less educated working class. He personally and directly influenced editorials and viewed the newspapers as the true means of communication about the political system. Scripp's son, Robert Paine Scripps, continued the newspaper legacy when his father died. When Robert died in 1938, one of the three key people to take over the newspapers was Roy Howard. Howard remained influential in what became the Scripps-Howard Newspapers, owned by the parent E. W. Scripps Company.

The E. W. Scripps Company, like many other major publishing enterprises, has now diversified into additional communications media, including broadcasting. But the personal style of journalism, evident when entrepreneurs such as E. W. Scripps was in *direct* control of his newspapers, has been replaced by corporate mergers and public ownership in which parent companies may look more closely at profits than at editorial lines. Surviving as a remnant of that past are some small-town dailies, which in certain parts of the country still exercise that personal style of journalism so popular with big dailies of the past.

THE CHANGING INDUSTRY

As we look at the growth trends of the newspaper over the past twenty-five years, we notice that circulation rose very slowly (Figure 2-18). The increase in circulation between 1946 and 1977 did not keep up with the general population growth.

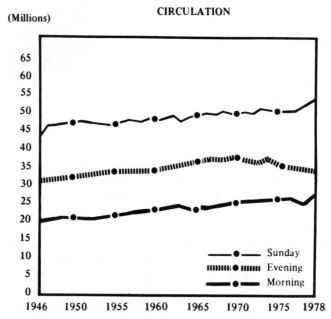

Figure 2-18 Daily newspaper circulation. (American Newspaper Publishers Association)

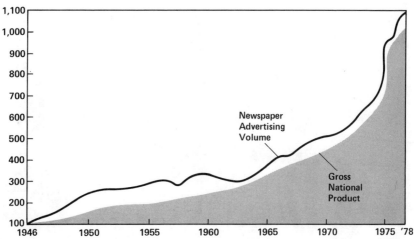

Index Of Growth (1946 Base)

Figure 2-19 Daily newspaper advertising volume. (American Newspaper Publishers Association)

This did not, however, spell financial gloom, quite the contrary. Income of most newspapers, through both advertising and sales, increased steadily. Newspapers still claim the major share of the advertising dollar. Economic data show that the growth of the newspaper industry has generally equalled and in several ways exceeded the growth of the economy (Figure 2-19). Expenditures for advertising for instance, have more than kept pace with the gross national product, and employment in the industry has expanded at a more rapid rate than have composite United States employment indicators. The success of the industry is due in large part to its adaptability to the new technology developed over the last fifty years. Supplementary features of the modern newspaper have also widened its appeal; such things as special features and syndicated colums grasp our attention just as much as news does. The evening sports page, "Dear Abby," "Ann Landers," and "Peanuts" all are lures for us to spend more time reading a daily newspaper. To boost circulation, many newspapers are appealing to more specialized audiences. Sectionals are becoming popular, and regional editions for suburban communities are adding to newspaper appeal (Figure 2-20). International editions also reach specialized audiences. For example, the *Wall Street Journal* publishes an Asian edition specializing in the economic news of Asia (Figure 2-21).

economic indicators

Along with the positive indicators have come signs of caution for newspaper publishers. A research study by the Bureau of Business Research and Service at the University of Wisconsin highlighted these concerns.[3] *First*, as consumers we

Figure 2-20 Sectionals are adding to the variety of newspaper content, helping many dailies to boost circulation and permitting advertisers to reach specialized audiences. (Courtesy, The Baltimore Sunpapers)

are finding it increasingly difficult to read more than one newspaper per day. We even are finding it difficult to read one newspaper per day. Newspapers are becoming larger; a major city edition may include sixty pages instead of the ten or twenty that comprised the major city editions at the turn of the century. *Second*, other media vie for our attention. We have at our disposal a wealth of magazines; we listen to the radio; we watch television; we receive direct-mail literature; and we go to the movies. *Third*, the shorter work week of many businesses and the new technology gives us more free time, longer vacations, and higher income to spend on recreational activities. Again, these activities take away from time spent reading. *Fourth*, deterioration of the central city means that we are not as apt to go downtown after dark and purchase an evening edition from the corner news-stand. The convenience of listening to the radio on the drive to work is another factor to be considered. *Fifth*, wire services carrying news and information from around the world are available at moderate fees to even the smallest newspapers, and these papers are taking advantage of this. Thus, their ability to carry national and international news cuts into the circulation of the major metropolitan dailies. *Sixth*, raw paper costs and labor costs are steadily increasing. Let's examine paper costs in more detail.

newsprint: cost and supply

Newsprint, the paper upon which newspapers are printed, has reached record consumption (Figure 2-22). A research study by the Bureau of Business Research and Service at the University of Wisconsin estimates newsprint consumption for 1980 will peak at 13 million tons, an increase of about six million from 1959.[4] But increase is only part of the story—cost of newsprint also has jumped because supply has not kept up with demand. There are many reasons for this economic disparity. One is the profit margins of paper manufacturers and suppliers. In the past, these merchants have proposed various cost-per-ton price increases. The newspaper industry justifiably complained loudly and effectively postponed rate increases for some time. Gradually, however, economic factors in the paper manufacturing and supply segments of the industry became depressed. With reduced profits, the manufacturers and suppliers could not expand and increase

Figure 2-21 (Dow Jones & Company, Inc.)

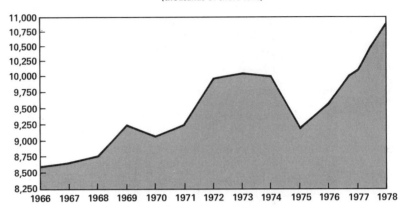

Growth In Newsprint Consumption
(thousands of short tons)

Figure 2-22 Newsprint consumption. (American Newspaper Publishers Association)

production. Finally, about 1971, everything came to a head. The gap between supply and demand began to close. The manufacturers and suppliers increased prices. The energy crisis arrived, and labor disputes developed which affected everyone from lumberjacks to shippers. Supplies dwindled. Costs soared.

As Canadian supplies began to dwindle, the United States's suppliers had to make up the difference.[5] The north central states, with newsprint production up 1,151 percent, carried most of the burden. To cut shipping weight and to make the same tonnage produce more paper, the industry is experimenting with new ways to retain paper strength while making it lighter. Breakage, however, is a big problem. The lighter stock cannot withstand the stress of high-speed presses. Moreover, very thin newsprint causes a "see through" effect which makes the finished newspaper difficult to read.

To cut costs, some newspapers are cutting the size of their pages. One of the most drastic reductions was that of the *Christian Science Monitor*, which switched to a tabloid format half the size of past editions. *Monitor* subscription prices also rose. Other newspapers cut pages and cancelled features. Even a reduction in margins can save thousands of dollars, depending on the size of the newspaper.

living with labor and new technology

New techniques in printing mean new equipment, new expenses, and new personnel to learn the trade. If labor unions are affected, technology can be forced to creep at a snail's pace when the unions try to protect jobs. The threat of strikes is common when skilled workers are fired because technology has made their jobs obsolete. When such strikes do occur, the result has been serious damage to the newspaper. Strikers have been accused of smashing presses to stop a newspaper from being printed by scab (nonunion) employees. This action may have several consequences: the newspaper may either shut down, print the editions elsewhere, bow to union demands, or a combination of all three. Personnel costs for the average newspaper now run between 50 and 60 percent of the total operating expenses. When labor costs approach the latter figure, cuts in other areas generally need to be made. For at this point, profit margins shrink, and the expense of new technology can become prohibitive.

newspaper advertising

Before the impact of television, the fall of every year was a boom time for newspapers. It was new car time, and to announce their new models, the major auto manufacturers would purchase advertising in newspapers of every size. For the smaller newspaper, it was big and important money. Yet in the last ten years, the small newspapers have seen the auto makers' money vanish. Such has been the way of most national advertisers' media buying habits. They have concentrated their purchases on the larger metropolitan dailies and television, while withdrawing their national advertising from smaller newspapers. Newspaper advertising in general, however, is increasing, and newspapers still outdistance radio and television in their share of the advertising dollar (Figure 2-23). Estimated expenditures for 1980 are $9.8 billion. The major share of that figure is attributed to local newspaper advertising, an increase of more than 100 percent in both categories. National advertising expenditures have not enjoyed similar gains. While 1980 estimates are for $1.5 billion, that is an increase of only slightly more than $.5 billion dollars from 1960 expenditures. Comparably, national advertising on television has soared.

Despite the increase in advertising expenditures, some forecasters offer only cautious optimism about the future of the newspaper industry.[6] Not that an immediate danger of depression looms, but the industry must realize that it is

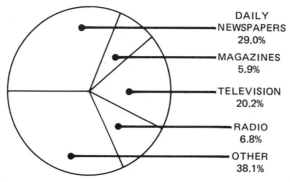

DAILY
NEWSPAPERS
29.0%

MAGAZINES
5.9%

TELEVISION
20.2%

RADIO
6.8%

OTHER
38.1%

Figure 2-23 Newspaper's share of the advertising dollar, compared to other media. (McCann Erickson, Inc. and American Newspaper Publishers Association)

living in an era of rapidly changing social and economic conditions. In chapter 1 we studied the theoretical development posited by Maisel that would link our existence in a postindustrial society with an increase in specialized media. With the advent of new technology and changing life styles, will we change the way we "consume" today's typical newspaper? Will our life style changes also evolve more rapidly than the newspaper industry can compensate for them? The ability of a newspaper to survive thus will depend on freeing itself from tradition, facing the reality of competing media, and understanding the changes that might have to be made.

THE ELECTRONIC NEWSROOM

If you had been a large city newspaper publisher in the early 1900s, you would most likely have set your news copy by the linotype or "hot type" method. With linotype, the linotype operator works at a typewriterlike keyboard. There is a series of steps, some performed by the operator and some performed automatically by the machine. The end product of the process is a line of type that has been cast in molten metal (thus the name "hot type"). These lines of type, or "slugs," are assembled into pages, and finally a special curved metal plate is made for rotary presses. In a small newspaper, printing is done from the original type in a flatbed press.

from hot to cold type

Linotype machines did not eliminate any of the processes in typesetting, but they did mechanize and accelerate typesetting. Because of increased speed and efficiency in typesetting the news, publishers could produce larger newspapers and produce them faster than when type was set by hand. With the exception of the steam-powered printing presses, linotype machines did more than any other invention to launch the newspaper industry forward into the twentieth century.

The invention of lithographic printing, commonly called "offset," to augment letterpress printing, increased printing efficiency in the 1950s. Offset differs from letterpress printing in the following ways: (1) a photographic image of the finished page is used to produce a (2) smooth surface plate from which to print the newspaper; the image is not transferred to the paper by raised typefaces.

The advantages of offset printing for the newspaper publisher over letterpress are lower cost of offset plates and better quality of printing, especially illustrations, that can be obtained.

The 1970s brought another change to the typesetting process—the computer. Computer-set type is also called "cold type." The operator types the copy on the computer's electronic keyboard. The computer sets the type electronically, using a memory system to position every letter in place. Each line and margin is set according to the input commands in the computer. The output is strips of special paper with columns of type just as they will appear in the newspaper. These strips are then pasted up in columns on a "mechanical" for each page. Headlines can be added by hand or programmed in the computer, and illustrations are put in by hand. The entire page is then photographed and ready for the next step, the production of the offset printing plate.

goodbye to typewriters?

Electronic keyboards and visual display terminals (VDTs) that look like television screens have been interfaced with the computer and are actually replacing typewriters in the newsroom (Figure 2-24). Reporters now type their copy on electronic keyboards and watch the letters appear before them on the VDTs. They can automatically "store" their story in the computer for later perusal by an editor. The headline writer than uses the computer to call up the story and prepares a headline for it. With yet another push of a button, the completed story is electronically set in type, photographed on the photosensitive printing plate, and rolls off the press minutes later. Although the newspaper looks much the same as the one composed by linotype, the actual process is radically different—it has become a product of the electronic revolution.

Most major newspapers have made the change to cold type and are adding computer technology to their newsroom. Publishers can justify the change by

Figure 2-24 Visual display terminals (VDTs), also called cathode ray tubes (CRTs), are replacing the typewriter and becoming commonplace in major newspapers and other media. (Courtesy, Dow Jones & Company, Inc.)

reduced labor and materials costs. Labor unions, however, are slowing the transition in many areas as they try to protect the jobs of workers who operate the older machines. Bound by union contracts, publishers cannot fire a linotype operator the way they fired the typesetter at the turn of the century—at least without inciting a strike. As these employees retire or can be retrained, more newspapers will undoubtedly switch to electronic printing.

For the journalist, computer technology brings two advantages. First, more money can be devoted to the actual process of gathering and reporting the news, since fewer people are needed to actually produce the paper. This does not mean that converting to computer technology will necessarily mean an increase in the reporting staff. However, there are some cost savings that can usually be realized. Second, computers speed up the process of placing a news story into print. If there is a 10:30 A.M. deadline in order for news to roll off the press and hit the street by 5:00 P.M., reporters will obviously be unable to get a late breaking story into print. With the arrival of radio and television, media that can air news as it is happening, this time factor has become even more crucial. Now, along with having the edge over radio and television in the amount of coverage that it can give to an event, the newspaper has more time to report complete and accurate stories to its readers.

Figure 2-25 Laser and satellite technology are permitting newspapers to reach regional audiences simultaneously with current information and specialized reporting features. (Courtesy, Western Union)

computer technology in advertising and distribution

Computer technology also has become a part of other phases of newspaper publishing, such as advertising and distribution. If you are a business executive and want to place an advertisement in the evening edition of your local paper but want to reach only one part of the city, a computer-based distribution system will put your ad in newspapers going exclusively to that section of the city, and you will be charged for the appropriate circulation. Even satellites and microwave transmission systems are part of the production of large newspapers. A facsimile of a major metropolitan daily can be sent via satellite to another country and be incorporated into one of its newspapers. It is now possible for newspapers with regional editions, such as the *Wall Street Journal*, to use computers and satellite technology to transmit entire pages from one city to another, electronically, in a matter of minutes (Figure 2-25).

Electronic distribution systems give newspapers a flexibility never before possible. Little more than a century after a crude method of dots and dashes was utilized to send individual letters across a telegraph wire, satellites now link news bureaus all over the nation and can almost instantaneously transmit news stories to any of these bureaus. Computers can automatically set the stories into type and start the presses rolling. The development of cable television systems can be expected to open up new frontiers for newspaper distribution.

teletext

Future newspaper subscribers may be able to "tune in" the evening edition of the local paper on television instead of having it delivered. Using special on-air coders and decoders, a television transmission system called teletext is in use in many parts of the world and in experimental use in Salt Lake City, Utah. Supplementary information ranging from movie schedules to supermarket prices are available. In actual use, a subscriber would simply select from an index list the "electronic page" to be placed on the television screen (Figure 2-26). By the twenty-first century, the era of the paper carrier may be a thing of the past.

EXPANDING ENTERPRISES

Independent newspapers are finding themselves the target of acquisitions by large newspaper corporations who are expanding their influence and ownership.

newspaper chains

Major companies such as the New York Times Company, the Times Mirror Company, Scripps-Howard, and Gannett are just some of the companies who own much more than either a single newspaper or, indeed, just newspapers

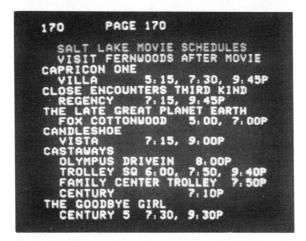

Figure 2-26 The experimental teletext system first introduced in the United States by Bonneville International of Salt Lake City could be a prototype of the electronic newspaper of tomorrow. The home subscriber can select from an index of different "pages," and then, by punching the correct code, can "call up" the full page of information. (Courtesy, Bill Loveless, Bonneville International and KSL-TV)

(Figure 2-27). For example, the Times Mirror Company owns the *Los Angeles Times*, Long Island's *Newsday*, the *Dallas Times Herald*, and the *Daily Pilot* in Orange County, California, among others. Gannett owns over seventy newspapers throughout the United States. It has even purchased entire chains of newspapers. In fact, 60 percent of the daily newspapers in the United States are owned by newspaper chains.

Part of the reason for the increase in chains is the necessity to invest

NEWSPAPER GROUP CIRCULATION TOTALS

	Weekday	Sunday
1. Knight-Ridder	3,699,896	4,312,702
2. Gannett	3,322,476	1,930,774
3. Tribune (Chicago)	3,208,128	4,267,839
4. Newhouse	3,190,341	3,546,844
5. Dow Jones	1,907,523	257,120
6. Scripps-Howard	1,873,930	1,544,581
7. Times Mirror	1,790,820	2,132,119
8. Hearst	1,407,933	2,176,849
9. Cox	1,212,743	1,224,676
10. Thomson (USA)	1,064,786	523,262
Total	22,678,576	21,916,766

Figure 2-27 Newspaper group circulation totals for the top ten group chains. (Source: *Editor and Publisher*)

operating profits from existing papers which may average as high as 25 percent to 30 percent. One of the most publicized acquisitions was when Australian businessman Rupert Murdock took over a myriad of New York publishing interests, including the *New York Post, New York Magazine,* the *Village Voice,* (Figure 2-28), and *New West Magazine.* Murdock's previous publishing record of borderline sensationalism worried some American journalists that too many media and their accompanying influence were in his hands.

diversified holdings

Many modern newspapers, much like other corporate conglomerates, have diversified into areas surprisingly different from publication of the local edition. The *Peoria Journal Star* of Peoria, Illinois, for example, has a rapidly developing broadcasting chain and publishes such magazines as *Shooting Times.* Dow Jones and Company, Inc. gives the reading public the *Wall Street Journal* and *Barron's National Business Financial Weekly.* In addition to publishing, its specialized services include the Dow Jones-Bunker Ramo News Retrieval Service, Inc., a jointly operated computerized news retrieval service available to stock brokerage firms, banks, and other businesses. The AP-Dow Jones Economic Report in conjunction with the Associated Press operates an international wire service. Operating twenty-four hours a day, six days a week, news is gathered by AP and Dow Jones and sent out around the world through AP facilities. Also part of the Dow Jones enterprises is the Ottaway Newspapers, Inc., a wholly owned subsidiary, and Dow Jones Books, yet another enterprise.

pros and cons of the media conglomerate

There are arguments both for and against the wisdom of such major holdings under one roof. Some argue that this arrangement seriously hampers the public's *ability to gain access* to the media. This is especially true when the media

the village VOICE

Copyright © 1978 The Village Voice   VOL XXIII No 12   THE WEEKLY NEWSPAPER OF NEW YORK   MARCH 20, 1978   60¢

WHO WANTS TO BE A HOROWITZ?

BY SEDGWICK CLARK (P. 36)

Death of a Young Poet

By Ianthe Thomas

They found her dead under a blue suede coat in the hall closet. She was curled in a ball, her legs tucked against her body, her head resting on her knees. The pearl-gray knit sweater she wore was soaked through with blood and her jeans covered with vomit.

On Friday, February 10, 1978, in New Jersey, Sudeka Harrison took 15 Valiums and slashed her wrists with a broken bottle. She was 15 years old.

Sunday, January 1, 1978: Mama say Linda to me Sudeka my name. Bunky know it, he say, no Grandma, her Sudeka. I got Natty Dread and diary for Christmas. Me, Sudeka, that's me. Somebody, Somebody, Bunky cry. He don't get truck. No woman, no cry, Bob sing. That's me. I tell them my new name. They laugh, these jokes. But I will write everyday like Jamal say. Don't forget the past Jamal say. Marley the people man. He sing Trenchtown Jamal say Trenchtown here. Little darling don't shed no tears. No woman, no cry. Sudeka. SUDEKA. SUDEKA AND JAMAL. Love forever.

The girl looking down from the photograph had a square face, the edges blurred by deep-set eyes. The bottom lip was slightly curled, her cheekbones flattened, Ethiopian-like, with hair that was parted

Poem for Jamal by Sudeka	In the ghetto we stand. what we see? Misery falling like rain

down the center in strong, thick, black braids. Sudeka at 10 years old.

Her mother remembers the day the picture was taken. It was a hot summer birthday party for a cousin. Sudeka had made the cake, coloring it a deep blue. She was so embarrassed that she hid in the kitchen. The relatives began chanting, "Bring on the baker," and finally she came out to their applause.

Mrs. Harrison squeezes her eyelids between her thick fingers, pressing the tears back. She takes the photo down from its nail on the living-room wall. She speaks very softly of how she made Sudeka quit school and get working papers. She *Continued on page 26*

MARGOT HENTOFF 'LOOKS' AT SOHO LOOKS (P.5)

An Exclusive Interview with Ralph Nader

Up Against the Iron Bladder

"The dyed-in-the-wool reactionaries never get worn down. They can best be described as men with iron bladders in iron cages. They're always there on the floor, they always vote the big-business way, they never get tired, they don't resign. The Allens never quit, the McClellans never quit. The Stennises never quit. They're iron bladders and iron cages."

BY COCKBURN & RIDGEWAY (P. 12)

Figure 2-28 Under publisher Rupert Murdoch, *The Village Voice* acquired a new layout style. (Reprinted by permission of *The Village Voice*. Copyright © The Village Voice, Inc., 1978)

holdings are in the same community. Concerned over this issue, the FCC has moved in to break up combinations of newspapers, television, and radio outlets when all are owned by the same party and serve the same people. Place yourself in the position of a politician running for office, who discovers that a certain journalist works for more than one medium. Perhaps the journalist writes a political column for the newspaper and also anchors a major radio newscast. You might feel that crossing this reporter could seriously jeopardize your campaign's publicity efforts either in the newspaper or on the radio station, and unfavorable publicity in one medium would surely be reflected in the other. Another argument against multiple holdings is the lack of *incentive to improve facilities*. If a newspaper-owned radio station is merely a hobby for the newspaper management, then even if the station is neglecting its community's needs, its personnel are underpaid, and its morale is low, the newspaper may be tempted to retain the status quo.

What the increase in newspaper chain acquisitions means to the public is still open to question. Certainly serious dangers can result. The tip-off comes when the ownership of the chain decides to use the newspapers as a unified editorial voice. A head office directing all newspapers in the chain to carry a certain editorial or to take a specific editorial line is all that is necessary to put the Justice Department on the alert for antitrust violations, to say nothing of the serious implications of monopolistic control of information.

Despite these drawbacks of monopolistic ownership, other examples reveal that rival media under the same owner can be as fiercely competitive as two football teams. When the same boss oversees both and can readily make a comparison, the incentive for excellence can far outweigh any concern over the identity of the owner. Similarly, when a broadcast division, a magazine division, and a newspaper division have an equal voice and vote in a board of directors meeting, and when each, in the presence of the others, must be accountable for its own operating procedures and profits, each will put forth maximal efforts.

The newspaper industry has remained prosperous, in some instances because of these diversified investments. Moreover, there is no indication that the public's desire for news is waning. For as both government and international politics become more complex and as new communication technology puts each individual in touch with people all around the world, newspapers and their allied services will continue to be a vital and prosperous part of the world economy.

SUMMARY

Newspapers are an important social and economic force in society. An outgrowth of the "posted bulletins" of early Italy, newspapers evolved from single sheets of paper locally distributed to multipage products with international distribution. In Germany, the first newspapers appeared in the early seventeenth century; in England the single-sheet corantos were being published by 1621. These were among the first newspapers to fit Otto Groth's standards for a true newspaper, which included being published periodically, mechanically reproduced, accessible, timely, and having varied content with continuity of organization.

American colonial newspapers contained mostly commercial news and were published by licensed printers who received government subsidies. Yet that content was changing. John Peter Zenger was tried for seditious libel after criticizing the governor's stand toward the Indians. Found not guilty, the Zenger case was indicative of the changing face of journalism which eventually culminated in a free press.

The minority press in America developed in the nineteenth century with such newspapers as *Freedom's Journal* published by blacks and the *Cherokee Phoenix* published by American Indians in the Southeast. Women journalists also made their mark on early newspapers, with such names as Nellie Bly and Ida Tarbell becoming legends in their own right. It also was the era of the "penny press," of inexpensive newspapers with sensational news stories. Big city dailies that adopted the style of the penny press introduced "yellow journalism."

By the twentieth century, newspapering was gaining credibility with the founding of professional associations. The first half of the twentieth century also saw a decline in the individual influence of the early publishing entrepreneurs, a gradual change to newspapers owned by large corporations with public stockholders, and newspapers as expanding enterprises. News gathering also changed with the growth of press associations such as United Press International.

Current economic indicators have seen a continuation of newspaper profits but only a gradual climb in circulation. To help the latter, newspapers are attempting to reach specialized audiences with suburban editions and increased use of sectionals. In addition, today's newsroom is equipped with video display terminals and computers instead of typewriters and filing cabinets.

OPPORTUNITIES FOR FURTHER LEARNING

BOLLIER, DAVID, *How to Appraise and Improve Your Daily Newspaper: A Manual for Readers.* Washington, D.C.: Disability Rights Center, 1978.

BOND, DONOVAN H., AND W. REYNOLDS McLEOD, *Newsletters to Newspapers: Eighteenth Century Journalism.* Morgantown: West Virginia University School of Journalism, 1977.

DOWNIE, LEONARD, *The New Muckrakers.* New York: Mentor Books, 1978.

EMERY, EDWIN, AND MICHAEL EMERY, *The Press and America.* Englewood Cliffs, N.J.: Prentice-Hall, Inc., 1978.

FILLER, LOUIS, *The Muckrakers.* University Park: Pennsylvania State University Press, 1976.

FOX, WALTER, *Writing the News: Print Journalism in the Electronic Age.* New York: Hastings House, 1977.

GOTTLIEB, ROBERT, AND IRENE WOLT, *Thinking Big: The Story of the Los Angeles Times, Its Publishers and Their Influence on Southern California.* New York: G. P. Putnam's Sons, 1977.

HOHENBERG, JOHN, *The Professional Journalist.* New York: Holt, Rinehart & Winston, 1978.

LEWIS, ALFRED ALLAN, *Man of the World: Herbert Bayard Swope: A Charmed Life of Pulitzer Prizes, Poker and Politics.* Indianapolis: The Bobbs Merrill Co., Inc., 1978.

MARZOLF, MARION, *Up from the Footnote: A History of Women Journalists.* New York: Hastings House, 1977.

PICKETT, CALDER, *Voices of the Past: Key Documents in the History of American Journalism.* Columbus, Ohio: Grid, Inc., 1977.

ROBERTS, CHALMERS, *The Washington Post: The First Hundred Years.* Boston: Houghton Mifflin Company, 1977.

SHAW, DAVID, *Journalism Today: A Changing Press for a Changing America.* New York: Harper & Row, Publishers, Inc., 1977.

SMITH, ANTHONY, *The Newspaper: An International History.* London: Thames and Hudson, 1979.

WILLIAMS, HERBERT LEE, *Newspaper Organization and Management.* Ames, Iowa: Iowa State University Press, 1978.

3

Magazines

The last quarter of the nineteenth century fostered the climate for the birth of what we today view as the modern magazine. The United States had survived the War Between the States, and its economy had made a new fiscal start that signaled the industrial revolution. Economic and geographical expansion brought with it a sharpened social awareness. Fields could be plowed beyond the Alleghenies, and people knew that they were part of the excitement that caught up thousands in the trek to reach the new western frontier. The new generation's background consisted of more than Main Street, U.S.A., for they were familiar with the great railroads which spanned the continent, the telegraph which brought messages from afar, and the newspaper which was published by rotary press with far greater speed and efficiency than its predecessors did in the earlier part of the century.

FINDING AN AUDIENCE

As the nation prospered, a growing audience began to yearn for entertainment, entertainment that took the form of magazines. Entrepreneurs immediately realized that if they could provide light, diversionary reading at nominal prices, they could capture this mass audience. And they did. The magazine publishing boom began. Between 1865 and 1885, the number of periodicals jumped from 700 to 3,300.[1]

As competition developed, so did trends in pricing and content. The name of the game was circulation. Circulation lured advertisers who could pay to reach a mass audience. The price was high enough to allow a decrease in subscription prices, making magazines still more attractive to the public. Distribution also became more efficient, as the rails spread their network into hitherto inaccessible rural areas. Many magazines specifically sought a mass audience, just the opposite of what happened fifty years later.

PROSPERITY AND TRANSITION

America's phenomenal industrial growth during the early twentieth century also helped spur the magazine publishing industry. The era saw major strides in corporate expansion and the ability to produce mass goods for the consumer. With that ability came the need to make the consumer aware of these goods and of the various brand names of the products on grocery shelves, in new car showrooms, on clothes racks, and in furniture stores. Magazines filled the bill, and advertisements filled magazines. Although there were ups and downs, many of the publications achieved wide national acclaim. Among them were *Life*, *Look* and *The Saturday Evening Post*. The classic issue of prosperity was the *Saturday Evening Post* of December 7, 1929. "Weighing nearly two pounds, the 272-page magazine kept the average reader occupied for twenty hours and twenty minutes. From the 214 national advertisers appearing in it, the Curtis publishing company took in revenues estimated at $1,512,000."[2]

For the mass circulation magazine, the glory of that era did not survive. Television already loomed on the horizon. It signaled the growth of specialized magazines and the decline of mass circulation publications. The exact time of this turning point is debatable. The mass national magazines survived the golden era of radio and at first seemed to hold their own with television. Advertising revenues for *Life* increased in the early 1960s. "A single issue of *Life* in October, 1960 carried $5,000,000 worth; another in November, 1961 had revenues of $5,202,000.[3] But the figures were deceiving. A period followed in which many industry spokespersons argued that television was making gains on the magazine publishers; magazine publishers countered that more than ever was being spent on advertising—magazines were not only holding their own, but gaining. To some extent, both arguments were correct. Magazines in general were still experiencing a period of growth, but television was bound to make an impact. It finally dealt a fatal blow to the mass circulation magazines. Skyrocketing postal rates also contributed to their demise.

DECLINE OF MASS CIRCULATION MAGAZINES

Inability to direct themselves to a specialized audience was another reason for the demise of such well-known magazines as *Look* and *Life*. These were magazines in the true sense of the word "mass," having something within their pages that was of interest to everyone. With the advent of television, however, advertisers could reach the same mass audience as *Look* and *Life* did, but more cheaply and more efficiently. Besides cutting into the major advertising revenues of the mass magazines, television also surpassed them in distributing visual messages on a mass scale. The new medium also could offer both motion and sound accompaniment. With increased operating costs, mass circulation magazines folded. The *Saturday Evening Post* shared the fate of the other mass circulation magazines.

REINTRODUCING FAMILIAR PUBLICATIONS

After reading the last paragraph, you may stop and say, "Wait a minute. I just saw *The Saturday Evening Post* on the newsstand." You are right. In the past few years you probably have spotted some of these magazines, such as *Life, Look,* and *Country Gentleman*. Each represents an unusual trend in publishing that applies to a select few of some of the biggest titles to grace magazine history. But do not be deceived into thinking those editions are reaching the same mass audience they did thirty years ago. They are not. What publishers have done is to purchase the names of the major publications and then reintroduce them into the marketplace, but to a much more specialized audience than they were reaching before they folded. The new publishers are able to capitalize on the name familiarity of the former publications, yet do not have to compete with television for the mass audience. What has been created instead are specialty magazines with familiar titles.

For example, after *The Saturday Evening Post* folded, it was purchased by the Ser Vaas family of Indianapolis. The new Curtis Publishing Company, operating out of a different city and with a different staff, introduced a new edition of *The Saturday Evening Post*, with quality articles and top illustrators (Figure 3-1). Instead of trying to reach the mass audience of the former publication, the new *Post* is directed at a more conservative element of American life and contains many of the same sort of illustrations that its predecessor had. Its secret is that it has been able to control its circulation and distribution systems. Had the old *Post* been able to accomplish this same feat early enough, it might never have disappeared from the scene (Figure 3-2). But most of the circulation magazines persisted too long in trying to reach a mass audience so that they were unable to make the drastic shift to a specialized audience in time to avoid insolvency.

The *Saturday Evening Post* was not the only magazine revived by the Curtis Publishing Company. A very shrewd gamble paid off when the company

Figure 3-1 Lucian Lupinski, artist in residence at the *Saturday Evening Post*. Creative illustrations are an important part of contemporary magazine publishing. Lupinski says, "An illustrator must be versatile in several styles, and be able to adapt to a style. . . ." He also points out that understanding a story you're illustrating is important. Learn what visual images come from the script; then convey these onto canvas.

reintroduced *Country Gentleman* magazine (Figure 3-3). Initial circulation had reached more than 100,000 before the new magazine ever left the printer. That continued to swell to more than 300,000 as *Country Gentleman* effectively reached the "gentleman farmer" of the 1970s and 1980s. That "farmer" may own only a half acre and buy a small riding lawn mower instead of the full-size tractor the reader of *Country Gentleman* (Figure 3-3) years ago would have purchased. Such products as building supplies for home repair and remodeling, lawn seed, and other suburban home owner products found the *Country Gentleman* the ideal medium to reach this specialized audience.

In 1978, Time-Life brought back *Life* Magazine. Based on the experience of other popular publications such as *People*, the new *Life* was designed for the more contemporary life style and the affluent reader than its mass-circulation predecessor was. Advancements in printing and photojournalism also permitted the new *Life* to be an even more "picture oriented" publication than the old *Life* was. *Look* also was revived and even adopted regional covers to attract readers.

Still famous magazine titles like *Collier's* remain to be reintroduced. But the potential is there, so do not be surprised if you happen to spot them at the newsstand someday.

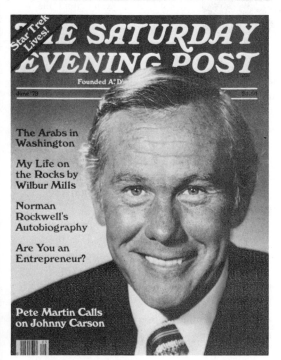

Figure 3-2 Three eras of the *Saturday Evening Post* during the twentieth century. Top left, the *Post* as it appeared on July 4, 1900; top right, the *Post* of May 1, 1954, with artist John Falter's painting of "Stan the Man" Musial signing autographs; and at left, the *Post* in 1979, highlighting the cover photo of Johnny Carson. (Reprinted from the *Saturday Evening Post*. © 1900 & 1954 The Curtis Publishing Company. Reprinted with permission from the Saturday Evening Post Company, © 1979)

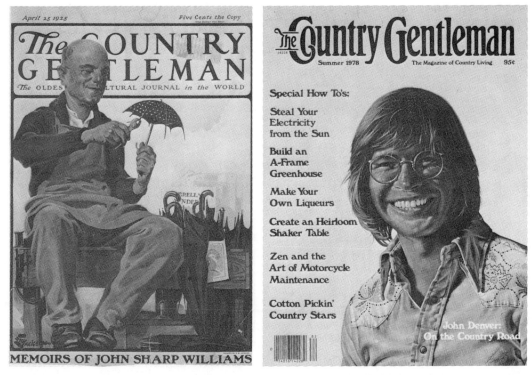

Figure 3-3 *Country Gentleman* is typical of the magazines which have been reintroduced successfully. Catering to the suburban homeowner, the new *Country Gentleman* capitalized on the solid reputation of its predecessor and provides articles of interest to people who own much less acreage than the farmers who comprised the readership of past decades. (Reprinted from *Country Gentleman*. © 1925 The Curtis Publishing Company. Reprinted with permission from The Country Gentleman Company, © 1978)

MODERN MAGAZINE PUBLISHING: THE SPECIALIZED AUDIENCE

Not all publications were destined for the fate of the old mass circulation periodicals. Many made the necessary changes to reach the highly specialized audiences that modern magazine publishing demands. For example, *Business Week* offers advertisers a select group of management level readers by regularly refusing to take subscriptions from nonmanagement level readers. Even living in a certain section of the country may determine if you qualify for a specialized magazine subscription. *Sunset* (Figure 3-4) magazine, called "the magazine of Western living," is directed to readers in the Pacific coast states and Nevada, Arizona, Idaho, and Utah. If you want to subscribe to the publication but do not live in the West, you have to pay more. As a result, advertisers know that by purchasing an ad in *Sunset*, they can concentrate on this western audience and will not be paying for circulation to other parts of the country that might not be as interested

Figure 3-4 Reaching a specialized geographical audience, *Sunset*, called the "magazine of Western living," features articles of the Western United States with a concentration on vacation spots, festivals, recipes, home construction, and home decorating. By keeping its circulation tightly controlled, *Sunset* survived the rough transition period that many magazines faced with the advent of television.

in their advertising. The same is true for *Southern Living* magazine for the southern audience.

special editions

Many magazines publish numerous special editions to reach those specialized audiences. What may appear to be one nationally distributed magazine is actually several specialized publications under the same cover. For example, *Time* magazine publishes both demographic and regional editions. An advertiser wanting to reach college students can advertise in the *Time* which is distributed primarily to college students, or *Time* offers its *Time* Z and *Time* A+ editions (Figure 3-5). *Time* Z stands for "zip codes." Time Z is directed to subscribers in 1,414 of the United States's most affluent zip code areas within metropolitan markets. The average family income in these zip code areas is $37,200. Thus if you were an advertiser with a product appealing to high-income buyers, the *Time* Z edition might be a good place to put your advertisement. An even more elite audience can be reached through the *Time* A+ edition. The A+ edition is directed at business and professional people, 600,000 of them. The average household income of *Time* A+ subscribers is $54,000: 93 percent of the subscribers have been to college. Again, *Time* A+ is providing advertisers with a very affluent audience.

Another example of specialized editions is *Sports Illustrated*. Not only does the magazine publish four regional editions—East, West, South, and Midwest—but it also publishes a "homeowners edition," limited to 640,000 subscribers in zip-code areas that show the highest concentration of home owners. In addition, it offers special "insert editions" to advertisers, with such special

TIME Z.

Z stands for ZIP Codes, and zeroing in on the markets that buy the most of the best.

Affluence has its geography.

A mere 20% of the nation's residential ZIP Code areas buy 73% of all the California chablis sold in America, 57% of all the dishwashers, 47% of the top-selling Scotch, 43% of all the life insurance policies—and so on, through virtually every category of goods and services you can name. As real estate agents have known for years, location is everything.

That's why TIME Z was created.

TIME Z reaches 1,200,000 TIME subscribers (average household income: $37,200) living in 1,414 of the nation's most affluent ZIP Code areas—all located in metro markets.

It's the biggest, ultraselective media buy around. With this curious and useful consistency: that the higher the neighborhood income level, the greater the penetration of TIME Z. In some cases, it's 25-30%.

As a marketing tool, TIME Z could make the crucial difference between hoping your advertisement will go to the right neighborhoods, and making sure that it will.

Case histories on the performance of TIME Z make heady reading. If you'd like to see some—or if you just want some information—call your TIME representative, or Jack Higgons, Associate Advertising Sales Director, at (212) 556-7811.

TIME Z		Subscriber Characteristics	
Circulation:	1,200,000	Average Household Income:	$37,200
B&W Page Rate:	$15,940	Attended College:	89%
4-Color Page Rate:	$24,705	Professional/Managerial:	79%

There's a right TIME for every advertiser.

Figure 3-5 *Time's* Zipcode reach. (Courtesy Time Magazine)

insert features as the U.S. Tennis Open and the Grand Slam of Golf. A manufacturer of tennis rackets, for instance, might find the U.S. Tennis Open insert
edition an excellent place to advertise.

regional editions

We mentioned the regional editions of *Sports Illustrated*. Other publications are
realizing the advertising appeal of regional editions. *Playboy* has eastern, central,
western, southeastern, southwestern, New York metropolitan, Chicago metropolitan, Los Angeles metropolitan, San Francisco metropolitan, and urban
market editions. The centerfold is not any different in the New York metropolitan edition than in the Los Angeles metropolitan edition. But an advertiser
wanting to reach only the New York audience can do so by buying advertising
space in just the New York metropolitan edition.

international editions

Playboy, along with its regional editions in the United States, also is among those
magazines that publish international editions. Along with its overseas military
edition, *Playboy* publishes foreign editions for France, Italy, Germany, Japan,
Mexico, and Brazil. But this time, different centerfolds do appear in certain
foreign editions. Some countries prohibit the bold displays used in the United
States. The magazine also has different titles, being called *Caballero* in Mexico
and *Homen* in Brazil.

Another magazine boasting international editions is the *Reader's Digest*. It
not only publishes editions in English but also in French, Dutch, German,
Spanish, Italian, Portuguese, Danish, Finnish, Norwegian, Swedish, Chinese,
and Japanese. In all, this magazine of good reading publishes thirty-five different
editions in thirteen different languages, reaching sixty million readers outside the
United States.

Two other familiar publications with international editions are *Cosmopolitan* and *Good Housekeeping*. Both have Spanish language editions. *Cosmopolitan's* Spanish edition looks much like the English-language edition. The front
cover is identical but a closer look reveals the Spanish-language subtitles (Figure
3-6). For *Good Housekeeping*, the title is *Buenhogar*. American advertisers who
want to reach the Spanish audience and Spanish advertisers find the magazines an ideal medium to reach the Spanish-speaking audience both in the
United States and Mexico (Figure 3-7). The magazine is independently edited. It
stresses family life, children, and self-improvement and is sold in 22 countries.

new target audiences: new publications

The magazine industry is much more than a series of specialized editions. New
publications are cropping up which are devoted entirely to very select audiences.

Perhaps nowhere is this trend more evident than in magazines directed

Figure 3-6 (© 1979 by the Hearst Corporation, New York, N.Y.)

toward today's changing woman, following her every mood from sports to professions. One of the first of these publications was *Ms* magazine. In chapter 1, we saw the front cover of *City Woman*, published for professional women living and working in the city. Still another specialized publication, this one appealing to a state identity, is *Texas Woman* (Figure 3-8). Others include *Professional Women* and *New Woman*. To give you an example, a look at demographic characteristics of *New Woman* reveals that 84.7 percent of its readers are working women. *Essence* appeals to an even more select audience, professional black women.

Business executives have always been a prime target audience for magazines. These individuals usually make major buying decisions and have higher than average incomes. Reaching this audience is the first aim of another specialized magazine, *Chicago Business* (Figure 3-9). Published by Crain Com-

Figure 3-7 *Buenhogar*, the Spanish *Good Housekeeping*

munications, Inc., *Chicago Business* is an excellent example of a magazine appealing not only to the specialized audience of business people but also refining that even further to reach business people in Chicago. Geared to more general audiences are the many city magazines that have appeared in recent years (Figure 3-10).

We discussed *Time's* ability to reach college students through a specialized edition, but one of the more novel examples of reaching college students is published by University Communications, Inc. The company publishes the *Directory of Classes* for selected colleges. The college supplies the company with its class schedule, and the company, in turn, sells advertising in the *Directory*. Reaching the college student is a difficult media problem since media attention habits change at that time. The hometown newspaper may no longer be available, the hometown radio station may not be within range, and loyality to other media may vary since class schedules and different living conditions can intervene.

CHARACTERISTICS AND TYPES OF MAGAZINES

Magazines are of four principal types—*farm, business, consumer,* and *religious magazines.* Each has subcategories. For example, farm publications consist mainly of *state* and *vocational* publications. State publications are directed toward a particular geographic area, such as the *Montana Farmer-Stockman* and

Figure 3-8 *Texas Woman,* specialized woman's magazine.

The Pennsylvania Farmer. Vocational farm publications, on the other hand, are directed toward a particular type of farmer, and include such magazines as the *Citrus and Vegetable Magazine* and *Dairy Herd Management* or *Beef* (Figure 3-11).

Business publications include *professional* magazines such as those pertaining to law, medicine, or education. Here the publisher may be a professional organization such as the American Dental Association. *The Quill*, official publication of the Society of Professional Journalists—Sigma Delta Chi, is an example of a professional magazine. Another subcategory of business publications includes *trade* magazines for specific businesses, such as the *Hardware Retailer.*

A third subcategory consists of *industrial* publications. Edited for specific

Figure 3-9 *Chicago Business.* Specialized magazine for Chicago business people.

ALSO: The "Golden Ghetto" of Carmel/America's First Union Depot

Indianapolis

JULY 1978/$1

Figure 3-10 *Indianapolis,* typical of a city magazine.

industries, they can include magazines directed to specific processes, for example, manufacturing or communication. Two examples of industrial publications of the printing and broadcasting industries, respectively, are the *Printing News* and *Broadcast Management and Engineering. Institutional* business magazines also abound, such as *Hotel-Motel News.* Publications that are sent to a group of people belonging to an organization are usually termed *house organs.* Copies of house organs may be sent to the news media for public relations purposes. In content, the house organ will consist mostly of information of special interest to its select readers.

In addition to these major categories of business publications, you should understand the difference between *vertical* and *horizontal* publications. Vertical publications reach people of a given profession at different levels in that profession. For instance, a major vertical publication of the radio and television industry is *Broadcasting.* Its content is geared to every person working or interested in

Figure 3-11 A specialized farm publication, *Beef*.

the broadcasting industry, whether it be the television camera operator, the radio station manager, or even the advertising executive who needs to know about new FCC regulations affecting broadcast commercials. Horizontal magazines, on the other hand, are aimed at a certain managerial level but cut across several different industries. *Business Week*, for example, is directed at management level personnel in many different facets of the business world. Two other examples of magazines directed at management include *Forbes* and *Fortune*.

Consumer magazines are usually of two types: specialized and general. Magazines directed at audiences with an interest in a special area, such as *Sailing* or the *Model Railroader*, are *specialized* magazines. *General* magazines are directed to people with more varied interests. *Playboy* would fit into this category.

Religious publications also have various subdivisions, usually based on specific religious denominations. Typical religious publications include *The Catholic Voice, The Jewish News, The Episcopalian, The Lutheran*, and many more regional publications that deal with specific denominations within a city.

MARKETING MAGAZINES

Magazine publishing overall has enjoyed a steady growth (Figure 3-12) both in number of publications and in circulation. Considering the increasingly competitive state of mass media, the growth is commendable, and many factors have contributed to this growth. In marketing a magazine to its intended audience, many marketing considerations must be kept in mind. These include such things as reader loyalty, the audience, the advertiser, and economic considerations.

the audience and the advertiser

Tough problems and decisions await the publishers of specialty magazines. For instance, when a market analysis reveals that an audience profile is changing, both publisher and advertisers may need to take immediate action, most of it based on hypothetical projections. Advertisers who buy space in the hope of reaching a specific audience as verified by market data must now decide whether or not to switch media.

Put yourself in the position of an advertising manager, say of your school magazine. According to market date, the audience you are reaching is the school

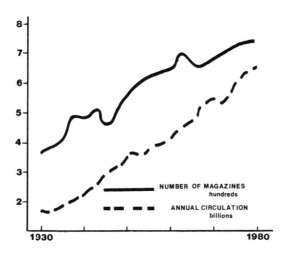

Figure 3-12 Magazine growth. (Source: Audit Bureau of Circulation and Magazine Publishers Association, data thru 1978. Included are comics, plus all general and farm non-ABC magazines listed in Standard Rate and Data Service)

audience. Suddenly your audience begins to shift. Your magazine's circulation remains the same, but student interest now begins to ebb while subscriptions among the housewives living near campus increase. Your first reaction may be, "So what?" Your advertisers simply do not want to reach housewives, that's what. They want to reach the students. What do you do? Do you change the editorial or news content of the magazine to reflect the needs of the student audience? That might work, but what if the trend is already too deeply rooted, and by changing the content you would not regain the students, but you would lose the housewives in the process. By now your circulation has dwindled, and advertising rates must be cut. But in order to stay in business and to meet expenses you must keep the same advertising rate. Tough decisions? Absolutely. Now imagine how hard it is for magazine publishers dealing with millions of dollars in revenue and millions of readers.

magazine reader loyalty

A major reason for the overall steady growth of magazines has been their ability to adapt with remarkable efficiency to the changing media habits of readers and to the unpredictable changes in the economy. Magazines also have fared well because of their ability to reach specialized audiences, audiences whose *loyalty* is considered fairly steadfast. Stop and consider your own media experiences. Naturally you watch television, if not as much when in school, then certainly when you are at home in the evening, on weekends, during the summer, or on vacation. But do you have a loyalty to one channel? Probably not. You switch freely from channel to channel. However, if you have a keen interest in a hobby, you may very well have a strong loyalty to a magazine devoted to your hobby. If you enjoy skiing, you might regularly read *Ski;* if you are a gun enthusiast, you might regularly read *Shooting Times;* a horse enthusiast might subscribe to *Western Horseman* or the *Chronicle of the Horse.* You may even be so involved in your hobby that you avidly read the editorial content of the magazine. Editorials may champion financial support for the United States Olympic team, gun control, or new interstate commerce regulations for transporting horses over state lines.

How strong is your own loyalty to a magazine? Would you sacrifice reading one issue of the newspaper each week to continue the opportunity to read your favorite magazine? Would you give up the chance to watch a TV channel one or two nights a week so that you could continue to receive your favorite magazine? Regardless of your own answers, keep in mind that millions of people would react with a definite "yes" to these questions. A business executive, for example, might need an industry publication to understand business trends and to ensure his or her continued livelihood.

Additional evidence of the important relationship between a magazine and its reader is seen in a research study by Opinion Research Corporation, released through the Magazine Publishers Association. It indicates that over a six-month period 72 percent of the male readers and 79 percent of the female readers kept an issue of a magazine for future reference: 79 percent of the men and 78 percent of the women discussed an article or feature with another person, and 51 percent of the men and 68 percent of the women tried an idea suggested in an article.

economic considerations

In today's world of rapidly increasing costs for labor and paper, an acute awareness of the expenses of magazine production also is important. Figure 3-13 examines the typical dollar spent on producing a magazine. We find approximately 8¢ out of every dollar is spent on postage. That figure is continuing to spiral upward, and as it does, money must be subtracted from other areas of production. Postage rates are forcing publishers to look for ways to cut the costs of distribution through such means as newsstand sales. *People* magazine, for example, is sold principally through newsstands. Yet for other magazines, their limited appeal prohibits this means of distribution. The average newsstand would sell so few issues of the publication that the use of shelf space to display it would be unjustified.

Paper costs also continue to eat away at the production dollar, accounting for 18¢. Many magazines are reducing their actual dimensions in an effort to save paper costs and to prevent their magazines from being listed as "outsized" by the Post Office. In fact, many publications on today's newsstands are at least one-third smaller in width and length than they were ten years ago.

The remainder of the magazine dollar allocates 14¢ for administrative costs, 31¢ for editorial and manufacturing functions, and 29¢ for sales, including advertising and circulation.

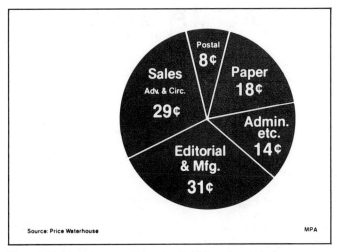

Source: Price Waterhouse   MPA

Figure 3-13 Magazine costs. (Magazine Publishers Association)

Costs have prompted some magazine publishers to join together to help each maintain a strong position in the market and cut costs. The Society of National Association Publications (SNAP) is one vehicle that helps publishers cut costs, in this case by sharing cover designs. The magazine *Hardware Retailing* published an issue featuring a cover design of Uncle Sam eyeing a consumer. The title of the special issue was "Consumer Protection . . . How Far Is Too Far." This cover was subsequently made available to any other member of SNAP who wanted to copy it. The other publishers needed only to substitute the title of their own magazine. Four others did, including *Mutual Review,* whose issue was entitled "A Look at Government-Industry Cooperation."

Despite these higher costs, magazines are predicted to fare better than both newspapers and network prime-time television in offering advertisers a lower cost per thousand in the coming years. Cost per thousand (CPM) is the cost of reaching one thousand people with one advertisement. Using 1977 as a base year, industry predictions see the cost per thousand for magazines rising 31 percent by 1981. But newspapers are predicted to rise 41 percent (Figure 3-14), compared with 77 percent for prime-time television (Figure 3-15).

This does not necessarily mean that if you were to go out and purchase a commercial on television or an advertisement in the newspaper that it would necessarily cost more than a magazine advertisement. We are talking about projected increases in CPM, not necessarily in the cost of advertising. But in an era of increased advertising costs, the cost of magazine advertising is not expected to increase at the rate that other media will. One major reason is the availability of magazines and the increasing number of magazines creating a good competitive climate. In many large markets you only have one choice in purchasing

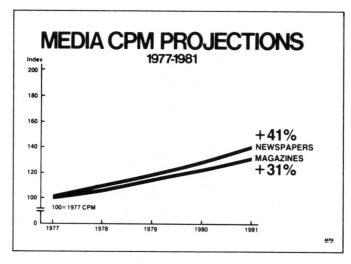

Figure 3-14 (Source: Foote, Cone & Belding and Magazine Publishers Association)

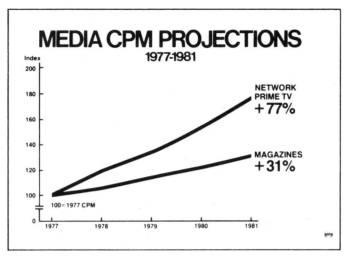

Figure 3-15 (Foote, Cone & Belding and Magazine Publishers Association)

newspaper advertising. Moreover, until we have more commercial television networks, there is no indication that the cost of prime-time television is going to level off significantly.

In addition, magazines also can offer advertisers and audiences some distinct advantages. Examining the education of magazine readers (Figure 3-16), we see that better educated people are more apt to read magazines than to watch television. Similarly, we see in Figure 3-17 that the higher income individual also is more apt to read magazines than to watch television.

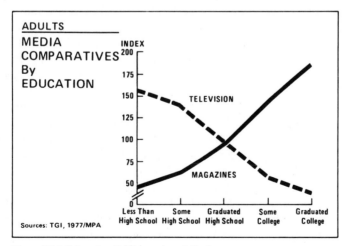

Figure 3-16 (Magazine Publishers Association)

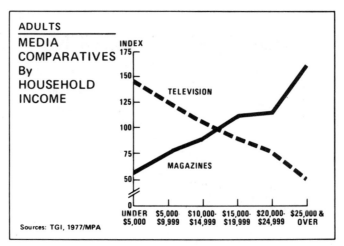

Figure 3-17 (Magazine Publishers Association)

Despite these economic considerations, the loyal readership of magazines, the magazines' ability to identify and to reach highly specialized audiences, and the willingness of those audiences to pay high prices for speciality magazines, suggest that magazines will continue to enjoy growth in circulation and income.

SUMMARY

Modern magazines trace their roots to the latter part of the nineteenth century when they became the first true entertainment medium, for at that time no radio or television signals crowded the air waves, and not every community was blessed with a movie theater. Magazines began to fill the void and gradually attracted advertising. As they grew in size and popularity, their success was closely tied to circulation. The more issues the magazines sold, the more advertisers they could attract and the more they could charge for advertising. But by the 1950s, television had acquired a sure foothold as the new "mass" medium, and it was not long before advertisers who wanted to reach a mass audience could do it more cheaply on television than in magazines. As a result, some of the true mass circulation magazines, such as *Life, Look,* and *The Saturday Evening Post* were forced to shut their publishing doors. Even though some of these were later revived, they were completely new magazines, for television had ushered in the era of specialized publications.

Today, magazines have at their disposal a variety of methods to reach specialized audiences. *Time,* for example, publishes special editions to reach the college student and the business person, among others. *Sports Illustrated* publishes special insert editions containing special information on the U.S. Open Tennis Championships or the Indianapolis 500. Regional editions permit advertisers to reach readers in certain select regions of the country. *Playboy* and *Reader's Digest* are two magazines that utilize the international edition option. Reaching special target audiences is still another way that specialized magazines flourish. The working woman is one example for which such publications as *City Woman* and *New Woman* are published.

Tough decisions await publishers of speciality magazines. Reader loyalty, competition, and economics are just some of these considerations. On the other hand, magazines have a projected lower growth in CPM than television or newspapers, and magazines reach an audience with higher education and income than television does.

OPPORTUNITIES FOR FURTHER LEARNING

HAMBLIN, DORA JANE, *That was the Life*. New York: W. W. Norton & Co., Inc., 1977.

Handbook of Magazine Publishing. New Canaan, Conn.: Folio Magazine Publishing Corp., 1978.

How and Why People Buy Magazines: A National Study of the Consumer Market for Magazines. Port Washington, N.Y.: Publisher's Clearinghouse, 1977.

KELLEY, JEROME E., *Magazine Writing Today*. Cincinnati: Writers Digest, 1978.

KIMBROUGH, MARVIN, *Black Magazines: An Exploratory Study*. Austin: Center for Communication Research, University of Texas, 1973.

MEYER, SUSAN E. *America's Great Illustrators*. New York: Harry Abrams, 1978.

NELSON, ROY PAUL, *Articles and Features*. New York: Houghton Mifflin Company, 1978.

RIVERS, WILLIAM L, *Free-Lancer and Staff Writer: Newspaper Features and Magazine Articles*. Belmont, Calif.: Wadsworth Publishing Co., Inc., 1976.

SCHREINER, SAMUEL A., *The Condensed World of the Reader's Digest*. Briarcliff Manor, N.Y.: Stein & Day Publishers, 1977.

WOLSELEY, ROLAND E., *The Changing Magazine: Trends in Readership and Management*. New York: Hastings House, 1973.

WOLSELEY, ROLAND E., *Understanding Magazines* (2nd ed.) Ames: Iowa State University Press, 1969.

4

Book Publishing

When radio and then television became mass media, pessimists made dire predictions about the future of books, similar to the prognosis they had made for the mails upon completion of the Atlantic Cable. They suggested that we would become a visual society attuned to the giant screen instead of to the printed page. The satirical movie *Fahrenheit 451* portrayed a future in which television would be the giant controlling medium and in which it would be illegal to possess books.

Although such a state is not beyond the realm of possibility in anything less than a free society, books have stood the test of time. They have survived and carry with them an important part of society's development. From Chaucer's *Canterbury Tales* to the latest best seller, books have remained an important part of our lives. We learn from them, we are entertained by them, and we possess them. They have survived major reforms among people and nations. Books have been the object of political suppression and the stimulus for champions of liberation. They have been among the cherished possessions of kings and have helped lay the foundations of republican government. Radio and television programs come and go; at best we may remember a catchy word or phrase, or a fleeting image may haunt our memory. A book, however, like a good friend, can be looked up again and again without tiring of its acquaintance.

BEGINNINGS OF BOOK PUBLISHING

The Saxons in the fifth century published some of the earliest books. They consisted of thin animal skins crudely bound together. The animal skin was called *vellum* and was a major improvement over the clay tablets used to communicate messages thousands of years earlier. Later in the cloisters and abbeys of medieval Europe, monks laboriously copied the Scriptures, embellishing them with crude hand-engraved illustrations. These early scrolls contained script sometimes extending their entire length, much of which was arranged in columns. These rolled scrolls were gradually replaced by manuscripts folded in accordionlike stacks, with wooden boards attached to the first and last pages. Then came the idea to punch holes into and stitch one side of the folds. From this process came the practice of "binding" individual sheets of paper between covers. Early binding actually consisted of flexible hinges to which the pages were attached with linen threads. When leather became the chief material used for book covers, bookbinders began bordering these covers with their trademarks of patterns rolled on with small wheel-like tools called *rolls*. These rolls were similar to those used by today's leathercraft workers to engrave belts, wallets, and other products. Needless to say, with so few books available and with considerable time and effort expended in their production, they were very valuable.

Figure 4-1 The early bookbinding shop shows the workers (left to right) beating the folded sections of the book, stitching the book, trimming the edges on a ploughing press (Figure 4-3), and pressing the edges on a standing press (Figure 4-4). (From *DIDEROT* and courtesy, *The Printer in 18th Century Williamsburg*. Williamsburg, Va.: Colonial Williamsburg, 1955)

With increased use of the printing press during the sixteenth century, composition changed drastically. Engraved wooden blocks became printing plates to produce illustrations. Books could now be mass produced—of course on a scale we would consider moderate indeed. These early books were mostly hardback volumes, with content concentrating on religion, the writings of the ancient Greeks, and the trades. The audience for the early hard-bound volumes again was not the mass audience. It consisted mostly of students who would borrow the books and pass them on from one class to another, the religious orders of the day, or the elite and wealthy who could afford the luxury of buying books.

The book publishing industry was centered on the local bookbinder's shop. Figure 4-1 and Figure 4-2 show two views of an early bookbinder's shop. In Figure 4-1, the man on the left is beating the folded sections of a book so that they will lie flat. He is using a wooden hammer and large wooden block in much the same way a blacksmith uses a hammer and anvil to shape metal. The folded sections of the book then are stitched on a crude stitching frame, operated by the woman on the right.

The two people at the right of Figure 4-1, are using a ploughing press (also seen in Figure 4-3) and a standing press (also seen in Figure 4-4). The ploughing press sat on a rectangular frame and was used to trim the edges of a newly sewn book. The worker on the far right is using the standing press to press a stack of

Figure 4-2 Notice in this illustration of a colonial bookbinder the hand tools on the back wall. The tools are used to "engrave" the ornate borders on leather bound books. The standing press is at the left, and immediately behind it are shelves with sheets of uncut leather. (Courtesy, Colonial Williamsburg)

Figure 4-3 A closer view of the ploughing press which "trims" the book. The pages are clamped firmly between the two top horizontal beams, then the knife secured in the "plough" cuts the rough, uneven pages off the book, leaving the edges of the pages even and smooth. (*The Bookbinder in 18th-Century Williamsburg*. Williamsburg, Va.: Colonial Williamsburg, 1959)

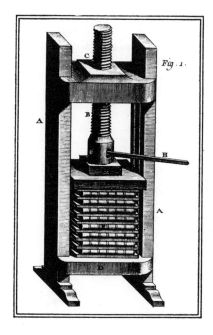

Figure 4-4 A closer view of the standing press shows the books stacked with "press boards" between each book and the large handturned wood screw applying pressure to the wood block on top the stack. (*The Bookbinder in 18th-Century Williamsburg*. Williamsburg, Va.: Colonial Williamsburg, 1959)

bound and trimmed books. The standing press used a large corkscrew to press a plate against the stack of books.

Figure 4-2 shows a typical colonial bookbinder at work. Here you can see a closer view of the standing press with its large wooden corkscrew. Notice that on the table there is a much smaller press used to hold a single book. On the shelves by the window are uncut sheets of leather used for book covers, and on the wall behind the bookbinder are the rolls used to imprint borders and designs on the covers. The bookbinder usually was in the village printing shop which, naturally, also sold books.

PUBLISHING AND "BINDING" IN COLONIAL AMERICA

The beginnings of the book publishing industry in America can be traced as far back as the seventeenth century, when the developing colonies needed to distribute laws, propositions before government, and other official documents approved by the Crown.[1] Often these "booklets" were published by officially approved printers in whose shops the bookbinders also worked. In fact, government printing and publishing contracts constituted the major trade of colonial printers. Additional income was obtained by printing religious publications, such as psalm books or collections of sermons. Often these "published" books were single copies, nothing resembling mass distribution.

Bookbinders in colonial America spent much of their time binding publications for private citizens who retained the only copy of the work. Some jobs were binding books written by the customer ordering the binding. Other books were Bibles, which often were rebound and passed on from generation to generation. If we had walked into the bookbinding shop of Joseph Royle in Williamsburg, Virginia in the summer of 1765, we could have visited with a customer wanting a song book bound, another wanting a prayer book bound,

---

THOMAS BREND,
BOOKBINDER AND STATIONER,
HAS for SALE, at his shop at the corner of Dr. Carter's
large brick house, Testaments Spelling Books, Primers,
Ruddiman's Rudiments of the Latin Tongue, Watts's
Psalms, Blank Books, Quills Sealing-Wax, Pocket-
Books, and many other articles in the Stationery way.
Old books rebound; and any Gentlemen who have paper
by them and want it made into Account Books, may
have it done on the shortest notice.

Figure 4-5 (Courtesy, Colonial Williamsburg)

Thomas Jefferson might have stopped by to request that a history of Virginia be bound, and two ministers might have come to have their Bibles rebound.

In addition to customer-ordered books, a lucrative side of the business was the publication of blank ledgers and account books. These, along with stationery items, kept the colonial bookbinder in business. If we had read the *Virginia Gazette* on August 19, 1780, for example, we would have seen an advertisement placed by Thomas Brend offering to sell spelling books, psalm books, pocket books, blank books, and account books (Figure 4-5).

The changes in early colonial bookbinding followed those of early colonial newspapers. After independence was declared, both increased the diversity of their content and their distribution.

MASS TEXTBOOK PUBLISHING

A quarter-century after American independence, William Holmes McGuffey was born in Claysville, Pennsylvania. He later became known as one of the great educators of the time and advanced through various positions including public school teacher and professor of languages and then served as president of Cincinnati College and later Ohio University, at Athens. But what McGuffey was best known for was his creation of elementary school textbooks known as the McGuffey Eclectic Readers (Figure 4-6), readers designed to teach good pronunciation and reading ability. McGuffey readers were an institution, not only in education but in book publishing as well. In all, between 1836 and 1857, McGuffey wrote six readers designed for different levels of achievement. Based on gradual learning and always carrying a moral message, they were designed so that the student could graduate to the next level of reader after completing the preceding one. As they became more and more popular, new editions were published and survived well into the first decade of the twentieth century.

Considering the times, the approximate circulation of 122 million copies of McGuffey's readers is phenomenal. Today, the original readers are collectors' items and are on the shelves of antique shops. In their time, they set the stage for a new era of book publishing that went beyond the classroom to the general public.

THE DIME NOVELS

The impetus for publishing on a mass scale occurred shortly after 1850 when there were both the means and the desire to produce books that would become the foundation for much of the current publishing industry. At that time, a New York publisher named E. F. Beadle decided that he could sell books if they were cheap enough and if they satisfied the public's desire for entertainment and good literary prose. He started with the publication of a ten-cent paperback song book.

McGUFFEY'S PRIMER.   39

LESSON XXXIII.

pull   eärt   g̅o̅ats   Bĕss
       ŭp   rīde   hĭll
              u̯

Bess has a cart and two goats.
She likes to ride in her cart.
See how the goats pull!
Bess is so big, I think she
should walk up the hill.
The goats love Bess, for she
feeds them, and is kind to them.

Figure 4-6 Page from the *McGuffy Reader*. The *Reader* became one of the most widely read and universally adopted early elementary textbooks.

Shortly thereafter, he ventured into other paperback "dime novels" (Figure 4-7), which became best sellers even by the modest standards of the late 1800s. Beadle's novels were not long—only about seventy-five pages—and most of them were about the American pioneer.

A search for an escape into fantasy was what made dime novels into best sellers. They contained little truth but continued to prosper even into the Civil War when troops found the books good company on long hikes. Many other companies also ventured into dime-novel publishing, and although the thrill of the original dime novel diminished, it left a sizeable impression on the history of book publishing. To it we owe the modern concept of the book as a medium of mass communication.

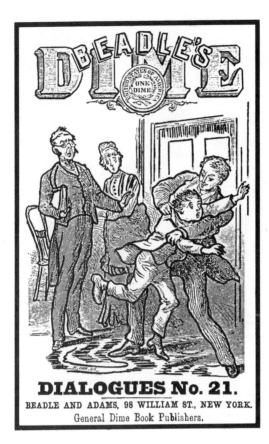

Figure 4-7 Beadle's "dime novels" were the forerunner of the modem paperbacks. Their content ranged from Western tales of adventure beyond the Alleghenies to "Dialogues" which could be adapted to amateur theatrical productions.

MASS MARKET PAPERBACK BOOK PUBLISHING

In a suburb of Dayton, Ohio, a former advertising executive sat down at his typewriter in the mid-1970s and began writing a series of paperback books. Under contract to his publisher and stringent deadlines, author John Jakes (Figure 4-8) typed the first pages of the American Bicentennial Series. The series would literally shake the roots of the book publishing industry.

Jakes's opportunity to write the series came after he had written approximately fifty science fiction novels under the pen name of Jay Scotland. They had been moderately successful, but provided only enough income for Jakes to continue his "hobby" of writing.

The American Bicentennial Series was released first in paperback. That in itself was a first in American book publishing, since the common practice for major best sellers was to release them originally in hardback and later in paperback. But then no one knew Jakes's novels would be best sellers.

Finally, the first of the series rolled off the presses. Titled *The Bastard*, it

Figure 4-8 Writer John Jakes (left) and actor John Jakes (right) as he appeared in the television miniseries of his best selling paperback novel, *The Seekers*, part of the American Bicentennial Series about the life of the fictional Kent family. Not only did the books set publishing records, but the miniseries, released through syndication, produced additional evidence that quality television drama can find a significant national audience without initially being released via one of the major commercial networks. (Copyright 1979, Universal City Studies, Inc., all rights reserved. Provided through the courtesy of JOVE Publications, Inc.)

traced the beginnings of the fictitious Kent family from their roots in France and England and then to America. It also triggered a chain of events that set records in American book publishing. *The Bastard* (Figure 4-9) was followed by other titles—*The Rebels, The Seekers, The Furies, The Titans, The Warriors, The Lawless,* and *The Americans.* The series became so popular that Jakes became the first author to have three books on the *New York Times* best seller list within one year. It was not long before the series had sold more than 15 million copies, and the publishing industry was taking another look at paperback book publishing. Some of Jakes's novels were later combined and released in hardback, and syndicated television features beginning with *The Bastard* were released to independent television stations, achieving a ratings success.

The success of John Jakes and his Bicentennial Series was indicative of both the potential and the present appeal of paperback book publishing. Today, it is a major part of the book publishing industry and is receiving increased distribution, production, and promotional support.

distributing paperbacks

One reason for the success of today's paperback book industry is its distribution system. Anytime you can distribute easily and inexpensively information that the public wants, then you have a chance for success. The first chapters of the paperback book success story are easy transportation and wide availability. The distribution system, although not as efficient perhaps as that of radio or television, is still not cumbersome by any means.

Because of this ease of distribution, paperback books also have become an instrument of persuasion and, in some cases, propaganda. For example, politicians running for office may find that they can add to their prestige by writing a book that details their career in office. The book can be assembled into approximately one hundred pages and distributed on a mass scale to as many potential voters as funds permit. The cost of producing the book is minimal, and distribution can be through political workers carrying an armload door to door.

Portability is part of the reason you, as a consumer, chose a paperback book to accompany you on your last trip. It was light, and you could carry it for a long time even though you were walking through bus stations or airport corridors. You also could hold it easily or set it on the edge of your seat.

Paperback books also can be bought at places other than book stores. Sir

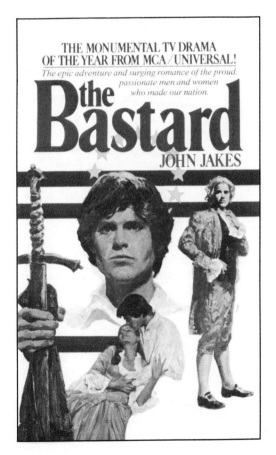

Figure 4-9 *The Bastard* was the first book of the Bicentennial series written by John Jakes. When the television miniseries appeared, the cover was adapted to reflect the characters in the television production. (JOVE Publications, Inc.)

Allen Lane, publisher of the famous Penguin books, during a visit to America in the early 1930s, surmised that if he could make buying books as easy as buying any other novelty, he could reach a substantial, untapped market of readers. Sir Allen managed to negotiate a contract with the Woolworth stores to distribute his Penguin books.[2] The venture proved successful, and the new distribution system clinched the success of his enterprise. Today, you can find paperback books in virtually every type of retail establishment imaginable, from gas stations to grocery stores.

promoting paperbacks

Along with distribution advantages, mass market paperbacks now emphasize promotion that rivals the best of Madison Avenue's marketing schemes. Today, a paperback book reaches the marketplace with a coordinated effort including everyone from the bookstore clerk to the consumer. For example, the best seller *Coma*, a medical thriller, was released to bookstores with a whole array of promotional aids. "Tie-ins" included an attractive floor display for bookstores to increase reader interest at the place of purchase. A special marketing booklet with scenes from the film was included. That in itself is a new phenomenon in book publishing—having book and film (sometimes even television) rights and production schedules all completed before the book is released. *Coma* T-shirts were part of the campaign, and posters showing movie scenes were available for bookstores, as were shopping bags with *Coma* printed on them and a special gimmick, *Coma* surgical masks. For the bookstore with the best display came a prize from the publisher.

Other promotional tie-ins also contribute to a book's success, whether paperback or hardback. The appearance of authors on television talk shows can definitely boost sales. Promotional agents work hard to get the authors on programs that can promote the books at both local and national levels. Advance copies of the book are distributed to reviewers, bookstore clerks, and other people who can promote the book. Radio, television, and billboard advertising also can be part of the marketing compaign. All combine to make contemporary book publishing a radically different business from what it was twenty years ago. Literary agents auction off top manuscripts in the millions of dollars, television rights can bring even more money, and movies add still more to an industry that certainly has adapted well to the competition of new media in the marketplace.

NEW FORMATS

In addition to paperbacks, publishers have started experimenting with new formats in book publishing. Two of these are personalized books and "fotonovels."

personalized books

Personalized books are composed and printed entirely by computer. The computer stores a complete text of the book but with programming arranged so as to permit the addition of specific names and places into the text. When the book is printed, the person ordering the book can request that certain names, dates, addresses, and places be incorporated into the text. For example, a parent wants to order a book for a child. Let us assume that the child has a family pet, a brother, and a sister and lives in a small community. We shall call her Nancy Smith, the dog will be named Laddie, and the family will live on Peach Street. When Nancy's parent orders the book, all of this information is given to the publisher, who in turn programs the computer to personalize the book for Nancy. When Nancy opens the book, it reads: "This morning, Nancy and her dog Laddie were walking home on Peach Street when Laddie began barking loudly." The story then continues with the names of the characters the same as those of Nancy's actual brothers, sisters, and relatives. There is more to this concept than novelty, however. What has given them significant educational value and use as learning tools are the interest and motivation that children acquire when they see their names in print.

fotonovels

The fotonovel is part printed text, part picture book, and part comic book. It developed as a spin-off to television and movies and includes still pictures from the movies or programs, accompanied by short lines of text or dialogue. *Star Trek* recently provided some of the most popular material for fotonovels. Acclaimed for years in Europe, fotonovels are relatively new to North America. But with the increased use of television, they are a natural commercial complement to entertainment programming. Promotional tie-ins often include releasing both the fotonovel and the television series at the same time and coordinating bookstore and retail outlet advertising (Figure 4-10) with television promotional efforts.

ISSUES IN THE BOOK PUBLISHING INDUSTRY

In the rapidly changing world of corporate decisions, the future of the book publishing industry hinges on many important issues.

distribution, printing, paper

The energy crisis has taken its toll in book-publishing expenditures as it has on the costs of operating other print media. Unlike radio and television, however, which can broadcast their messages over the air waves, the book-publishing industry must transport its messages by truck, ship, train, and plane. Each of

89

Figure 4-10 Marketing display for Bantam Books' Fotonovel of the Star Trek series. (Courtesy, Bantam Books)

these sources of transportation will naturally continue to increase its rates as the cost of fuel continues to rise. When a book leaves the warehouse, many people handle it, and many vehicles transport it. The labor costs of loading books onto trucks, the cost of purchasing the trucks to haul them, the cost of gasoline to run the trucks, the salaries paid to drivers, the cost of labor to unload the books, and the increased rental costs to display them in a bookstore or wherever else they are sold all have burgeoned. This has triggered everything from bankruptcy to consolidation.

More and more printers are realizing the value of their skills and the importance of good printing to the overall production of a book. Labor unions are negotiating contracts that add higher salaries and new fringe benefits.

As other print media do, book publishers also face soaring paper costs. The chief villain is the inflated cost of energy and natural resources necessary to manufacture paper. Added to this are higher labor costs. In many cases, the market for books simply will not bear the essential price hikes to offset completely these paper costs. As a result, the difference has appeared in shrinking profit columns. This does not mean that book publishing is about to vanish from the American scene. It can, however, translate into lean years for stockholders until prices level off, for paper can represent as much as one-half the expense of publishing a book.

new ventures: new income

We already have seen how the paperback book industry is booming because of major promotional efforts. In addition, the industry is branching out into new, profitable areas. For instance, Bantam Books has developed a new gift books division. In a major commitment to this type of publication, Bantam hired Ian Ballantine, the founder of Ballantine Books, out of retirement to head the new division, called Peacock Press. The Peacock Press publishes gift books with excellent reproductions of quality art prints (Figure 4-11).

Retailing for a fraction of the cost of competing publications, these specialty items have literally stolen the market. Paperback originals by established authors are also increasing the potential of this upcoming offshoot of the industry.

Even unusual undertakings can become profitable with imagination, research, and a little luck. Ballantine Books, for example, published a packet of blueprints for the starship *Enterprise* from the popular "Star Trek" television series. More than a half million packets were sold. Publishing sets of books or reissuing books in gift covers also has proved successful. A popular book may beget sequels, and after five or so have been published, a gift-box arrangement of an entire set can lure new readers and new buyers to bookstore shelves. Even the illustrations can turn into popular collection pieces. Norman Rockwell's paintings, which for many years decked the covers of the *Saturday Evening Post*, have

Figure 4-11 High quality printing processes have helped produce a consumer demand for gift books. (Covers of titles published by Peacock Press/Bantam Books © Bantam Books, Inc., 1975)

been published and republished in collectors' editions. Special collections of circus stories, Christmas stories, Easter stories, recipes, and numerous other items have proved interesting reading and profitable book publishing ventures.

REGIONAL PUBLISHING

Some publishers predict that future economic constraints on distribution will generate growth in regional publishing—books appealing to a particular region. As a regional book publisher, you would not seek out manuscripts that appeal to a national readership but, rather, to a specific regional market. For example, instead of publishing a book about farming, you instead might publish one about farming in New England or in the Midwest. Similarly, instead of publishing an all-American cookbook, you might accept a manuscript about southwestern cooking. Although the market for regional books is more limited, sales density can be higher because of generally greater interest. Most important, distribution costs drop as the publisher concentrates on a specific region, say the East Coast. Many major publishing companies already have developed regional distribution systems, and some smaller companies are exclusively regional. One of the more successful regional presses is the Caxton Press of Caldwell, Idaho. Its primary distribution area, the Northwest, is also the focal point of its readership. Caxton has made recent inroads into what has become known as *coffee table books*— handsomely designed, oversized volumes with color pictures—selling for as much as fifty dollars or more. Other publishers maintain similar regionalism within their published titles. The University of Tennessee Press, for instance, concentrates on books on the heritage and people of that region. Its list of titles also includes books on the War Between the States.

FUTURE MANAGEMENT DECISIONS

The future manager of any publishing enterprise will need to monitor constantly the industry's cost factors. Besides production and distribution costs, the industry has fundamental cost factors such as sales and advertising. Here, the key is to attract and to keep enthusiastic and dedicated people who have the discipline to work well without much supervision and who enjoy working on a commission basis. These people keep a firm in business. But, as with every other cost, the expenses incurred by a sales staff are increasing. In any publishing venture, there are only so many excess dollars to go around after basic publishing expenditures. Thus, at some point management must decide if it can raise the commission paid to the sales staff without raising the price of the book.

Other management decisions also will affect profit. Knowing a book's market is crucial, because the larger the number of volumes that are printed, the smaller the cost per copy. However, it costs just as much to print books that do not sell. One key to success in a new venture is not to overrun the initial printing, that is, to avoid unsold books being returned from bookstores. Again, distribution costs apply to sold as well as to unsold books. In addition, management faces unexpected costs that might develop before the book reaches the bookstores, such as a truckers' strike that would necessitate shipping some books by air freight. All of those factors can dramatically change the economic picture of any publishing venture.

SUMMARY

The roots of book publishing can be traced back to the Saxons in the fifth century. Making accordionlike folds and binding the edges, the book concept gradually evolved because of the advantages of stitching the loose pages together. From the limited distribution of hand-copied manuscripts of the monks, the printing press and moveable type began to transform book publishing into a mass medium.

Book publishing's colonial American roots were closely tied to the printing industry. Colonial bookbinders using such equipment as ploughing and standing presses bound books on special order for individuals and the government. Mass production books as we know them today could be bought only in England.

The first real impact on mass publishing came with the work of E. F. Beadle, who pioneered the famous "dime novels" which became popular in the late nineteenth century. Beadle's novels were about seventy-five pages long, sold for a dime, and contained short plays or tales of the West. Lane discovered the secret of modern paperback book publishing—that inexpensive works available in many different retail establishments could be a profitable publishing venture.

Author John Jakes is responsible for introducing a new era in contemporary paperback publishing with his American Bicentennial Series. It proved that a major novel could be successfully released in paperback without first appearing in hardback. Jakes's bicentennial novels, the first of which was titled *The Bastard*, not only sold in the millions of copies but also had some of the largest first printings in book publishing history.

Paperbacks have succeeded because of their inexpensive price, inexpensive distribution costs and multiple places of sale, such as drugstores and grocery stores. Major promotional efforts also are closely tied to a book's success and can include everything from T-shirts to television commercials. In addition, book formats also appear on bookseller's shelves. Computer-produced books, called personalized books, and fotonovels are becoming popular. Future decisions affecting the industry will center on such issues as distribution costs, regional publishing, and labor and printing costs.

ANDERSON, CHARLES B., ed., *Bookselling in America and the World: Some Observations and Recollections*. New York: Quadrangle/The New York Times Book Co., Inc., 1975.

ARMOUR, RICHARD, *The Happy Bookers*. New York: McGraw-Hill Book Company, 1976.

ARNDT, KARL J. R., AND MAY E. OLSON, *The German Language Press of the Americas, Volume I: History and Bibliography. 1732–1968, United States of America*. New York: Unipub, 1976.

BARKER, NICOLAS, *The Oxford University Press and the Spread of Learning: An Illustrated History*. New York: Oxford University Press., 1978.

BENJAMIN, CURTIS G., *A Candid Critique of Book Publishing*. New York: R. R. Bowker Company, 1977.

BRUCCOLI, MATTHEW, AND E. E. FRAZER CLARK, JR., *Pages: The World of Books Writers, and Writing*. Detroit: Gale Research Co., 1977.

COCHRAN, WENDELL, *Into Print: A Practical Guide to Writing, Illustrating, and Publishing*. Los Altos, Calif.: William Kaufmann, Inc., 1977.

DESSAUER, JOHN P., *Book Publishing: What It Is, What It Does*. New York: R. R. Bowker Company, 1974.

DUKE, JUDITH S. *Children's Books and Magazines: A Market Study*. White Plains, N.Y.: Knowledge Industry Publications, 1979.

FEBVRE, LUCIEN, AND HENRI–JEAN MARTIN, *The Coming of the Book: The Impact of Printing 1450–1800*. Atlantic Highlands, N.J.: Humanities Press, Inc., 1977.

HACKETT, ALICE PAYNE, AND JAMES HENRY BURKE, *80 Years of Best Sellers: 1895–1975*. New York: R. R. Bowker Company, 1977.

PETERS, JEAN, *Book Collecting: A Modern Guide*. New York: R. R. Bowker Company, 1977.

RICE, STANLEY, *Book Design: Systematic Aspects*. New York: R. R. Bowker Company, 1978.

RICE, STANLEY, *Book Design: Text Format Models*. New York: R. R. Bowker Company, 1978.

STEINBERG, S. H., *Five Hundred Years of Printing*. Baltimore: Penguin Books, 1974.

TEBBEL, JOHN, *A History of Book Publishing in the United States, Volume I: The Creation of an Industry, 1630–1865*. New York: R. R. Bowker Company, 1972.

TEBBEL, JOHN, *A History of Book Publishing in the United States, Volume II: The Expansion of an Industry, 1865–1919*. New York: R. R. Bowker Company, 1977.

TUROW, JOSEPH, *Getting Books to Children: An Exploration of Publisher–Market Relations*. Chicago: American Library Association, 1979.

5

Radio

While the print media continued to influence world opinion, reaching millions of people with information and entertainment, the twentieth century signaled the era of electronic communication. In many ways, it also changed the habits of media consumers. People began to spend more and more time with a new novelty called radio. Although they temporarily left it for the phenomenon of television, they returned, and radio once again prospered. Today, over 8,000 radio stations operate in the United States alone. Radio reaches every corner of the globe, bringing the latest pop music to a large metropolis or information about fertilizer to a remote tribal village. Radio is unique in its portability as well as its ability to reach us while we do different things or even while consuming other media. The soothing background music of a classical FM station adds to the atmosphere of a library reading room. The latest rock music bounces from the speaker of a nearby transistor radio while a teenager leafs through a favorite magazine at the beach. And a car would practically be naked without its radio.

Much different from the tubes and wires that held together the early stations of the 1920s, today's radio station is a complicated combination of electronic sophistication and creative mastery. Radio commands more than just the attention of the audience; it also commands the imagination. But radio's ability to conjure up creative imagery also has disadvantages. Images triggered by auditory stimuli, perhaps more than visual cues, depend heavily on the listener's own experience. For the child in the ghetto, for example, the sound of a crackling fire might create a vision of a burning tenement house. For a child from a well-to-do family, it might recall an open hearth fireplace in a sunken living room or the crackling logs beyond the doorstep of a motor home. Radio's coverage of civil unrest has suffered from the same drawback, resulting in the criticism that it is not objective and accurate. A news report about a shouting demonstrator and a milling crowd could easily give the impression of a mob out of control in the minds of many listeners.

With all of this criticism, though, radio has the ability to communicate messages with special qualities. Intangible products, for instance, can sell well on radio. Thus, the added "visual costs" of television sometimes are unnecessary, and less expensive radio advertising can do the job with equal effectiveness. Moreover, radio journalism is experiencing considerable new growth and recognition. When did this medium of radio begin? We shall begin our discussion in the late nineteenth century.

THE BIRTH OF WIRELESS: MARCONI

By the standards of the late nineteenth century, Guglielmo Marconi was born of wealthy parents. On their estate in Italy, he experimented with the theories of

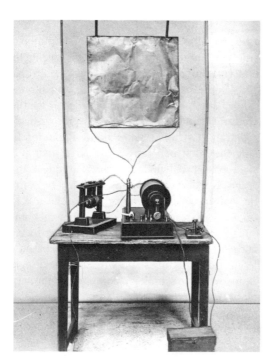

Figure 5-1 Marconi's early transmitting device used in the first experiments of wireless in Italy and later England. The large tin sheet served as the antenna. (The Marconi Company Limited, Marconi House, Chelmsford, Essex)

Figure 5-2 Guglielmo Marconi seated at his transmitter in New-foundland where the first trans-Atlantic wireless communication took place. (RCA)

Heinrich Hertz until his father's patience grew thin with the boy's constant dinner conversations of wireless telegraph possibilities. Finally, hoping to either encourage him or to apply the experiments to some constructive conclusion, Guglielmo's father loaned him the money to buy equipment necessary to outfit an attic laboratory. Equipped with the basics (Figure 5-1), Marconi successfully proved Hertz's theory of electromagnetic waves by making a compass needle turn at the same time a spark jumped between two wires on the other side of the room. Constructing a more elaborate transmitter, Marconi next successfully transmitted signals across the hillside outside the family home near Bologna. With his mother, he then traveled to England and successfully demonstrated the device to and received support from the British Post Office Department. He patented the new "wireless telegraph" on June 2, 1896.

At twenty-three years of age, Guglielmo Marconi was fast gaining world recognition for his experiments that linked islands off the British Isles to communication with ships at sea. Familiar with the long historic work of Samuel F. B. Morse in America, Marconi realized the full potential of his invention would occur only with a transatlantic wireless link. After an unsuccessful attempt at a transatlantic broadcast between England and the New England coast, he later tried again from Signal Hill, Newfoundland (Figure 5-2). There, at Signal Hill on the afternoon of December 12, 1901, a kite antenna and crude spark-gap receiving unit heard the letter S repeated through the earphones. Newspapers and magazines throughout the world heralded the historic event. With this success, Marconi developed a series of companies which dominated the wireless market. In fact, he was accused of monopolistic tendencies because of his refusal to permit ships with other companies' equipment to communicate with shore stations and other ships equipped with his wireless equipment. But despite criticism, his work brought wireless far beyond the realm of experimentation.

IMPROVING WIRELESS

Marconi's invention was the application of a basic principle, sending electromagnetic Morse code. But Marconi was only the first in the long line of contributors to the invention of radio.

Fleming and de Forest

One of the biggest hurdles to be conquered was the receiving apparatus. It was bulky with an enormous antenna necessary to receive the minute electrical impulses. One of the early breakthroughs in this area is credited to J. Ambrose Fleming, who in 1904 patented a special, two-element receiving tube called the Fleming Valve. The device controlled the "flow" of electricity much like a valve controls the flow of water, greatly amplifying the incoming radio signals. It was improved upon by another inventor, Lee de Forest (Figure 5-3), who added a third element. His tube, the *audion,* in principle is still in use today and was the main component of radio before the invention of the transistor. Although both de Forest and Fleming ended their careers still feuding with each other over the patent rights to the vacuum tube design, the work of both men was critical to radio's development.

voice broadcasting

While Fleming, de Forest, and even Marconi were conducting their historic experiments, a Kentucky farmer named Nathan B. Stubblefield also made history by transmitting the first voice via wireless using a method called "induction." It had little promise because it worked well only over short distances. Stubblefield's first demonstrations took place in 1892, but his work never had any significant application. He was still experimenting with his little publicized device when a professor at the University of Pittsburgh named Reginald A. Fessenden joined with some local entrepreneurs and successfully broadcast music to ships at sea on the night of Christmas Eve, 1906. With the help of a General Electric engineer named Ernst Alexanderson, a large alternator was used successfully to transmit the sounds of "O, Holy Night" between the coast of Mas-

Figure 5-3 Lee de Forest examining the developments of the vacuum tube which he helped pioneer with the invention of the audion. (AT&T)

sachusetts and the West Indies. In 1908, de Forest also conducted experiments in voice broadcasting with successful demonstrations from Europe.

RADIO COMES OF AGE

With the advent of voice broadcasting, radio matured quickly. The takeover of the industry by the federal government during World War I actually gave broadcasting an additional boost. Although the efforts were directed to war defense communication, the takeover forced all companies that were once competing with each other to share their knowledge. Everyone was thus immune from patent infringement suits, and thousands of amateur radio operators and war-trained telegraph operators swelled the ranks of early radio experimenters.

the early stations

It was not long before people began to envision radio as much more than just ship-to-shore communication, and experimenters began to apply radio as a medium for the masses. Generally recognized as the first commercial station to sign on the air was an experimental venture in 1909 built by Dr. Charles David

Herrold, which later evolved into KCBS. With studios in San Jose, California (Figure 5-4), the station broadcast mostly advertisements of Dr. Herrold's School of Radio.

Another pioneer station signed on as WHA at the University of Wisconsin at Madison, becoming the first major noncommercial broadcasting station. Its regularly scheduled programming dates back to 1919, the same year RCA was formed. Today, WHA continues as one of the leading public broadcasting stations in the United States. Under its experimental call letters 9XM, early listeners heard such programs as extension college courses by radio, the University of Wisconsin Glee Club, farm news, and even courses on how to build your own radio receiver. It eventually was joined by WHA-TV.

Two other stations are included in what historians consider the foundation of radio in America. On August 20, 1920 at 8:15 P.M., two records were played on an Edison phonograph with the speaker horn directed into a microphone connected to a de Forest transmitter. This experimental broadcast of WWJ, the *Detroit News* station, worked so well that it was followed the next day by a broad-

Figure 5-4 The early studios of Charles David Herrold's station in San Jose, California. (Herrold is standing in the doorway.) (KCBS radio, Gordon R. Greb, and The Sourisseau Academy of San Jose State University)

Figure 5-5 WWJ's early mobile news unit which served both the radio station and the newspaper. (Courtesy, WWJ)

cast of the Michigan election returns. The event captured attention with its newspaper-radio mobile unit. (Figure 5-5).

In November the same year, station KDKA in East Pittsburgh, Pennsylvania signed on with the election returns of the Harding-Cox race. The flagship station of what was to become known as the Westinghouse Broadcasting stations, or "Group W," KDKA has frequently been dubbed the first radio station in the United States. Actually, it was the first station with regularly scheduled continuous programming, but the publicity surrounding its inaugural broadcast that November night began its claim to fame. However, if you were to travel to either San Jose, Madison, Detroit, or Pittsburgh, you would find commemmorative plaques claiming *first* broadcasting honors for each of these pioneer stations.

competition and cross-licensing

In 1916, a former employee of the American Marconi Company, David Sarnoff (Figure 5-6), wrote his new boss at RCA (Radio Corporation of America) a memo:

> I have in mind a plan of development which would make radio a "household utility" in the same sense as the piano or phonograph. The idea is to bring music into the house by wireless. . . . The receiver can be designed in the form of a simple "Radio Music Box";. . . supplied with amplifying tubes and a loud speaking telephone, all of which can be neatly mounted in one box. . . .
>
> Aside from the profit derived from this proposition, the possibilities for advertising for the company are tremendous for its name would ultimately

Figure 5-6 David Sarnoff as he appeared in 1912 at the wireless station of the American Marconi Company. (RCA)

be brought into the household, and wireless would receive national and universal attention.

Like many memos, this one went largely unheeded. But KDKA's broadcast quickly changed all of that. Even GE (General Electric), RCA, and A.T.& T. (American Telephone and Telegraph), which had envisioned themselves the triumvirate of radio as a form of marine communication, what these companies thought the future of the medium would be, stopped short. Westinghouse had something here, something profitable.

The four companies soon secured agreements to share patents, manufacturing, and distribution. But the honeymoon ended when GE, RCA, and A.T.& T. also decided to sign on the air with their own stations. Westinghouse increased its broadcasting chain by adding such stations as WBZ, then in Springfield, Massachusetts, and now in Boston; WJZ in Newark, New Jersey; and KYW in Chicago, later assigned to Philadelphia. RCA started WDY in New York, and GE went on the air with WGY in Schenectady, New York.

WEAF: beginnings of commercial radio

The big headliner of early radio, however, belonged to A.T.& T. It signed station WEAF on the air in 1922 with the idea of toll broadcasting, meaning that anyone wanting to use the station's airwaves could do so by paying a toll. Queensboro Corporations, a local real estate company, was the first to try out the idea. It was not long before the print media began to criticize the practice, realizing the dangers of radio competition. The printing trade journal, *Printer's Ink*, said that advertising on radio would be offensive. WEAF disagreed. It secured a more favorable, less crowded frequency, and the advertising continued to roll in. It was evident A.T.& T. had discovered what David Sarnoff had predicted, commercial broadcasting was where the action was. Not satisfied with just WEAF, A.T.& T. began to license other stations, charging them a fee before permitting them to hook up to its long distance lines. It then organized groups of stations to give advertisers a discount on advertising, creating the first true broadcasting network, called "chain" broadcasting.

Finally, the agreements between the four companies began to erode as each started to pave its own way into the future of commercial broadcasting. The end result was the involvement of the Justice Department, charges of antitrust by the Federal Trade Commission, and A. T.& T.'s decision that the negative public opinion and expensive legal battles were not worth the trouble. The telephone company bailed out of the broadcasting business in 1926 and sold WEAF to RCA's separate subsidiary company, the National Broadcasting Company.

NETWORK RADIO

The start of NBC began a new era in broadcasting—the networks.

NBC

Two networks operated as part of the NBC system: the Red and the Blue. The Blue Network served stations on an exclusive basis as did the Red, but some stations negotiated contracts permitting them to draw programming from both. Both operated until the FCC became involved in 1941. In a special report titled the *FCC Report on Chain Broadcasting*, NBC was criticized for its financial holdings in a talent company that steered the best stars over to NBC. Finally, the breakup of the Red and Blue Networks was inevitable, and NBC reorganized the Blue Network into a separate corporation in order for it to be sold.

ABC

He made his money in Lifesavers candy, but when Edward J. Noble bought NBC Blue in 1943, he turned much of Livesavers' assets toward broadcasting. It was a sizeable challenge for the times. World War II was raging, and the country was in a state of economic uncertainty. But Noble pulled together his own management team, and on June 15, 1945, affiliates heard the network announcer open with: "This is the American Broadcasting Company."

In what turned out to be one of the most novel decisions ever to affect radio network programming, on January 1, 1968, ABC split its operation into four different networks. These were the American Contemporary Radio Network, the American FM Radio Network, the American Entertainment Radio Network, and the American Information Radio Network. The idea was to develop news programming to meet the needs of different types of radio formats. For example, the American Contemporary Network was designed to match the programming of contemporary-sounding stations. Sharp, quick tones preceded and concluded the newscast; stories were shorter and more direct; and the entire newscast was shortened to fit into the quick changes in sound and the fast transition that occurs on the contemporary station. The four-network concept has proved to be extremely successful.

CBS

CBS has its roots in a cigar company with an advertising manager named William S. Paley (Figure 5-7). Paley's cigar company had experimented with sponsoring a program on the UIB/Columbia radio network in 1927 and saw its business more than double. Paley, a year later at the age of twenty-seven, arrived in New York and bought the network that later became CBS.

Like the other networks, besides its regular entertainment and news pro-

Figure 5-7 William S. Paley. From the family cigar business, he moved full time into broadcasting and guided CBS to become the largest advertising medium in the world and the owner of numerous subsidiaries, ranging from publishing to retail sales. (Courtesy, CBS)

gramming, CBS experimented with broadcasts from trains, balconies, and underwater bathyspheres. There were some unexpected outcomes. A 1930 broadcast featuring George Bernard Shaw aired the playwright's comments without approving them beforehand. CBS officials gasped as Shaw began with, "Hello America! Hello, all my friends in America! How are you dear old boobs . . . " and ended up by praising Russia. When the broadcast was over, CBS decided it was in everyone's best interest to provide equal time for an opposing opinion.[1]

In 1930, Paul Kesten joined CBS as promotion manager and immediately began to whittle away at powerful NBC. First came a survey on radio listenership that refuted NBC's claim to be the most "listened to" network. Next came an era highlighted by a policy of attracting big-name radio personalities to CBS. This concept of using major entertainment to build up the business saw such stars as Bing Crosby and Kate Smith join CBS.

In 1935, a twenty-seven-year-old instructor from the Ohio State University received a telegram from CBS. It read, "I don't know of any other organization where your background and experience would count so heavily in your favor or where your talents would find so enthusiastic a reception."[2] The instructor's name was Dr. Frank Stanton. He accepted CBS's invitation and began to work for $55 a week doing audience measurements and research. Later, he too climbed CBS's success ladder to become one of the leading spokesmen for the broadcasting industry.

When World War II broke out, many CBS employees began to make names for themselves in broadcast journalism. Correspondents Eric Sevareid, Richard C. Hottelet, H. V. Kaltenborn, and many others reported from the front lines—a first in providing up-to-date wartime news coverage.

When the war ended, there again was a movement to develop competitive programming, and CBS spared little in competing head-on with NBC. In what became known as the great "talent raids," CBS literally bought such NBC talent as Red Skelton and Jack Benny. CBS also developed a sizeable chain of its own radio and television stations serving major markets. The combination of CBS's own stations, its network affiliates, and creative programming placed the network at the top in national popularity.

Mutual

The Mutual Broadcasting System started in 1934 as a cooperative arrangement among four stations: WOR in Newark, WXYZ in Detroit, WGN in Chicago, and WLW in Cincinnati. Mutual was the time-broker for all four stations. Advertisers buying commercial time on all four stations would pay the regular advertising rate, and Mutual would take 5 percent to handle the cost of promoting the network, line charges for network programs, and other expenses.

In 1936, Mutual added thirteen stations in California and ten in New

England. Two years later, it assimilated a regional network in Texas, adding 23 more stations to the chain. By 1940, Mutual had grown to 160 outlets.

Today, the network not only operates its original system but also has added the Mutual Black Network and the Mutual Information Network. Remaining an exclusively radio network, Mutual is owned by the Amway Corporation, known for direct sales of home cleaning supplies. Its programming includes such names as newscaster Fulton Lewis, III, son of the famed Fulton Lewis, Jr., who for years was a major attraction of Mutual. Also included in the Mutual programming schedule are such major sports events as Notre Dame Football, championship boxing, NFL football, PGA golf, and the Sugar Bowl.

National Public Radio

The roots of public radio go back to WHA at the University of Wisconsin, which signed on the air as the first noncommercial station. Noncommercial radio was soon trying its microphones on college and university campuses all across the country. Then in 1965, the Carnegie Commission for Educational Television conducted a major study of noncommercial broadcasting in the United States and recommended providing financial support for a national system of public broadcasting stations. The Public Broadcasting Act of 1967 appropriated $38 million for improving existing noncommercial stations and building new ones. Also formed was the Corporation for Public Broadcasting (CPB), a quasi-government agency selected to administer funds to public broadcasting stations.

The 1967 legislation made possible a special category of stations, called CPB-qualified stations, which met certain operating criteria, such as specified hours of operation and transmitter power. Although not all noncommercial stations are CPB-qualified, the 1967 act made all noncommercial stations "public" stations, in that they can secure grants from individuals and corporations to provide operating expenses. National Public Radio is the organization linking together all CPB-qualified stations by direct lines and satellite connections permitting network programming to reach all of those stations simultaneously. Essentially, NPR operates in the same way as other radio networks do except that it does not accept commercial sponsorship.

the role of radio networks

The role of radio networks in broadcasting is similar to that of television networks, except that the individual station is not as dependent on the network for programming. Radio has become a very specialized medium with considerable local programming directed to specialized and local audiences, and it is much less expensive to program local radio than to program local television. The recording industry provides countless hours of inexpensive recorded music which can fill local programming schedules. In addition, a single disc jockey can operate virtually all the controls in a radio station, including the transmitter, and originate local programming as well, all at the same time. Larger stations naturally require a larger number of personnel, but the operation of a radio station is much less complicated and less expensive than that of a television station, overall.

Radio affiliates are sometimes reimbursed for airing network commercials, although the contractual agreements with stations vary greatly. In many cases, the station may not realize a profit from affiliating with a network, but it feels that the network programming adds to the overall image of the station.

Despite their supplementary role, radio networks have thrived, even though many radio stations have no network affiliation. If the future of radio networks can be predicted from their ability to specialize, plus the burgeoning number of FM stations, all indications are that they will prosper. Also, we must keep in mind that the cost per thousand persons reached by radio advertising is low and that advertisers can aim at specific markets.

FM RADIO

Frequency modulated, or FM radio, operates at a higher frequency than AM, or amplitude modulated radio, does. As we shall learn later in this chapter, the higher frequency permits the signals to travel in a straight line, rather than bouncing them off the atmosphere in a zig-zag pattern. As a result and because of the type of modulation employed, FM signals are less susceptible to atmospheric distortion than AM signals are. That, plus other advantages, has made FM radio a growing, popular medium.

FM was invented by Edwin Armstrong while he was working at Columbia University in 1933. Its early application met with little enthusiasm because of the developing war and the radio industry's preoccupation with the threat of television. But after World War II ended, both the FCC and the industry began to take another look at FM. That second look became even more appealing in the 1970s, because the FCC had already allocated most of the available AM frequencies during the previous decade. FM still had a wide range of frequencies open for expansion.

The development of FM stereo also gave FM stations the ability to broadcast music of a quality and distinction previously limited to the stereo record player. FM stereo broadcasts the two tracks of a stereo record on two separate FM frequencies. A special FM stereo receiver picks up these signals. Even stereo news is coming into its own. With stereo speakers, a morning news interview with a local politician assumes immediacy as the interviewer's voice emanates from one speaker and the politican's from the other. When a reporter airs a report from the scene of a parade, the listener hears the parade bands first on one speaker and then gradually on the other speaker, as though the band were marching through her dining room.

Many industry professionals expect the real growth of radio audiences to be in FM. From a low figure of 35 percent of the radio audience in America's top twenty-five markets in 1973, Cox Broadcasting Corporation research predicts a majority figure of 55 percent by 1981 (Figure 5-8). Today it is not unusual for FM broadcasting stations to sell for millions of dollars, a price inconceivable in the 1960s.

PROGRAMMING

In 1923, Robert McCormick, editor and publisher of the *Chicago Tribune*, wrote his mother saying, "I have written to arrange to have an operator come to your room with a radio set and give you an exhibition. I don't think you will want to keep one, but you cannot help being thrilled at the little box that picks sounds from the air. . . . "[3] McCormick's *Chicago Tribune* had its own station, WDAP, which later became WGN, a major station in American broadcasting. The ambitious and creative people at WGN helped bring radio into its own. A warm May afternoon brought the microphone of WGN's A. W. "Sen" Kaney to the famed Indianapolis 500 auto race for seven hours of live sports broadcasting, the first time the Indy 500 had ever been heard on radio. In October of 1924, a crack of the bat kept listeners glued to their radios as sounds of Chicago Cubs and Chicago White Sox baseball came over WGN's air waves. That same month, the University of Illinois and the University of Michigan met for a football clash, again broadcast by WGN. The famed Scopes trial of 1925 heard WGN broadcast the voices of Clarence Darrow and William Jennings Bryan as they argued the case of the Tennessee school teacher, John Thomas Scopes, accused of teaching the theory of evolution.

becoming a mass medium

The next decades saw radio blossom into mass popularity. Variety shows, dramatic productions, and comedy series elevated such radio personalities as Jack Benny and George Burns to national stars. Radio heroes dominated the medium. "The Lone Ranger" (Figure 5-9), "The Shadow" (Figure 5-10), and many more

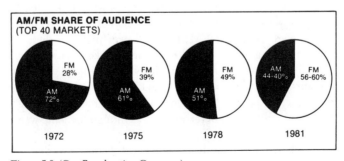

Figure 5-8 (Cox Broadcasting Company)

Figure 5-9 (Lone Ranger Television, Inc.)

kept listeners spellbound. Radio also developed as a news medium. A study by educator Wilbur Schramm in 1945 asked college students what medium they would most likely believe in the face of conflicting news reports. Radio led by far.[4] Broadcasts of events as they happened—the actual "sounds"of the news—made radio one of the most credible news sources. The radio schedule of the evening newspaper became important and popular reading for everyone, especially the radio critics' columns. When WSB in Atlanta pioneered the airways, the *Atlanta Journal* noted in wordy adjectives:

> As may be instantly surmised by a casual glance at telegraphic tributes printed elsewhere on this page today, Sig Newman, astonishing virtuoso of the saxophone, and his orchestra of New York, entrancingly aided by the vocal brilliance of Mrs. Susan Reese Kennedy, Atlanta soprano, not only took Atlanta but half of the United States by storm at WSB's 10:45 concert Monday night, following proportionate glittering success at the 7:00 radio debut of the *Journal's* radio telephone station.[5]

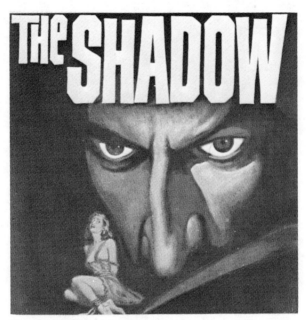

Figure 5-10 (Charles Michelson, Inc.)

For the time being, the thrill and novelty of radio were conveyed to the public by a press only too eager to cover every new programming and technical development of the new medium.

the medium becomes specialized

This massive audience appeal began to waver, however, when television made its appearance. Forced into new formats, radio began a period of transition. It found its niche as a "specialized" medium (Figure 5-11). Major radio networks that once carried entertainment programming began to specialize in news. Each station began to forge its own individual identity. An examination of radio stations in any major metropolitan area illustrates the extent to which this specialization has been accomplished. One station may specialize in Top 40 or rock music with top disc jockeys (Figure 5-12) while another may devote itself exclusively to foreign broadcasts. Still others may concentrate on educational programs or all-news formats. Starting at one end of the AM spectrum; your first encounter might be a "personality" station. By the time you had turned the dial to the other end of the spectrum, you would probably have heard a country-western station, a station that plays only hit records from the past, an automated station, a foreign language station, a top-forty station, and more than a dozen others. If you were to turn to the FM dial, you would hear an equally large selection among almost three dozen stations, each with its own identity.

educational radio

In many countries where television systems are not well developed, radio remains the dominant medium. Consequently, it has become a major teaching
medium for people in these underdeveloped nations. Researchers at the Institute
for Communication Research at Stanford University have compared the effectiveness of instructional media in various international locations. The institute
has tested both instructional radio and instructional television. In a summary
report, researchers concluded:

> There is nothing in the research evidence to cast doubt on the proposition
> that a motivated student can learn from any medium. One of the most
> surprising results to researchers was the absence of any clear and consistent
> evidence of difference between the efficiency of learning from the complex
> and costly media like television and the less costly ones like radio.[6]

Installation of relatively inexpensive transmitters in local areas enables radio to
disseminate information in the local language and to reflect local cultures. This
is especially important in areas in which social and cultural identities are
threatened. In the United States, many colleges and universities offer special
courses by radio. The University of Wisconsin School of the Air pioneered in
this area, and other schools that followed, such as Purdue University's WBAA,
offer credit by examination for radio courses. Public schools also have found
radio an inexpensive alternative to television. The South Carolina Educational
Radio Network serves public schools in South Carolina. Special multiple-

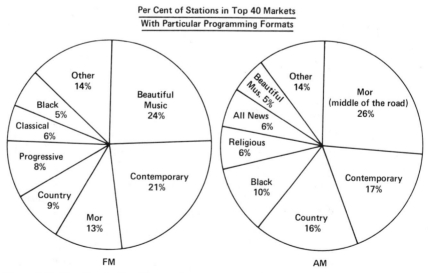

Figure 5-11 (Cox Broadcasting Company)

Figure 5-12 Larry Lujack, nationally famous disc jockey. Careers as disc jockeys range from minimum wage positions in small markets to slots in major cities which pay big money for stars like Lujack.

earphone listening systems (Figure 5-13) permit teachers to use radio as a supplement to classroom activities and learning experiences.

IMPACT OF RADIO

The medium that was once merely a theoretical vision of the late nineteenth century has now achieved a major impact throughout the world.

radio's acceptance and potential

Despite the enormous impact of television in the 1950s, radio has continued to grow and prosper. Since its early development in 1920, it has achieved and maintained growth rivaling that of all other media in the history of mass communication. Estimated percentages through the 1980s see growth up over 225 percent from that of the early 1950s. Despite a penetration of more than one radio for every person, radio set sales continue to climb. Almost 95 percent of all automobiles have radios, up from 55 percent in 1952.

We might well ask, with virtually every household equipped with more than one radio, why people continue to buy radios. One reason is that a transistor radio has become a widely accepted gift, coming in all shapes and sizes from complex shortwave sets, to combinations of radios and other gadgetry such as cigarette lighters, liquor decanters, and pencil sets. Miniaturization of parts has made it possible to place a radio in all kinds of imaginable items in the home, from intercoms to popular home entertainment combinations of television, AM/FM radio, and stereo record players. Moreover, increased use of FM bands has sparked still more sales. Now the public's appetite has been whetted for FM sets that can receive FM in stereo or quadrophonic, four-channel sound.

Radio is an especially strong medium among both the general population and specialized audiences. For example, the overall radio listening audience is larger than the television audience for a sizeable portion of the day. The highest audience measurement comes at approximately 8:00 to 9:00 A.M. local time, then it tapers off, climbing back up to a plateau between 3:00 to 7:00 P.M. local time. These "highs" are commonly called drive-time, when many people listen to radio while commuting to and from work. Television begins to take over the audience after 8:00 P.M. But among both high school and college students, radio is the primary mass medium. High school students spend an average of three and one-half hours per day with radio compared to two and three-quarters hours for television, thirty-eight minutes with newspapers, and twenty-three

Figure 5-13 Somewhat overlooked because of the predominance of television, educational radio serves a vital purpose in many curricula. Permitting the imagination to stretch to its limits, accountable educational radio programming can play an important part in supplementing classroom instruction. (South Carolina Educational Television and Radio Network and the South Carolina State Department of Education)

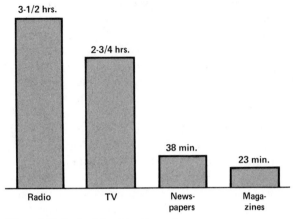

Figure 5-14 (Radio Advertising Bureau)

minutes with magazines (Figure 5-14). College students spend an average of two and three-quarters hours per day with radio compared to two hours with television, thirty-one minutes with newspapers, and twenty-one minutes with magazines (Figure 5-15).

radio's future perspective

The future of radio is bright both in terms of technological developments and the all-important economic considerations that face any mass medium. The ability of radio, for example, to reach a great number of people at a comparatively small cost has a distinct advantage over television. For corporations with small to

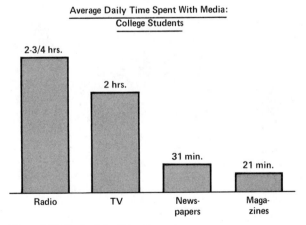

Figure 5-15 (Radio Advertising Bureau)

moderate advertising budgets, radio affords the opportunity to reach their public. Many radio news departments operate with a small number of personnel, a few inexpensive cassette tape recorders, and an automobile equipped with a two-way radio. For television news to function, it takes thousands of dollars worth of equipment, trained personnel for operating the equipment, and a costly television transmitter and studio equipment to edit, compose, and send the program to the viewers.

Stereo FM will continue to develop. The full potential of stereo news has yet to be tapped. It will permit radio to develop and stretch the audio picture of an event even beyond what television can do as a single video dimension. The medium has come a long way since Marconi first lifted his kite antenna above Newfoundland and received signals across the Atlantic. Throughout the world, radio serves the masses with entertainment, news, and instructional programming. It survived television and gained its own identity as a medium with distinct advantages and the ability to reach specialized audiences in our society.

SUMMARY

Chapter 5 examined the medium of radio. With over 8,000 stations operating in the United States alone, radio penetrates the lives of virtually the entire world population. The development of the medium is credited to a number of countries. In Italy, Guglielmo Marconi experimented with a crude spark-gap transmitter and sent signals over the hillside near his home. He later captured world attention by sending and receiving wireless signals across the Atlantic. In America, Fleming gave radio his two-element valve, and de Forest contributed his three-element audion. Voice broadcasting began as early as 1892 using a process called induction, but the primitive process had little promise. Practical voice application of the methods employed by Marconi were made by Reginald Fessenden in 1906.

As radio moved out of the experimental era, early radio stations began to apply the technology by bringing music and news to large numbers of people. In 1909, Charles David Herrold's station signed on the air in San Jose, and in 1919, WHA at the University of Wisconsin became the nation's first recognized noncommercial station. A year later, both WWJ in Detroit and KDKA in Pittsburgh crackled onto the air waves. The KDKA venture signaled a new entertainment and commercial application for radio, and it was quickly followed by other stations. A.T.&T. signed WEAF on the air but sold it to RCA in 1926. Out of that sale came NBC. NBC operated two networks until 1943 when it was forced to sell one of them, which became ABC. Two other networks, CBS and Mutual, also were part of the development of early commercial radio. For noncommercial stations, the National Public Radio began regular programming in 1971.

FM radio, once shelved by the industry in favor of the development of television, has overtaken AM radio in listener popularity. Both AM and FM have prospered because of radio's ability to adapt its programming to both the competition and the audience. Programming drama in the 1920s, 1930s, and 1940s, radio began to direct its programming to a specialized audience in the 1950s.

Today, the medium has reached nearly 100 percent saturation in the United States and is found in 95 percent of the country's automobiles. It commands our attention for the majority of the daytime hours and is the most listened to medium among high school and college students.

OPPORTUNITIES FOR FURTHER LEARNING

AITKEN, HUGH G. J., *Syntony and Spark–The Origins of Radio*. New York: John Wiley & Sons, Inc., 1976.

BARNOUW, ERIK, *The Golden Web*. New York: Oxford University Press, Inc., 1968.

BARNOUW, ERIK, *The Image Empire*. New York: Oxford University Press, Inc., 1970.

BARNOUW, ERIK, *A Tower in Babel*. New York: Oxford University Press, Inc., 1966.

BITTNER, JOHN R., AND DENISE A. BITTNER, *Radio Journalism*. Englewood Cliffs, N.J.: Prentice-Hall, Inc., 1977.

CLAUDE, BARBARA HALL, *The Business of Radio Programming*. New York: Billboard Publications, 1977.

DREHER, CARL, *Sarnoff: An American Success*. New York: Quadrangle/The New York Times Book Co., Inc., 1977.

DUNLAP, ORRIN E., *Marconi: The Man and His Wireless*. New York: Arno Press, 1971.

FANG, IRVING E., *Those Radio Commentators!* Ames: Iowa State University Press, 1977.

HOOD, STUART, *The Professions: Radio and Television*. North Pomfret, Vt.: David and Charles, 1975.

JULIAN, JOSEPH, *This Was Radio: A Personal Memoir*. New York: The Viking Press, 1975.

LICHTY, LAWRENCE W., AND MALACHI C. TOPPING, eds., *American Broadcasting: Book on the History of Radio and Television*. New York: Hastings House, 1975.

ROBINSON, SOL, *Radio Advertising: How to Sell It and Write It*. Blue Ridge Summit, Pa.: TAB Books, 1974.

STERLING, CHRISTOPHER H., AND JOHN M. KITTROSS, *Stay Tuned: A Concise History of American Broadcasting*. Belmont, Calif.: Wadsworth Publishing Co., Inc., 1978.

ULLYETT, KENNETH, *Ham Radio: A Practical Guide and Handbook*. North Pomfret, Vt.: David and Charles, 1977.

VYVYAN, R. N., *Marconi and Wireless*. Yorkshire, England: E. P. Publishing Limited, 1974.

6

Television

Television has been called everything from an educational panacea to a boob tube projecting images of a vast wasteland. People have labeled it biased, accurate, liberal, conservative, and have accused it of everything from wrecking the family structure to robbing us of our individuality. Somewhere in between all this lies the truth. One thing is certain. The medium has become one of the most powerful communicative forces in the history of civilization.

EARLY DEVELOPMENT

To appreciate the great technological strides television has made in the past decades, we need to examine the history of the medium. The concept of television can be traced back to 1839. In that year, French physicist Alexandre Edmond Becquerel observed the electrochemical effects of light.

Nipkow's scanning disc

In 1884, the German scientist, Paul G. Nipkow, devised a method by which a spiraling disc would pass over a picture and create a scanning effect. Nipkow punched holes in his disc to create the pattern of a spiral, beginning at the outer edge and circling toward the center of the disc. When the disc revolved, the holes would pass over the picture, and in one complete revolution of the disc, the total picture would be scanned. Nipkow transferred the light passing through each hole into electrical energy and transmitted this electrical energy through wires to a receiver that also had a synchronized disc connected to a transmitter. When the transmitter changed pictures at rapid intervals, a very crude picture with a semblance of motion could be achieved. Nipkow's device represented a mechanical adaptation of the principle used in the old penny arcade in which a series of cards would turn down, each with a slightly different picture than the one before it, thus creating the illusion of movement.

Mechanical television and the scanning disc processes continued to improve. Television entered into new experimental eras with greater picture clarity. By the 1920s, although very crude, pictures could be reproduced with high intensity lighting. Felix the Cat was the first star of the system which made Felix look more like a venetian blind than a cat and the sixty-line (Figure 6-1) system was a long way from the picture clarity that would follow with major developments in electronic television.

Zworykin and Farnsworth

It was not long before the television experimenters realized that the future of the industry could not be tied to the mechanical reproduction of visual images. The breakthrough into electronic television came in the 1920s and is credited to two

Figure 6-1 Felix the cat became television's first star as the crude scanning process resulted in a picture far inferior to modern transmission techniques. (RCA)

Figure 6-2 Vladimir Zworykin holding the iconoscope tube which helped usher in the era of electronic television. (RCA)

men, a Russian immigrant, Vladimir K. Zworykin (Figure 6-2), and an American, Philo Farnsworth. Zworykin was an employee of Westinghouse in Wilkensburg, Pennsylvania in 1919. It was there that the company gave him permission to work on a new device which used electrons to detect and transmit pictures instantly. The device was patented in 1923 and named the iconoscope television pickup tube. It signaled the end of television's mechanical era.

Improving the system was left to a schoolboy from Rigby, Idaho, who at age fifteen drew a blackboard sketch of a high-resolution scanning system. The boy was Philo Farnsworth, and he later shared the credit with Zworykin for fathering modern television. Farnsworth formed the Crocker Laboratories in San Francisco, later the Capehart-Farnsworth Corporation. Farnsworth eventually held more than 150 patents related to television, some common to all television receivers.

RCA, meanwhile, continued its own television experiments, which included opening an experimental television station, W2XBS in New York on July 30, 1930. In 1931, the company placed an experimental transmitting tower on top of the Empire State Building. These experimental transmissions permitted the development of a system producing a clearer picture than had been possible previously. Continuing its television experiments, RCA announced in 1935 that it would spend one million dollars for television field testing. It was a sizeable business venture at a time when there were few viewers and much progress still to be made before the system could approach significant home use.

experimental programming succeeds

In 1936, television receivers were able to pick up signals from a distance of one mile. In 1937, the antenna atop the Empire State Building went into "public" use, and NBC and RCA took television to the people. In an arrangement set up on the streets of New York passersby could stop and see the operation of the new invention. A broadway play, *Susan and God*, was televised from the NBC studios on June 7, 1938. It was also the year David Sarnoff, pre..ident of RCA, announced to a meeting of the Radio Manufacturers Association that television sets would go on sale to the public when the World's Fair opened in 1939. During that year, television signals were transmitted a distance of 130 miles from New York City to Schenectady, New York. A year later on the first of February, as members of the FCC watched, television pictures were sent from New York to Schenectady and then *rebroadcast* to other points in upstate New York. On a small and experimental basis, the first television network began that first day of February in 1940.

color, the freeze, and UHF

Three FCC decisions greatly influenced television's growth from the early 1940s through the early 1950s. They included the decision on a compatible color transmission and receiving system, the freeze on licenses and the resultant allocation of frequencies, and the support of UHF television stations.

Two broadcasting giants, CBS and RCA, battled for supremacy in color transmissions. Both had systems that produced color programming with acceptable results. CBS got the FCC's first go-ahead with a noncompatible system, one which permitted color pictures to be received on special sets that could not receive the same pictures in black and white. Meanwhile, RCA was developing a compatible system which permitted color programs to be transmitted so that they could be received in black and white on sets already in use. RCA sued CBS with a court order, and the appeals went to the Supreme Court where CBS's noncompatible system received its blessing. But CBS's jubilation was short-lived. The FCC, realizing the advantages of RCA's system and wishing to avoid a disruption of the industry's manufacturing efforts, reversed itself. Thus, RCA's system became the standard color system of modern television (Figure 6-3).

As the color debates were brewing, the FCC meanwhile had frozen all new television licenses in 1948 until it had time to study a plan for television's orderly development. It lifted the freeze in 1952. The results were that twelve channels were assigned to the very high frequency (VHF) band (channels 2 through 13), and seventy channels (13 through 83) were assigned to the ultrahigh frequency (UHF) band.

Figure 6-3 RCA's first color television receiving sets come off the assembly line in Bloomington, Indiana. (RCA)

Although the freeze cleared the way for the development of both VHF and UHF television, UHF stations operated at a tremendous disadvantage. Few sets had channel selectors beyond channel 13. Thus, although in theory the FCC hoped that television set manufacturers would keep up with the demand for UHF, the demand could not materialize because UHF stations could not stay on the air for financial reasons. It was a vicious circle. As a result, everything stood still until 1964 when the FCC required set manufacturers to install both UHF and VHF tuners on all sets. Although UHF stations still do not have as many viewers as VHF can muster, many are gaining in the marketplace as viable competitors. Most UHF stations are independent, and, as independent stations obtain quality programming through syndication, they are sure to give VHF stations a run for their advertising money.

developments in television technology: beyond the iconoscope

The iconoscope tube was only the beginning of television technology. Improvements in design led to the orthicon tube, which improved clarity, and the image orthicon tube, which allowed light levels to be used to pick up the visual image. The vidicon tube improved clarity and was more stable in capturing and holding the image. In color television, the plumbicon tube, a trademarked tube of the Amperex Corporation, permitted gains in picture clarity equal to the sensitivity of the human eye.

Recording the television picture also was of great concern to engineers. Early attempts used film. The first successful demonstration was in 1950 using Kodak film, a Navy camera, and a CBS receiver. Videotape recording was demonstrated by RCA in 1953, but it was Ampex Corporation's demonstration in 1956 at a NAB meeting that received the publicity. From that point on, videotaped recording continued to be improved through systems which now include cassette recorders with tape as small as one-quarter inch and which promises widespread use of even smaller systems in the future.

TRENDS IN TELEVISION PROGRAMMING

Television networks were essential to early programming. NBC, with the backing of RCA's financial support and technology, was one of the top competitors. CBS, with William Paley's administrative abilities, had by the 1950s become a powerful force in the industry. ABC, although an infant, kept pace with innovative programming, especially with sports programming in the 1960s and 1970s.

the golden era

The 1950s are generally considered television's golden era. It was a time of continual experiments, and the experiments were live. Television was innovative because almost everything was a "first." One of the pioneer stars was Milton Berle with his "Texaco Star Theater." The show was so popular that on Tuesday nights, restaurant owners without a television set could expect vacant tables. Comedy was also king with programs like "I Love Lucy," built around a zany redhead and her band leader husband. William Bendix starred in "The Life of Riley," one of the first shows to bring blue-collar comedy to television.

Children had the puppet show of "Kukla, Fran, and Ollie." For the slightly more serious child there was Jack Barry's "Juvenile Jury," and for the budding scientist there was "Mr. Wizard." Perhaps the most famous early children's program was "Howdy Doody" (Figure 6-4), featuring a puppet with a sidekick named Buffalo Bob and a group of kids in the studio audience called the "peanut gallery." The "Wonderful World of Disney" and the "Mickey Mouse Club" (Figure 6-5) were two other famous shows; the Disney show still remains popular. Even the original "Mickey Mouse Club" and "Howdy Doody" returned to modern television through syndication.

1960s: politics and space

If television were said to have been "in training" in the 1950s, it went to war in the 1960s. Few could have predicted the turmoil that television would capture in the 1960s. For the first time in history, it brought the trauma of political assassination to the world with the coverage of the assassination of President John F.

Figure 6-4 Early television programming had its share of children's shows, one of the most popular which was Howdy Doody. With a cast of characters centered around "Buffalo Bob" Smith, the puppet Howdy Doody and other puppets charmed youngers in after-school programming carried coast-to-coast. The show was later revived and syndicated. (Photo courtesy of Jack Drury Associates)

Figure 6-5 Jimmie Dodd and Roy Williams of the original Mickey Mouse Club. (© Walt Disney Productions)

Kennedy. It repeated the horror as it covered the assassination of civil rights leader Martin Luther King. And then Senator Robert Kennedy met death by an assassin's bullet while he campaigned in California for his own presidential bid. By this time, television was beginning to be blamed for the outbursts of violence that began rocking the country. As the decade drew to a close, that violence had spilled onto the streets and into living rooms as television covered the civil rights riots in the Watts section of Los Angeles and the student protests at the 1968 Democratic National Convention in Chicago. But most of all, it covered the bloody agony of American servicemen fighting an impossible, unpopular war in the jungles of Vietnam. Yet, although most of the decade was spent covering conflict, it ended with a triumph as television captured the first live coverage of man on the moon (Figure 6-6).

the 1970s

The trends of the sixties, both in national events and television's coverage of them, continued into the 1970s. The winding down of the Vietnam War and the pullout of American forces, the last remnants of campus protests, and the continuing saga of space travel all were a part of 1970s television. But that decade

Figure 6-6 Live television pictures of the Apollo Moon landing were sent back to earth on July 19, 1969. For television news, it seemed like a sharp contrast to the coverage of civil protest and the Vietnam War which had been regular television fare during the spring. (NASA)

Colgate-Palmolive Company

Policy Statement

*The Company's policy regarding violence in
television programming is printed below.
During February 1977, a copy of this statement
was sent to the chief executive officers of all
our advertising agencies and to the networks.*

**Policy Statement on Violent or Antisocial
Television Programming**
So there is no doubt about our policy regarding
violence in television programming, the
Colgate-Palmolive Company is releasing this
statement summarizing its policy and operating
procedures on this subject for the guidance of
television stations, television networks, and our
advertising agencies.

1. The Colgate-Palmolive Company does not
advertise its products in programs making
gratuitous or excessive use of violence. This
eliminates programs which include violence
which is not necessary to the development of
the program's characters or story line. It also
eliminates those programs which, although
some violence is an integral part of the story
line, feature unnecessary violent details,
brutality, or suffering.

2. The Colgate-Palmolive Company does not
advertise its products in programs which it
considers to be antisocial or in bad taste, or
which could stimulate antisocial behavior
through viewer imitation.

3. The Colgate-Palmolive Company has
charged its advertising agencies with the
responsibility of prescreening any questionable
program material and, if there is any doubt
about a program's suitability, it is to be referred
to Colgate for prescreening and decision.

Figure 6-7 Concern over sex and violence in television has caused some corporations to issue advertising guidelines disassociating their products from such programming.

had its own version of conflict—that of a nation testing the very roots of its foundation through the impeachment hearings of a president. Television was there, giving us continuity through Richard Nixon's resignation, Gerald Ford's succession, and Jimmy Carter's election to the White House.

Major new efforts in programming developed as the situation comedy so popular in the 1950s found its way back to television. Perhaps the leader in this trend was "The Mary Tyler Moore Show." The program made a successful run on CBS as the fictitious crew of a TV news department brought laughs and some serious issues to television. Audiences watched Mary Richards, played by Mary Tyler Moore, grow from a trauma-ridden single girl to a mature professional woman. The program became as popular in syndication as it was in its network run.

The 1970s also heard continuing criticism of television programming and saw a growing consumer movement. A critical and also popular view of television was offered by Canadian philosopher Marshall McLuhan, who said that the media was massaging us into a rear view way of thinking. More direct criticism of television began to develop as groups, such as Action for Children's Television, began to examine what was being shown to children and what could be done about it. Direct communication with and lobbying efforts at both the FCC and the networks made the organization and the consumer movement in general a visible force in the television industry. Some of the public's reaction to violence on television resulted in some major corporations issuing public statements that they would not sponsor violent programming (Figure 6-7).

As the 1980s begin, there is some indication that possibly serious attention could be paid to higher quality programming. ABC rose to the top of the ratings under the direction of programming executive Fred Silverman. When NBC lured Silverman away, Silverman suggested that in contrast to the action-filled (some called it sex and guts) programs that put ABC on top, NBC would reach the top slot through a new wave of quality programming that Silverman predicted would materialize in the 1980s.

CONSUMER PRESSURE AND SELF-REGULATION

What is the result of such public attention? Is it having positive or negative effects? For the consumer groups, there is now an impressive record of victories at high levels.

pressure on government and industry

The FCC has become very concerned with children's television, both programming and commercial content, and this has prompted voluntary changes within the industry. As happens in a country with a free press, the activities of consumer groups have been accorded considerable media attention even by those who are on the receiving end of the criticism. Some industry representatives complain that these groups are the ruination of the industry. They argue that the programs being aired are broadcast *because people want to see them.* They cite the impressive figures of the rating services to back their postulations and criticize the pressure groups for not understanding the first thing about the workings of the media in a free society. The consumer groups counter with the argument that pressure from the public is much more satisfactory than pressure from government. Gradually a citizen-industry working relationship is being constructed.

If consumer groups are to be successful, both they and the industry will have to keep in mind that overreaction leads only to polarization. The lesson is also pertinent to industry. When a community group becomes militant and refuses all compromise, then there is great reason to believe that they will isolate themselves from both the industry and other members of the community to the point of losing all previous gains. When industry representatives, on the other hand, charge consumer groups with irresponsible activity and do not engage in self-regulation, then they also will suffer the consequences of that same isolation. The lesson is pertinent to both industry and reformers. Consumer groups are a phenomenon that goes beyond the traditional role of the "unseen, unheard" consumer. If the dialogue that has been developed by these groups remains rational and responsible on both sides, then new channels of communication may open up to give the citizen more say in what reaches the family living room.

the NAB codes

While consumer groups continue to work toward better television programming, the industry points to its own efforts at controlling programming, especially for children. Both radio and television stations have the opportunity to subscribe to the "codes" of the National Association of Broadcasters (NAB), but membership is by no means universal, even though the codes have been in existence for decades and undergo constant revision.

The Television Information Office, an independent association partially funded by the NAB, has tried to bring the Codes' provisions to the attention of the public and broadcasters alike. Ads in major newspapers as well as flyers from the Television Information Office alert parents to programs that are endorsed by the NAB as suitable for children to watch.

code enforcement

Adherence to both the Radio and Television Codes is enforced by a systematic monitoring (either listening or watching) system. Subscriber radio stations are monitored near the time of their license renewal periods and TV stations are monitored twice each year. The NAB then notifies the station if it is operating within the guidelines established by the code authority. In certain situations, special attention will be paid to specific types of programming. If, for instance, the code authority feels that there has been an increase in certain types of questionable commercials at a station, then the authority may ask for the transcripts of those commercials. Along with determining a station's own self-regulatory posture, such detailed analysis keeps the authority cognizant of changes that may be occurring within the industry. Still, when a broadcasting station decides not to join the code, there is little the rest of the industry can do to pull it into line. When there is an economic crunch, a station may be less willing to turn down an advertisement dollar for a commercial unacceptable to the code. Similarly, if the difference between the profit and loss column of a station begins to shrink, management may cancel its subscription to the code altogether, thus saving the subscription fee.

When subscription support is present throughout the system, the real advantage of codes for the broadcasting industry is in two areas. First, they tend to deter dubious advertising and programming. Second, they can be an effective alternative to government regulation. The NAB keeps in close touch with the actions and the pulse of the FCC. Whenever possible, it will actively try to assure the FCC and other government agencies that there is self-regulation in the broadcasting industry and that government regulation is therefore not necessary.

TELEVISION JOURNALISM

The events of the 1960s also thrust television journalists into the limelight. In a sense they became seers, showing and explaining what was happening. Some of this record is less than satisfactory, specifically the overreactions in covering the heated chaos of protests and civil unrest. Unfortunately, the tendency to sensationalize these events still plagues the profession, both at the local and network levels. However, news programming, like the medium itself, was still maturing.

surviving the Red scares

As a social force, television news received attention and respectability in the 1950s. It was an era beset with irrational, patriotic fever, worried that the Communist movement had infiltrated into every segment of American society. This included the entertainment industry. Waving the banner of the Communist scare was Senator Joseph McCarthy. As he used the "Red" scare as a platform for political expediency, his rhetoric persuaded both the government and a number of private businesses to fire certain employees. The entertainment industry was hard hit by the impact of his purge when a right-wing publication, entitled *Red Channels*, published in June 1950 the names of 151 people associated with the Communist movement who also were in the radio and television industry. Many entertainers found themselves suddenly without work and their professional careers ruined.

It was television journalism that finally brought these abuses of civil liberties to the attention of the public and signaled the beginning of the end for McCarthy. Career journalist Edward R. Murrow (Figure 6-8) hosted the television news show *See It Now*. After an Air Force officer was asked to resign because of his relative's questionable Communist activities, Murrow went on national television presenting the case that the officer had been the victim of innuendo. Another show covered the case of Dr. Robert J. Oppenheimer, who lost his security clearance because of a political stand on nuclear energy. The *See*

Figure 6-8 Edward R. Murrow with one of the many interview guests, movie star Marilyn Monroe, who helped to make his television program, *Person to Person*, a success on early television. (WNET/THIRTEEN and CBS)

It Now program cast the first shadows of doubt on the legitimacy of the McCarthy purge. When the senator took on the United States Army in congressional hearings, television was there, and the public, already skeptical of McCarthy, watched his radical accusations. When it was over, McCarthy had been reduced to humiliation, and television journalism had gained a new legitimacy.

TV news and technology: microwave and ENG

Microwaves are ultra-high frequency waves which have been found very effective in carrying television signals and computer data over relatively short distances using line-of-sight transmission that does not bounce off the ionosphere. With relay receivers and transmitters approximately every thirty miles, the signals can be carried across unlimited distances.

Portable microwave systems have become an effective tool of local television programming, especially electronic news gathering (ENG). A portable microwave system consists of a motor van or truck equipped with portable batteries, television cameras, a small transmitter, and an antenna capable of sending signals via microwave (Figure 6-9). Back at the main television studio, another microwave antenna works as a receiving antenna for signals transmitted from the mobile van.

Small microwave horn antennas and a miniature transmitter about six inches long now can be mounted on a small tripod about three feet high (Figure 6-9). This portable tripod microwave transmitter is focused on the microwave transmitter in the mobile van (Figure 6-10), and the signal is then retransmitted back to the main studio. A television journalist with a portable camera (Figure 6-11) connected to this portable microwave system can walk anywhere and broadcast live reports. Clear glass does not destroy the signal, so it is possible to take the portable tripod system inside a building and point the transmitting antenna through the window toward the antenna at the mobile van.

The development of microwave systems has opened up new frontiers for television journalism. The city council meeting once reported on the evening news and in the evening newspaper now can be televised live. Members of the local zoning board can be held accountable to the public in a far more direct and immediate manner. You can view documentaries broadcast live from such places as the inside of a nursing home, the office complex of a corporate execu-

Figure 6-9 ENG Transmitter, Electronic News Gathering (ENG) has brought a new dimension to television news. Transmitters using microwave technology can send signals which relay the program back to the studio for retransmission to home receivers. (CBS)

Figure 6-10 A microwave receiver is mounted on a mobile van alongside the larger dish for the link-up to the news center at the television station. (CBS)

tive, the parking lot of a shopping center, or the middle of a ghetto. Mobile television news crews can provide live coverage from the scene of a major event within a few minutes after its mobile van arrives.

PUBLIC BROADCASTING

Along with the commercial networks, public broadcasting systems also are an essential part of the overall structure of broadcasting. Public broadcasting as defined here means *the operation of the various noncommercial radio and television stations in the United States*. The depth to which the public participates in these broadcasting complexes varies considerably, but the underlying purpose of these stations is to serve the public—not to operate at a profit. This does not mean that commercial radio and television stations do not serve the public; it means simply that staying in business, that is, making a profit, must be their primary concern. In many cases, commercial stations may be owned by a parent corporation that views them first as profit-making instruments. If they are not, then there is a good chance that they will be sold for more profitable ones. Since public radio stations are not under the same financial pressure as their commer-

Figure 6-11 Smaller cameras and microwave links permit live coverage of breaking news events. (Reprinted by permission of the Magnetic Audio/Video Products Division, 3M Company, St. Paul, Minnesota)

cial counterparts are, they can program to more select audiences without as much concern over losing a mass audience or over winning a spot in audience ratings. Public broadcasting stations usually operate with a sizeable portion of their budget coming from listener contributions, direct appropriations, and grants from foundations and corporations.

early stations and NET

Although public broadcasting has attracted serious attention only in recent years, as we learned earlier, the roots of the system began back in 1919 at the University of Wisconsin in Madison when the experimental radio station 9XM went on the air. In 1952, the FCC allocated exclusive channels for noncommercial television. Of these, 80 were located in the VHF range and 162 at the UHF end of the spectrum. This was just the help that noncommercial television needed to develop along with radio. Also in 1952, noncommercial broadcasting received a major financial boost when the Ford Foundation created the Educational Television and Radio Center. This later became the National Educational Television (NET), involved in producing educational programs for public television stations. In 1953, station KUHT at the University of Texas in Houston was the first noncommercial, educationally licensed television station to sign on the air. WQED-TV in Pittsburgh, Pennsylvania became the first community-owned, noncommercial television station to sign on the air. WQED-TV also is credited with supporting one of the earliest children's quality television programs on a noncommercial television station. One of the station's employees was Fred Rogers who took part in the creation of a show called "Children's Corner." The program first appeared in 1954, but it sparked a much more lasting and creative effort that materialized into a program called "Mister Rogers" on the Canadian Broadcasting Corporation and eventually "Mister Rogers' Neighborhood" (Figure 6-12) in 1965 on WQED-TV. Fred Rogers was directly responsible for all of the programs and has continued to star in "Mister Rogers' Neighborhood" while working closely with child psychologists in developing the popular program on public broadcasting But in the 1950s when noncommerical television needed to show its potential, Fred Rogers's programming inventiveness became a good example of what the medium could accomplish.

Figure 6-12 *Mister Rogers' Neighborhood,* which had its start in the 1950's, is still regarded as one of television's most successful children's programs. Fred Rogers, star and creator of the program, has served as an international consultant in children's television programming. (Copyright, Family Communications, Inc.)

the Carnegie commission and CPB

The next nine years saw noncommercial broadcasting develop rapidly. In 1962, Congress passed the Educational TV Facilities Act which provided $32 million over a five-year period to develop state systems of educational broadcasting.

In 1965, planning began for what was to become a major policy document affecting the development of public broadcasting in America. A major industry-wide study of public television was undertaken by the Carnegie Commission for Educational Television. The Commission was "asked to 'conduct a broadly conceived study of noncommercial television' and to 'focus its attention principally, although not exclusively, on community-owned channels and their services to the general public.' . . . The Commission will recommend lines along which noncommercial television stations might most usefully develop during the years ahead." The Commission, whose report was published in 1967, was made up of a broad spectrum of industry leaders. It reached the conclusion that a "well-financed, well-directed educational television system, substantially larger and far more persuasive and effective than that which now exists in the United States, must be brought into being if the full needs of the American public are to be served."[1]

the Public Broadcasting Act and CPB

Acting on that recommendation, Congress passed the Public Broadcasting Act of 1967. Among other things, the act allocated an appropriation of $38 million for the construction of facilities and the formation of a nonprofit corporation called the Corporation for Public Broadcasting (CPB). Specifically, CPB was charged with authorization to:

> Facilitate the full development of educational broadcasting in which programs of high quality, obtained from diverse sources, will be made available to noncommercial radio or television broadcast stations, with strict adherence to objectivity and balance in all programs or series of programs of a controversial nature;
>
> Assist in the establishment and development of one or more systems of interconnection to be used for the distribution of educational television or radio programs so that all noncommercial education television or radio broadcast stations that wish to may broadcast the programs at times chosen by the stations;
>
> Assist in the establishment and development of one or more systems of noncommercial educational television or radio broadcast stations throughout the United States;
>
> Carry out its purposes and functions and engage in its activities in ways that will most effectively assure the maximum freedom of the noncommercial educational television or radio broadcast systems and local stations from interference with or control of program content or other activities.[2]

134

The concept of public broadcasting had received the beginnings of a financial base. Now it could prosper and expand.

the Public Broadcasting Service—PBS

To help meet these goals, the CPB joined in cooperation with many of the licensees of noncommercial television stations in the United States in 1970 and formed the Public Broadcasting Service (PBS), which became the primary distribution system for programs serving public broadcasting stations. PBS is responsible for obtaining programs for national distribution from its member stations as well as from independent suppliers. In less than a decade, PBS has been responsible for a number of award-winning special programs as well as regular series, the most famous of which is "Sesame Street" (Figure 6-13). Along with its production and distribution system, PBS is also responsible for representing the interests of member stations before Congress and other governing bodies.

In 1979, the PBS membership of affiliate stations voted the recommendation to split PBS into three primary services with different programming and distribution responsibilities. A national or primary service is designed for prime-time entertainment and cultural programming; a regional and special-interest service is designed to feature the works of independent producers; and a third service is designed to provide informational and instructional programming for both in-school and home-study offerings.

Figure 6-13 Big Bird of *Sesame Street*. (Courtesy Children's Television Workshop)

affiliates, organizations, and licensees

In addition to NPR, PBS, and CPB, other key components of public broadcasting include affiliated stations, state systems of educational radio and television, program libraries, and producers. Noncommercial radio and television stations are of four basic types. There are those licensed to state authorities or commissions; community stations licensed to nonprofit community corporations; school stations licensed to school corporations; and university stations, usually licensed to the boards of trustees of both public and private colleges and universities.

Carnegie Commission II

A second study of public broadcasting was made in 1978 and was released in 1979. Officially titled "The Carnegie Commission on the Future of Public Broadcasting," it criticized the system now in operation and suggested numerous changes. Among these was eliminating the Corporation for Public Broadcasting and replacing it with a Public Telecommunications Trust, with a Program Services Endowment as a subsidiary of the trust. The trust would be a nonprofit, private, nongovernmental corporation, and the endowment would be dedicated to underwriting and developing quality programming for public radio and television.

Funding for public broadcasting would come partly from licensee or "spectrum" fees paid by commercial broadcasters. At the same time, the Carnegie II report took some pot shots at commercial broadcasters for not providing quality programming. Comments such as "the growing degradation of America's commercial communications media" and other phrases did not sit well with commercial broadcasters. At the very least they showed little political expediency since Congress will make the final changes in the system and since commercial broadcasters through the NAB can be a powerful lobby on Capitol Hill.

If the proposals of Carnegie II are carried out, the trust will be administered by nine trustees, as opposed to a fifteen-member controlling board of the CPB. Trying to insulate the trust from political pressures claimed to hinder the CPB, the new management structure would have the nine members chosen by a select panel including the librarian of Congress, the head of the National Endowment of the Arts and the National Science Foundation, the head of the National Endowment for the Humanities, the secretary of the Smithsonian Institution, and members from public radio and television.

TELEVISION'S IMPACT AND FUTURE

The public has widely accepted the medium ever since its first year of significant operation in 1948. Television's Bureau of Advertising estimates list television as commanding 48 percent of our time spent with media as opposed to 32 percent

136

for radio, 13 percent for newspapers, and 7 percent for magazines. Television set ownership increased dramatically after World War II. Networks began to develop major distribution systems at that time to reach affiliate stations in most areas of the United States and in many foreign countries. A. C. Nielsen estimates listed more than forty-three million households with televisions in 1950. By 1980, that figure has increased to approximately seventy million. In the United States, we averaged more than five hours of television consumption per day, per household, in 1963, and this increased to over six hours by 1980 (Figure 6-14). This translates into actual years spent in front of television by the time we reach adulthood.

Educational television (ETV) and instructional television (ITV) have been designed specifically to capitalize on the teaching-learning process in both education and industry (Figure 6-15). ETV refers to *any noncommercial television program*, whether or not the program is used for direct classroom instruction. ITV refers to *programming especially tailored for use in the classroom or in direct teaching*. Industries also have incorporated ITV into many areas of training. The ability to transmit ITV programs directly into the home makes it possible for many corporations to conduct home training programs. Similar programs have been developed through colleges and universities.

Much of the medium's impact cannot be measured in statistics. The changes in our life styles since the advent of television are too numerous and in some cases too subtle to measure fully. An international television spectacular from one country can set a new trend in another country's clothing styles. A breakfast cereal commercial may show someone participating in the sport of hang-gliding. The sale of the breakfast cereal soars, and so does the sale of hang-gliders. A stomach medicine is advertised as a man stuffs pizza into his mouth. The sale of the stomach remedy stays constant, but pizza sales increase. A student sits in the classroom and has little desire to learn from lectures. The

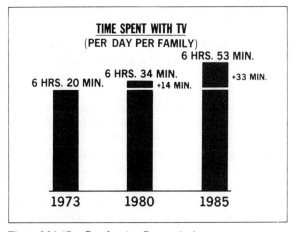

Figure 6-14 (Cox Broadcasting Corporation)

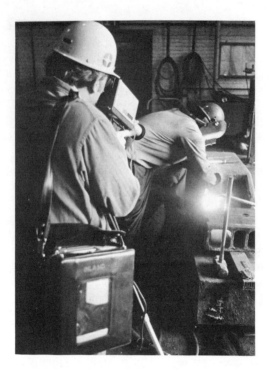

Figure 6-15 Television is becoming an increasingly important tool in corporations, where it finds applications ranging from the production of training programs, to customer sales aids, to internal communication and teleconferencing. (Inland Steel)

teacher introduces a televised segment into the lesson, and the student's interest and attention span increase. Researchers in a university prepare a comedy series to teach reading to underprivileged children. When their examples seem unreal to the children's preconceptions of television, the series fails miserably. All of these examples show that at present we are still unaware of the total impact of the medium. It has only been during the last decade that college students have become the first total-television generation, living with the medium from birth. What will occur when you become the first television-parent generation, and your children will be part of a home that has seen every member of the family molded by television since birth? It is easy to see why it is so important to realize the impact of the medium now and to become responsible consumers and molders of its future.

What television holds for society as it approaches the end of the twentieth century is open to considerable speculation. Already we can sit in front of "big screen" television, which can cover an entire wall. A special television receiver collects the signal and then projects it onto a wall like a slide projector. Research also has developed slim-screen television to replace the cumbersome models of the past that had television tubes as large as two feet thick. The new picture tubes are not much thicker than a picture frame and can be hung on the wall in much the same manner. Portable "mini-cams" and "microcams" give television reporters the flexibility of the radio journalist, although still not at the reduced cost that radio enjoys. Held easily with two hands, these small cameras permit live TV coverage of many news events that was previously impossible because of the difficulty in transporting cumbersome television equipment. Sideline interviews with football coaches, traffic-flow observations from a helicopter, and streetside interviews at a political rally thus have become commonplace. Although we may not see the wholesale marketing of Dick Tracy-type wrist televisions in our lifetime, the miniaturization of electronic components will increase television's portability.

Television programming also will change as cable television grows, making available more channels than are possible with direct, over-the-airways reception. We will see an increase in the amount of local access to cable television, and community groups will be responsible for this programming. Public television supported through public contributions and government subsidies from the Corporation for Public Broadcasting will be providing more alternatives to the mass appeal programs seen on commercial network television. The future of pay television on a mass scale is somewhat uncertain, but limited experiments have proved successful in a number of communities. A coin dropped into a slot in the top of your home television set permits you to see programming not available on other channels. All this adds up to more selective viewing, which, along with technological improvements, will be important to television's development as a medium of the future.

SUMMARY

Television's debut can be traced back to the work of Alexander Edmund Becquerel and the electrochemical effects of light. Practical application of principles transmitting visual information took place in 1884 with Paul Nipkow's scanning-disc transmitter and receiver. Vladimir Zworykin with his iconoscope tube and Philo Fransworth with his improved, high-resolution scanning system made the transition to electronic television. Other improvements in television tubes included the orthicon, image orthicon, vidicon, and plumbicon.

Television was introduced to the public at the 1939 World's Fair. Surviving the FCC's decision on an industry-wide color system, a freeze on licenses, and rules improving the development potential of UHF, the medium enjoyed its golden age in the 1950s. Programming ranged from the variety shows and comedies of the fifties, to the political turmoil of the sixties, and to the consumer movement of the seventies. Television journalism gained respect in the 1950s with such programs as "See It Now" and explored new horizons in the 1970s with electronic news gathering. Television's impact on our lives has been substantial, with steadily increasing amounts of time being spent with the medium.

OPPORTUNITIES FOR FURTHER LEARNING

AVERY, ROBERT K., AND ROBERT M. PEPPER, *The Politics of Interconnection: A History of Public Television at the National Level.* Washington, D.C.: National Association of Educational Broadcasters, 1979.

BARCUS, F. EARLE, AND RACHEL WOLKIN, *Children's Television: An Analysis of Programming and Advertising.* New York: Praeger Publishers, Inc., 1977.

BARNOUW, ERIK, *Tube of Plenty.* New York: Oxford University Press, Inc., 1975.

CATER, DOUGLASS, AND RICHARD ADLER, EDS., *Television as a Social Force: New Approaches to TV Criticism.* New York: Praeger Publishers, Inc., 1975.

COMSTOCK, GEORGE, STEVEN CHAFFEE, NATAN KATZMANN, MAXWELL McCOMBS, AND DONALD ROBERTS, *Television and Human Behavior.* New York: Columbia University Press, 1979.

FIREMAN, JUDY, *TV Book: The Ultimate Television Book.* New York: Workman Publishing Co., 1977.

HYDE, STUART W., *Television and Radio Announcing.* Boston: Houghton Mifflin Company, 1979.

NEWCOMB, HORACE, ed., *Television: The Critical View.* New York: Oxford University Press, 1979.

PEPPER, ROBERT M., *The Formation of the Public Broadcasting Service.* New York: Arno Press, 1979.

PRIMEAU, RONALD, *The Rhetoric of Television.* New York: Longman, 1979.

A Public Trust: The Report of the Carnegie Commission on the Future of Public Broadcasting. New York: Bantam Books, 1979.

SMITH, ROBERT R., *Beyond the Wasteland: The Criticism of Broadcasting.* Falls Church, Va.: Speech Communication Association, 1976.

STEDMAN, RAYMOND WILLIAM, *The Serials: Suspense and Drama by Installment.* Norman: University of Oklahoma Press, 1977.

STEIN, ALETHA HUSTON, AND LYNETTE KOHN FREIDRICK, *Impact of Television on Children and Youth.* Chicago: University of Chicago Press, 1975.

WURTZEL, ALAN, *Television Production.* New York: McGraw-Hill, 1979.

7

Photography and Photojournalism

In the early 1860s, the illustrated newspaper brought vivid, if not altogether accurate scenes of the Civil War to an anxious readership. Gradually, the woodcuts used to print these scenes were replaced by engravings and later, photographs. By the 1920s, photography was radically changing the newspapers' format. The camera also changed from the large, tripod-mounted models to the small, hand-held 35mm models capable of capturing "candid" shots of world leaders and celebrities.

CAMERA OBSCURA

History's first record of images being reproduced with light dates back to the ancient Greeks. Aristotle described light waves and how they behaved when projected through a small opening called an aperture. Later applications of Aristotle's principles were recorded in the Middle Ages when Francis Bacon used a dark room with a tiny opening in one wall to permit light to enter from the outside and to project an image on the opposite wall. The device used for these experiments became known as the *camera obscura*, which in Latin means "darkened chamber." Artists, including Leonardo da Vinci, are reported to have used

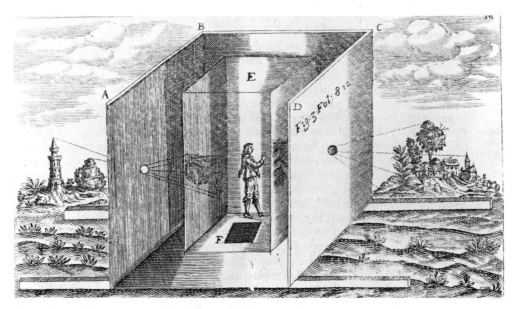

Figure 7-1 Camera obscura, a box-like room, was used to project images on the inside walls of the room. Artists many times used it as a guide for paintings and sketches. (International Museum of Photography at the George Eastman House)

the camera obscura to project images (Figure 7-1) into the darkened chamber where the artist would trace the image.

Gradually, the camera obscura began to be improved and reduced in size. What started out as a room became a large box. Then a piece of glass was added to the aperture, and a mirror was placed inside the box. The mirror reflected the image to the top of the box where another lens permitted it to escape and to be projected onto a wall. By looking directly into the lens on top of the box, the image could be viewed from outside the camera obscura. This latter principle is the same used in early cameras held at chest level while the photographer looked down into the viewfinder.

A PERMANENT IMAGE

Although the camera obscura had considerable use for the artist, it was not a camera capable of capturing permanent images. That did not occur until 1727 when German scientist Johann H. Schultze discovered that silver salts were sensitive to light. The process Schultze used, however, was not stable, and although a crude image could be captured, it could not be preserved. Closer scrutiny of the process resulted in Carl W. Scheele's 1777 discovery that the image captured on silver salts could be preserved longer with ammonia.

Niepce and Daguerre

Progress was slow until 1826 when, after a series of experiments, Frenchman Joseph N. Niepce succeeded in producing a permanent photograph (Figure 7-2), but the exposure time ran as much as eight hours.

Three years after this, Niepce joined in partnership with another Frenchman, Louis Daguerre. Daguerre, Like Niepce, also was attempting to create permanent photographs. Using copper coated with silver and exposed to iodine vapors, a photosensitive plate was produced. When exposed to light through a camera obscura and then brought into contact with mercury vapors, the plate produced the image seen by the camera obscura. The process was both quicker and of better quality than the process originally used by Niepce. Called *daguerrotype* (Figure 7-3), the process became popular in Europe and America and even was used for portrait photography. It was not long before explorers' expeditions were carrying daguerrotype cameras to capture the landscape of unexplored territory.

The only disadvantage of the daguerrotype was that only one daguerrotype could be made at a time. There was no process for reproducing more than one image, such as multiple positive prints from a single negative. That hurdle was overcome by British scientist William H. F. Talbot, who invented a light-

Figure 7-2 The first photograph, "Image from Nature," produced by Niepce in 1826, was called a heliograph. The gray area of the sky is actually the impurities of the metal. In the original, the sky appeared white, and the dark shadows showed more contrast. (Gernsheim Collection, Humanities Research Center, The University of Texas at Austin)

Figure 7-3 Daguerreotype camera. (International Museum of Photography at the George Eastman House)

sensitive paper. Talbot's paper was coated with salt and silver nitrate and from a single negative, multiple positive prints could be made. Talbot's process was christened *photography*. By 1841, Talbot had received a patent on an improved version of his paper film, calling the improved process *calotype*, and by 1844, Talbot's photographs had appeared in *The Pencil of Nature*, the first major book containing photographs. For the early world of photography, however, Talbot's ability to make multiple copies from a single negative of marginal quality did not appeal as much as Daguerre's single prints of almost perfect quality.

improving the photosensitive plate

The next two developments in photography were in the substance of the photographic plate. Frederick Scott Archer took glass and coated it with a wet substance called *collodion*. The *wet-plate* process was later applied to metal by an American, Hamilton Smith, who called them *tintypes*. There were further improvements in photography in 1871 when Richard L. Maddox invented a *dry-plate* process which meant less cumbersome developing equipment which in the past resulted in a wagon load of chemicals and apparatus when the photographer ventured into the field.

George Eastman

Although history records Hannibal Goodwin as the inventor of celluloid film, George Eastman, founder of the Eastman Kodak Company, will always stand out as having the greatest impact on photography and motion pictures. The year was 1877 when Eastman took an amateur interest in photography ard discovered the craft entailed being part chemist, part artist, and part mechanic. Producing pictures required much equipment and luck. Eastman, who at the time was working as a bank clerk in Rochester, New York, began experimenting with manufacturing "dry plates." Eastman invented a machine to manufacture the dry plates and with a partner, H. A. Strong, opened a business in a third-floor loft in Rochester to begin manufacturing the plates on a mass scale. The Eastman Dry Plate Company opened for business on January 1, 1881.

Three years later, Eastman jolted the photographic industry with his announcement that he had invented film rolls and a roll adapter which fit virtually every dry plate camera. Not having to change plates after every picture was a significant improvement but not as monumental as what happened in 1888. It was in that year that Eastman introduced a light, portable camera priced at twenty-five dollars and capable of holding film for one-hundred exposures. When the exposures were taken, the customer sent the entire camera back to the company where the film was extracted, developed, and the camera with new film was returned to the sender. The cost for replacing and developing the film was ten dollars. A year later, Eastman introduced the first commercial roll of film on transparent nitrocellulose backing.

Not satisfied with manufacturing a camera that contained film for one-hundred exposures, Eastman set out to make photography a truly "mass medium." What was needed was a camera that anyone could afford and simple enough for anyone to use. The price of his early camera, twenty-five dollars, was inexpensive compared to previous studio models, but still out of reach of the average person. For the most part the only people really engaged in photography were studio photographers and people who could afford the high-priced camera with roll film. Finally after much product research and testing, Eastman introduced the world to the Brownie camera (Figure 7-4), a simple box camera with a price tag of only one dollar. Now photography was available to almost everyone, and the company that had started as a manufacturer of dry plates was into worldwide distribution of its products (Figure 7-5).

Figure 7-4 Early ad for a Brownie camera. Mass production made both the Brownie and popular photography available to the masses.

Figure 7-5 Improvements on the original Brownie still kept the same box-camera concept and inexpensive price. (Photo: Greg Rice, DePauw University News Bureau)

EARLY ILLUSTRATED REPORTING

Despite the changes in the development of still photography in the 1800s, using photographs in the daily production of the newspaper waited until later.

sketch artists and illustrated newspapers

The roots of photojournalism grew from the work of artists, not photographers. The appetite for these sketchbook reporters was whetted by such events as the War Between the States in the United States and after it, the massive westward expansion. When photographs were used, they became the guide that engravers used to make woodcuts, which in turn, were printing plates. Debate ensued between photographers and printers alike on which method, the sketch artist or photographer, would become the mainstay of the illustrated press.

But while the debate continued, events meant that illustrated newspapers and their artists would flourish. Often criticized for glorifying battle and portraying an unrealistic picture of events, the sketch artists still found a waiting public. Illustrated newspapers, started in the 1850s, flourished with the war. Most prominent were titles such as *The Southern Illustrated News, Harper's Weekly,* and *Frank Leslie's Illustrated News* (Figure 7-6).

Even papers not accustomed to using pictures became conditioned to new layout styles. For these papers, the maps of the Civil War battles and troop movements demanded composition different from the thin columns commonly used for type. Gradually, two and three columns were used to display maps large enough to identify roads, paths, and tiny, unknown hamlets made famous by the war.

Along with the Civil War, the movement to the western frontier created another appetite for illustrations. Again the sketch artist prevailed. Names such as Charles Graham and Allen C. Redwood embellished weeklies with drawings of outlaws, cowboys, and the western experience. Graham, who was one of the best known national news artists of the late 1800s, traveled throughout Montana and Idaho sketching Indians. Redwood, who fought with the Confederates, traveled and sketched Idaho and Washington after the Civil War.

Although better known for his famous paintings than his work as a sketch artist for newspapers, Frederic Remington helped bring scenes of the West to eastern newspapers and magazines. One of the most responsible artists of his day, his scenes were not the glorified exaggerations produced by some of his peers. Illustrations by Remington appeared in such publications as *Century Magazine*

Figure 7-6 The illustrated newspaper did much to make pictures an important part of journalism and paved the way for acceptance of photographs as illustrations. **(Leanin' Tree Publishing Co.)**

and *Collier's Weekly*. When the Spanish-American War broke out, he was sent to Cuba as a war correspondent by the Hearst papers.

Another product of the West was artist Charlie Russell. Like Remington, he is more famous for his paintings than his illustrations, although Russell's pictures did appear in publications. Longing to be a cowboy, Russell left home in St. Louis for the West and remained to live among the cowhands of Montana and the Indians of Canada. For capturing the life style of both groups, few equaled Russell's talent for depicting the hard, calloused, but sometimes fun-loving life of the open range. While writers created glamour and intrigue of the West, Russell, Remington, and others made a realistic appraisal of a land that many easterners saw only in pictures.

One of the most complete chronicles of Western life in the late 1800s and 1900s occurred, not on the pages of newspapers, but in a tiny photographic studio located in Wallace, Idaho. There, T. N. Bernard photographed not only commissioned portraits of the people of the rich silver-lead mining region, but the town, its surrounding area, the mines, and anything else that made a good subject. When his business of the 1890s grew too busy to manage, he telegraphed

Figure 7-7 "Bridge Wreck." One of over 5000 photographs which were the work of pioneer photographers T. N. Bernard and Nellie Jane Stockbridge. (Bernard-Stockbridge Photographic Collection of the University of Idaho Foundation, Inc.)

his photographer sister-in-law in Chicago and asked her to join him. She did, and Nellie Jane Stockbridge continued to photograph the people of Northern Idaho well into the 1960s (Figure 7-7). But it wasn't until her death in 1965 that her work gained recognition on a wide-scale. At that time, the University of Idaho became the beneficiary of over 200,000 negatives from the Bernard-Stockbridge photography business, and, through the efforts of the University of Idaho Foundation, cataloguing and copying of the negatives began in earnest. The result is a rich depository of material for scholars of both early photography and the history of the Pacific Northwest.

PHOTOGRAPHY MAKES AN IMPACT

By the late 1800s, the photographer had managed to become part of the reporting process, albeit not in newspapers. Government collections, books, and private exhibits were the showcase of the photographer-reporters. What the photograph could do for reporting, however, was shown by a massive photo project headed by Mathew Brady.

Mathew Brady

Many illustrators captured the Civil War, but Mathew Brady and his staff did it on a grand scale. Brady's interest in photography grew from a boyhood fascination that matured through associations with Samuel Morse, who, along with inventing the telegraph, had an interest in optics. Morse introduced Brady to Daguerre in Europe, and in 1844, Brady came back to New York and opened his own photography studio using daguerrotype. By 1860, he had met and photographed Abraham Lincoln. When the Civil War broke out, Brady received presidential approval to photograph it. With Secret Service protection and now using the improved wet-plate process, he and his assistants traveled from the battlefield to battlefield bringing reality to a war the sketch artist often misrepresented. Although the newspapers did not benefit from his photographs, since there was no rapid photoengraving process, his work remains one of the important beginnings of photojournalism.

Brady also left his mark on photography and photojournalism by giving us some of the best photographs of prominent figures (Figure 7-8). Along with Lincoln, he also photographed Jefferson Davis, John Tyler, John Quincy Adams, James Polk, and Franklin Pierce. Brady, or his assistants, are also credited with photographs of such noted people as Mary Lincoln, wife of the President and Susan B. Anthony, women's suffrage leader.

Mathew Brady brought photography out of its experimental stages into being a recorder of history. But the invention that brought photographs to mass communication was the halftone.

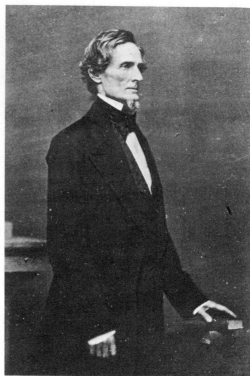

Figure 7-8 Two of Brady's famous photographs are these of Abraham Lincoln (left) and Jefferson Davis (right). (International Museum of Photography at the George Eastman House)

the invention of the halftone

For the newspaper publisher of the 1870s, photographs were nice, but there was no fast and practical way to put them in print. Even when used as tracings for engravers, the cutting and edging of a good engraving took time—too much time for the demands of instant news the telegraph brought to newspapers. But all that began to change in March, 1880, when the *New York Daily Graphic* published its first line halftone picture showing a scene in Shantytown, New York (Figure 7-9). The halftone process permitted the printer to capture the full tonal range of a photograph, something not possible before. An improved halftone process used two pieces of acid-coated glass with tiny parallel lines cut on the glass. When the two pieces of glass were placed so the lines were perpendicular to each other, it formed a "screen" effect that in turn was used to impose the tonal variations of a photographic negative onto a printing plate (Figure 7-10).

There is a debate over who contributed the most to developing the halftone. Two people stand out as particularly important. One is Frederic E. Ives

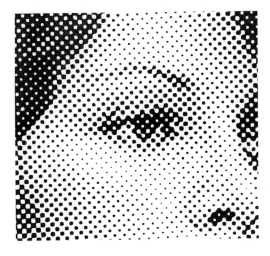

Figure 7-9 A halftone image is created using a screen process with different amounts of ink adhering to the printing plate. At a distance, the illustration becomes an eye. Close up we can see the various "dots" created by the halftone screen. In this halftone, both vertical and horizontal lines were used to create the screen, whereas in Figure 7-10, only vertical lines were used.

Figure 7-10 A halftone engraving of a photograph titled "Scene in Shantytown" appeared in the New York *Daily Graphic* on March 4, 1880. It marked a new frontier in newspaper illustrating. (Newspaper Collection, The New York Public Library, Astor, Lenox and Tilden Foundations)

who worked at Cornell University and is credited with making the first halftone reproduction in 1878. He continued to improve the process, while simultaneously a photographer named Stephen H. Horgan worked on a way to use the halftone process in newspaper publishing, specifically for his employer, the *New York Daily Graphic*. It was Horgan who prepared and published the Shantytown picture and made the use of halftone practical on the rotary press.

With the ability to publish quality photographs with speed, the importance of the photographer to journalism increased dramatically.

THE TABLOIDS

As photography began to improve, more and more people became aware of the capabilities of the medium, and organized professionals banded together to promote their craft. Early efforts by Alfred Stieglitz resulted in the formation of Photo-Session, a cooperative group of photographers who, through 1917, published and displayed a wide variety of photographs.

After World War I, newspaper publishers took time to view the growth of the illustrated tabloid newspapers of England and realized that a handsome profit awaited the publisher who could combine good photography with reporting. Unfortunately, it was not journalism's finest hour. With strong competition among tabloids, sensationalism became the norm, and there were ample opportunities, too. Motion pictures were just coming into their own, and the life of the celebrity filled gossip pages. In Germany, a new camera called the Leica was placed on the market. Much smaller than the older models, the new 35 mm Leica was small enough to catch candid photographs of politicians, movie stars, and everyone else who could be caught in an embarassing position.

Edwin and Michael Emery in their book *The Press in America* succinctly describe the era:

> The national experiment called Prohibition brought rumrunners, speakeasy operators, and gangsters into the spotlight, and they were interesting people. Al Capone, Dutch Schultz, Waxey Gordon, Legs Diamond, and their rivals were sensational copy. Socialites caught in a speakeasy raid made good picture subjects.
>
> Tabloid editors feasted, too, on stories about glamorous and sexy Hollywood and its stars—Rudolph Valentino, Fatty Arbuckle, Clara Bow. They glorified in the love affairs of the great and not-so-great—Daddy Browning and his Peaches, Kip Rhinelander, the Prince of Wales. They built sordid murder cases into national sensations—Hall-Mills, Ruth Snyder. They glorified celebrities—Charles A. Lindbergh, Queen Marie of Rumania, Channel swimmer Gertrude Ederle. They promoted the country's sports stars—prizefighter Jack Dempsey, golfer Bobby Jones, tennis champion Bill Tilden, football coach Knute Rockne, and home run hitter Babe Ruth.[1]

With Joseph Medill Patterson at the helm, the *Illustrated Daily News* became one of the first New York tabloids, with its inaugural issue on June 28, 1919. Hearst launched another tabloid, the *Daily Mirror* in 1924. Magazine publisher Bernarr MacFadden bought the *Daily Graphic* and turned it into a tabloid. But the pinnacle of the photo-oriented tabloids came on January 14, 1928 when a full-page picture of convicted murderess Ruth Snyder being electrocuted at Sing Sing appeared with a caption reading "exclusive closeup of Ruth Snyder in death chair at Sing Sing as lethal current surged through her body."

Photojournalism had gained such popularity by the late 1920s that some publishers had syndicated photographs of major news events (Figure 7-11) and would send them to subscribers for posting in such places as hotel lobbies,

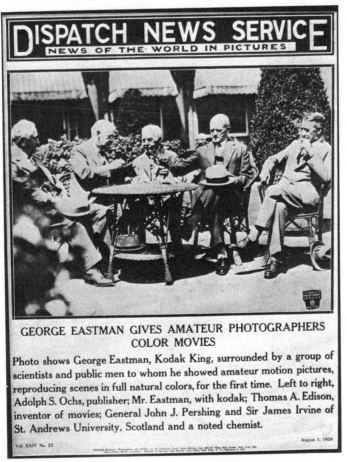

DISPATCH NEWS SERVICE
NEWS OF THE WORLD IN PICTURES

GEORGE EASTMAN GIVES AMATEUR PHOTOGRAPHERS
COLOR MOVIES

Photo shows George Eastman, Kodak King, surrounded by a group of scientists and public men to whom he showed amateur motion pictures, reproducing scenes in full natural colors, for the first time. Left to right, Adolph S. Ochs, publisher; Mr. Eastman, with kodak; Thomas A. Edison, inventor of movies; General John J. Pershing and Sir James Irvine of St. Andrews University, Scotland and a noted chemist.

Vol. XXIV No. 23   August 1, 1928

Figure 7-11 Gracing everything from barber shops to hotels and store windows, the news poster become a popular attraction of early photojournalism.

restaurants, and barber shops. These "instant news" one-page sheets lasted until radio news began to take over as the new instant medium.

MAGAZINES AND DOCUMENTARY PHOTOGRAPHY

Other tabloids in other cities prospered, but many eventually went out of business, including New York's *Mirror* and *Graphic*. But photography and photojournalism were growing, and it was the magazines that brought the camera to new heights in mass communication.

Life and Look

When Henry R. Luce launched *Life* magazine in 1936 (Figure 7-12), it quickly became the standard of photojournalism. Although showing its own brand of sensationalism by printing such things as sequence pictures of the top of a man's skull being removed for a brain operation, it prospered with the expert photographic talents of such well-known names as Margaret Bourke-White and Alfred Eisenstaedt. Eisenstaedt has one of the longest associations with the magazine, over thirty-six years. He is credited with over 1,700 stories and 90 covers for *Life*. He joined *Life* eight months before its first issue and rejoined them at the age of eighty when *Life* was reintroduced. As we learned earlier, the original *Life* fell victim to the mass appeal and lower cost-per-thousand of television. *Look*, first appearing in 1937, copied *Life*'s picture style. It also succumbed to television but appeared again in 1979 with different covers for different regions of the country. Both magazines are considered standards in photojournalism.

still photography as documentary

While *Life* and *Look* radiated the importance and acceptance of photography magazines, a man named Roy Emerson Stryker made history in the photographic division of the Farmers Home Administration. Founded in 1935, it showed what could be done with documentary photography, the graphic recording of events, conditions of society, and its people. Documentary photography is a statement, an impact, a commentary, yet an accurate portrayal. And for documentary photography, few eras could equal the Great Depression of the 1930s. Roy Stryker made a permanent history of these tragic times of poverty and gave documentary photography a permanent place in modern photojournalism.

More recently, a project of the 1970s called project Documerica brought photographers (Figure 7-13) together to record the ecological condition of the country. Stryker in the 1930s and Documerica added still more to the importance of photography and photojournalism.

Figure 7-12 *Life* magazine, perhaps more than any other publication, brought the photojournalist to the forefront and permitted a significant amount of latitude in photo layout and reproduction. Shown is the cover of the first issue of *Life* as it appeared in 1936. (Margaret Bourke White, LIFE Magazine, © 1936, Time, Inc.)

THE FUTURE

Photography and photojournalism matured far beyond the crude images of Niepce and the Civil War pictures of Mathew Brady. There have been major developments in cameras, lens, and film. Even small-town dailies are well equipped to adapt layout designs to capture the full impact of good news photography (Figure 7-14). Color photography is a vital, if not major force in photo-

Figure 7-13 The Environmental Protection Agency's Project Documerica set out to record the effects of our industrial growth and expansion on the environment. Reminiscent of the Farm Security Administration's photographic record of the 1930's Great Depression, the EPA project provided a contemporary chronicle, again using the skill of the photographer. (EPA-DOCUMERICA-Gil)

journalism. Such scientific breakthroughs as Polaroid's instant developing and the printing industry's color offset presses promise to bring more and more color photography to a variety of publications.

Today, just as media are becoming more specialized, so is the work of the photographer. Depending on the publication or on the company, a photographer can spend a career specializing in specific types of photography such as food, fashion, and farming.

What about the future? Will new media delivery systems mean new demands and markets for the photographer? What will the new technological advances in photography mean? Alfred Eisenstaedt was asked that question and replied: "You can buy the most modern equipment, lenses, cameras, etc., but you still need the eye and the brain behind the camera. It's not the camera that takes the picture, it's the person with the brain and the eye."[2]

SUMMARY

Photography had its beginnings with the camera obscura, a crude, boxlike device used to project inverted images. A lens was added to the camera obscura, and

Figure 7-14 Modern layout designs permit the full impact of photographs, as evidenced by this award-winning front page from a small town daily. (Eric Bernsee and the *Banner-Graphic*, Greencastle, Indiana)

photosensitive plates were invented to capture the image permanently. The first permanent photograph is credited to Joseph Niepce who later, with his partner Louis Daguerre, perfected the photosensitive plate and shortened the exposure time necessary to take pictures. The photosensitive plate was improved still further by such people as Frederick Scott Archer, Hamilton Smith, and Richard Maddox. George Eastman produced an inexpensive camera and roll film, bringing photography in reach of the average citizen.

The earliest photojournalism began during the Civil War when photographers such as Mathew Brady made realistic pictures of battle scenes, tempering the exaggerated and glorified examples drawn by some sketch artists of the period. After halftone printing processes made rapid and accurate reproduction of the photograph possible in newspapers and other publications, photography became much more a medium of mass communication. Although it suffered from the sensational reporting techniques of the early tabloids, photojournalism matured and was represented with distinction in such publications as *Life* and *Look* and in the documentary photography of Stryker in the Great Depression and the 1970s Docuamerica Project for ecology. Today, new technology in camera, lens, and film have aided the photographer. As other forms of mass communication have become more specialized, so has the work of the modern photographer.

OPPORTUNITIES FOR FURTHER LEARNING

BLODGETT, RICHARD, *Photographs: A Collector's Guide.* New York: Ballentine Books, 1979.

CAVALLO, ROBERT M., AND STUART KAHAN, *Photography: What's the Law.* New York: Crown Publishers, Inc., 1976.

COE, BRIAN, *Cameras From Daguerreotypes to Instant Pictures.* New York: Crown Publishers, Inc., 1978.

CRAVEN, GEORGE M., *Object and Image: An Introduction to Photography.* Englewood Cliffs, N.J.: Prentice-Hall, Inc., 1975.

CURRENT, KAREN, *Photography and the Old West.* New York: Harry N. Abrams, 1979.

DAVIS, PHIL, *Photography.* Dubuque, Iowa: William C. Brown Co., Publishers, 1975.

EDEY, MAITLAND, AND CONSTANCE SULLIVAN, eds., *Great Photographic Essays from Life.* Boston: New York Graphic Society, 1978.

EDON, CLIFTON C., *Photojournalism.* Dubuque, Iowa: William C. Brown Co., Publishers, 1976.

GOULD, LEWIS L., AND RICHARD GREFFE, *Photojournalism: The Career of Jimmy Hare.* Austin: University of Texas Press, 1977.

LANGFORD, MICHAEL, *The Step-by-Step Guide to Photography.* New York: Alfred A. Knopf, Inc., 1978.

POLLACK, PETER, *The Picture History of Photography: From the Earliest Beginnings to the Present Day.* New York: Harry N. Abrams, Inc., 1977.

STARK, ROBERT, AND LYNN DANCE, *Nebraska Photographic Documentary Project.* Lincoln: University of Nebraska Press, 1977.

THOMAS, ALAN, *Time in a Frame: Photography and the Nineteenth-Century Mind.* New York: Schocken Books, Inc., 1977.

WELLING, WILLIAM, *Photography in America: The Formative Years, 1839–1900.* New York: Thomas Y. Crowell Company, Inc., 1978.

Motion Pictures

If we walk back to the nineteenth century, we will not see shopping centers with movie theaters tucked away between department store entrances and ice cream shops. We will not see neon signs flickering names like Roxy or Rivoli between rows of flashing lights. We will not see marquees listing the choices at Cinema I, Cinema II, Cinema III, and Cinema IV. Neither will we find plush cushioned seats, wide screens, or sound-encased theaters. What we will see are movie parlors and curious theaterlike establishments called nickelodeons and store-front theaters. We will encounter people like Thomas Edison. And as we begin our walk toward today, we will meet other familiar people like Lee de Forest and George Eastman.

TOWARD REPRODUCING MOTION

Film really began in the minds of people who came long before the film pioneers. The attempt to capture and recreate motion can be traced to the beginnings of civilization when cave drawings depicted a horse with eight legs, the fleeting arrow from a hunter's bow, or carefully detailed drawings of kings with one foot outstretched to suggest a walking motion.

159

images and sequence

Early attempts at photographing and reproducing motion were crude. Eadweard Muybridge came close when he photographed a running horse with a series of cameras. Connected to each camera along a track was a trip cord, and when the horse ran by, it tripped the cords and the cameras, giving Muybridge a series of photographs of the horse in various stages of running. The French next developed a single camera that could take twelve pictures in a second. What was still lacking, however, was a film and a camera capable of taking rapid pictures of moving objects, pictures that when developed could be "played back" for an illusion of motion.

Edison's contributions

Despite George Eastman's contributions to photography and the development of film, it took the inventive and practical mind of Thomas Edison to appreciate fully the potential of Eastman's new film, the film with the transparent nitrocellulose support. With an associate, William Dickson, Thomas Edison invented a workable motion picture camera in 1888. A year later, the two were successfully taking and projecting motion pictures. By 1891, Edison had constructed a crude motion picture studio at his workshop and headquarters in West Orange, New Jersey. The studio was a tarpaper shack dubbed "Black Maria" (Figure 8-1), but it was the beginning of the commercial motion picture industry in America. From Black Maria came a series of very short films on such subjects as Buffalo Bill, a strong man, a dancer, and a Chinese laundry. The camera capable of recording these short subjects was called the *kinetograph*. The projector, which was actually a large contraption with a hole to view the picture show, was called the *kinetoscope*.

Edison viewed his inventions more as novelties than as something that would sweep the world as a mass medium. His attitude proved to be a costly mistake. His refusals to improve his inventions and to protect them by patents opened the door to commercial exploitation. In fact, Edison had to rely on his industrial might even to stay in the motion picture business. The kinetoscope parlors, everything from buildings to store fronts, were converted into these rooms where dozens of the machines were lined up for paying patrons to view about fifty feet of film, all that the kinetoscope could hold. Eastman, who was supplying film for studio still photography and amateurs had not yet produced reels longer than fifty feet. What Edison did not know was that in France, two brothers would soon make his device obsolete, almost overnight.

projection: the Lumière brothers

Auguste and Louis Lumière were brothers who worked with their father's business manufacturing photographic plates and film. Using the technology they

Figure 8-1 Edison's early studio, the Black Maria. (U.S. Department of the Interior, National Park Service, Edison National Historic Site)

learned from Edison's work, they set out to improve both the kinetoscope and kinetograph. They succeeded in developing a camera much more portable and less cumbersome than Edison's, one that could print and project pictures with a crude yet intermittent motion. The invention was named the *cinematographe*.

In 1895, the Lumière brothers produced their first film entitled *Leaving the Lumière Factory*, the content of which was what the title implied. On December 28, 1895, they opened their first movie theater in the basement of a Paris cafe, and the motion picture industry began. The impact of the new medium, even with its shaky photography, caused quite a stir. One of the Lumières' most famous films, *The Arrival of a Train* made theatergoers cringe in their seats as they watched the huge steam locomotive approach on the screen. Other famous *Lumière* films included *Feeding Baby* and the more humorous *L'Arroseur arrosé*. The latter showed a gardener with a water hose and a boy coming behind the gardener and stepping on the hose. When the water stops, the gardener looks down the nozzle of the hose at the moment the boy steps off the hose. The gardener gets wet. The audience laughs. As you can probably detect, even simple humor was amusing since the mere presence of motion before the eyes of the audience created a heightened emotion capable of being triggered by the slightest response.

For the Lumière brothers, the potential of the new invention was never fully realized. They were far more impressed with the mechanical workings of their "scientific" discovery than they were with its ability to make money. They produced films that used the reality of the outdoors and the real lives of people. Most were between thirty and sixty seconds long and sufficient to entertain early film enthusiasts. Critics view the films of the Lumières as being much more creative than those of Edison who used more stilted presentations suitable to the confines of his early makeshift studio.

Back in the United States, Edison quickly realized that his kinetoscope was doomed because of the popularity of the Lumières' projection system. The Edison organization shrewdly managed to secure the rights to an American improvement on his own machine. An inventor named Thomas Armat had discovered the same principle that the Lumière brothers used, an intermittent projection of film to produce the illusion of motion. So using their combined corporate and scientific reputations, Edison and Armat went into business together with Armat receiving a percentage of the sales of his projection system which Edison announced as belonging to his own company. Called the *vitascope*, the device was introduced as part of a vaudeville program on April 23, 1896 at Koster's and Bial's Music Hall in New York. It signaled the beginning of the movie theater in the United States.

When admission reached a nickel and theaters opened exclusively for movies, the era of the *nickelodeon* was born. More and more films were produced as the owners of the nickelodeons tried to satisfy the unsatiable thirst for films. Keep in mind that the average show consisted of a small selection of very "short subjects" and meeting the demand for new material kept production humming.

Edison eventually tried a series of legal power plays to push other producers and manufacturers out of the market. One of his claims to ownership was what was called the *Latham loop*, which entailed the film being positioned on the projector with a small loop to permit a flexible tension as it passed in front of the lens. The loop is still used today, and although a rather simple principle, it was the cause of countless legal battles. Armat later fell out with Edison and sued him over ownership of the vitascope. But whatever the outcome of these power plays, the motion picture business was now an established entity.

expanding the story line: Méliès and Porter

Among many, two other people left their imprint on early motion pictures. One was a Frenchman named Georges Méliès who added the dimension of special effects to film. A magician by trade, Méliès secured a camera and projection device and began producing films as early as 1896. Soon he became an international distributor, quickly eclipsing the work of the Lumières. Méliès's most famous film, *A Trip to the Moon*, showed a group of scientists and chorus girls launching a rocket to the moon. The rocket is seen hitting the "eye" of the man in the moon, and the space people encounter moon people. Some of the special effects Méliès incorporated in the film include the earth rising on the horizon

Figure 8-2 Scene from "The Great Train Robbery." (U.S. Department of the Interior, National Park Service, Edison National Historic Site)

and a trick photography scene of moon people disappearing in smoke. Méliès went on to produce numerous fanciful pictures showing his talent for special scenery, if not the most imaginative use of the camera.

Another landmark film was the product of one of Edison's employees, Edwin S. Porter. Porter produced *The Great Train Robbery* (Figure 8-2) and numerous other films that were a direct product of Méliès's influence on world cinema. *The Great Train Robbery* is famous for its introduction of narrative to early films. It told a story and inaugurated the technique of *cross-cutting*, piecing together different scenes in a composite story line, to a fourteen-scene film which lasted just short of twelve minutes. An earlier Porter film, *The Life of an American Fireman*, used similar editing techniques, but not knowing exactly how the last scene was edited caused *The Great Train Robbery* instead to emerge as the singular example of the narrative style. A sequence of scenes was not new to film. That had appeared before in Méliès's films. But in Méliès's films, especially *A Trip to the Moon*, the action progressed from one scene to another—from constructing and launching the rocket on earth to its landing on the moon. In *The Great Train Robbery*, viewers visit the telegraph office not once but twice at different times in the film, first for the outlaw to tie up the operator and later for the operator to be discovered. For the nickelodeon audience, this scene was a marvel, and people could not get enough. Thus began an industrial revolution in the production, distribution, and showing of motion pictures. Silent films had arrived.

D. W. GRIFFITH AND THE SILENT ERA

By the turn of the century, the technology and creativity of motion pictures were beginning to mesh. Longer narratives and sophisticated techniques became the norm. But for the industry, this meant stiff competition, so stiff that nine companies, including Edison's, joined together in 1908 to form the Motion Picture Patents Company to oversee all aspects of the motion picture industry. It also was the time when the talents of motion picture producers and directors were given their just recognition. Perhaps none was more highly regarded than David Wark Griffith.

the technique

Intending to be a serious stage actor and playwright, D. W. Griffith found his aspirations and the demand for his work somewhat at odds. After he unsuccessfully tried to sell some of his material to the Edison studio, Edwin S. Porter convinced him to try his hand at film acting. He did and played the lead role in the film *Rescued from an Eagle's Nest*. But more importantly, Griffith landed a job as assistant to a director when a shortage of help and a demand for films gave many studio employees a jack-of-all-trades experience. Griffith was no average assistant, however. He had an energy and a will to learn that gave him a reputation among studio people that he could be counted on and that he would put in the hours to get the job done. It paid off.

He was given a chance to direct, and his attention to dramatic flow impressed even the studio heads. With more and more films under his belt, Griffith was slowly beginning to change the way motion pictures were made. He scheduled rehearsals before final shootings and concentrated on producing scenes that carefully followed the progress of the film. His first film, *The Adventures of Dollie*, utilized a high-angle shot that gave the film a new dimension. But this was only a hint of the man's talents.

Gradually Griffith graduated from single-reel films to the longer versions that gave him more latitude for experimentation. By 1914, he was firmly entrenched as a brilliant director, respected by the motion picture industry around the world. He had not only realized the tremendous potential of the camera to capture the intense emotions of the actors but also the flexibility of different camera angles and shots to communicate these emotions to the audience. Until Griffith's time, the camera had been primarily a silent witness to theaterlike productions. It was not any longer. Griffith carried three important elements to their full potential: (1) the use of the camera (2) scene and costume design and (3) editing. In using the camera, he effectively employed the close-up, medium, and long shot to give the audience many different perspectives on a scene. Such shots were designed to add to the story line as well as to the feeling of the picture. A battle scene shot from a distance, for example, could show the size of the armies and the terrain on which they fought. A medium shot could show the fierce fighting in the trenches, and a close-up could show the emotion on a soldier's face as he met the enemy and death.

Similar mastery was displayed in his editing techniques. Louis D. Giannetti, in his book *Understanding Movies*, classifies Griffith's editing techniques as *cutting to continuity, classical cutting,* and *thematic montage.* Cutting to continuity is editing the action so as to preserve its flow without showing all of the action. In its very simplest form, a modern example would show someone boarding an airplane, the airplane taking off, a shot of the person in his or her seat, the plane landing, and the person walking out of the airport. Griffith brought to the screen a smoother yet more dramatic continuity than had been seen previously. The "dramatic" aspects of his films were highlighted further by his classical cutting. Some of Griffith's most famous scenes were chases or rescues that he carefully edited to control both time and space to prolong the climactic moment of suspense. Or, using the thematic montage technique, Griffith would unify a central theme of his film, regardless of the different scenes or camera shots. For example, different periods in time can be edited together to capture a central theme. Actors in a live scene while the camera flashes back to one actor's memory of previous romantic encounters is an example of thematic editing.

The Birth of a Nation and Intolerance

Of all of the films produced by Griffith, he displayed the greatest talent in *The Birth of a Nation* and in *Intolerance* (Figure 8-3). They remain today the most discussed and studied of Griffith's works. *The Birth of a Nation* could be called the first "docudrama" in that it traced in dramatic terms the history of the United States through the Civil War and Reconstruction. That in itself was a first, because history had previously been limited to books. Although critics deplore the blatantly racist theme of the picture, which centered on the Ku Klux Klan and postwar racial strife, it is still considered a brilliant cinematic work. Costing $125,000 and requiring fifteen weeks to shoot, it opened in Los Angeles in 1915.

In comparison, Griffith's film, *Intolerance,* presents some of the best cinematic examples of thematic montage. *Intolerance* was an extravaganza even by today's lavish standards. Originally begun as a film titled *The Mother and the Law* that dealt with life's injustices, the piece was expanded into four scenerios in different time periods which were edited together in an attempt to show the existence of injustice over time. The four scenerios consisted of the city of Babylon constructed with lavish sets and hundreds of extras, the age of Christ and the conspirators against him, Protestant-Catholic strife in Renaissance France, and murder and child stealing in modern America. In typical Griffith fashion, the four parts of the film that kept the audience jumping between each period all were brought together by editing a "unified" conclusion.

For all of its acclaim over the years, however, *Intolerance* had its pitfalls. *The Birth of a Nation* had brought Griffith considerable criticism because of its

Figure 8-3 Although its audience found it difficult to comprehend, "Intolerance" provided a classic example of an early spectacular. (National Film Information Service, Academy of Motion Picture Arts and Sciences)

social implications; *Intolerance* was an attempt to show that social strife had been with us through the ages. Unfortunately, it did not refute the criticism of *The Birth of A Nation*. In addition, it proved to be too complex for its audience. Griffith had attempted to carry even further his skills in camera technique, editing, and lavishly detailed sets. But in doing so, he went beyond the ability of his audience to understand the film. In other words, it flopped. Because it was so lavish, Griffith had to put his profits from *The Birth of A Nation* into *Intolerance*, which spelled financial trouble. No longer a financially independent producer, Griffith was forced to seek outside financing for future films.

Ironically, the motion picture industry went through a similar experience in the late 1960s when *The Sound of Music* was produced with a budget in the range of $20 million. It was highly successful. Believing that the key to big audiences and big profits was similar spectaculars, the industry spent huge sums on films that, like *Intolerance,* flopped and placed some of the biggest motion picture companies on shaky financial ground.

The Birth of a Nation and *Intolerance* were the pinnacle of D. W. Griffith's career as a director. By having to secure outside financing, he lost some of the independence of producing what he wanted, how he wanted, and with the production schedules he wanted. But besides this, times were changing. The roaring twenties were not noted for their love of Victorian theatrical epics of the kind that Griffith produced. Two of his films that were popular just as the twenties arrived were *Broken Blossoms* and *Way down East.* The former showed rare compassion and gentleness somewhat unusual for Griffith's tradition of social upheaval. *Way down East* presented one of the most popular rescue scenes complete with a damsel in distress heading over a giant waterfall.

The arrival of sound in motion pictures signaled the beginning of the end for Griffith, for it was a technology that he did not master, as he had the camera lens. The powers in the movie industry also felt that Griffith had failed to sense the changing tactics of the movie audience. Nevertheless, the man had a profound affect on the entire concept of film and still does.

SILENT COMEDY: SENNETT AND CHAPLIN

It was one of D. W. Griffith's understudies who began a silent-era tradition of bringing comedy to the silver screen. Mack Sennett was much like Griffith in the paths their cameras took and what led them to fame as directors and producers. With a background in acting and little success in vaudeville, Sennett ended up at Biograph working under Griffith as an actor. It was with the Keystone film company that Sennett was able to begin producing his first love, silent comedy.

Sennett paid little attention to the narrative story telling and continuity for which Griffith was noted. Rather, he had one objective, to produce comedy through purely physical action. It was not important if the scenes fit together in any real sense of forward motion, nor critical that a social message be presented. Sennett cared only that actors and objects be combined in a way that gave the audience as many chuckles as possible in as little time as possible. The famous Keystone cops became one of his trademarks, the focus of his directing style being on three primary methods. One method was to take a melodramatic plot and insert strategically placed gags in it. Another was to take a particular location and stage all the gags there. For example, a single room might contain a slippery bananna peel, a board ready to knock someone on the head, a bucket placed where someone will step in it, and glue all over the floor. Another approach was to fit individual gags into the theme of the picture, such as a movie director trying to instruct a half-witted actor.

Two other Sennett trademarks were his use of fast-motion film and characters whose fast-paced antics tickle the funny bone. The secret was to direct an actor to act out gags in a mechanical fashion, record the action at one speed, and project it at a faster speed, thus achieving the robotlike comic effect. Machines also were important to a Sennett comedy. An automobile crashing into and knocking over everything in its path was even more outrageous with an illusion of a fast speed of eighty miles per hour.

Of all who worked with Sennett, none captured the hearts and box office popularity of America as Charlie Chaplin did (Figure 8-4). It was 1913 when Chaplin went to work for Keystone at a salary of $150 per week and a year's guaranteed salary. His small, thin frame was perfect for the mechanical tin-soldier look Sennett wanted, and the director used Chaplin effectively in a number of comedies. While with Keystone, Chaplin began to develop a character called the "tramp" that would make him a star. The little man with a cane, moustache, derby, and baggy pants, Charlie Chaplin shared with audiences the disappointments, frustrations, and constant confrontations with the obstacles of life. But it was after leaving Keystone that he was able to realize his potential.

In 1915 he was offered and accepted a salary of $1,250 per week to act, direct, and produce for the Essanay company. In Essanay's *The Tramp*, Chaplin

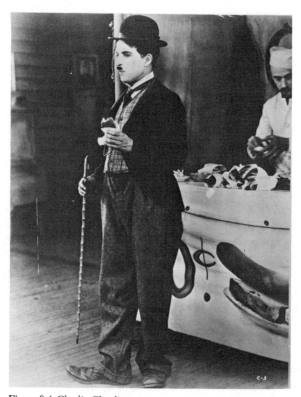

Figure 8-4 Charlie Chaplin.

comes to the rescue of a beautiful woman, played by Edna Purviance, only to lose her love to her handsome boyfriend. Yet, unlike the Sennett style that progresses rapidly from gag to gag, Chaplin moved with more deliberation, milking a scene for all the humor it could offer before going on to the next one. His films also contain more continuity and composition than Sennett's do. For instance, in *The Tramp*, Chaplin acted through four complete scenerios protecting the girl from other tramps, working for the girl's father on their farm, stopping a robbery of the farm, and losing the girl.

The pretty girl and the downtrodden tramp became the theme of many Chaplin pictures. Chaplin himself came from a life of poverty and had a keen awareness of social injustices. This added quality, well portrayed in his pictures, made him a popular favorite. Today, his films still are studied and enjoyed in theaters, coffee houses, and on college campuses.

LAUREL AND HARDY, KEATON, AND LLOYD

The popularity that Sennett and Chaplin brought to comedy was echoed by other stars of the silent era. Among comedian teams, two men named Stan Laurel and Oliver Hardy were among the best (Figure 8-5). Laurel's and Hardy's comic style was in the tradition of Sennett and Chaplin. Downtrodden and against the world, they managed to tackle it head-on. Although starting out in pictures separately, they worked well with each other. Critics did not regard them as having the depth of style of Chaplin, but their "team" approach nevertheless kept audiences entertained well into the sound era.

Called the "Great Stone Face," Buster Keaton began in pictures in 1917 and became a master at portraying an individual able to succeed through ingenuity. Many times confronted with mechanical obstacles from trains to boats, he would use them to get an upper hand. His appeal was his straight-faced reaction to unsurmountable circumstances while keeping audiences on the edge of their seats with his hair-raising stunts. In *Sherlock Jr.*, we see a movie projectionist fall asleep, dreaming that he is playing the hero in a series of daredevil stunts. Critics consider Keaton's best film to be *The Navigator.* Here he ends up as a dumbfounded millionaire adrift on an ocean liner with one other passenger, played by Kathryn McGuire. Before the picture ends, they end up in the drink after being attacked by cannibals. Unfortunately, the one hurdle Keaton could not conquer was sound. When talkies arrived, he moved behind the camera and worked as a script doctor, never to have his talents extended beyond a few short appearances as an extra.

A third well known comedian of the silent era was Harold Lloyd, who combined some of Chaplin and Keaton in a straightman image. For Lloyd, the character was Lonesome Luke, also the title of many single-reel films produced between 1915 and 1917. Movie scenes carried Lloyd, however, more than Lloyd carried the scenes. In *The Freshman*, a tiny thread on his tuxedo begins to

Figure 8-5 Laurel and Hardy. (© Freelance, Lansdale, PA)

unravel and carries the action through a hilarious romp in which the tuxedo falls apart. With the public taste whetted by Chaplin and Keaton, Lloyd had no trouble finding an audience for his antics.

OTHER STARS, PRODUCERS, DIRECTORS

This also was the era of giant epics, lavish sets, and big money, especially with the monumental *Ben Hur.* Starting production in Italy, it finished in California where M-G-M's home office could keep an eye on expenditures. The total cost of a staggering $6 million was not entirely recovered from box office receipts.

Horror films had their day with Lon Chaney starring in such pictures as *The Monster*, a story about a mad doctor who captures motorists for experiments in bringing back the dead. Other Chaney hits included his 1923 *The Hunchback of Notre Dame* and his 1925 picture, *The Phantom of the Opera.*

Sex made its appearance in a number of early films. *Sinners in Silk* in 1924 had Hedda Hopper's drinks spiked so that the villain could take her home for the evening. In those days, wild intentions were mostly thwarted, however. Greta Garbo excited early audiences in such films as *The Temptress*, in which she played a loose woman who drove men to murder. In *Flesh and the Devil*, Garbo teamed up with John Gilbert for some of the hottest love scenes of the 1920s.

Pickford and Fairbanks

The "sweetheart" of early films was Mary Pickford. Labeled "the first movie star" and "America's Sweetheart," her Hollywood ventures included marriage to Douglas Fairbanks and life on their estate named Pickfair. Born in Canada, she started her career acting with stock companies before she joined D. W. Griffith. She later became one of the partners with Griffith in founding United Artists. Her "sweetheart" role was nurtured by such films as *Tess of the Storm Country, Rebecca of Sunnybrook Farm, Poor Little Rich Girl,* and *Little Lord Fauntleroy.* In 1929, her performance in *Coquette* won her an Academy Award.

Douglas Fairbanks was a hero with so much energy that Griffith's directing seemed to confine rather than to display his talents. With physical attractiveness and roles that made him the chief romper through pirate ships and Sherwood Forest, Fairbanks was a movieland star of the first order. He was at his best when he was physically involved in the scene, whether it be crashing through windows or swinging from ceilings. He was John Wayne, Tarzan, and a Latin lover all rolled into one. *Robin Hood, The Three Musketeers,* and *The Mark of Zorro* all made Fairbanks a famous male symbol of the 1920s.

Ince, De Mille, von Stroheim

The king of the silent Western thrillers was Thomas Ince. Known more as a producer than as a director, he realized early the power of the great outdoors, especially the West. With stagecoaches, posses, Indians, and blazing but mute gun battles, he brought the Western hero to the silent era. Ince is respected for his ability to combine shoot-'em-up action with a tight story line that did not get lost in the shuffle. Careful editing to preserve that story line also became his trademark, instead of editing for emotional highlights as Griffith and Sennet did. Representative of his major Westerns are *War on the Plains, Custer's Last Fight,* and *Hell's Hinges,* all produced between 1912 and 1916. So intent on producing films set in lavish landscapes, he arranged for 18,000 acres of land on the Pacific to be leased for *War on the Plains.* The tract was christened Inceville.

Also realizing the lavish possibilities of the West was Cecil B. De Mille. De Mille became famous for his spectaculars, such as *The Ten Commandments,* and his films that catered to liberal morals as in *Why Change Your Wife?* Although his films received high praise when they were released, he slipped out of grace among contemporary critics for his appeal to the masses and his preoccupation with studio profits. Nevertheless, just his longevity as a director has made him an indelible part of film history.

Somewhat in contrast to De Mille was Eric von Stroheim. Von Stroheim, a popular actor and later director, brought some very long, yet quality films to the early screen. *Foolish Wives* and *Greed* were two of his longest films, running seven and nine hours, respectively. He also brought *uncompromising detail* to films and would sacrifice nothing to create the tiniest display of realism. Although his films have not played to nearly as many audiences as De Mille's have over time, the critics have been kinder to von Stroheim because of his devotion to this detail while remaining at odds with studio accountants over costs and shooting times.

LAVISH SETS, LAVISH SCENERY

The public's hunger for movies, the overnight profits, and the bullish attitude toward the future of films are readily seen in some of the lavish expenditures and

Figure 8-6 With the development of major motion pictures came major studios with huge sets, such as this replica of a Chicago street.

sets that the major studios constructed (Figure 8-6). For example, Universal Studios kept a complete zoo, drawing on everything from elephants to pets. At one time it housed thirty lions, ten leopards, a sizeable share of elephants, numerous monkeys, horses by the hundreds, and an array of dogs and cats.

Twentieth-Century Fox had entire streets and villages constructed for its productions. It started in 1925 when William Fox purchased a ranch for cowboy star Tom Mix. A western street became part of the Mix set and was shortly joined by a European city for *Sunrise,* a French village and battleground for *What Price Glory?* and a Parisian set for *Seventh Heaven,* all on the back lot. A scale model of an ocean liner seen from blocks away was constructed for *Metropolitan.* Surviving for thirty years because of its flexibility was the famous New England street with its stone church, courthouse, and gabled houses. The Erie Canal set was constructed for Henry Fonda's *The Farmer Takes a Wife* and a Honolulu set for Warner Oland's *Charlie Chan* series.

THE INTERNATIONAL INFLUENCE

Although our discussion of motion pictures to this point has centered on American actors and directors, we need to mention the impact that motion pictures made in other parts of the world. Two countries stand out for their cinematic contributions. Germany and the Soviet Union.

Germany and The Cabinet of Dr. Caligari

After World War I, Germany brought its fledgling film industry under the complete control of the state and organized it into what was known as the Universum Film A.G. (UFA). With massive studios at Neubabelsberg near Berlin, UFA's goal was to join the power of film to domestic "uplifting" and international influence. Although originally more a war policy than a creative one, the latter eventually materialized as German directors captured the desolate state of the German people following the European conflict. The emotional impact they made stirred sensations in international film circles, beginning with *The Cabinet of Dr. Caligari* in 1920, Dr. Caligari, played by Werner Krauss, is a demented physician with mental powers over his patients, powers that can hypnotize them into performing lunatic acts in the most grotesque fashion. This was a horror film with far more realism than anything the American directors had dared to make. For the unsophisticated viewer, the film is an escape into fantasy. For the critic in search of symbolism, the film unearths a wealth of comparison to political suppression and tyranny.

If *Caligari* jolted the senses, other German films went on to show a mastery of technology that the Americans found tough to match. Cameras were used in every conceivable way to illustrate emotion. Strapped to an actor's chest, placed on camera dollies to follow the action, and hung from a trapeze, they went everywhere a viewer or a viewer's eyes could go.

Dominating German films was the theme of a depressed people caught in hopeless straits against both the real and surreal. Fritz Lang's *Destiny* with souls going through a stone wall surrounding a cemetery, Paul Leni's *Waxworks,* and F. W. Murnau's *Nosferaty* on the Dracula theme all are representative of the oppressed horrific themes. Even the future world of Lang's *Metropolis* reflects a city with human catacombs beneath the street.

As German films began to play in America, they not only became popular but also spurred American directors to become more creative and bold in their own endeavors. For Germany, however, the creative era was short-lived and is considered to have ended when Hitler took power in the 1930s.

Russia and Potemkin

Like Germany, the Soviet Union developed a sizeable state-controlled film industry after the Russian Revolution. By 1917, film was an instrument of propaganda but one that still nurtured creative talents. International acclaim was

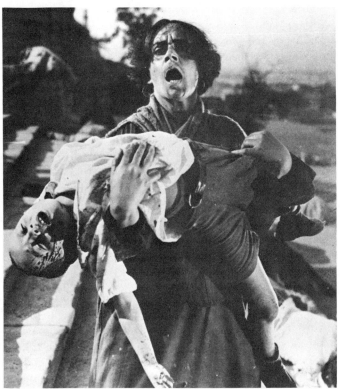

Figure 8-7 The mother and child from "Potemkin." (National Film Information Service, Academy of Motion Picture Arts and Sciences)

achieved through the successful use of the thematic montage, refined and perfected from the foundation laid by Griffith. Carefully editing for sequence and
emotion, the Soviets used the broad expanse of natural scenery with the thematic
montage to capture a new realism in film. It was perhaps best displayed in Sergi
Eisenstein's *Potemkin* (Figure 8-7). The story of symbolic revolt and revolution,
it takes place on the ship *Potemkin* where a mutiny of the crew symbolizes the
revolution against oppression. The theme fit in well in the postrevolutionary
Russia of 1925. Five parts of the film are skillfully edited through thematic
montage into a theme of *unity* against political dictatorship. The film is further
heightened by classical cutting techniques. In a scene from the first part of the
film, a sailor eating infested meat sees the words "Give us this day our daily bread"
inscribed on a plate and smashes the plate in frustration as the action is highlighted by ten different camera shots.

Other Soviet films and personalities displayed similar creativity. Vsevlod I.
Pudovkin brought a more relaxed approach to film with attention to the individual. Comedy in *Chess Fever* and empathy in *Mother* were part of his reper-
toire. Although clinging to the revolutionary themes of Eisenstein and Pudovkin,
Alexander Dovzhenko chose surrealism in which people and objects are distorted
from reality. In his *Arsenal*, bullets from a firing squad have no effect on a
prisoner, symbolizing the ability of the spirit to withstand the oppressor.

France and Un Chien Andalou

In France, surrealism reached its height with the work of artist Salvador Dali and
director Luis Bunũel. Their film, *Un Chien Andalou*, carries the shocking and
absurd to new peaks with objects out of place and the camera deliberately focused
on special effects to jolt the audience. A dead donkey on a piano is one example,
but tame compared to a portrayal of a straight razor slicing across a woman's
eyeball.

French surrealism treated life as an irrational dream with its directors
making no apologies for their film's content or even trying to justify any symbolism. The shocking scenes of *Un Chien Andalou* have somewhat masked the
displays of other French films. However, the artistic movements of the era still
exerted a massive influence on European directors and audiences as political
strife, revolution, and the bloodshed of World War I spilled over from real life
onto the big screen.

the Passion of Joan of Arc

Climaxing the silent era was a French film of international proportions. *The
Passion of Joan of Arc* was produced by Carl Dreyer whose association with the
UFA brought his talents to France where he was joined by German craftsman
and designer Hermann Warm and Polish photographer Rudolph Mate. Starring
as Joan was the Italian actress Falconetti. The key to *Joan's* success, even in the

beginning days of sound, was the use of the camera to catch facial expressions. For instance, the close-up shot masterfully captures every turn of her eye, every tear, and every agony. The special effects of Joan burning at the stake, not so much gruesome as they were expressionist and packed with intense empathy, brought audiences the world over to appreciate what the camera could do. And audiences would need to remember that versatility, because with the arrival of sound would come a degree of restraint on directors and producers that had been present only at the very beginnings of film.

THE ARRIVAL OF SOUND

Sound joined film as early as 1889 when William Dickson introduced to Thomas Edison sound on a disc system. But not until the end of World War I was there any significant development.

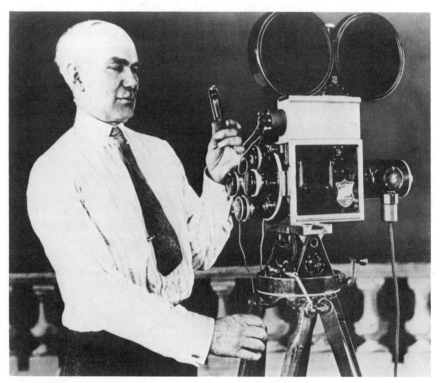

Figure 8-8 Lee de Forest with a sound film camera. De Forest's audion contributed as much to the motion picture industry as it did to broadcasting. (AT&T)

technology

Two different systems premiered in early sound pictures. The famous "audion" tube that Lee de Forest invented to amplify the incoming electromagnetic waves of a radio receiving set appeared again in the 1920s as an amplification system for sound motion pictures (Figure 8-8). De Forest also invented a method through which sound could be recorded directly on the film in perfect synchronization with the picture. This system, introduced in 1922, was called *phonofilm* and was similar to a German process called the *tri-ergon process*. The other system was developed by Western Electric and used a disc recording in synchronization with the picture. Called *vitaphone,* it would not become the standard of the industry, but it would drastically change it.

Vitaphone, after being offered to numerous studios, was finally purchased by the almost bankrupt Warner Brothers. Warner started out by producing a series of sound short subjects, or "shorts," with vitaphone, using a few talking dignitaries of the film industry and some musical scores. The first feature length film with the system was *Don Juan* in 1926. Warner's almost instant success came on the night of October 6, 1927 when the film *The Jazz Singer* starring Al Jolson opened in New York. Although not the first sound film, it did use synchronized sound to tell a story. Audiences loved it.

Meanwhile, Twentieth-Century-Fox started producing sound films with a system closely resembling Lee de Forest's. Called Fox Movietone News, the early "journalism" shorts were gradually replaced by feature films produced in Fox's Movietone City, a special studio complex built for sound in 1928. By 1930, movie theaters around the country had converted to sound. While technically it moved motion pictures far into the future, artistically it left them behind.

restraint on creativity

Cameras that had once roamed sets and had gone along with riding posses now were frozen in cement. They had a new device to contend with—a microphone. The camera could not rove because the microphone could not rove with it. In addition, the director's habit of shouting directions now had to be muzzled. But they adapted. The camera became encased in a special soundproof box, and the director learned to use everything from signs to sign language to communicate with the actors. And the studio audience, which once had filled the balconies of the silent movie studios, was kept out entirely. The most abused character in all of this was the cameraperson who had to be locked up inside the soundproof cage with the camera.

Unfortunately, movie audiences did not give the studios much incentive to adapt to sound creatively. Early sound films with their stilted camera shots and lack of action were a novelty, just as film itself had been in the days of the Black Maria. People came to hear actors talk and guns shoot. Never mind that actors huddled together straining their voices toward a concealed microphone; never

177

mind the crackling quality of voices picked up and reproduced on primitive equipment; never mind the return of the theater sets. Stars and directors of the silent era cringed at what was happening to the medium. There was no place for the trifles of Chaplin's tramp nor the stunts of Buster Keaton.

transition: actors and directors

For actors, sound became a frightening experience of mammoth proportions. Stars of the silent era dropped like flies, victims of the new technology. When a hero of action sounded like a whimpering coward, his career could end with a ten-minute audition. When a romantic actress talked with sloppy English and battered accent, beauty could not salvage a crumpled career.

But reliance on theater for scripts also brought new stars with the voices to make the transition. One of vitaphone's finds was Lionel Barrymore (Figure 8-9). For Barrymore, the microphone was a friend. It captured his resonance and gave the audience just what it wanted. Delores Costello starred with Conrad Nagle in *Glorious Betsy* and brought a contrast of the male and female voices to the screen (Figure 8-10). In *The Lights of New York* in 1928, Helene Costello and Cullen

Figure 8-9 Lionel Barrymore's (right) wide-stage experience made him a find for Vitaphone productions. Buster Collier, who also gained experience on stage, appears here as Barrymore's son in the film "The Lion and the Mouse."

Figure 8-10 Emphasis between the masculine and feminine voice played an important role in "Glorious Betsy," which starred Dolores Costello and Conrad Nagel.

Landis sat "very close" so the single microphone could pick up their dialogue, even though the picture consisted of little more than the camera shots of the pre-Griffith era.

Fortunately, the creative void did not last too long. Soundproof cages were replaced by more manageable soundproof camera covers. Two directors unshackled the industry with their creative and technical breakthroughs. Rouben Mamoulian accomplished with *Applause* in 1929 a feat that sounds simple by today's standards. First, he separated sound from picture in the original filming. Using a camera crane for aerial shots of New York's Penn Station, he added the sound later. Second, Mamoulian used two microphones instead of one. Using a sound mixer, dual microphones permitted new latitudes in positioning actors as well as scenery.

The second director to break the sound barrier was King Vidor. With his production of *Hallelujah!* Vidor put the camera into a chase through a swamp, then later added the sound of squishing mud and animals. Distant shots of blacks in the fields of the South were accompanied by the singing of spirituals, which made it seem as though microphones were in the cotton bushes.

At last the motion picture industry was managing to wed sound to film, even though the products were a bit like a newborn fawn, beautiful to look at but with a lot of growing up to do.

HOLLYWOOD: THE 1930s TO WORLD WAR II

With the creativity of sound released from its cages and an audience again becoming sophisticated, film moved into its second generation. Some critics feel that film grew faster in these years than it ever would again. As a new medium experimenting with itself, virtually all of the shots used in today's pictures and much of the sound techniques came from this time. By the 1930s, the town called Hollywood was a lavish dreamland where millions were made and stars were born. And the public began to idolize these stars. To examine this era, let's look at some of the producers, the films and the stars that were part of it. Keep in mind that it was a time when the big Hollywood studios like M-G-M, Warner Bros., Columbia, and Twentieth Century Fox were big, big business. Movies were mass produced, and their audiences clamored to the theaters. Remember also that television was not around to keep audiences at home. That came later and drastically altered the motion picture industry.

Film in the 1930s had reached a Waterloo with sex and violence, just as television today is feeling the pangs of citizen group pressure. After the risqué 1920s, civic and religious leaders began blaming the movies for society's ills. In 1934, a Catholic lay leader, Joseph Breen, was added to the board of the Motion Picture Producers and Distributors Association, which had been founded as a self-regulatory commission in 1922, headed by President Harding's postmaster general, Will Hays. Although there was still plenty of action, it was Breen's responsibility to determine what society should see and what it should not. Fortunately for Breen and the industry, the lack of competition from television, the novelty of sound, and the new achievements in color photography kept people interested in the movies.

animation: the work of Walt Disney

Walter Elias Disney entered Hollywood not as an actor or director like so many before him, but as an artist. A cartoonist from Kansas City, Disney started producing short, animated cartoons called Laugh-O-Grams. Then with animal characters, he set out to produce cartoons which mimicked the real world. By the time his career had matured, Disney had collected a record number of Academy Awards and had moved beyond cartoons to feature films known for their family entertainment value. The profits his company amassed stand today in such monuments as Disneyland in California and Walt Disney World in Florida.

What brought Walt Disney's productions to the national public's eye was his 1928 cartoon, *Steamboat Willie*. It introduced a character eventually named Mickey Mouse who went on to become one of the biggest stars in motion picture history. In *Steamboat Willie*, Disney put Mickey on a steamboat, bringing music out of everything from a cow's teeth played like a xylophone to the drumming sounds of garbage cans. The picture was a success because cartoon characters did not need the peculiar microphone arrangements of real characters.

Rather, they could roam at will, and sound could complement, not constrain. Following the success of *Steamboat Willie*, Disney's *Silly Symphonies* series combined music with animated dance and preliminary attempts at color. Then after three years of work on the project, Disney captured the hearts of the world as he set to animation *Snow White and the Seven Dwarfs*. Here the screen could capture much of the great techniques of directors and actors alike. With the use of animated close-ups, the audience was able to see the flawless beauty of Snow White and the varied expressions of the Seven Dwarfs. After all, how could any real life film character compete with Sleepy, Dopey, or Grumpy? Disney was showing Hollywood and the world what he could do, and there was no one who could match him.

Many critics feel that his most creative efforts were unleashed in his 1940 production of *Fantasia* (Figure 8-11). Here Disney set his cartoon characters loose to dance and to act out the themes of great works of classical music. For example, Hyacinth Hippo dances with Ben Ali Gator to Ponchielli's "Dance of the Hours." Then Mickey Mouse, as Dukas's "Sorcerer's Apprentice," bewitches brooms to do water-carrying chores. Filmed in Technicolor, which now was able to bring the complete spectrum of color to the screen, *Fantasia* still stands as a classic example of the ability of animation to mix sound, sight, and color together as only animation can.

Disney continued to produce cartoon features. The little fawn *Bambi* both

Figure 8-11 Walt Disney's "Fantasia" combined the work of the artist and the musician in what some consider to be the Disney studio's best example of animation. (© Walt Disney Productions)

enchanted and scared the daylights out of young audiences in 1942. *Pinocchio* made any child think twice about telling a lie, and *Dumbo* became a symbol of hope for children who doubted their importance. After World War II, Disney began adding real people to his cartoons. In *Song of the South*, animated birds and animals flirted with real people. By the 1950s, Disney was working on Disneyland, and his films had expanded to include family features and nature documentaries.

the stars

The 1930s also proved that the silent films did not have a corner on the comedy market. Comedy was alive and well, even among the female stars like Mae West. Her original roles displayed her buxom appearance and unrestrained sex appeal, but restrictions from the Hays office and Breen kept her reined in through much of her career. One of her best appearances was in *My Little Chickadee* with comedian W. C. Fields. Fields was to sound what Chaplin had been to silents. He possessed both the voice and the physique to garner a laugh. He became known for his highly articulated speech and natural deviousness in comic portrayals. Along with *My Little Chickadee*, some of his most famous films include *The Bank Dick* (Figure 8-12) and *Tillie and Gus*. Matching Fields in comic routines were the Marx brothers. Groucho, Harpo, and Chico had the irrever-

Figure 8-12 W. C. Fields. (Copyright, Raymond Rohauer)

ence of Fields, the style of Chaplin, and were able to play one against the other in such films as A *Night at the Opera* and *Duck Soup*.

Romance and intrigue arrived when Paramount Studios director Josef von Sternberg found Marlene Dietrich. The match worked financial wonders for Paramount. Dietrich became the star of shadows and mystery, lover and loved. Among others she played in *The Blue Angel, Blonde Venus,* and *The Devil Is a Woman*. Born in Berlin, Dietrich became an American citizen in 1937 and was honored during World War II for her overseas entertainment efforts.

Gary Cooper and Clark Gable also entered films in the thirties, Cooper, playing in famous roles opposite Dietrich, and Gable, who won an Academy Award in 1934 for *It Happened One Night*, were symbols of the macho male.

Other stars making their presence felt in the thirties and early forties included Jimmy Stewart, Jean Harlow, Spencer Tracy, Jackie Cooper, John Wayne, James Cagney, Humphrey Bogart, and Rita Hayworth. Joan Crawford starred in *No More Ladies*, while Robert Young of modern television fame and Betty Furness of consumer fame starred together in the 1936 M-G-M production of *Three Wise Guys*. Johnny Weismuller, meanwhile, romped through the jungle in the *Tarzan* movies. Then Myrna Loy starred in *The Barbarian* which included a racy nude bathtub scene. Fred Astaire and Ginger Rogers entertained audiences whenever they danced together, and Edward G. Robinson entertained them by being the original tough guy. Names such as William Powell in *The Thin Man*, Peter Lorre in *Mad Love*, Judy Garland in *Broadway Melody 1938*, and Greta Garbo in *Ninotchka* and *Camille*, all kept movie audiences flocking to the theaters. Even with the Great Depression of the early thirties, when attendance took a massive but temporary dip, the movies survived.

But the stars were only one of the attractions. It was the directors who made the industry and, consequently, stardom possible.

the directors

In addition to being known for consistently casting Marlene Dietrich in his films, Josef von Sternberg was most at home with intrigue set in seamy places. From the foreign legion to the back street night club, von Sternberg loved focusing his shadows and dull lights on shady characters and bewitching women.

Breaking out of the studio into the freedom of the open spaces, John Ford used people and scenery in contrast with each other. In films like his most notable *Informer*, Ford used the camera to emphasize the facial expressions of the middle class in their life of survival and fight against the idle rich or political injustice.

Carrying contrast to the inner self, Howard Hawks (Figure 8-13) was most comfortable with actors of the Douglas Fairbanks era. But Hawks went beyond action to the psychological. Here the contrast was between courage and cowardice.

Even the genius of Alfred Hitchcock (Figure 8-14) received its first real

Figure 8-13 Howard Hawks.

Figure 8-14 Alfred Hitchcock, recognized as one of the great directors of movie intrigue, is famous for such titles as "Psycho," "The Birds," and "Frenzy."

appreciation in the 1930s. The master of such later shockers as *The Birds* and *Psycho*, Hitchcock brought these audiences such thrillers as *The Man Who Knew Too Much* and *The Thirty-Nine Steps*.

Gone with the Wind and Citizen Kane

Two films that stand out as "the" movies of the early sound era, however, are *Gone with the Wind* (Figure 8-15) and *Citizen Kane* (Figure 8-16). The former is considered so because of its lasting appeal to the masses, the latter because of its lasting appeal to critics and students of film.

Based on Margaret Mitchell's book of the same title, *Gone with the Wind* was the dream child of producer and studio head David O. Selznick. As soon as Mitchell's book became a best seller, Selznick bought the screen rights for $50 thousand, intending the movie to be his company's masterpiece. Later he voluntarily doubled the amount after profits on the film soared. But it was not long before the Selznick organization needed both financial and artistic help. The public wanted Clark Gable for the leading role, but Gable had a contract with

Figure 8-15 "Gone With the Wind" was an epic production of the late 1930s, famous for numerous cinematic accomplishments. Well publicized was this embrace between Rhett Butler (Clark Gable) and Scarlett O'Hara (Vivien Leigh). (From the MGM release GONE WITH THE WIND © 1939, Selznick International Pictures, Inc. Copyright renewed 1967 by Metro-Goldwyn-Mayer, Inc.)

Figure 8-16 Orson Welles in "Citizen Kane." (National Film Information Service, Academy of Motion Picture Arts and Sciences)

M-G-M. Undeterred, Selznick convinced M-G-M to place $1 million into the picture and to release Gable to star in it, giving the film company the distribution rights and half the profits in return. Even the *New York Times* became interested in the picture, lamenting in an editorial that the first actress chosen to play opposite Gable, Norma Shearer, declined the role. Vivian Leigh became the beguiling Scarlett O'Hara instead.

Throughout its production, the American press constantly ran stories about the upcoming event, generating enough anticipation that regardless of what the final product was, America was ready to see the movie. Sidney Howard was hired to do the screen play but died before the picture was finished. Such well known writers as Ben Hecht and F. Scott Fitzgerald were called in to finish the script. When the picture was officially released in 1939, it immediately filled theaters both in America and abroad. During World War II, there were lines at box offices in England even during the raids. Among the records set by the film were its running time of two hours and forty-two minutes and its collection of ten Academy Awards. Since its release, it also has chalked up the distinction of being one of television's biggest film spectaculars and has earned M-G-M close to $200 million.

If *Gone with the Wind* stands as the picture of this era with the most mass appeal, *Citizen Kane* stands as the film most heralded for its accomplishments in cinema. The director, who also saw to it that he starred in it and had a direct hand in virtually every phase of the production, was young Orson Welles. Welles had become famous through theater and his 1938 *War of the Worlds* radio broadcast. *Citizen Kane* was his first, his best, and practically his last fling at pictures.

Opening with shots of Charles Foster Kane near death, recalling his life, it moves to a shot of a small sled bearing the name of "Rosebud." Rosebud becomes a symbol of the film, contrasting the love and play of Kane's childhood to his adult life in pursuit of material things. Kane becomes a powerful and ruthless newspaper executive who will do anything to create a story, increase circulation, and boost profits. He tries to buy everything, including love, and spends much of his life in a California castle filled with museum artifacts, the symbols of his materialist life. Faintly resembling the life of William Randolph Hearst Sr., the picture uses lighting and angle shots to the limit to accentuate the ferocious temperament of Kane and the massive walls of his castle. The film, despite its dismal box office showing, is still a popular favorite of film studies programs.

FILM THROUGH THE FIFTIES: CHANGES AND TRENDS

World War II had an unusual effect on the movies. Directors produced government films, people escaped the realities of war by attending those pictures that Hollywood did turn out, and it postponed the inevitable breakup of the theater chains and distribution systems that the antitrust forces soon dissolved. It also took the industry's mind off a new invention that RCA's David Sarnoff had introduced at the 1939 World's Fair. That invention arrived in the fifties and with it, dramatic changes for motion pictures.

transition to television

A business faced with monumental and almost overnight competition will do some unusual and hasty things to survive. Some work; some do not. Film was no exception. What could the industry do to counteract a movie screen that had been reduced to twenty-one inches and placed in the living room? How could motion pictures compete with "I Love Lucy" and the "Texaco Star Theatre," with Ed Sullivan and Milton Berle? It tried novelty, novelty in the form of *cinerama*.

Cinerama was more a process than a picture. Using multiple cameras and projectors, the audience was offered a visual spectacular with a huge screen expanded to ten times its usual size and "wrapped around" the audience. Peripheral vision made it all seem incredibly real. The first cinerama captured the visual feeling of clutching in the front seat of a roller coaster as it thundered up and down and around the curves, all in living color. Cinerama worked, but on a limited scale because only a select group of theaters were big enough or went to the trouble of buying equipment for it.

The next novelty was three-dimensional pictures, or 3-D. Using separated images on the screen and bringing them together with the muted hues of a pair of special 3-D glasses, the audience looked more like a group of Martians with space goggles than like theater patrons. The idea did not work well because the movies that used the process were as bad as the glasses. Some of the most famous 3-D films were *It Came from Outer Space, Bwana Devil, House of Wax,* and *Creature from the Black Lagoon* (Figure 8-17).

Creature from the Black Lagoon, however, managed to take its place among some of the better science fiction features of the 1950s. John Baxter writing in *Science Fiction in the Cinema* called it "brilliant underwater photography." Even the relationship between the creature, Gill-Man, and the woman he desires managed to elicit positive reactions from critics. The film is still a popular feature of science fiction festivals and is distributed in its original 3-D version.

With the expense of cinerama and its limited distribution possibilities, and the short-lived novelty of 3-D, the industry next tried *cinemascope*. First introduced by Twentieth-Century-Fox in the biblical story *The Robe,* cinemascope

Figure 8-17 One of the original 3-D films, "Creature from the Black Lagoon," still plays frequently on college campuses.

expanded the width of the screen to a two to five ratio but did not wrap it around the audience as cinerama did.

Along with cinemascope came new sound systems with names such as Warnerphonic and Kinevox Stereo. Other marketing labels attached to sound-visual sensations included Visterama, Vista Vision, Vectograph, and Vitascope. But through all the gimmicks and all the novelties, it became clear that if audiences were going to keep coming back, the industry needed more than wide screens, glasses, and fancy names. It needed big pictures.

spectaculars

One solution was to produce epic pictures of proportions too big to be ignored by the public and the press. One of the first of the fifties was *Quo Vadis*. At a cost of $7 million, it was filmed in Rome where a cast of 5,500 extras took part in a march to Nero's palace. Director Mervyn LeRoy guided Robert Taylor, Deborah Kerr, Peter Ustinov, and Leo Genn through scenes that saw them co-starring with no less than twenty lions and two cheetahs. The success of *Quo Vadis*, which earned for M-G-M the most money it had seen since *Gone with the Wind*, made it clear that spectaculars had promise.

Another profitable spectacular was a remake of *Ben Hur*. This time, M-G-M sunk $15 million into it as Charleton Heston raced chariots, again on location in Rome. Back home the movie won twelve Academy Awards.

The lure of the spectacular created a different kind of reaction at Twentieth-Century-Fox. There *Cleopatra* went into production on the basis that a big event picture could not go wrong. It did. *Cleopatra*, starring Elizabeth Taylor, Richard Burton, and Rex Harrison, came out as the first and most lavish spectacular of the 1960s, but it flopped and cost the studio millions.

other solutions

Another solution to television and something the movies did rather well, was social commentary. *Blackboard Jungle* brought to the screen the theme of juvenile delinquency with switch blades and confrontations in schools. Then an unknown actor from a small town in Indiana came to the screen in *Rebel without a Cause*. James Dean (Figure 8-18) became the symbol of the teenager searching for identity, adventure, love, and life. After Dean was killed in an automobile crash, he became almost a spiritual guru of the teenage scene, and movie magazines for years played up his image.

Because television was faced with even more content restrictions than the motion picture industry was, movies sought to exercise what freedom of expression they did have to the limit. Elizabeth Taylor and Paul Newman starred in Tennessee William's play, *Cat on a Hot Tin Roof*. From the plantation country of the deep South, a story of romance and tension unfolds as Paul Newman, the husband, refuses to make love to his wife, played by Elizabeth Taylor. Implied

Figure 8-18 Killed in an exploding automobile crash, James Dean became a film martyr for many teenagers of the 1950s.

homosexuality is the result with outstanding performances by both stars. Taylor then teamed up with Rock Hudson and James Dean for a temptuous love affair in the movie *Giant*. Sex symbol Mamie Van Doren also kept the theaters steaming with *The Beat Generation, Girls Town*, and *Born Reckless*.

The ever popular Westerns padded the box offices, especially when cast with major stars like John Wayne. Jimmy Stewart ended up in the Alaska gold fields in *The Far Country* and on the railroad in *Night Passage*. Western hero Audie Murphy starred in such films as *The Duel at Silver Creek* and *Destry*. Victor Mature rode along in *Chief Crazy Horse*, Rock Hudson trailblazed in *Seminole*, and Jeff Chandler shot it out in *Pillars of the Sky*. By the time the 1960s rolled around, motion pictures had adapted to television so well that they were beginning to permit the medium to buy selected films for broadcast use and even attempted to produce some television movies themselves.

THE MODERN ERA: FINANCIAL TRANSITION

Financially, the movie industry also began to change after the 1950s. In a nutshell, box office flops and big expenditures spelled financing.

big bank financing

Sharp financial business managers have not always sat behind the desks of the motion picture corporations. Before television, creative geniuses, or movie barons, as they were known, ruled the movie kingdom, and there was nothing that could not be sacrificed for the sake of creativity. If a picture went over its budget in adding the necessary glamour to suit the director's whim, over it went. The difference between then and now was that money seemed to stretch further in those days.

Competition from television, however, required new management and new thinking within the industry. It thus entered a transitional period that brought management keen financial minds, people who could talk the language of accountants and bankers. Although creative talent was and continues to be the backbone of the industry, "dollars and cents" people began to make the final decisions.

At the same time, money became scarce, and financial risks became much greater. And remember, the industry was entering the era of the spectacular. The *Sound of Music* (Figure 8-19) was a typical example of a picture that went all out with script, stars, and financial backing in the $20-million-dollar range. Fortunately, it was extremely successful at the box office. As we have seen, such

Figure 8-19 Julie Andrews starred in "The Sound of Music," one of many films that became part of the big budget, bank-financed movie spectaculars. (SOUND OF MUSIC Copyright © 1965 Twentieth Century-Fox Film Corporation)

movies created the theory that big scripts, big stars, and big money automatically meant big box office receipts.

To obtain big money, the industry approached leading financial institutions to secure loans. But banks were not used to lending money under the risks common to the motion picture industry. So the industry had to prove that responsible management and financial safeguards were inherent in any given film enterprise. One of the banks' greater concerns was budget overruns. To counter this, film companies had to show that even though a director or producer might have a tremendous desire to shoot a special scene for a special effect, he or she would not jeopardize the budget. After all, the financial luxury of waiting thirty days for the weather to clear to achieve the proper lighting and scenery was not something upon which banks looked favorably. In order to further appease the banks, the industry also rearranged its contractual agreements with actors and actresses. The rule had been to guarantee a star a certain amount of money before the picture ever went into production, regardless of how well the movie did at the box office. Instead, film companies now began to offer the stars a percentage of the box office receipts.

Some banks did give credit to some of the larger film makers on the basis of past film successes. For instance, a typical film company may produce twenty-five films in a year, five of which may prove quite successful, another five may be financial disasters, and the rest may come somewhere near the break-even point. On balance, then, the company's profit record seems a reasonable credit risk.

Film companies also could offer the banks collateral in the form of *in-the-can* films—movies which already had been run in movie theaters but whose income was still assured from re-releases and release to television. This was the type of collateral that appealed to banks. The fallacy, however, was in the formula. Big money did not necessarily mean big profits. Three New York banks found that out after they arranged a credit line of over $70 million to one major company for four movies, only one of which was profitable. In fact, some of the most popular bank-financed titles, such as *Hello Dolly*, did not live up to their financial expectations. As a result, some banks backed out of the movie financing business.

low budgets and big profits

A happy ending was in sight, however. Although some of the big-budget movies were bombing at the box office, some low-budget pictures, those in the three- to five-million-dollar range, were on the upswing. Two which turned the heads of the industry were *M.A.S.H.* and *Butch Cassidy and the Sundance Kid*. Paul Newman and Robert Redford helped the latter considerably. It meant a new formula was possible, one with only one of the formerly essential ingredients— big stars. In some cases, even big stars were not necessary, as Tom Laughlin proved in *Billy Jack*. So, almost as fast as spectaculars appeared on the scene, they disappeared.

Today, movies in the seven-million-dollar range are permitting many producers and directors to experiment with their creative talents without endangering the financial structure of a movie company. This development also has allowed individual investors to get back into the movie financing business. People and organizations with a few million dollars to lend can reap tremendous profits if the movie is a success, yet they need not place their own corporate structure on the line in case of failure. This attitude also has given rise to more creative production flexibility, for if too tight a financial rein is placed on a production, creativity can suffer as well as quality. Today's producers have found that they can produce pictures of exceptional quality on reduced budgets, and the public is willing to accept them, sometimes even more eagerly than the spectaculars.

ACCENT ON YOUTH

The 1960s brought turmoil to America with the unpopular Vietam War, the civil rights movement, the drug scene, and campus protests. Perhaps at no other time in recent history was a generation of young adults in such a quandary. The

Figure 8-20 Dustin Hoffman and Katherine Ross in "The Graduate." (Embassy Pictures)

movies, which had been trying to find a theme and an audience to match it, stumbled onto this young adult audience.

First came the beach movies of the early 1960s with themes of California and sun. Teenagers were dancing, loving, swimming, and playing volleyball by the ocean, while bikinis were featured in such films as *Beach Party*, *Beach Blanket Bingo*, and *How to Stuff a Wild Bikini*. Elvis Presley took up the role in *Spinout* playing a singer and race driver.

Then as the decade progressed, an unknown star named Dustin Hoffman teamed up with Anne Bancroft and Katherine Ross, another unknown, in the picture *The Graduate* (Figure 8-20). Hoffman, who was an instant hit, portrayed a young college graduate who finishes his senior year without a job and little more going for him than his parents' rich friends, all giving him advice. His problems are compounded as he falls emotionally for Mrs. Robinson's daughter, played by Katherine Ross, and sexually for Mrs. Robinson, played by Anne Bancroft. Hoffman followed *The Graduate* with a starring role in *Midnight Cowboy*, a story about a male derelict and his friend, played by Jon Voight.

The epitome of pictures of the sixties generation was *Easy Rider*, starring Dennis Hopper and Peter Fonda. It brought to the screen the contrast between the establishment and the nonconformists, between clean living and drugs, all wrapped in the theme of directionless youth.

Thomas Laughlin continued the nonconformist theme in his portrayal of *Billy Jack*, a nonviolent hero who, when pushed far enough, could still stand up and fight. The story of an Indian war veteran on a reservation, *Billy Jack* became a cult movie by the 1970s, spawning two sequels, *The Trial of Billy Jack* and *Billy Jack Goes to Washington*. World-of-mouth promotion campaigns and surprisingly low production costs made these films a huge success.

DIRECTORS LEAVE THEIR MARK

While movies were catering to their young adult audience with nonconformist themes and low budgets, still other films reassured the critics that creative directors had not all gone to the beach. The genius of Stanley Kubrick had emerged as early as 1962 in the movie *Lolita*. He enhanced that recognition, although not necessarily for a better picture, in *Dr. Strangelove, or How I Learned to Stop Worrying and Love the Bomb*. In *Dr. Strangelove*, country-western star Slim Pickens portrays a crew member on an Air Force bomber that mistakenly heads to Russia to drop its load. But the movie that propelled Kubrick into world fame was his 1968 production of *2001: A Space Odyssey* (Figure 8-21). Stars did not make the picture; Kubrick's creation of future interplanetary civilizations did, and without gimmicks. Kubrick carried his wild illusions further in *A Clockwork Orange*, a film about a futuristic society with sexual mannikins and perversions of violence.

Examining the inner self and the search for reality, Italian director

Figure 8-21 Stanley Kubrick's "2001: A Space Odyssey." (From the MGM release 2001:
A SPACE ODYSSEY © 1968 by Metro-Goldwyn-Mayer, Inc.)

Michaelangelo Antonioni brought to the screen such well-known pictures as his
1966 *Blow Up*. Two sex scenes in the movie caused such a stir that in South
Dakota, a local Baptist minister demanded the film be banned from the city
theater. A much deeper meaning than the sex, however, is the search by a
photographer to find meaning in his life. That meaning had been treated earlier
in Antonioni's *Red Desert*, in which a woman examines her life in relation to the
people and things surrounding her.

Director Federico Fellini's films brought an explicit visual realism to the
screen, achieving a height of emotional vigor difficult to match. The human
condition reflected in both individuals and society in his films was presented in
sometimes shocking form. Fellini explored the mind in his 1963 production of
8½, dwelt on fanciful illusions in *La Dolce Vita*, and expanded this in *Juliet of
the Spirits*. On location in Rome, Fellini shot *Fellini Satyricon* and *Roma*,
which display the cynicism and grotesqueness for which he is noted.

Other directors of the 1960s and 1970s who stand out for their individual
achievements include Franklin Schaffner, who directed George C. Scott in one
of his most powerful roles, in *Patton* (Figure 8-22). The expert use of camera
techniques created a larger-than-life leader of men who displayed both a fanatical
love of war and an equal contempt for the bureaucracy that created it. Interest-
ingly enough, it managed to appeal to both the hawks and doves of the Vietnam
War era. Roman Polanski received rave reviews directing Mia Farrow in *Rosemary's Baby* and brought the underworld of the 1930s to life in *Chinatown*.
William Friedkin directed *The French Connection*, a powerful film about an
international drug ring, and the *Exorcist*, an equally powerful movie about
mental powers. Francis Coppola brought us *The Godfather*, while Alfred Hitch-

Figure 8-22 George C. Scott in "Patton." (PATTON Copyright ©
1969 Twentieth Century-Fox Film Corporation. All rights reserved.)

cock directed Tony Perkins and Janet Leigh in *Psycho*. Peter Bogdanovich's *The
Last Picture Show* was another favorite of the film set. And David Lean, who had
been well accepted as a director in the 1940s and 1950s, directed the beautiful
1965 production of *Dr. Zhivago* as well as the 1970 production of *Ryan's
Daughter*.

DRAWING CARDS: VIOLENCE AND SEX

While the peace movement was flourishing, the motion picture industry was
swelling with violence. In the bullet category, *Bonnie and Clyde* took top honors. Directed by Arthur Penn and starring Faye Dunaway and Warren Beatty,
the gangster movie climaxed with machine guns riddling the two stars. More
vintage firearms were used in director Sam Peckinpah's *The Wild Bunch*. And
raw guts and guns came to the screen as a new star named Clint Eastwood spent
time looking down both ends of a gun barrel in such pictures as *Hang 'Em High*
and *Joe Kidd*. Eastwood then donned more modern garb for some equally violent
scenes in *Magnum Force* and *Dirty Harry*. Steve McQueen starred as a police
officer in *Bullet*, noted for its famous chase scenes.

The audiences that violence could not lure to the box office, sex did.
Midnight Cowboy had an X rating. Jane Fonda lay nude inside a science fiction
love-making tube in *Barbarella*, and *A Clockwork Orange* detailed future sex.
Swapping sex was the theme of *Bob and Carol and Ted and Alice*. For further
instructions, along came *A Guide for the Married Man*. Prostitution appeared in

such films as *Irma La Douce*, starring Jack Lemon, and sexual fantasy was the theme of *Belle de Jour*. Two films, *I am Curious Yellow* and *Carnal Knowledge*, contained such explicit scenes that they provoked court cases testing the power of censorship. Yet even harder core sex appeared in the 1973 production of *Last Tango in Paris* starring Marlon Brando. Receiving attention as more serious X-rated films of the era were Gerard Daminao's *Deep Throat* and *The Devil in Miss Jones*.

EMERGING BLACK FILMS AND BLACK STARS

By the 1960s and 1970s, race relations were being treated with some degree of reality. Stars such as James Earl Jones, Lola Falana, Roscoe Lee Brown, and James Brown helped to focus this reality.

Of all the black stars, however, Sidney Poitier probably did more to call attention to the black actor as a serious star with major audience appeal. Poitier was a hit in Ralph Nelson's production of *Lilies of the Field*. He then played a powerful role in *In the Heat of the Night* as a black New York police detective who is stranded in a small southern community. While he is there, the detective finds himself working on a murder case with the town's bigoted white police chief, played by Rod Steiger. The film brings realistic racial tension to the screen but concludes with a lesson in racial harmony. Still another Poitier film is *To Sir with Love*, in which he plays a school teacher who wins the respect of white students in trouble. In *Guess Who's Coming to Dinner*, he portrays a doctor marrying into an aristocratic, white family.

Other black stars followed Poitier's lead, helping black films to be acclaimed in their own right. Singer Diana Ross starred as Billie Holiday in the well received *Lady Sings the Blues*, and Pamela Grier played in *Coffy*, *Foxy Brown*, and *Sheba Baby*. From television to recordings, Richard Roundtree's role in M-G-M's *Shaft* had audiences intrigued with a new hip private eye. The actor even starred in two spin-off sequels: *Shaft's Big Score* and *Shaft Goes to Africa*. The screen had come a long way from the racist 1915 production of *The Birth of a Nation*.

NEW EPICS

If three types of films could best represent the 1970s, they would be disaster films, shark films, and science fiction. The former found their way onto the screen with *The Poseidon Adventure*, which showed an ocean liner sinking with most of its passengers trapped inside. This ocean adventure was followed by fire in *The Towering Inferno* and by crumbling buildings in *Earthquake*. Airplanes and dirigibles also became part of the act. Fear at 30 thousand feet was so successful for the movie *Airport*, starring Dean Martin and George Kennedy, that it begot

Airport 1975. In this film, Jack Smight directed box office favorites Charlton Heston, George Kennedy, and Karen Black in this adventure about a stewardess flying a Boeing 747 after a small plane crashes into the jet's cockpit. Its success even spawned *Airport 1977* and yet another, *Airport '79*, which featured the fast flying Concorde jet.

A more realistic approach to big action suspense was played by George C. Scott in his role of a German colonel assigned to travel with the dirigible *Hindenburg* to try to prevent sabotage. Using original footage from the actual Hindenburg crash, the picture was one of the better disaster epics, winning an Academy Award for special effects.

Although they produced their own low budget copies, *Jaws* and *Jaws II* kept many theaters in the black during the seventies. *Jaws* was the brainchild of author Peter Benchley who wrote the book and publicized it in serial form in a leading magazine. Released at the beginning of the summer of 1975, it was not long before the "Jaws" fad took the country by storm. The film was successful enough to give Universal City Studios a 25 percent share of the United States and Canadian film market for 1975 and to become the all-time box office record breaker (Figure 8-23). For producers Richard Zanuck and David Brown and director Steven Spielberg, it meant millions in personal income.

As for science fiction, few films could equal the dazzling display of special effects in *Star Wars*. With a likeable pair of robots, *Star Wars* was the sleeper film that broke all-time box office records. It was pure fantasy, but it brought forth a new wave of interest in science fiction and a definite wave of

Figure 8-23 (From the Motion Picture "JAWS," Courtesy of Universal Pictures)

Figure 8-24 Sean Connery and Karl Malden climb through rubble in "Meteor." (© 1978 American International Pictures, Inc. Courtesy: Columbia Pictures Merchandising)

profits. Followed by the more realistic but equally majestic *Close Encounters of the Third Kind*, creatures from outer space were becoming bigger stars than earthlings. The success of *Star Wars* and Steven Spielberg's *Close Encounters of the Third Kind* was followed by the news that the cast of the television series *Star Trek* had been reassembled for a major motion picture.

American International kept the reality of *Close Encounters* and the science fiction genre alive with their 1979 release of *Meteor* (Figure 8-24), starring Sean Connery of James Bond fame and other major stars such as Natalie Wood, Karl Malden, Brian Keith, Martin Landau of television's *Space 1999*, and Henry Fonda. Similar science fiction fare arrived with *The Humanoid*, in which a world of tomorrow is menaced by a super human force. How far into the 1980s the science fiction craze will last is only a guess. In 1979, "special effects" director Spielberg had turned his attention back to nostalgia with *1941*, a comedy about a Japanese submarine's unannounced appearance off the California coast.

1980s: THE CARTOON AS FEATURE FILM

What else is in store for film in the 1980s? The beginning of the decade will introduce the characters of the comics. Columbia Pictures bills its 1981 film *Annie* (Figure 8-25) as "the top movie musical of all time." Patterned after the popular comic strip feature "Little Orphan Annie," as well as the Broadway hit by the same name, *Annie* already has to its credit seven Tony Awards, including best musical, and the New York Drama Critics Award for Best Musical. With

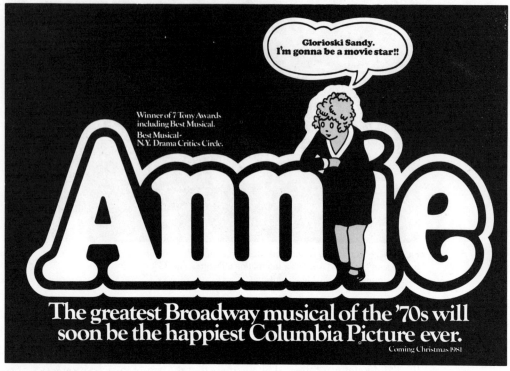

Figure 8-25 Full length cartoons, such as "Annie," showing a return of major animated features for the early 1980s. (© 1979 Columbia Pictures Industries, Inc. Courtesy, Columbia Pictures Merchandising)

news of *Annie*, other film companies quickly bought the rights to additional comic characters. If the trend is successful, the 1980s could see a whole motion picture series of "Terry and the Pirates," "Spiderman," "Flash Gordon," "Popeye," "Buck Rogers," and "Dick Tracy."

SUMMARY

In theory, we can trace motion pictures back to the era of pictographics when cave paintings attempted to express the illusion of motion. By the 1800s, motion pictures became a reality as Thomas Edison invented the motion picture camera in America, and the Lumière brothers in France invented a projection device. Early films were short and easily satisfied their patrons. Gradually, as directors like D. W. Griffith and Mack Sennett offered more creative camera techniques and story lines, the public thirst for films grew, and makeshift studios were built to accommodate production of these new films. People especially developed an interest in movie stars. Charlie Chaplin, Buster Keaton, Laurel and Hardy, Mary Pickford, and Douglas Fairbanks were among the early idols.

In 1927, sound was introduced to motion pictures, and they became a novelty all over again. But creativity stood still as sound moved forward. Finally, Mamoulian placed two microphones at different locations, thus unleashing the constraints that had plagued directors and actors.

Even through the depression of the 1930s, the movies flourished. Studio profits were plowed back into bigger productions and lavish sound stages. World War II promoted the boom. Then in the 1950s, film met a new competitor—television. Panic attempts to lure audiences back to the movies came up with such novelty technology as 3-D, cinerama, and cinemascope. Movies also adapted with a series of low budget films, a few spectaculars, and themes of juvenile delinquency.

The 1960s and 1970s witnessed changes in the financial structure of movies as studios were purchased by corporate conglomerates more concerned about profits than about creativity. Bank financing also became common, although some box office failures were too much for conservative financiers. The movies themselves began to search for an audience and found it in young adults. Pictures about the "now" generation thus became the vogue, followed by sexual liberation and violence. Disaster epics, shark films, and science fiction seemed to characterize the 1970s, and prospects for the early 1980s see a new trend in full-length feature cartoons.

OPPORTUNITIES FOR FURTHER LEARNING

BOHN, THOMAS W., AND RICHARD L. STROMGREN, *Light and Shadows* (2nd ed.). Sherman Oaks, Calif.: Alfred Publishing Co., Inc., 1978.

BONDANELLA, PETER, ed., *Federico Fellini: Eassays in Criticism*. New York: Oxford University Press, Inc., 1978.

DICKSTEIN, MORRIS, ed., *Great Film Directors: A Critical Anthology*. New York: Oxford University Press, Inc., 1978.

EIDSVIK, CHARLES, *Cineliteracy: Film among the Arts*. New York: Random House, Inc., 1978.

FRY, RON, AND PAMELA FOURZON, *The Saga of Special Effects*. Englewood Cliffs, N.J.: Prentice-Hall, Inc., 1977.

GIANNETTI, LOUIS D., *Understanding Movies*. (2nd ed.). Englewood Cliffs, N.J.: Prentice-Hall, Inc., 1976.

GRANT, BARRY K., ed., *Film Genre: Theory and Criticism*. Metuchen, N.J.: Scarecrow Press, Inc., 1977.

GUNTER, J., *Super 8: The Modest Medium*. Paris: UNESCO, 1977.

LEESE, ELIZABETH, *Costume Design in the Movies*. New York: Fredrick Unger Publishing Co., In., 1977.

LONDON, MEL, *Getting into Film*. New York: Ballentine Books, Inc., 1977.

McCabe, John, *Charlie Chaplin*. New York: Doubleday & Co., Inc., 1978.

Mast, Gerald, and Marshall Cohen, eds., *Film Theory and Criticism*. New York: Oxford University Press, 1979.

Monaco, James, *American Film Now: The People, The Power, The Money, The Movies*. New York: Oxford University Press, 1979.

Ryan, R. T., *A History of Motion Picture Color Technology*. New York/London: Focal Press, 1978.

Sampson, Henry T., *Blacks in Black and White: A Source Book on Black Films*. Metuchen, N.J.: Scarecrow Press, Inc., 1977.

Sitney, Po Adams, *Visionary Film: The American Avant-Garde,1943–1978*. New York: Oxford University Press, 1979.

9

The Recording Industry

What images come to mind when we think of the recording industry? The support for virtually every type of electronic mass communication, the industry is synonomous with multimillion dollar studios, rock bands, promoters, albums, concerts, stars, excitement—and perhaps heartbreak. To the musicians it means Nashville, London, Chicago, New York, Paris, and Los Angeles. To the electronic engineer it is echo chambers, reverbs, microphones, and synthesizers.

SCOPE OF THE RECORDING INDUSTRY

The recording industry today is an international, billion-dollar enterprise. In the United States alone, more than 1,200 companies are producing and releasing records and tapes; approximately 2,600 different record and tape labels are sold; 60,000 stores sell records and tapes; approximately 73 million phonographs are in use; and in any one year, as many as 2,600 albums and 6,200 singles will be released. Retail sales of records in the United States are in excess of $2 billion dollars annually. In fact, the United States is the largest consumer of recorded music with approximately 36 percent of the world market. What types of music are the most popular? Contemporary music by far, accounting for over 61.4 percent of sales. Country music follows with 11.7 percent. Figure 9-1 examines

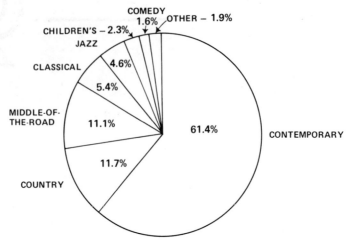

Figure 9-1 Record sales by music type. (Source: *Billboard* magazine and the Recording Industry Association of America)

other musical types, showing that middle-of-the-road music accounts for 11.1 percent, classical for 5.4 percent, jazz with 4.6 percent, children's music at 2.3 percent, and comedy with 1.6 percent.

To understand how the recording industry achieved such success, we need to go back before radio, before disc jockeys, even before the phonograph.

PRERECORDING ERA: BROADSIDES AND SHEET MUSIC

The first use of music as a means of mass communication is credited to the print medium. Long before the concept of electronics, a new song was *published* on paper and inserted inside a decorated cover to be played on the piano or other appropriate musical instrument of the time. Published meant just that, produced by a printing press and distributed the same way a book would be published and distributed. Music publishing in the eighteenth century took the form of *broadsides*, which were musical editorials on some important political event of the day and were printed on a rather large sheet of primarily rag content paper, hence its name.[1] The broadside's purpose was not actually to publish music but rather to act like a newspaper "extra." Inside would be news of the day and the accompanying comical verse set to a familiar tune satirizing some newsworthy event.

Sheet music, those separate publications devoted entirely to musical selections, arrived later as the American Revolution whetted appetites for patriotic songs. *The Yankee Man of War*, in honor of the deeds of the famous Captain John Paul Jones, and *The Liberty Song* were typical of songs in the late eighteenth century. Some of the songs first appeared in newspapers, then if their popularity warranted it, they received separate publication status as sheet music.

Typical of these was the song *Independence*, first published in the *Freeman's Journal*, a full month before the signing of the Declaration of Independence in 1776. Another popular tune of the era was the famous *Yankee Doodle*. Actually, this song was in existence before the American Revolution, having been part of a larger selection published as part of a comic opera in 1767. It evolved as a separate song about 1780, published in London under the title *Yankee Doodle or (as Now Christened by the Saints of New England) The Lexington March* (Figure 9-2). Instructions were given to the effect that "the Words to be sung thro' the Nose, & in the West Country drawl and dialect."

The War of 1812 also produced its share of sheet music favorites. The most famous American tune is credited to author Francis Scott Key, who wrote what became our national anthem during the defense of Fort McHenry near Baltimore. Although the verse is credited to Key, the tune itself had appeared in many versions prior to 1814. Titled *Anacreon in Heaven*, the tune was composed by the Englishman John Stafford Smith and appeared as early as 1798.

Sheet music remained the usual method of music distribution in the nineteenth century, and the politics of the times produced a wide selection of

Figure 9-2 The first separate version of "Yankee Doodle" published as sheet music in London about 1780. Numerous variations of the verse were published in later years in Boston, New York, and Philadelphia. (Source: Harry Dichter and Elliott Shapiro, *Handbook of Early American Sheet Music 1768–1889*. New York: Dover Publications, Inc., 1977)

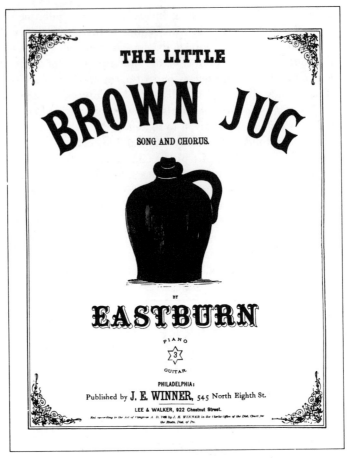

Figure 9-3 "The Little Brown Jug" was one of the popular sheet music selections of the late 1800s and was published by J. E. Winner of Philadelphia in 1869. Notice the decorative corners of the cover. Engraved borders, many in color, were a feature of early sheet music publishing. (Source: Harry Dichter and Elliott Shapiro, *Handbook of Early American Sheet Music 1768–1889*. New York: Dover Publications, 1977)

popular songs. Presidential campaigns were naturals for sheet music publishers. The most popular selections were marches such as *President John Quincy Adams's Grand March*, published by G. E. Blake of Philadelphia about 1825, and then there was the *Fillmore Quick Step* published by Miller & Beacham of Baltimore in 1856, and the *Lincoln Quick Step*, published by Lee and Walker of Philadelphia in 1860. Even tobacco provided themes for such sheet music as *The Light Cigar* and *Think and Smoke Tobacco*.

The Civil War continued the sheet music craze, and both the war and the celebration of its conclusion packed music sellers' shelves. One of the most enduring songs appearing in sheet music between 1860 and 1869 was *Dixie* by Dan Emmett, appearing under the original title of *I Wish I Was in Dixie's Land* by Firth, Pond & Co. of New York and later reproduced, some say "pirated," by P. P. Werlein of New Orleans. Werlein changed some of the lyrics, as typified by this first line of the Firth edition, "I wish I was in de land ob cotton," which the Werlein edition changed to, "I wish I was in the land of cotton." Another popular favorite was *The Little Brown Jug* (Figure 9-3), published by J. E. Winner of Philadelphia.

Sheet music continues today to be sold by most major retail stores, and the recording industry is still plagued by people pirating songs and selling them through infringing on their copyright. But the widespread practice of pirating began to diminish when the international copyright agreements were reached in 1891 and President Benjamin Harrison issued the U.S. International Copyright Proclamation on July 1 of that year. By then the era of sheet music was beginning to feel the effects of competition from an odd-looking machine called the phonograph.

BEGINNINGS OF ACOUSTICAL RECORDING

The story of the phonograph began in Thomas Edison's small laboratory in West Orange, New Jersey (Figure 9-4) where he worked on a device to improve the telegraph.

the phonograph: Edison and Cros

The problem was to devise a way in which the dots and dashes of the Morse telegraph could be captured on a paper that later could be played back. Edison was fascinated by communication. The Western Union Telegraph Company was using his improved carbon transmitter in competition with Bell and had developed a system in which four telegraph signals could be sent over the same wire. As Edison played the "paper tape" back to hear the Morse code, the increased speed sounded much like rhythmic tones of the voice. An idea developed. Why not record the human voice in the same way that the Morse code had been recorded? In 1877, although the exact date is somewhat obscured by history, Edison sketched a crude drawing and had his assistant manufacture the machine that Edison envisioned would "talk back" to its speaker. The device consisted of a metal cylinder around which Edison wrapped a form of tin foil. Connected to a diaphragm was a needle which touched the tin foil. A second diaphragm and needle were used for playback. As the cylinder turned, the needle would vibrate on the tin foil, making an indentation. This indentation would then reproduce the sound when the needle first was returned to its starting position, then played back over the cylinder. The question was, would it work? With exacting care, Edison placed the needle in position, and as he hand-cranked the cylinder, recited the poem "Mary Had a Little Lamb" into the diaphragm. The playback stylus was placed in position, and as Edison turned the crank, he was "taken aback" by the little machine saying "Mary Had a Little Lamb." Using the Greek words for "sound writer" the new invention was christened the *phonograph* (Figure 9-5).

History has confirmed that Edison later took the machine to the editorial offices of *Scientific American*. There under the witness of eager reporters, he demonstrated the phonograph. One eyewitness said, "The machine inquired as to our health, asked us how we liked the phonograph, informed us that *it* was very well, and bid us a cordial good night. These remarks were not only perfectly audible to ourselves, but to a dozen or more persons gathered around." On

Figure 9-4 Thomas Edison in his lab in West Orange, New Jersey. On the table is an improved version of the cylinder phonograph he invented in 1877. (U.S. Department of the Interior, National Park Service, Edison National Historic Site)

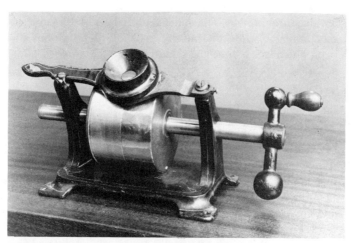

Figure 9-5 Edison's original phonograph, patented in 1877, consisted of a piece of foil wrapped around a rotating cylinder. The sound waves of the voice as Edison spoke into a recording horn (not shown) caused a vibration which in turn caused the stylus to cut grooves into the tin foil. The first sound recording was Edison reciting the poem, "Mary Had a Little Lamb." (U.S. Department of the Interior, National Park Service, Edison National Historic Site and the Recording Industry Association of America)

Christmas Eve, 1877, Thomas A. Edison filed for a patent on the phonograph. Sound recording was born.

It is interesting to note that while Edison was busy inventing the phonograph, a Frenchman already had conceived the idea, although he had never managed to apply it practically. Charles Cros, a poet and tinkerer, wrote a paper in which he envisioned a "phonograph" that would record speech and play it back for the listener. Cros's idea was quite similar to Edison's and used a stylus to imprint a groove in a disc. Edison's machine used a cylinder. Cros never built the device that he imagined but did file a sealed paper describing it with the Academie des Sciences. He later requested the paper be read, presumably on hearing the news of Edison's machine in the United States. Although both men had the same idea and both used the term phonograph, Edison remains the recognized inventor of sound recording with the cylinder machine that cited "Mary Had a Little Lamb."

Despite its accomplishments, the phonograph was far from becoming the medium of home entertainment that it is today. The little tin foil cylinder wore out after a few plays, and it only took a couple of minutes for the stylus to travel the length of the cylinder. Still, it looked profitable, and Edison formed the Edison Speaking Phonograph Company in 1878. One of his backers was none other than Gardner Hubbard, Alexander Graham Bell's father-in-law. The phonograph became the hit of the vaudeville circuit as entertainers demonstrated it to audiences willing to pay for the privilege of hearing a few words of prose or a few measures of song. The entire venture lasted less than a year, and although it was profitable while the novelty lasted, Edison's commitment to the electric light, plus a lack of time and resources, sent the whole idea into early retirement, at least temporarily.

the graphophone: Bell and Tainter

It is understandable that with Alexander Graham Bell's father-in-law backing Edison's venture, Bell would keep an eye on the phonograph's development. After winning the $10 thousand Volta Prize from the French government for the invention of the telephone, Bell founded the Volta Laboratories in Washington, D.C. in 1880. There he hired an English relative, Chichester Bell (Figure 9-6) and an American technician named Charles Tainter to begin work improving the Edison machine. They developed an improved version of the phonograph and called it the *graphophone*. The graphophone differed from the phonograph in two important ways: (1) the cylinder used a wax coating instead of tin foil, which permitted a clearer sound though one not as loud as the phonograph, and (2) the stylus or needle encasement floated on the wax cylinder. Bell and Tainter were not interested in stealing Edison's idea, but Edison apparently did not think so. When Bell and Tainter visited him with their new invention, he decided that the two men had invaded sacred territory.

Bell and Tainter wanted Edison to help them perfect, market, and manu-

Figure 9-6 Chichester A. Bell, cousin of Alexander Graham Bell, who worked on sound recording in the Volta Laboratories. He teamed up with Charles Tainter to improve on the Edison machine by developing the graphophone. (AT&T)

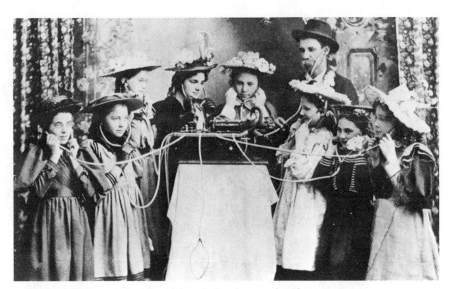

Figure 9-7 An improved version of the cylinder phonograph with multiple earphones, permitting upwards of ten people to listen at the same time. (Recording Industry Association of America)

facture their graphophone. But Edison, suddenly faced with competition, developed a new interest in the phonograph. Meanwhile, Bell and Tainter gained financial support from a group of Washington, D.C. business executives and formed the American Graphophone Corporation in 1877. Acquiring a treadle to replace the hand crank, the new graphophone hit the market as a definite step above the phonograph. Edison counterattacked by adding an electric motor to his phonograph and incorporating solid wax cylinders that could be shaved and reused. Subsequent refinements resulted in a machine with multiple earphones which permitted upwards of ten people to listen at the same time (Figure 9-7).

Before the corporate war heated up, a Philadelphia businessman decided to enter the sound recording business and gained control of the distribution rights for both the phonograph and the graphophone. Jesse Lippincott had the right idea, but he went about it the wrong way. Taking his cue from the telephone company, he decided the best way to make money was to lease the machines instead of letting people buy them. Lippincott divided the country into territories, but it was not long before the whole venture began to collapse. The only territory making any money was that assigned to the Columbia Phonograph Company, which had secured the distribution franchise for Washington D.C., and could service the government offices with dictating machines.

Soon some poor, rebellious salespersons on the West Coast threw corporate image to the wind and started leasing the machines to a San Francisco saloon. There, patrons began to stand in line to plug a nickel into the machines and be "talked to" by the phonograph (Figure 9-8). What was supposed to be the

Figure 9-8 A view of one of the phonograph parlors which helped popularize recordings during the 1890s. These machines were the forerunners of the home phonograph and the jukebox. (Library of Congress and Recording Industry Association of America)

distinguished mechanical contribution to the offices of the country became the bawdy boon to the saloon business. Yet, despite their interest in the amusing apparatus, saloons did not rescue the American Graphophone Company. It went the way of the tin foil phonograph. The lone survivor was the Columbia group which kept its fiscal head above water and gained control of the Bell-Tainter patents. The new venture became known as Columbia-Graphophone.

the gramophone: Berliner and Johnson

While the graphophone and phonograph were confronting each other, a German immigrant and a machine shop operator were preparing to steal the show with the third addition to the sound recording family, the *gramophone*. Emile Berliner (Figure 9-9) landed in America as a penniless immigrant from Germany and was self-educated in the science of physics. He first invented an improved telephone transmitter, which was the forerunner of the modern microphone. Bell Telephone paid him for the patent and put him to work. Almost ten years later, he took a leave of absence from Bell and went to work improving the phonograph. The most dramatic improvement came in changing the way that the stylus recorded sound. The second change was to use a disc instead of a cylinder.

Figure 9-9 Emile Berliner, who arrived a pennyless immigrant from Germany, educated himself in physics. He invented an improved microphone for the telephone. But his most famous work occurred with the invention of the disc recording device called the gramophone. (RCA)

Figure 9-10 The Berliner gramophone of 1893, manufactured by the U.S. Gramophone Company of Washingotn, D.C., was one of the early disc phonographs on the market. Hand powered, it required the operator to crank the handle up to a speed of about 70 revolutions-per-minute in order to get a satisfactory playback. (Smithsonian Institution and the Recording Industry Association of America)

Figure 9-11 Original painting of "His Master's Voice," which became the trademark of the Victor Talking Machine Company and
later, RCA Victor. (RCA)

It was now time to begin marketing and selling the new device. For that, a
Camden, New Jersey machinist named Eldridge Johnson joined Berliner, and
the two formed the Victor Talking Machine Company. Berliner received 40
percent and Johnson 60 percent of the stock. Not only did the gramophone
(Figure 9-10) ornament people's living rooms, but Johnson also began importing
the famous European Red Seal records of famous opera stars. They were expensive, about $5.00. Enrico Caruso was one of the first to record, and the event in
1902 gave a new legitimacy to sound recording. Other opera stars were quick to
follow. Now the public could obtain quality recordings and purchase reasonably
priced machines with which to listen to them. Along with good music, Victor
also obtained a world famous trademark, "His Master's Voice," the picture of a
terrier named Nipper listening to a gramophone. The trademark (Figure 9-11)
was originally painted by Francis Barraud and sold to the European affiliate of
Victor. Johnson realized the appeal of the art, secured an American copyright for
the logo, and used it on Victor records.

The final breakthrough in early acoustical recording came in 1905 when
Columbia introduced disc records with songs on both sides. The dual-sided
records originally sold for 65¢ and could be played on any disc machine. Columbia promoted the dual-sided recordings in ads which read, "Columbia *Double-*
disc Records! Double discs, double quality, double value, double wear, double
everything except price! Don't put your record money into any other!"

Although the popularity of acoustical recording spread widely, it was seriously limited in its reproduction of quality sound. Because the sound was imprinted on the record through the impact of sound waves on the recording stylus, performers had literally to shout into the microphone. Heavily draped and highly confined recording studios were employed, and, in some cases, even the musical instruments were altered so that a satisfactory recording could be made. Sounds from string instruments could not be reproduced clearly; thus many orchestras would substitute brass and woodwind instruments for better sound reproduction. One altered instrument was the Stroh-violin (Figure 9-12), which employed a special acoustical horn permitting directed amplification of the sound and greatly aiding the recording process. Because of all the makeshift apparatus, though, inventors realized that the future of recorded sound was in finding a way to record and amplify sound through an electrical, not an acoustical process. The breakthrough came just as radio was becoming a home medium.

Joseph P. Maxfield and electrical recording

Joseph P. Maxfield and other members of the Bell Laboratories began experimenting with electrical recording processes in 1919. Other companies also were

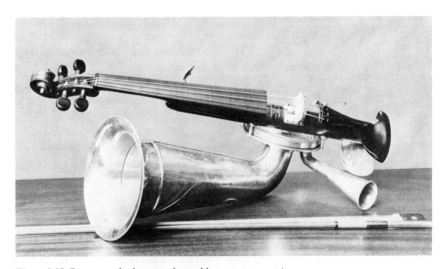

Figure 9-12 Because cylinder records could not capture string sounds faithfully, brass and woodwinds were frequently substituted for strings at recording sessions. The Stroh-violin, an acoustically amplified instrument, was designed especially for cylinder recordings. Smithsonian Institution and the Recording Industry Association of America)

working on this, including the English Columbia and His Master's Voice, formerly the Gramophone Company, Limited. Their main goal was to find a means of electrically amplifying sound. Three things were needed to accomplish the task: (1) a condenser microphone that would provide greater clarity than the horn did and would reduce the loss of volume and quality of sound as it passed to a (2) vacuum tube amplifier that would amplify the sound and transmit it to (3) an electromagnetically powered cutting stylus. If perfected, listeners could hear everything from the most subtle sounds of a symphony orchestra to the true undistorted sounds of a marching band.

By 1924, Maxfield had perfected the process, and recording companies quickly jumped in line for licenses permitting them to develop commercially the new process for the home consumer. The first company to reach the home playback market was Brunswick with its Panatrope machine in 1926. Soon such names as Electrola and Radiolas began to crop up in advertisements as companies such as Victor marketed the home playback devices. Prospects looked promising enough for RCA to purchase a major portion of Victor in 1929 and to move for a formal merger in 1930. Although the long-term benefits were substantial, the short-term were disastrous.

rise and fall of depression profits

Neither radio nor the recording industry foresaw the economic consequences of the 1929 stock market crash. For the recording industry, it was a catastrophe, primarily caused by radio, which was free to the listener. The medium that was to be the "advertiser" for the recording companies' products appeared at first to be its demise. Movies did not help either. Escaping the realities of famine and unemployment, crowds flocked into theaters to watch the silver screen. Based on figures of the Recording Industry Association of America (RIAA), recording industry retail sales, which had reached $75 million in 1929, had plummeted to $5.5 million by 1933.

But in the same year, the industry started to regroup. With the repeal of Prohibition in 1933, the nightclub trade, the bars, and the cocktail lounges once again returned to the neon facade of the business district. With them came juke boxes. First manufactured by Automatic Music of Grand Rapids, Michigan in 1927, the names on the flashing, push-button record players were such industry standards as Capehart, Seeburg, and Wurlitzer. Through juke box exposure, record sales began to climb back to respectability, reaching $26 million in 1938. Radio networks, meanwhile, were beginning to see future tie-ins with the broadcasting industry. CBS even purchased the Columbia Phonograph Company. Recordings by major stars made famous by radio were snatched up quickly in the record stores, and familiar coporate names began to appear on recording labels, such as RCA Victor, Columbia, and Decca.

battle of the speeds

Also brewing at this time was the "battle of the speeds." RCA in 1931 had unsuccessfully launched a long-playing 33 1/3 rpm (revolutions per minute) record, substantially improving the ability to record such major productions as musicals and symphonies. The trouble was that the records wore out after a few plays. Some 33 1/3 recordings were used in World War II to send radio programs overseas, but for the most part, the long-playing record was of little value to either the recording industry or the broadcasters. Then in 1948, Dr. Peter C. Goldmark (Figure 9-13) of CBS invented a long-playing, long-lasting 33 1/3 rpm record. Accompanied by lightweight tone arms and special microgroove cutting techniques, the new records began to catch on. Success did not come overnight, however, because arch rival RCA created chaos one year later by introducing the 45 rpm disc. With three speeds to choose from—78, 33 1/3, and 45—the public reacted by not buying much of anything. Finally, Columbia released its famous 33 1/3 recording of *South Pacific*, and the public demand for the disc sent the era of 78 rpm into the past. RCA was not licked, however. Juke box operators found the durable, lightweight 45s with the big holes just right for the coin operated machines. To be safe, radio stations bought equipment with all three speeds.

Figure 9-13 Dr. Peter C. Goldmark is shown in an early picture dramatizing the increased capacity of the long-play 33⅓ r.p.m. record, which he helped develop. The music contained in the stack of 78 r.p.m. records on his left can be recorded on just the long-play albums Dr. Goldmark is holding. (Columbia Records)

Finally, 45s found a home in single hit records, and 33 1/3 records were ideal for musicals, symphonies, and operas.

TAPE, TELEVISION, AND STEREO

The recording and broadcasting industries became involved with much more than just discs. The Allied forces during World War II discovered that the Germans had made great strides in recording on magnetic tape, and the technology was brought to America. Now for broadcasting, even the 33 1/3 rpms were running second to what the capabilities of tape could offer. Tape gave even the smallest radio stations the ability to record, playback, erase, and rerecord everything from local newsmakers to studio trios. Editing also was possible, down to a note or syllable. Radio newscasts began to use the actual sound of the news, edited into short audio "actualities" which fit easily into the shorter time slots evolved during radio's competition with television. Today, the cartridge tape plays inside the radio studio, the home, the car, and even the boat. Radio broadcasting and sound recording have achieved not just a relationship, but a marriage.

What about television? It sent radio into a tailspin, and the recording industry did not have much comfort either. There were dire predictions once again for both industries. RIAA figures show that record sales, which had hit $224 million in 1947, plunged to $173 million in 1949. In fact, they did not return to 1947 levels until 1955. Radio advertising fell, and the radio networks consequently could not afford live talent. What they desperately needed was a cheap supply of quality radio programming. Coming to the rescue was the 45 and the 33 1/3 which had made significant inroads into the home market. The two industries started to revive.

Moreover, television did not have stereophonic sound, which had been successfully developed in 1931 by Englishman A. D. Blumlein. Stereo records made their debut in 1958. Audio Fidelity, a small recording company, led the way in producing stereo records. As people began to understand the possibilities of sound separation, the demand for stereo records increased. FM stereo received the FCC's approval in 1961, opening up more new stereo avenues. Today, quadraphonic, four-channel sound has become commonplace in the recording industry and is undergoing experimentation for adaptation to full-scale broadcasting, and AM stereo is on the horizon.

THE RECORDING ARTIST: A RISING IDENTITY

Although the changing technology of the recording industry was an important part of the history of recorded music, the transition between songs and performers was equally important. At the turn of the century when the novelty of the phonograph was in full bloom, people were not as interested in performers as they were in specific songs. Today, a recording artist is what the public wants; the songs follow. People pay as much as $20 to attend a rock concert, not because they want to hear a given song but because they want to hear and see the star. The same holds true when someone enters a retail establishment and buys an album; it is the artist who counts.

But, back in the 1880s, records did not even carry the name of the artist. It was the song people purchased. Names like George W. Johnson, a popular black performer, George Schweinfest, a piccolo soloist, and George J. Gaskin, an Irish tenor, were destined to obscurity although their recordings were hits at the turn of the century. Then there was Russell Hunting who recorded Irish dialect stories and received fame in recording industry management circles but never as a recording star. It took opera favorites like Enrico Caruso to change the industry, to see the name of the recording artist appear on the record label, and to see performers paid royalties instead of a fee for each recording session.

Entrepreneurs also capitalized on the industry's growth. An enterprising Englishman named Louis Sterling became rich by recording musical shows and selling the recordings to lonely soldiers in World War I. These were the first of the "original cast album shows," which included such favorite tunes as Irving Berlin's *Watch Your Step*. World War I also saw the introduction of jazz recordings, with the public snapping up those by jazz artists King Oliver, Kid Ory, and later Louis Armstrong.

Changes in technology, specifically electrical recording, brought a new wave of artists called *crooners*. Crooners were performers who sang in soft romantic tones, something that was impossible with acoustical recordings. Among the early favorites were Rudy Vallee, Bing Crosby, and Frank Sinatra. When film began to incorporate sound, recorded music again received attention as musical scores from motion pictures came into vogue. When Al Jolson appeared in the movie *The Jazz Singer* in 1928, every song in the film became an instant hit.

By the 1930s, the big bands were in full swing. Names like Benny Goodman, Jimmy and Tommy Dorsey, Harry James, Glen Miller, Artie Shaw, and Woody Herman were the hottest sounds around. Their popularity continued through the 1940s, receiving a big boost from radio which, ironically, also signaled their demise by ushering in the next big era, the age of rock and roll.

ROCK AND ROLL

The 1950s brought forth a revolutionary new musical concept—"rock and roll." It changed the music industry, it helped change radio, and it provided some of the largest profits that the entertainment world had ever seen. Its beginning is credited to a combination of fast-paced country-and-western music combined with rhythm and blues. Its first international hit belonged to Bill Haley and the Comets and their song "Rock around the Clock." It also began to narrow its

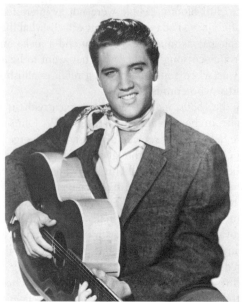

Figure 9-14 Elvis Presley.

Figure 9-15 The Beatles. Their tour of America in 1964 provided the major emphasis for British rock in the United States.

appeal to teens and young adults. Middle-aged people were attracted to the novelty by Elvis Presley's (Figure 9-14) first appearance on national television, but it was the younger audience that became devoted fans of rock music and performers. By the time the Beatles (Figure 9-15) arrived in the 1960s, these young fans were complete rock converts. Meanwhile, the middle-aged recording fan had become a voice almost too small to be heard in the consumer market.

Disciples of the new music made up the larger portion of the population who tuned in rock radio stations to hear the "Top 100," the "Top 40," the "pick hit of the week," the "number one song" in the area, and the occasional "oldies but goodies" which were never too old to be out of the real era of rock music. The music industry's new commodity commanded a loyalty and a following that sent thousands to concerts from Woodstock to the Thames. Because of radio's adaptability, it drew the same overwhelming loyalty, and disc jockeys became popular stars in their own right. Transistors even made it possible to take rock music and a favorite radio station almost anywhere.

But rock music did more than acquire its devotees—it also changed our culture. With the Beatles came long hair and then still longer hair with the countless rock groups that followed. People began to realize that rock and roll was a true cultural expression and not a passing fad.

From its beginnings with Bill Haley and the Comets through Elvis Presley, rock and roll itself began to specialize. Today there are different rock forms from middle-of-the-road rock, which has a beat not unlike that of the original rock, to

Figure 9-16 The rock group KISS. (Aucoin Management, Inc.)

hard rock, and the even harder acid and progressive rock. Groups such as *Kiss* (Figure 9-16) brought a new dimension to rock with wild costumes, popular music, and broad appeal to a contemporary audience.

DISCO

While rock and roll played to the beat of the young audience of the 50s and 60s, the late 70s spawned a new generation of music lovers. They listened, danced, bought records, and danced some more to disco. Disco music had its roots, much like rock and roll, in the beat of rhythm and blues, the repeated tempo, and the sounds of drums and brass fermented by synthesizers.

the dance beat

Where it all started few agree on, but the dance seemed to precede the music. Evolving from the jitterbug of the earliest rock, to the twist, to the hustle, the disco dance steps managed their way into clubs and dance halls before disco music came along. The rock-fueled dance craze spawned in the 50s tapered off in the 60s, and was gradually replaced by the rock concert. People did not stop dancing altogether, they just listened more. The acid and progressive rock of the 60s did not lend itself to dancing—at least not like disco does. But as though somehow penned up in the psyche of the public was a steaming desire to get back to the dance floor. Disco popped the cork, let out the emotion, and brought the public out of their seats and back to the dance floor. What people wanted were simple beats and hard pumping sounds—sound to which bodies could move. At just about 125 beats per minute the formula jelled, and disco music plunged onto the scene, first in the off-beat bars and hole-in-the-wall dance clubs, then onto the record charts and Wall Street. Before long, disco was big, big business, with big stars and big audiences.

the stars

New stars emerged as charter members of the disco era. Expressing the animal beat of a bump-and-pump rhythm, Donna Summer began to capture the sensuous side of the disco beat with her recording "Love to Love You Baby" released in 1975. Donna Summer was as hot on stage as on an album. Tour and television appearances soon added to her mass appeal. Even in small-time night clubs, amateur talent tried to woo audiences by imitating Summer and her sound.

From the solo performances of Donna Summer followed The Village People—six men whose on-stage costumes produced a cowboy, construction worker, Indian policemen, motorcycle jockey, and soldier. Their 1978 songs "Y. M. C. A." and "Macho Man" became instant hits. By now, established stars saw the handwriting on the wall—disco was more than a quick passing fad.

Even names like Rod Stewart and Dolly Parton found their way into disco. And studio technicians, working with an assorted array of vocals and sound tracks, put together disco hits comprised completely of technology.

new role for the disc jockey

The public's acceptance of a disco song often comes first in the night clubs, where the key person to its success is the disc jockey. The disc jockey's evening transplant from the radio station to the dance floor is not new. Rock saw the same phenomenon, but the d. j.'s performance was different. There the disc jockey at a dance did not do things much differently than at the radio station. A song was introduced, it ended, the next song was introduced, it ended, and so on through the evening. With disco, the disc jockey is the artist behind the painting, the person with an appreciation and deep knowledge of music who blends one song into another without ever missing a beat or forcing the dancer to concentrate on a transition.

Some disc jockeys on big-city radio pull in hundreds of thousands of dollars for their talents *away* from the airwaves. Some have left radio entirely to become the producing technicians behind some of the biggest record company hits.

MAKING A HIT RECORD

How does an idea become a hit record? It starts at one of the *performance rights societies*, such as Broadcast Music, Inc. (BMI) or the American Society of Composers, Authors, and Publishers (ASCAP). Association with these organizations is important because they become responsible for collecting royalties. They collect licensing fees from broadcast stations, airlines, or rock groups that perform songs.

demo and master recording sessions

After the performing rights societies comes the *publishing company*. The publishing company arranges for a *demo session* and provides the basic accompaniment to put a song on tape. After the manager and some of the staff of the publishing company listen to the tape, they decide whether or not to arrange for a *master session*. This session is immensely important. To achieve authentic reproduction of every sound, the recording is done on a major control console having as many as thirty or more channels with a trained recording engineer and full orchestral accompaniment (Figure 9-17). The master session requires an investment by the publishing company of many thousands of dollars. After the master session, the tape is sent to be made into a *master record*, usually a 45 rpm, and from this, thousands of records are pressed and readied for distribution.

Figure 9-17 Recording studio control console. (Photo: Yael Brandeis, Courtesy, Le Studio)

Figure 9-18 Sophisticated computer technology resulting in "digital recording" has the potential to bring a new era to recorded music. (Soundstream and Telarc Records)

Modern production methods also employ a process called *direct-to-disc* that eliminates the tape-to-disc transfer.

Computers have also entered the very foundation of the recording process with *digital recording* becoming the wave of the future (Figure 9-18). With digital, the range and clarity of reproduction is greatly enhanced. High and low notes are virtually distortion free, a feat with which other methods cannot compete. With digital, the distortion occurring from standard recording onto magnetic tape—mixing sounds in the studio, transferring the tape to a master disc, using the master disc to press other records—is eliminated. As the sound is originally produced by, say, an orchestra, the computer can sample the sound waves picked up by the microphone as many times as 50 thousand times in one second. Each "sampling" is assigned a numerical value and, along with other "samplings," produces a numerical model of the sound. The numerical values comprising the model can be stored in the computer and called back when the recording is made. Sounds can still be mixed, just as they can with magnetic tape. But distortion—creating characteristics of magnetic tape such as flutter and varying tape speed—is eliminated. Although direct-to-disc methods also eliminate many of the problems encountered with tape, the need still arises for the artist to perform perfectly, since post-performance correction cannot be made on the disc.

promoting the record

Promotion is the next step. So far, there is no one interested in buying the record. But the publishing company plans to change that and sends complimentary copies of the record to radio stations all over the country, hoping the disc jockeys will listen to it, like it, and begin to play it. This process is not as easy as it sounds. At an average radio station, the record will be in competition with more than two hundred other records each week. At many stations, unless the artist is known, the record will not even be taken out of its cover. However, if someone does decide to play the record, and if it begins to generate requests for air play, then the next step is watching for it to appear on the charts of the industry's trade magazines.

the charts

Let's assume that it does appear on one of *Billboard* magazine's hit charts (Figure 9-19). Now the chances for success, although not guaranteed, suddenly become a thousand times greater. As we shall learn later in this chapter, the *Billboard* charts are a detailed summary of a recording's popularity. Once a song appears on the chart, it has a much better chance of receiving air play on radio stations, of being recognized by program directors and disc jockeys, and finally of being purchased by the public.

However, before you run out to buy a guitar and head for Nashville,

Billboard SPECIAL SURVEY For Week Ending 6/10/78
(Published Twice A Month)

Billboard Best Selling Jazz LPs ®

This Week	Last Report	Weeks on Chart	TITLE Artist, Label & Number (Distributing Label)
1	1	18	**WEEKEND IN L.A.** George Benson, Warner Bros. 2Wb-3139
2	2	34	**FEELS SO GOOD** Chuck Mangione, A&M SP 4658
3	3	18	**RAINBOW SEEKER** Joe Sample, ABC AA 1050
4	4	25	**LIVE AT THE BIJOU** Grover Washington Jr., Kudu KUX 3637 (Motown)
5	5	10	**SAY IT WITH SILENCE** Hubert Laws, Columbia JC-35022
6	7	5	**CASINO** Al DiMeola, Columbia JC 35277
7	6	5	**MODERN MAN** Stanley Clarke, Nemperor JZ 35303 (CBS)
8	NEW ENTRY		**ELECTRIC GUITARIST** John McLaughlin, Columbia JC 35326
9	9	12	**WEST SIDE HIGHWAY** Stanley Turrentine, Fantasy F-9548
10	10	10	**LOVE ISLAND** Deodato, Warner Bros. BSK 3132
11	8	5	**LOVELAND** Lonnie Liston Smith, Columbia JC 35332
12	24	3	**BALTIMORE** Nina Simone, CTI CTI 7084
13	14	5	**JUST FAMILY** Dee Dee Bridgewater, Elektra 6E-119
14	15	8	**BURCHFIELD NINE** Michael Franks, Warner Bros. BSK 3167
15	13	18	**HERB ALPERT & HUGH MASEKELA** Horizon SP 728 (A&M)
16	17	5	**SPINOZZA** David Spinozza, A&M SP 4677
17	12	18	**HOLD ON** Noel Pointer, United Artists UALA 848-11
18	27	3	**INNER CONFLICTS** Billy Cobham, Atlantic SD 19174
19	25	3	**BOP-BE** Keith Jarrett, ABC IA 9334
20	38	3	**SPYRO GYRA** Spyro Gyra, Amherst AMH 1014
21	23	12	**LOVE WILL FIND A WAY** Pharoah Sanders, Arista AB 4161
22	NEW ENTRY		**EVERYDAY, EVERYNIGHT** Flora Purim, Warner Bros. BSK 3168
23	NEW ENTRY		**HEART TO HEART** David Sanborn, Warner Bros. BSK 3189
24	21	8	**LET'S DO IT** Roy Ayers, Polydor PD1-6126
25	35	3	**BRAZIL—ONCE AGAIN** Herbie Mann, Atlantic SD 19169
26	22	51	**LOOK TO THE RAINBOW—AL JARREAU LIVE IN EUROPE** Warner Bros. 2BZ 3052
27	NEW ENTRY		**SKY BLUE** Passport, Atlantic SD 19177
28	20	31	**HEADS** Bob James, Columbia JC 34896
29	16	13	**THE MAD HATTER** Chick Corea, Polydor PD 1-6130
30	11	18	**THE PATH** Ralph MacDonald, Marlin 2210 (TK)
31	19	5	**PEG LEG** Ron Carter, Milestone M9082 (Fantasy)
32	18	16	**FUNK IN A MASON JAR** Harvey Mason, Arista AB 4157
33	NEW ENTRY		**MAGIC IN YOUR EYES** Earl Klugh, United Artists UA LA 877
34	NEW ENTRY		**DON'T ASK MY NEIGHBORS** Raul de Souza, Capitol SW 11774
35	32	10	**ROSEWOOD** Woody Shaw, Columbia JC 35309
36	NEW ENTRY		**GLIDER** Auracle, Chrysalis CHR 1172
37	31	3	**MOONSCAPES** Bennie Maupin, Mercury SRM-1-3717
38	33	57	**FRIENDS & STRANGERS** Ronnie Laws, Blue Note BN-LA730-H (United Artists)
39	28	18	**EASY LIVING** Sonny Rollins, Milestone M-9080 (Fantasy)
40	26	8	**THAT'S WHAT SHE SAID** Flora Purim, Milestone 9081 (Fantasy)

Figure 9-19 One of the weekly *Billboard* charts indicating a song's popularity. Appearing on the charts and rising into the top slots can mean big money to people involved in producing the record. Such things as money charged for concert appearances, the frequency of airplay, and record sales can be influenced by a song's position on the *Billboard* charts.

remember two things: those who do make it to stardom are few and far between, and the time that transpires between the first signing with the publishing company and reaching stardom may be decades. Although glamorous and profitable, the recording industry has many risks.

UNDERSTANDING CHARTS AND PLAYLISTS

It is Monday morning, and every disc jockey, radio program director, recording company executive, artist, composer, and everyone who has anything to do with the music industry is literally consuming every word of the *Billboard* chart published in *Billboard* magazine.

billboard

The typical *Billboard* chart lists ten important pieces of information which, when surveyed over time, can indicate how well a particular performer or group is doing, how well a particular recording company is faring, and the prospects for a record becoming a hit (Figure 16-4). For instance, assume the hit song you are following is "Sunset," recorded by Mary Doe. It might appear on the chart as follows:

675 SUNSET
Mary Doe, Apple 1201 (Capitol) (Tre-Hollis, BMI)

The first two numbers on the chart indicate the record's standing for the current and the previous week, respectively. In our example, "Sunset" has moved up from seventh place to sixth place. This information immediately tells you that the recording is becoming more popular or is "climbing the charts." As program director at a radio station that is airing "Sunset," you might, on the basis of this listing, increase the frequency of air play of the song, for example, from one to two air plays every hour. You might also give it some additional buildup, such as your own station's "pick hit of the week." All of these decisions, which may seem little more than radio "jargon," are daily judgments that actually can be reflected in profits or losses of hundreds or thousand of dollars, for the slightest change in a radio station's programming can prompt the listener to switch stations or to change listening patterns entirely. When this decision is translated into rating shares, which then affect advertising dollars you can see how this "jargon" becomes very expensive.

The third important number on our listing represents the number of weeks the song has been on the charts, in our example, five weeks. This information indicates how fast the song climbed to its present position. The remainder of the information tells the name of the song; the label and number, which in our example is Apple 1201 and very important if you must order it; the distributor's label, which in our example is Capitol; the publisher of the song, which for "Sunset" is a company called Tre-Hollis; and the licensee, which is BMI.

playlists

Playlists are similar to the *Billboard* charts except that they are published by individual radio stations and reflect the popularity of songs in that station's immediate listening area. They usually are found in most record stores posted in a conspicuous place next to the record display racks. Many times they contain supplementary information, such as the latest "gossip" on station air personalities. They are distributed by direct mail and are important promotional literature for many radio stations. Playlists also are an excellent way for stations to assure themselves of obtaining free records for air play. In fact, when the energy crisis created a shortage of the petroleum products used to make records, some recording companies informed campus radio stations that they could not afford to send them any more free promotional records unless they received playlists in return.

Along with retail record outlets in any market, station playlists usually are mailed to major recording companies, record distribution companies, certain artists and performers, and other radio stations. Just as the recording industry scans the *Billboard* charts, it also reviews playlists, especially those of the major radio stations. In essence, being first on the playlist of some of the larger radio stations in the United States is equal in importance to being first on the *Billboard* charts.

syndicated charts and playlists

In addition to station playlists and the *Billboard* charts, other charts and services are used by the industry to gauge the success of its products. Some private individuals, mainly authoritative and knowledgeable program directors or disc jockeys, make up their own syndicated record charts and playlists. Such charts and playlists are detailed and can reflect the rise of an obscure recording in a small market, thus indicating how it might do nationally.

ECONOMIC ISSUES

The road to a hit record is becoming more expensive, affected by everything from price wars among record distributors to shortages of vinyl, the material used to manufacture records. In between is the consumer, whose fickle buying habits send many a recording artist into unemployment and promoters back to the drawing board. To the average consumer, records are a luxury, and the industry tends to sway with the economy. When the economy is up, record sales are up; when the economy is down, then record sales either drop or consumers change their buying habits. For instance, singles may outsell albums simply because they are cheaper, and people wanting a certain hit sound may not want to spend the extra money for added sounds. The segments of the industry are interrelated. Artists, through their contracts with recording companies, are not as flexible in the marketplace as artists in some other media are. Whereas an author may easily go to different publishing companies, a recording artist is usually signed to one company and remains there until his or her contract runs out or is bought out by another company. The companies themselves are also involved in related areas of the industry, such as distribution, retail sales, and promotion. As a result, the entire industry is affected by its component parts, many of which may be controlled by a single corporation. Expenses are mostly in two areas—promotion and distribution.

promotion costs

Only on rare occasions does a record make it big on its own without the recording company launching a major promotional campaign. The cost of these promotional campaigns and all of their various aspects can be in the millions of dollars. For example, recording companies purchase a substantial number of commercials to introduce new artists. They also pay fees for performers to appear on prime-time television programs. They purchase blocks of tickets at rock concerts to give away to fans and purchase outdoor advertising (Figure 9-20). Large record companies will join with promoters to stage concerts and dance fests featuring major rock stars. All of these promotional efforts have a single goal: to give the artists ample exposure and thus attract attention to their recordings.

Figure 9-20 Generating sales of a major recording means a well coordinated advertising campaign, often using different media. Here a billboard advertisement is used to promote the rock group CHICAGO and their album, "Chicago X." The billboard is on a gold background with red lettering showing a mock bar of chocolate candy being unwrapped. (Institute of Outdoor Advertising)

Another heavy expense is keeping an artist or rock group soluble until they have a major hit record and can pay their own expenses. The recording industry is much like a crowded airport with planes flying in a holding pattern. With only so much room for planes to land at any one time, the rest have to stay airborne until they have the opportunity to land. Similarly, many recording artists are kept in business until there is an opportunity for them to penetrate the market; public demand dictates that only so many of them can be popular at any one time. All recording companies make major investments in talent, some of which never pay off.

distribution

The distribution system for records is quite similar to that for books and has many of the same costs. Transportation is one. Shipping of recording discs and cassettes is done by truck, and increased fuel prices affect the distributors' and eventually the consumers' costs. The distributor also must estimate the demand for the recording to avoid the costly process of returning unsold recordings. On top of this, price wars have complicated the distributors' woes. Record retail outlets are very much like gas stations. They buy from wholesalers but also can discount their merchandise. A market that has not only price but also time limitations placed on it can suffer considerable loss from such tactics. A popular recording artist, for example, will have a hit on the charts for a limited time only. It is during this period that the public will purchase his or her record. Signs with "big tape discounts" and "cut-rate prices" abound, and consumers invariably find that shopping around does pay. Although the record companies have been accused of cooperating in this, the FCC has been strongly against interfering, stating that recording companies must compete in a free market.

Overall, the recording industry has shown the ability to weather most of the economic storms it has faced—partly because it also has a system of royalty agreements suited to different outlets such as bands, juke boxes, radio stations, and airline music systems, to name a few.

pirating

In addition to price wars, the recording industry also must contend with *pirated tapes*—illegally recorded music sold in violation of copyright agreements and contractual agreements with artists. Pirate companies have been the target of both the industry and the Justice Department. Although there have been some major crackdowns, the practice continues. Pirate operations will record songs of popular artists directly from a broadcast or from other recordings and then sell the tapes at a big discount. Profits are considerable, since pirate companies pay neither royalty fees nor the cost of distribution. Most are operated on a regional or even local basis with few outlets, thus eliminating most middleman fees. All that is needed is duplicating equipment and a retail outlet to sell the merchandise. After that, it is mostly profit. The fines for the offenders, however, are stiff, and a jail sentence can be an accompaniment.

SUMMARY

Chapter 9 examined the billion-dollar recording industry, starting with its roots in the seventeenth century when musical selections first appeared in broadsides and as published sheet music. Thomas Edison is credited with inventing the first workable phonograph in 1877, which used a tin foil-covered cylinder upon which indentations were made from a stylus connected to a large recording horn. Chichester Bell and Charles Tainter made substantial improvements on the machine and named their improved recording device the graphophone. It also used a cylinder but one made of wax.

A German immigrant named Emile Berliner teamed up with craftsman Eldridge Johnson and invented the first workable disc recorder, called the gramophone. Commercial development of acoustical recording devices continued through the early twentieth century while the machines tried to find a profitable market, appearing as everything from dictating machines to fads of saloons and phonograph parlors.

By 1924, radio had become a home medium, and Joseph P. Maxfield introduced the first electrical recorder. Now sounds could be amplified much more than was possible with acoustical methods, and the result was a tonal clarity never before achieved. The improvements made the phonograph the newest home entertainment medium. Although the Depression slowed the growth of the industry, it bounced back and remains an important part of both home entertainment and broadcasting.

Along with the technology came the identity of recording stars. Early opera favorites such as Enrico Caruso were to be followed by such greats as Al Jolson, the big-band sounds, the jazz favorites, and crooners. By the 1950s, rock and roll arrived, and by the late 70s, disco was obtaining mass popularity.

The making of a hit record is part of a step-by-step process that has many more failures than successes and is tied to the economic issues facing the recording industry. The concept of a hit record starts at the performance rights society and goes from there to the publishing company, where recording sessions are followed by major promotional efforts, possibly leading to retail sales.

OPPORTUNITIES FOR FURTHER LEARNING

CHAPPLE, STEVE, AND REEBEE GAROFALO, *Rock 'n' Roll is Here to Pay*. Chicago: Nelson-Hall Publishers, 1977.

CLARK, DICK, AND RICHARD ROBINSON, *Rock, Roll & Remember*. New York: Thomas Y. Crowell Company, Inc., 1976.

CLARKE, GARRY E., *Essays on American Music*. Westport, Conn.: Greenwood Press, 1977.

CSIDA, JOSEPH, *The Music/Record Career Handbook*. New York: Billboard Publications, Inc., 1975.

DAVIS, CLIVE, WITH JAMES WILLWERTH, *Clive: Inside the Record Business*. New York: Billboard Publications, Inc., 1975.

DENISOFF, R. SERGE, AND RICHARD A. PETERSON, eds., *Change*. Chicago: Rand McNally & Company, 1972.

DICHTER, HARRY, AND ELLIOT SHAPIRO, *Handbook of Early American Sheet Music 1768–1889*. New York: Dover Publications, Inc., 1977.

DUNN, LLOYD, *On the Flip Side*. New York: Billboard Publications, Inc., 1975.

GELATT, ROLAND, *The Fabulous Phonograph: 1877–1977*. New York: Macmillan, Inc., 1977.

HENDERSON, WILLIAM, *How to Run Your Own Rock and Roll Band*. New York: Popular Library, 1977.

McCUE, GEORGE, ed., *Music in American Society, 1776–1976: From Puritan Hymn to Synthesizer*. New Brunswick, N.J.: Transaction, Inc., 1977.

PALMER, TONY, *All You Need Is Love: The Story of Popular Music*. New York: The Viking Press, 1976.

RUST, BRIAN, *The American Record Label Book*. New Rochelle, N.Y.: Arlington House, 1978.

SHEMEL, SIDNEY, AND M. WILLIAM KRASILOVSKY, *This Music Business*. New York: Billboard Publications, Inc., 1977.

SMITH, BILL, *The Vaudevillians*. New York: Billboard Publications, Inc., 1976.

STAMBLER, IRWIN, *Encyclopedia of Pop, Rock and Soul*. New York: St. Martin's Press, Inc., 1976.

TITON, JEFF TODD, *Early Downhome Blues: A Musical and Cultural Analysis*. Urbana: University of Illinois Press, 1977.

WEISSMAN, DICK, *The Music Business: Career Opportunities and Self-Defense*. New York: Crown Publishers, Inc., 1979.

WHITCOMB, IAN, *After the Ball: Pop Music from Rag to Rock*. Baltimore: Penguin Books, 1974.

10

Advertising and Public Relations

As either industry professionals or future consumers of mass communication, we should be aware that there are many people responsible for the messages disseminated by mass communication. There are people and organizations whose primary responsibility is to produce and prepare messages, especially commercial messages. Advertising agencies are one of the most important and active organizations that influence every facet of mass media.

Along with studying advertising and ad agencies, this chapter will examine public relations.

FUNCTIONS OF AD AGENCIES

Ad agencies first appeared in the late nineteenth century when newspapers began to rely less on government subsidies and more on commercial advertising to survive. The improved distribution systems of railroads and highways made newspaper advertising an attractive means of reaching a large number of people. Yet advertising still met resistance, not from consumers but from merchants who felt it was unorthodox to market their products in any way other than in a storefront display or a simple, typed paragraph in the paper. The creative ads in the pages of today's newspapers and magazines were unheard of in the late

1800s, mainly because the foundation for such an inventive service had yet to be laid. The newspaper publisher was concerned mainly with publishing, and the merchant was concerned mainly with running a business. There needed to be someone in the middle, someone who could develop the creative message necessary to take the merchant's product out of the typed column and into the limelight of reader attention. Early efforts at advertising were made by copywriters at the local newspaper. As the importance of their function was realized, however, they became independent agents, specialists whose talents were in great demand. Businesses realized that they needed the assistance of these specialists to compete successfully in the marketplace.

This modest beginning was the foundation of modern advertising and the ad agency. Today, ad agencies are found in virtually every major city in the world, and their role in stimulating economic growth is solidly established. To understand advertising, we need to examine the four principal functions of an ad agency: talent, research, distribution, and monitoring feedback.

talent

The basic function of an ad agency is providing *talent*. The creative efforts of the art director, the marketing savvy of the media buyer, the detailed analysis of the research director, and the political understanding of the campaign director are just a few examples of the many abilities ad agency personnel have to offer. A business, organization, or person will contract the services of an ad agency to help market a product. The product may be soap, the corporate image of a multimillion dollar company, a political figure, or a nonprofit organization.

research

The second function is research. In order to distribute the message to the public successfully, the agency first must know all that it can about the product. Imagine you are responsible for handling the advertising for a major lumber company. The company wants to develop an advertising campaign for a new by-product it has developed. This by-product is small chips of bark which previously have been burned as waste. It is your job to plan the advertising campaign.

One of your first jobs is to research the product and the company. You must learn everything you possibly can about both. Your research must even take you close to the heart of the firm's inner operations. In order for you to make effective advertising judgments that may involve thousands of dollars, you must know how that firm works. Occasionally research may reveal certain questionable business operations, dealings that may force your agency to withdraw from handling the campaign. Handling a disreputable firm's advertising may leave your agency with the problem of collecting money for your services, to say nothing of a lawsuit for fraudulent advertising and possible tangles with the

Federal Trade Commission. This research into the company and its product is called *product research*.

    Market research is the second type of research. It aims at finding the potential market for the new product. You will need to know if there are other products on the market that can successfully compete with your client's product. You will want to know where the customers for the product can be found. You will want to know the characteristics of your potential customers. Are they home owners? Are they apt to do their own gardening and yard work, or do they hire professional gardeners to do these tasks? Answers to these questions are part of market research.

distribution

The third important function is *distribution*. Here you will decide what type of *message* you are going to create for the company and what *media* will be most helpful in sending this message to the public. Let's assume that your research into the company's background gives it a clean bill of health and that you decide to continue with the account. You have learned that the bark chips make a good bedding to place around shrubbery. Next, you conduct further research into a possible name for the bark chips. Your research strikes a positive note on the name "Barko!" The name is catchy, it is easily remembered, and it carries the substance of the product into the name.

    Now comes the decision on how to tell the "Barko!" story to the public. It is time to call a meeting of the agency's department heads.

Account Executive: The lumber company has decided to market the small wood chips that are waste material when bark is ground off the logs. The chips are a few inches long and come in all shapes. They'll bag them in fifty pound sacks and we're calling it "Barko!"

Research Director: We've investigated the product and the market as thoroughly as possible. The bark chips are great for placing around shrubbery. We see the market as basically home owners who do their own gardening and yard work.

General Manager: It's a good account all around. The lumber company has been in business for fifty years, and they have an excellent credit rating. Any ideas on how to tell the story?

Art Director: I think some pictures toned with soft brown shades will tell the story best.

Production Director: OK, but don't go too far; color television has more potential than brown. Let's consider using some bright yellows, oranges, and greens.

Art Director: Since this stuff comes in all shapes and sizes, perhaps we could arrange a cartoon character around it.

General Manager: That's cutting our budget close. Cartoon production is too expensive with this account.

Photographer: We could shoot some sharp photography of sunlit patios with Barko around the shrubbery.

Copywriter: That might work well. We could develop a series of commercials to stress seasonal outdoor decorating.

Media Buyer: I envision running some ads in the syndicated section on gardening in the Sunday paper and tying in the theme to evening television and radio. Perhaps some billboards would also be helpful. In addition, I feel a brochure sent to all the gardening outlets in the state would be an excellent sales piece.

This conversation illustrates some of the numerous considerations in planning an advertising campaign. Notice how the development of the commercial message encompasses the creative talents of many people. Precisely because it would be too time consuming and costly to develop this expertise within the lumber company, its management hired the ad agency. Moreover, the people at the ad agency can look at the company's product objectively. They are not as closely associated with the product or the company so they can point out possible negative aspects of the product that should be considered.

monitoring feedback

The fourth function of an advertising agency is *monitoring feedback*. Although this may be accomplished in various ways and is not always included in the ad agency's contract, it can be an important part of the business-media relationship. Perhaps retailers receive complaints about Barkos. Perhaps there is a rival product, and the public is confusing your product with its competition. By monitoring consumer feedback, a decision on whether or not to revise the message, the medium, and/or the target audience can be made.

The preceding paragraphs have given us a brief look at the operation of an ad agency. As the business of reaching the public with information about new products becomes increasingly complex, the work of ad agencies becomes more and more important. No longer can a firm make a decision merely to advertise in a storefront window or in the local newspaper. Complex multimedia buying decisions, the psychology of attitudes toward styles and color combinations, and the ability to coordinate advertising messages across many different media all demand talent—talent based on the ad agency's years of expertise.

Many large, diversified corporations supplying national and international markets are developing their own ad agencies right within the company. These *in-house* agencies serve much the same function as an independent ad agency except that they deal exclusively with that company's products. Although there is some danger in being "too close" to the company and its line to treat them objectively, such dangers have not deterred the growth of in-house agencies.

If an advertising campaign has the backing of effective talent, research,

Figure 10-1 (General Cigar & Tobacco Co.)

distribution, and feedback, it has the best chance of succeeding. Today, more and more specialized advertising is developing, demanding new creativity by advertising personnel. Although some of the simplest campaigns have, over the years, been tremendously effective—campaigns like Mail Pouch Tobacco (Figure 10-1) and its painted barns—new campaigns demand specialized talent. For example, in many areas attorneys are advertising for the first time, and special consulting and advertising firms are devoting their talents to the law profession (Figure 10-2). Celebrities are used more and more in ads, and not only the

Figure 10-2 Advertisement for legal services.

Figure 10-3 Football star O. J. Simpson advertising Hertz Rent-A-Cars. FTC guidelines specify such celebrities must also use the products they advertise. (© Hertz Systems, Inc., 1975. Reprinted by permission)

Figure 10-4 Spanish language advertising retains a cultural identity while reaching a specific audience. (OMAR)

creative talents of an ad agency but legal talents are required to understand the regulations of complex contracts between stars and the products and agencies with which they are associated (Figure 10-3).

Ad agencies are developing to reach ethnic audiences and some of the most effective advertising includes ads written in the native language of the target audience (Figure 10-4). All of these specialized campaigns are creating new demands on agencies and are requiring new talents for people who work in advertising.

ECONOMICS OF AD AGENCIES

Two arguments can be heard by agency personnel whenever they gather. One executive will claim his or her agency is doing well because the economy is doing well. Another will claim that because the economy is in bad shape, businesses are advertising more, and thus the agency is doing well. Both arguments are valid and reflect some of the concerns of being in a business that is "in the middle."

ad agency income

Much of the income of an agency comes from the discounts it receives from media. Most discounts, which are in effect agency commissions, are approximately 15 percent. With the exception of newspapers, which generally still refrain from giving agency discounts, this percentage is fairly standard in all media. By the way of illustration, assume that you are advertising "Barkos" and that your ad agency is going to spend $10,000 advertising "Barkos" in a gardening magazine. You contact the gardening magazine and purchase a $10,000 full-color insert. After the ad runs, the gardening magazine bills your ad agency for $8,500 ($10,000 minus 15 percent). Your ad agency pays that bill and then bills the company that manufactures "Barkos" for $10,000. When the manufacturer pays its account, your agency has received $1,500 income in the transaction. Of course, the agency's costs must come out of the $1,500, so that this is by no means clear profit. The American Association of Advertising Agencies estimates that in a typical large agency, media commissions represent about 75 percent of the agency's income. In smaller agencies, the percentage drops to as low as 55 percent. The reason for this difference is that large agencies usually cater to large markets where a thirty-second radio commercial may cost $250. Fifteen percent of $250 makes a nice commission. But smaller agencies in markets where $10 buys a thirty-second spot simply cannot exist on the commission alone. They must have other income.

Other income can be realized through an agency's own percentage charges. For instance, an agency may have a printing job to complete for a client. The printer allows the agency a 20 percent discount on the job to attract and keep the agency's business. We shall assume the nondiscount rate for the printing job is $500. With the 20 percent discount, the agency is billed only $400 ($500 minus 20 percent). The agency then bills the client for $475, keeping $75 as a commission. Although the client still pays a fee over and above what the agency is charged, the client is still receiving the service at less cost ($25 less) than if he or she had placed the printing order directly with the printing company.

Some ad agencies have even entered into special arrangements with manufacturers in which they not only handle a company's advertising, but also process orders for goods and services provided or sold by that company. For instance, an ad agency might handle the advertising for a new cooking utensil. In the media campaign, the agency purchases ads in leading homemaker magazines and issues press releases to media outlets that might give the new product free publicity. The agency then processes the orders for the new product and takes a commission on the gross sales, such as $5.00 on each utensil sold. These arrangements are not a general practice with all ad agencies, but they have proved successful for smaller agencies that have a limited market in which to secure accounts. Other income has been realized by agencies conducting executive workshops, sales training seminars, and other activities.

Within the agencies, there are many different arrangements for commissions and income. Any agency-client relationship, of course, rests on an agreement that is mutually satisfactory. Some agencies, for instance, provide different classes of service in accordance with clients, needs, wishes, and, most importantly, budgets. More experienced personnel and those with proven creative abilities may be enlisted to serve clients wanting the best service possible. Newer personnel may be engaged for lower quality, less expensive projects. Some large accounts from which the agency receives a major share of its income will receive top-of-the-line service simply because of the importance of retaining such a lucrative account. Different services within the agency also can affect the final cost to the client. For example, additional use of the secretarial force does not raise the cost of the total package anywhere near as much as extra hours of an art director's talent.

public relations

Agencies with extensive public relations work will command a larger proportion of their client's dollars than agencies concerned mostly with placing media buys. Public relations services for a client include such things as meeting with media representatives on behalf of the client, sending press releases to media, visiting trade fairs, organizing promotional luncheons, and so on. Whenever such activities are involved, there is less outflow of cash for media buys and more retained within the agency. The actual amount of these "services" can account for as much as 50 percent of an agency's income.

future costs of making impressions

One factor that will largely determine the income of ad agencies in the future is the actual cost of advertising—placing a message with a particular medium to reach a target audience. Let's examine how one medium, television, will require more of the ad dollar to reach a target audience, women, between now and 1985. This future perspective was offered at a meeting of the Association of National Advertisers by Andrew Kershaw.[1] It illustrates how the cost of reaching women is increasing, but that the impressions—the number of times a person is reached by an ad—are decreasing. Figure 10-5 shows that in 1965, a $5-million ad budget spent on daytime network television would have reached all women, eighteen years old and over, ninety-six times that year. However, that same ad budget in 1985 will reach that same audience only twenty-four times. The cost of keeping up with the 1965 impressions also becomes substantial. Figure 10-6 illustrates how the increase will be almost 300 percent for daytime network television. In other words, in 1985 it will be necessary to spend $20 million in daytime network television to make the same ninety-six impressions per woman that $5 million

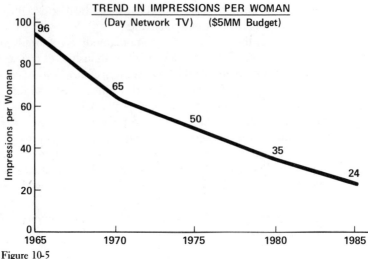

Figure 10-5

bought in 1965. Similar cost effectiveness is felt in nighttime network television. It will be necessary to spend $14.6 million in nighttime network television advertising in 1985 to make the same thirty-eight impressions per woman that $5 million purchased in 1965. An expenditure of $5 million in nighttime network television in 1985 would make only thirteen impressions per 100 women. Kershaw points out that "advertising budgets are not going to grow at that rate" and that "research budgets are not going to grow at that rate." Kershaw's prediction for the future?—a necessity for more effective advertising and, in the case of

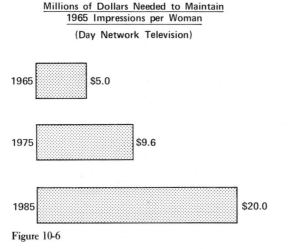

Figure 10-6

television, shorter commercials. The talents of the ad agency seem to be assured of an even more receptive market.

the agency's position

The agencies themselves, however, are in the unique position of remaining flexible and of still making money despite increasing costs. There are two important reasons for this. One is that the ad agency takes its commission from the overall purchase price of the advertising. If the cost of purchasing advertising time increases, then the agency's commission increases proportionately. Second, in a highly competitive market that takes advertising glamour for granted, most businesses find themselves willing to spend gigantic sums only to obtain the most for their advertising dollars.

TYPES OF ADVERTISING

The most common types of advertising are *standard advertising* and *public service advertising*. In addition, contemporary social issues and governmental regulations have induced new types of advertising. Among these are *social responsibility advertising, counter-advertising, corrective advertising, advocacy advertising,* and *image advertising*. Let's examine the different types of advertising in more detail.

standard advertising

Standard ads appear in all media and are financed by the company or organization that has products to sell or services to render. The motive is to sell and to create in the consumer a feeling of need and desire for a product or service. Decisions as to the type of message the ads will use, in what media they will be placed, and how often they will appear in the media are usually made by the manufacturer or distributor, sometimes in conjunction with an ad agency. Once these decisions are made, time or space is purchased, and a contract is signed specifying such things as the number of times the ad will appear, when it will appear, and in the case of billboards, at what location. There is usually some type of tangible market feedback to judge the ads' effectiveness, such as the number of sales resulting directly from the ad. Standard advertising is the financial lifeblood of commercial mass media.

public service advertising

Public service advertising supports nonprofit causes and organizations. Time or space for this type of advertising is provided free as a service to the public by the print or broadcast media. Most public service advertising is to solicit contributions of either time or money for the nonprofit enterprise. Contributions to organizations such as the Red Cross are received almost exclusively through public service advertising.

Federal regulations demand that a certain amount of broadcast media time be devoted to public service programming. Public service announcements (PSAs), more evident in American broadcasting than anywhere else, run a regular schedule with the commercials. They usually last anywhere from a few seconds to five minutes, the most common lengths being thirty or sixty seconds.

Prime time on broadcasting networks devoted to PSAs is a valuable commodity worth many thousands of dollars. As a result, there is considerable competition among nonprofit organizations to obtain exposure for public service advertising.

Public service advertising in the print media is concentrated mainly in those magazines that devote free space to nonprofit organizations. Although there is no legal requirement for the print media to do so, most magazines cooperate with the Advertising Council and contribute advertising space. Major outdoor companies also cooperate with nonprofit organizations and provide public service space. Outdoor companies, however, expend considerable effort in designing and pasting up the bulletin. Moreover, they must usually foot the rental for the property on which the bulletin is displayed.

social responsibility advertising

A screech of tires, the sound of smashing glass, twisting metal, and the plea to "drive safely." This message is the subject of radio and television messages which are especially plentiful during holiday seasons. The safe driving ads and others which admonish us to act responsibly belong to social responsibility advertising. These ads are usually sponsored by either a nonprofit organization such as the National Safety Council, not linked to any one industry, or special public relations organizations representing a particular industry.

An example of the latter is the Distilled Spirits Council of the United States, Inc. The Council is the public information and research arm of the distilled spirits industry. A major campaign of the Council through its Licensed Beverage Industries division is to instill responsibility in drinking (Figure 10-7). Its advertisements have a dual purpose: raising the public's consciousness about drinking, and informing the media that the industry is taking an active role in promoting a responsible attitude toward alcohol consumption. The major thrust of this campaign came just after cigarette commercials were banned on television. Although, because of the NAB Codes, advertisements for hard liquor seldom appear in broadcasting, there is nothing to prevent a major anti-drinking campaign from developing in a fashion similar to the anti-smoking campaign. Perhaps if the cigarette industry had provided a "responsibility in smoking" advertising campaign, cigarette ads would still be running on radio and television. The distilled spirits industry is thus applying the extremely effective public

You're old enough to drink.
But are you mature enough?

The legal voting age has been lowered recently.
So has the legal drinking age in many areas.
Both trends show growing confidence in the maturity of our young citizens.
But with every privilege comes a responsibility.
Young men and women who choose to exercise the privilege of social drinking, should learn to exercise a sense of responsibility. Above all, they should not pressure friends who choose not to drink.
This new generation is the best-informed, best-educated in our history. We hope it will drink responsibly. The vast majority of older Americans do.
If you choose to drink, drink responsibly.

LICENSED BEVERAGE INDUSTRIES
Division of Distilled Spirits Council of the United States, Inc.
485 Lexington Avenue, New York, N.Y. 10017

Figure 10-7 Social responsibility advertising.

relations technique of combatting poor publicity before a significant image problem can arise.

There are many other types of social responsibility advertising besides the two we have already mentioned. Significant campaigns to use natural resources responsibly have become common, and land use planning, fire prevention, and wildlife management are just three examples. Energy conservation has also received wide exposure in ads sponsored by nonprofit industries and in some cases the energy companies themselves.

counter-advertising

One of the most controversial types of advertising is counter-advertising, advertising directed *against* a product or service. Counter-ads directed against *specific* products are rarely seen on a national scale. Nevertheless, industry and public concern over such ads has become significant. Advocates of counter-advertising claim that standard advertising does not sufficiently inform the public to enable

consumers to make intelligent buying decisions; counter-ads are therefore necessary to counteract some of the allegedly unwarranted claims found in standard
advertising. Some familiar counter-ads are those which warn against abusive
collection practices by credit agencies, the dangers of air and water pollution
(Figure 10-8), and cigarette smoking.

Broadcasters have put up considerable resistance to counter-advertising.
The National Association of Broadcasters as well as the Television Information
Office, both professional groups representing the broadcasting industry, have
opposed widespread requirements for stations to run counter-ads.

The effectiveness of counter-advertising is still moot despite recent research
efforts. Bayer aspirin counter-ads apparently made Bayer users adopt a more
cautious attitude toward the product, but the statistical figures were not significant.[2] There was no indication that in a real-life situation attitudes would have
changed significantly, that peer group decisions about the product might have
contradicted the effectiveness of the ads, or that the decrease in favorable attitude
would have remained over time.

Counter-advertising remains a concern of mass media. The interpretation
of the Fairness Doctrine in broadcasting, the possibility of lawsuits against other

Figure 10-8 Counter-advertising.

media, and the liability for broadcasting and printing unfounded claims in product advertisements certainly are not taken lightly by media executives. At the very least, the issue of counter-advertising has made media management stop, consider, and scrutinize the content of advertising.

corrective advertising

"Super bloopers make your feet run faster." "This vitamin cures all ills." "Thirst-quench has better nutrients than any other drink." Exaggerated claims such as these are prime targets for corrective advertising, which are attempts, usually instigated by regulatory orders, to correct false or misleading advertising.

Many government agencies participate in policing advertising claims, including the FCC, FTC, and the Food and Drug Administration, but the agency responsible for ordering corrective advertising is the FTC (Figure 10-9). The others assume more of a preventive role. The Food and Drug Administration, for instance, has established strict rules of ingredient disclosure, thus guarding against deceptive food and drug labeling. Similarly, the FCC strongly encourages radio and television station management to reject advertising that may be deceptive.

The classic case of corrective advertising occurred in 1971 when the FTC reached an agreement with the ITT Continental Baking Company to correct advertising that implied that eating the company's Profile Bread would result in weight loss. According to the FTC, Profile Bread was no different from other breads except that the slices were thinner. The baking company was ordered to stop using weight loss as a pitch and to spend part of its advertising budget over a one-year period to tell the public that its bread was not an effective weight reducer. The result was a television commercial with the script:

> I'd like to clear up any misunderstandings you may have about Profile Bread from its advertising or even its name. Does Profile have fewer calories than other breads? No, Profile has about the same per ounce as other breads. To be exact, Profile has 7 fewer calories per slice. That's because it is sliced thinner. But eating Profile will not cause you to lose weight. . . .

The FTC also ordered the maker of Listerine mouthwash to start including in its advertising a statement to read, "contrary to prior advertising, Listerine will not prevent colds or sore throats or lessen their severity." The company denied that it had claimed the mouthwash was a cold cure and readied an appeal.

Obviously, there are arguments for and against corrective advertising. Supporting arguments claim that the ads are necessary to put the "bite" on companies that readily defy regulatory measures. In addition, they are necessary to inform the public that misleading claims do appear and that therefore the consumer should be more critical of advertising. Negative arguments say that years

---

ADVERTISEMENT

WALL STREET JOURNAL
February 10, 1978

FTC NOTICE

As a result of an investigation by the
Federal Trade Commission into certain allegedly
inaccurate past advertisements
for STP's oil additive, STP Corporation
has agreed to a $700,000 settlement.
With regard to that settlement,
STP is making the following statement:

It is the policy of STP to support its advertising with objective information and test data. In
1974 and 1975 an independent laboratory ran tests
of the company's oil additive which led to claims of
reduced oil consumption. However, these tests
cannot be relied on to support the oil consumption
reduction claim made by STP.

The FTC has taken the position that, in making that claim, the company violated the terms of a
consent order. When STP learned that the test data
did not support the claim, it stopped advertising
containing that claim. New tests have been undertaken to determine the extent to which the oil additive affects oil consumption. Agreement to this
settlement does not constitute an, admission by STP
that the law has been violated. Rather, STP has
agreed to resolve the dispute with the FTC to avoid
protracted and prohibitively expensive litigation.

February 10, 1978

Figure 10-9 Corrective advertising.

will have passed by the time the wheels of the enforcement process begin to turn
and a misleading advertiser has been made to retract claims it has made for its
product. Others claim that people are attracted by the novelty of the corrective
ads, which call their attention to the product rather than to the corrective message and that the regulatory purpose of the ad is therefore defeated.

advocacy advertising

Closely related to counter-advertising is advocacy advertising. Whereas counter-
advertising is normally directed at a particular objectionable product, a company

producing such a product, or an industry responsible for creating a societal ill, advocacy advertising champions preventive action against illegal or illegitimate activities affecting the public welfare. Ads raising our awareness of heroin addiction, the rising crime rate, and impoverished conditions in the ghetto are all examples of advocacy advertising. In most cases, advocacy advertising is sponsored and paid for by an organization which wants to be associated with community involvement. The ads may or may not be directed toward the sponsor's own business interest. The Distilled Spirits Council, which we learned has sponsored the responsibility in drinking ads, has also warned against the ills of moonshine liquor. Moonshine is illegal but can also cut into the profits of licensed distillers.

Advocacy advertising is finding more and more sponsors as companies and organizations want to gain the added benefit of directing a message against a common fault of society while at the same time keeping their name visible to the public.

image advertising

For many corporations, especially oil companies, image advertising has become very important. It is part of many companies' natural public relations function. They may go to great lengths to show how they were working to protect or reclaim the environment during drilling and exploration. Such scenes as waterfowl flying in front of an oil rig or the rays of a setting sun across reclaimed grassland are designed to create a favorable corporate image. Other image advertising is more direct and deals head-on with issues confronting a particular company or industry. Mobil Oil has taken a particularly strong stand in its ads, frequently clashing with journalists' positions on the oil industry and Mobil.

ADVERTISING APPEALS

As consumers of mass communication, understanding advertising also is understanding the different appeals used in advertising messages. Two of the most common appeal to an individual's values and basic needs.

value appeals

Values are broad-based characteristics of a population defined as *standards that influence individuals to choose between alternative behaviors.* Values are a product of our early childhood development and hence are not easily changed. Since they form the basis for many of our decisions, appeals to our value structures are very common in mass communication.

Most researchers have defined the range of values into six broad categories: *aesthetic, humanitarian, intellectual, materialistic, prestigious,* and *religious.* Looking at each of these values separately, we can recognize the value-oriented appeals found in advertising. For example, aesthetic appeals attempt to evoke a

Figure 10-10 Aesthetic value appeal. (Produced for Vail Associates, Inc. by Advantage Vail. Photo by Peter Runyan)

sense of beauty and grace in our environment (Figure 10-10). Humanitarian value appeals are some of the most widely used in advertising and can reach across cultural boundaries. Love and respect of people are the basis of humanitarian appeals (Figure 10-11). Intellectual appeals on the other hand, are based on an individual's love and respect for knowledge.

Some of the most dominant and most frequent value appeals found in advertising are those directed to materialistic and prestige values. We are an acquiring people who enjoy having possessions and the money to purchase them. Our orientation into materialism begins when we acquire our first toys and continues from there. Regardless of whether or not materialistic values are dominant, people usually make decisions based on their "money's worth." Similarly,

Figure 10-11 Humanitarian value appeal. (American Telephone and Telegraph Company, Long Lines Department)

prestige values are closely matched to our desire to obtain some form of power and position among our peers. When an advertising campaign equates wearing a certain suit with leadership, it is appealing to our desire for prestige.

Appeals to religious values are not used as frequently in advertising as other value appeals are. It is difficult to relate consumer product demand to the worship of a supernatural being. Religious appeals are used principally to persuade people to attend church or to make religion more relevant to their daily lives. Religious appeals are most strongly felt by those whose value orientation is predominantly religious; for example, as a group, the elderly tend to be more oriented toward religion than some younger generations are (Figure 10-12).

"There's nothing I can do. I'm just one person."

Do you really think God is going to let you get away with that?

If you feel one person is too insignificant to help make the world a better place, then work together with others at your local church or synagogue. Example: in Montana, one congregation was disturbed by the lack of adequate housing for senior citizens in the area. Through its perseverance, a non-profit building with 111 homes is now a reality. There are lots of things you can do, too. The God we worship expects more from us than sympathy and good intentions.

Start treating your brothers and sisters like brothers and sisters.

RELIGION IN AMERICAN LIFE

A Public Service of This Magazine & The Advertising Council   Ad Council

Figure 10-12 Religious value appeal.

**Give him a Christian Dior shirt and tie for Christmas.
And stay home New Year's Eve.**

*Think of the most elegant name in fashion.
Think of the man in your life. Wouldn't they look great together?
Christian Dior for this Christmas, this New Year's Eve,
and all year long. At fine stores everywhere.*

Figure 10-13 Sex appeal in advertising. (C. F. Hathaway Company)

appeals to basic needs

Everyone shares certain biological and psychological needs. The three basic ones are *food*, *shelter*, and *sex*. We need food to live, we need protection from the elements to survive, and we have a biological sex drive to enable the species to survive. Much of the content of advertising is designed to appeal to these needs. Food products, for instance, consume a sizeable portion of most media advertising income. It is no accident that among children, Ronald McDonald is the most recognizable character next to Santa Claus. Breakfast cereals predominate on Saturday morning television, and savory sauces precede, permeate, and parcel the evening news. Exhausted athletes quenching their thirst with fruit drink and families barbecuing steaks in the back yard all are part of food product advertising.

Another common appeal and sometimes a controversial one, is sex appeal in advertising (Figure 10-13). It can be subtle, as in a commercial for eye glasses, or more direct, as in some advertisements in leading men's and women's magazines. All are based on the fact that people are sexually attracted to each other. Multimillion dollar industries have developed around cosmetics, hair coloring, after shave lotions, padded bras, toothpaste, bikinis, toupées, perfume, and hard liquor, to name a few. Some of the most successful sex appeal themes have been used to market health foods and diet drinks.

The women's rights movement has had some strong criticism for sex-appeal advertising. In one state, protests arose over the use of a billboard advertisement in which a woman dressed in black velvet was used to sell hard liquor, likening its taste to the soft touch of velvet. In another case, when singing star Susan Anton showed up in a men's locker room selling Muriel cigars, one television network even refused to air the commercial (Figure 10-14).

Shelter, like food, is somewhat limited and is usually directly related to building products or similar items. Often combined with materialistic values, such shelter-oriented ads as good investments in a home, long-lasting weather siding, leakproof shingles for the roof, or dual-pane insulated windows are common. Occasionally, motels and hotels have also used the shelter appeal on a theme of "coming in out of the storm."

Again, it is important to remember that seldom are any of the appeals we have discussed used exclusively. For instance, as you sit in front of your television set or read the evening newspaper, the message that states that the new car is priced $500 cheaper also says it will add prestige to your life, will probably enhance your sex appeal, and has beauty equivalent to a fine artistic masterpiece. Likewise, the appeal for your vote on the city bond issue will more than likely stress that your children's health and education are at stake and that you will save gasoline by not having to take your garbage to the city dump. As consumers of

Figure 10-14 (DKG Advertising, Inc. and Consolidated Cigar Corporation)

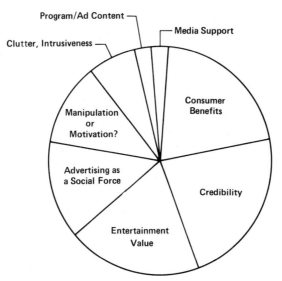

Figure 10-15 The extent to which opinion about each issue contributes to overall attitudes towards advertising.

mass communication, you should become familiar with these various appeals and learn to identify them. With this knowledge, you will be able to make more intelligent and critical judgments of the issues and products the appeals are designed to support.

OUR PERCEPTIONS OF ADVERTISING

How do we feel about advertising? The answer to that may depend on how we have been taught to react to advertising and to the quality of advertising in the area in which we reside. The American Association of Advertising Agencies (AAAA) has studied the issue and found that our opinions of advertising are principally influenced by the advertising we see on television. Naturally, newspaper, radio, and magazine advertisements also have their effect. Direct mail and billboards contribute the least to our opinions of advertising. The AAAA study also showed that the issues about which we are most concerned are advertising's credibility, entertainment value, advertising as a social force, and consumer benefits (Figure 10-15). We are concerned about how advertising manipulates and motivates us, its clutter and intrusiveness, its content, and media support of advertising as an institution. Of these, our negative opinions center on its credibility, content, intrusiveness, and its ability to manipulate and motivate us.

Advertising has been criticized by some for turning us into a materialistic society, isolating the poor who cannot afford the majority of products splashed across billboards, the television screen, and countless other media. Advertising also has been held responsible for creating an artificial demand for products that we do not need and in some cases are actually harmful to us. Counter-advertising, corrective advertising, and social responsibility advertising have emerged from this concern to change the tide of mass persuasion more toward the public's welfare and away from commercial exploitation. Ad executives speaking on college campuses are fielding questions about why the agencies are continually producing ads that show women in their traditional roles as house-wives and childbearers, thus supporting the status quo and perpetuating tra-ditional role models for young children. These and many other considerations will remain important concerns. One thing is certain—advertising is a major force in our society. It is an important part of media content and has perhaps a greater effect on our lives than any other type of media message. For this reason, it is important to know as much as possible about all types of advertising mes-sages.

PUBLIC RELATIONS

Public relations is directly related to advertising. In fact, there is only a very fine line distinguishing them. Whereas advertising is concerned with selling a prod-uct, public relations is concerned with creating a favorable image for the com-pany that produces the product. As responsible consumers of mass communica-tion, we need to be aware that many of the messages we receive through the mass media are concerned with public relations. The thin line between public rela-tions and advertising is evident when a fast-food chain sponsors a bike-a-thon for a national charity. In the charity ads, the food company's name and trademark are used in the same way that they are used to sell sandwiches, yet the message solicits participation in the bike-a-thon. What the company is trying to do is create a favorable impression for itself as well as interest the public in its product.

philosophy of public relations

Why bother with public relations? Why not just concentrate on selling sandwiches? That may be satisfactory if the company's only goal is to sell sandwiches at their current locations. But what if the chain wants to expand? Perhaps the next community in which it plans to build a restaurant has had bad experiences with a similar food chain. As the request for the company's restau-rant comes before the zoning board, there is much negative reaction to the application. However, the company officials remind the board and the con-cerned citizens about their involvement in local charities with their national bike-a-thon. This public relations event may be just what is needed to garner approval for the building application.

A major criticism of public relations is that too often it is similar to shutting the barn door after the horse has escaped. Effective public relations programs should help *prevent* problems in image and public opinion before they occur, not afterwards.

Many public relations firms work closely with professional organizations that act as a voice for certain industries. National organizations such as the American Gas Association work to help identify critical issues concerning the gas industry and to gain public support for the industry through national campaigns. The Mortgage Bankers Association represents much of the banking industry and actually presents journalism awards for stories related to banking. The contest, along with publicizing the banking industry to the news media, also promotes special features, articles, and documentaries carrying the message of the financial world to the public.

Professional organizations on the state level also carry on public relations campaigns and media awards programs. For example, the Indiana Public Health Association conducts an annual awards contest to recognize media organizations for excellence in three categories: best in-depth factual presentation of a health matter, best promotional activity on a health matter, and best support given to public health programs on a continuing basis.

As with any media award given by an association whose first function is public relations, a question of ethics immediately arises: Should a journalistic medium compete for public relations awards?

Public relations will continue to be important to mass communication, especially because the media themselves are important in forming public opinion. Public relations will be a vital function of organizations whose best interests are served by favorable publicity.

the publicity function

Publicity is another important aspect of public relations. In most cases, publicity deals directly with the gatekeepers who control the flow of news. The forces directed toward such gatekeeprs can be tremendous. These people are usually bombarded with telephone calls from press agents, piles of press releases on everything from new products to politicians, tickets to free dinners at which a politician is appearing or a company is delivering its latest annual report, and countless other tactics from people and organizations all trying to receive free media exposure. If they successfully receive this free exposure, it often is more valuable than media exposure obtained through advertising campaigns. For example, a feature article of a new product in a national magazine may elicit a much greater reader response than an advertisement for the new product. Readers who see the product in the feature article are not resistant to its message as they may be to the message in an advertisement. If a politician makes a favorable impression on the evening news, the publicity can be much more credible than if he or she appears in a paid political advertisement.

Those whose job it is to obtain free publicity work very hard at it, sometimes with limited results. In many news rooms, personnel are so accustomed to press releases that they often do not bother to open certain mail. The letterhead is enough to tip them off. In most cases, the press releases are tossed away because the person trying to obtain free publicity has done one of two things. This person has probably first inundated the media with almost daily press releases. Rarely does a single subject or politician warrant that much publicity. After all, if you were a regular reader of a newspaper and saw that every issue had a story about a local congressman or congresswoman, you would begin to grow somewhat suspicious of the paper's credibility. Second, many press releases try to masquerade as news. The press release begins with a lead sentence that might be used to introduce a major international event; the second paragraph reveals, however, that the politician is simply speaking to the ladies' aid society. The gatekeeper thus loses trust in the source of the press release and tends to shy away from future releases.

Publicity, when it is effective, can reap many rewards. One of the more successful publicity campaigns was in Oregon where a teacher at a community college invented an "executive toy." This toy was made with a line of steel balls hung in a row on individual strings from a small wood frame about nine inches square. Using Newton's Third Law of Motion, which says that for every action there is an equal and opposite reaction, you pull one of the steel balls back, let it go, and the steel ball at the other end of the line will bounce while all the other steel balls remained stationary. Beverly Green, president of Green/Associates Advertising, Inc., was responsible for successfully marketing the gadget through free publicity. The publicity campaign included sending letters, press releases, and samples of the novel toy to newspapers, television stations, and magazines throughout the United States. The toy appeared in such publications as *Playboy*, *Newsweek*, *Boy's Life*, and *House Beautiful*. It also appeared on such national television shows as the "Today Show", Johnny Carson's "Tonight Show," the "Merv Griffin Show," the "Joey Bishop Show," and the "Steve Allen Show." This media publicity brought the toy to the attention of millions of people, of whom 200,000 purchased their own by the end of the first year of production.

This is just one example of how free publicity was used to market a product. The channels of mass communication are limited, so the competition is fierce. Yet when you can gain exposure on the media, it can have far-reaching results.

SUMMARY

Advertising agencies are responsible for many of the commercial messages in the mass media. The main asset of the advertising agency is talent. The creative talents of such people as the production director, research director, general manager, photographer, copywriter, media buyer, and account executive are all combined. This "team" of creative people works to call the attention of the public to a product or service. Along with talent, the ad agency uses research, distribution, and monitoring feedback.

There also are many different types of advertising. Standard advertising, the most common, attempts to persuade us to purchase certain products and services. Public service ads are those devised by nonprofit organizations to answer a public need. Social responsibility ads seek to warn us against the dangers inherent in the excessive use of some product. Counter-advertising concentrates on warning consumers about alleged fraud or misrepresentation in advertising. Corrective advertising is employed when an enforcement agency has determined that a previous ad has misrepresented a product. Image advertising, on the other hand, operates much like public relations. Overall, advertising is accepted as an important part of any economic system, and a large majority of the population feels that it creates better products for society. Advertising messages continually surround us. Our value structures, attitudes, and basic needs affect how we perceive these messages.

Public relations campaigns are the most effective when they help prevent problems before they exist. Working closely with professional organizations and the news media is part of a good public relations program, and some products have even been marketed successfully through public relations alone.

OPPORTUNITIES FOR FURTHER LEARNING

AAKER, DAVID A., and JOHN G. MYERS, *Advertising Management.* Englewood Cliffs, N.J.: Prentice-Hall, Inc., 1975.

BLOOM, PAUL N., *Advertising Competition and Public Policy: A Simulation Study.* Cambridge, Mass.: Ballinger, 1976.

CHASE, COCHRANE, and KENNETH L. BARASCH, *Marketing Problem Solver.* Radnor, Pa.: Chilton Book Co., 1977.

DeLOZIER, M. WAYNE, *The Marketing Communications Process.* New York: McGraw-Hill Book Company, 1976.

DUNN, S. W., and A. M. BARDAN, *Advertising: Its Role in Modern Marketing.* Hinsdale, Ill.: The Dryden Press, 1978.

Evaluating Advertising: A Bibliography of the Communications Process. New York: Advertising Research Foundation, 1978.

EWEN, STUART, *Captains of Consciousness: Advertising and the Social Roots of the Consumer Culture.* New York: McGraw-Hill Book Company, 1976.

FOWLES, JIB, *Mass Advertising as Social Forecast: A Method for Futures Research* Westport, Conn.: Greenwood Press, 1976.

HARRIS, MORGAN, and PATTI KARP, *How to Make News and Influence People.* Blue Ridge Summit, Pa.: TAB Books, 1976.

LEYMORE, VARDA LANGHOLZ, *Hidden Myth: Structure and Symbolism in Advertising.* New York: Basic Books, Inc., Publishers, 1975.

LITTLEFIELD, JAMES E., ed., *Readings in Advertising: Current Viewpoints on Selected Topics.* St. Paul: West Publishing Co., 1975.

NEWSON, DOUG, and ALAN SCOTT, *This is PR: The Realities of Public Relations.* Belmont, Calif.: Wadsworth Publishing Co., Inc., 1976.

PRESTON, IVAN L., *The Great American Blow-Up: Puffery in Advertising and Selling.* Madison: University of Wisconsin Press, 1975.

QUERA, LEON, *Advertising Campaigns: Formulation and Tactics.* Columbus, Ohio: Grid, Inc., 1977.

ROSS, ROBERT D., *The Management of Public Relations: Analysis and Planning External Relations.* New York: John Wiley & Sons, Inc., 1977.

SETHI, S. PRAKASH, *Advocacy Advertising and Large Corporations: Social Conflict, Big Business Image, the News Media, and Public Policy.* Lexington,

WEINER, RICHARD, *Profession's Guide to Publicity.* New York: Richard Weiner, Inc., 1976.

WRIGHT, JOHN S., DANIEL S. WARNER, WILLIS L. WINTER, JR., and SHERILYN K. ZEIGLER, *Advertising,* 4th ed. McGraw-Hill Book Company, 1977.

11

Mass Media News

Of all the messages processed through mass communication, news is certainly one of the most important. But the news we read in the evening newspaper or watch on television does not reach us through a set of formulas. Many forces are at work in this process, including human forces which are subject to mistakes, misjudgements, misunderstandings, and biases.

In this chapter, we shall study the qualities of news, what affects its dissemination, and those forces that affect the gatekeepers who process it. We shall begin by examining the difference between gatekeeper chains and gatekeeper groups.

THE GATEKEEPER CHAIN

There is a *gatekeeper chain* when more than one gatekeeper processes the same news story with a *limited amount of feedback* from other gatekeepers in the chain. To understand the concept, imagine that you are a newspaper reporter assigned to the scene of a flood (Figure 11-1). You interview people, survey the damage, and write up the report. You (G_1) then call your story back to the city

desk reporter (G₂) who takes down all the information and rewrites your story to
read:

> The Clearwater River overflowed its banks today near the downtown sec-
> tion of Pineville. First reports are that two persons sustained minor injuries
> and three homes were destroyed.

The city editor (G₃) then reads the story and changes it to:

> Flash flooding hit Pineville today as the Clearwater River overflowed its
> banks, destroying homes and injuring residents in the area.

Now the story goes to a major wire service bureau in the state. The bureau
receives a continual inflow of information from all over the region and uses this
information to prepare a report for its subscribers. At the wire service, a reporter
(G₄) works to collate all the information about flood damage. Reports are coming
in from all over the state, telling of property damage and numerous injuries.
Compiling all of this information, the wire service story is sent to subscribers and
reads:

> Flash floods swept over the state today doing millions of dollars in damages
> and injuring more than 100 persons. Pineville and other cities were hit by
> the sudden storms.

Obviously, the story that reaches the wire service subscribers is entirely
different from the one you originally reported from the scene at Pineville. Nevertheless, word for word, there have been millions of dollars in damages, more
than 100 persons have been injured, and Pineville is one of the communities
which has been hit. On the other hand, a person who read the wire service
description and had relatives in Pineville could easily have been left with the
impression that the town had been swept off the map. Rearrangement of the

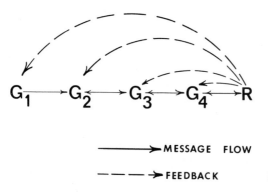

——————→ MESSAGE FLOW

— — — —→ FEEDBACK   **Figure 11-1** Gatekeeper chain.

Maybe More, Maybe Less Who Knows?

What if you held a political rally and lots of people came? Fob James Jr. did, but no one is exactly sure how many.

At Saturday's barbecue and rally, workers say they served 6,000 plates of barbecue. Yet some folks went back for seconds, or even thirds, and some didn't eat at all.

Capt. Ronald Dunson of the Opelika Police Department, giving a requested, unofficial estimate, said between 6,000 and 8,000 persons attend-

ed. Yet the Auburn High stadium, where the rally was held, has a seating capacity of only 4,000, and at no time Saturday night was it full. On the other hand there were those who spent the time mingling above the bleachers, and never did sit down.

There was no "official" count, so the crowd size, we surmise, was somewhere between the "few hundred" reported by a radio station in Auburn, and our maybe-too-generous 6,000 to 8,000.

Figure 11-2 (*Source: Auburn-Opelika News*)

factual material, minor changes made in the story by the various gatekeepers, and the merging facts at the wire service all led to a variation in the story.

News distortion in a gatekeeper chain can be frequent, especially when a central clearing house for information, such as a wire service or other news bureau, has conflicting information from which to compile a report. Crowd estimates can be particularly difficult (Figure 11-2). Different news organizations covering the same story can report significant variations in the estimates of a crowd. A political rally, protest, convention, or other news event may look either like a small gathering of a few friends or a large assembly, depending on who is looking. When these variations are transmitted back to the wire service, there is bound to be distortion.

THE GATEKEEPER GROUP

Now we shall examine a *gatekeeper group* (Figure 11-3). Gatekeeper groups can operate at any point within a gatekeeper chain. The advantage that such groups have is that they permit interaction among gatekeepers. Interpersonal communication among members of the group results in greater accuracy, simply because the information can be discussed and checked before it is disseminated to the public. The message is clarified, changed, rewritten, and evaluated by each member of the group.

Consider what might have happened to the flood story at any point in the

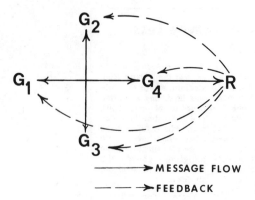

Figure 11-3 Gatekeeper group.

gatekeeper chain if there had been a gatekeeper group. The conversation among the group might have sounded like this:

OK, what have you been able to pick up?
Well, it wasn't too bad at Pineville, just some homes lost.
I checked with the sheriff, and he said the two injuries were to children.
Were they hurt very badly?
No, but the family dog drowned and a ten-year-old girl almost drowned trying to save it.
That might be good to note. Stories like this can become too impersonal.
Good idea. I wouldn't have thought of that.
I'll write up a draft, and then you can check it over.
OK. I'll see if there's an update.
The interaction permitted a check and a recheck of the story's content.

Gatekeeper chains and gatekeeper groups have many different combinations. The presence or absence of either does not mean news distortion *will* occur. It simply means it *can* occur, and as consumers or practicing professionals of mass communication, we should be aware of this potential.

New developments in electronic journalism have eliminated certain uses of the gatekeeper group without necessarily producing distortion. For instance, a television news correspondent in a foreign country may send a filmed report by satellite to a news bureau in New York. From there, the report may be transmitted to a regional distribution center and then retransmitted to subscribing stations. The filmed report remains relatively unchanged from the time it was originally prepared. The only real distortion might be technical "noise," such as visual or audio interference.

Although the gatekeeper chain and gatekeeper group are in a sense a "road map" of the flow of news, other factors are pertinent to *how news is diffused* into society and *how we react* to it.

NEWS DIFFUSION

News diffusion is defined as *the process by which news is disseminated to the receiving public*. To understand news diffusion, let's see what happens when the story about the flood reaches the public. An executive of a fertilizer company buys a copy of the paper at a newsstand, reads the story about the flood, and is alarmed at the reported damage to farms owned by a number of his customers in the heart of the flood region. He goes back to the office and immediately tells his colleagues about the flooding. They in turn tell other colleagues, and within a ten-minute period, almost the entire office is clustered around the radio to hear news updates on the flooding.

The experience of the fertilizer company executive illustrates what happens when news of high value reaches the public. In this case, the news was disseminated through interpersonal communication. Then, those who heard about the event through interpersonal communication turned to the mass media for additional information. Within a relatively short time, it had reached many other people who also were affected by the event. To recapitulate, when news of high value enters a social system, (1) it diffuses very rapidly; (2) much of the diffusion process is through interpersonal communication; (3) there is a tendency to search out mass media to learn more about the event; and (4) there is a desire to tell other people about the event.

Now let's consider what might occur when the news is of low value. Let's assume the executive purchased the newspaper, but that this edition contained a story about an economic upturn in agricultural industries. When he returns to the office, the sales manager walks in, and the executive tells her about the economic forecast he has just read. She replies with a quick "that sounds good" and continues with her work. About half an hour later, another colleague goes out for a coffee break, returns with the same edition of the newspaper, and reads about the predicted economic upturn. He mentions it to the executive who says he already has seen the item. About this time, some members of the sales force stop by the office to ask about new accounts. The sales force leaves, and there is no mention of the item in the newspaper. Meanwhile, the radio plays softly in a corner of the office. Now ask yourself, what is different about the diffusion of news in this case?

First, we can see that although the economic forecast affected the employees of the fertilizer company, it was not of immediate concern to them as was the news of the flooding. Second, the diffusion process occurred less through interpersonal communication and more through individual purchases of the evening newspaper. Third, no one hurried to gather round the radio to hear the latest updates. As the radio continued to play background music, many people in the office remained completely unaware of the news. Comparing the diffusion patterns of the two events, we see that both interpersonal and mass communication participated in the diffusion process, but that these varied depending on the value of the event.

Many other factors will affect news diffusion: the time of day an event occurs; when an item is released by the media; to what audience and through what medium it is first released; and the education, age, sex, and other demographic characteristics of the audience, to mention a few.

SOURCE AND MEDIA CREDIBILITY

Ever since the ancient Greeks noted that a message delivered by one spokesperson had more impact than the same message delivered by a different spokesperson, the concept of *ethos* or credibility has been accorded much attention. Research into interpersonal communication has investigated how the source of a message can affect its reception, a concept called *source credibility*. We know, for instance, that the leader of a nation will have more credibility when talking about foreign policy than the factory worker expounding on his preferences to a hometown audience. The factory worker, on the other hand, may have more credibility than the national leader when the subject is factory production. Besides the effects of message and source on the ultimate reception of a message, we must also reckon with the role of different media. Their contribution to a story's believability is called *media credibility*.

Research has suggested some general trends about media credibility, trends that *do not* necessarily remain constant but do reflect the public's perception of the news media. For example, in the 1930s when radio first appeared as a medium, it quickly jumped ahead of newspapers as the most credible news source. Whether it was really more credible or contained fewer inaccuracies than newspapers is debatable. Yet the public clearly preferred hearing the news over the radio, and there were several reasons for this. First, the medium was new. Second, the dimension of sound added a realism to mass communication that was even reflected in Franklin D. Roosevelt's increased political stature. His "fireside chats" were not only novel but also instrumental in cementing a closer bond between the people and the president of the United States.

On Halloween night in 1938, radio's credibility as a mass medium was vividly demonstrated when actor Orson Welles broadcast his famous radio drama, *The War of the Worlds*. Its theme was a takeover by spaceships from another planet of the East Coast of the United States. Despite repeated announcements that the play was merely a radio drama, Welles succeeded in producing mass panic among thousands of listeners, who actually waited in fear for the Martians to swallow their community. Even today's highly refined television techniques cannot command this same blind belief.

Since the 1930s, research has examined the public's changing perceptions of media credibility. We know, for example, that newspapers have regained much of the overall credibility that they lost to radio in the thirties and early forties. We have also seen television surge ahead as today's most credible medium. *However, we should be cautious in assuming that messages received via other types of mass communication are therefore less credible.* Television's enormous credibility is attributable not only to the tremendous impact it has on our lives but also to its two dimensions of sight and sound. People also spend more time with television than with any other medium.

However, it is also important to consider each message and source separately in judging media credibility. For example, few members of the financial community would contest the fact that the *Wall Street Journal* covers economic news more credibly than any television station does. However, if you were to ask a rodeo rider which medium he considered more credible for rodeo news, *Rodeo Sports News* or his favorite television station, *Rodeo Sports News* would undoubtedly be the winner.

Certain characteristics inherent in different media lend themselves to different types of messages. The ability of television to capture the motion and color of major sporting events is unequaled by any other medium. A detailed contour map necessary to understand a complex story on the environment can, on the other hand, hardly be reproduced on a television screen.

FORCES AFFECTING NEWS SELECTION

Although we may feel that after reading a newspaper and a news magazine, listening to various radio newscasts throughout the day, and watching a local and national television news program, we have been exposed to all the news that could possibly happen in one day, such is not the case. Reporters are constantly faced with a multitude of stories from which to choose, scores of events to report, and a myriad of decisions to make about what should and should not appear in print or on the air. Why are some stories chosen and others are not? Why do some stories carry pictures and others do not? Why are some stories on the front page or lead a broadcast while others are either buried or do not ever appear? All of these questions are summarized by one: What forces affect gatekeeper decisions?

economics

With the exception of noncommercial media, such as campus radio stations or some campus newspapers, most media are commercial, profit-making businesses. Our context is the free world countries where the majority of media operate as free enterprises. And an economic fact of life is that these media must make a profit or go out of business.

For example, the ability of a newspaper to afford to send investigative reporters to cover a story will have a direct bearing on the type and amount of information the public receives. Labor costs and newsprint costs also affect the operation of a newspaper. Perhaps economic considerations might force a newspaper to reduce the number of pages. Even if it does cut back, however, the number of advertising pages, the newspaper's bread and butter, will probably not be affected. News will be what suffers.

Economics can affect messages on other media. Television stations can be very expensive to operate. Purchasing and maintaining electronic equipment as well as trained personnel can be costly. Like newspapers, television has certain basic operating costs. Engineers, directors, and producers all draw on the station's payroll. The evening anchorperson is not trained to repair a $100,000 color camera. In television, when personnel cuts take place, the news department may be the first to go.

Radio is no different. In some cases, economics can play havoc with this medium. At many radio stations, one or two persons staff the entire news department. Eliminating one position may reduce the department's ability to cover news by fifty percent. Economic considerations such as permission to make long distance telephone calls and freedom from other on-air duties at the station all can affect how well a news team can gather and disseminate news to the public.

legal restrictions

The media most affected by legal restrictions are radio and television. One example of these legal shackles is the Fairness Doctrine, which requires radio and television stations to present all sides of a controversial issue. Although this may seem like common sense, it can place a station in a position of "bookkeeper," such as when a group of California stations found themselves faced with actually measuring the time given certain issues and then providing an equal amount of time for the opposing side. Moreover, the issues must be balanced over all types of programming, not merely advertising or editorials. News programming is included under this umbrella, as is entertainment programming. We shall learn more about these legal restrictions in other chapters.

Nor are newspapers immune from regulations. A reporter can be called to testify in a criminal case and be requested to reveal the sources of confidential information. Although the reporter can refuse the request and will usually win a contempt of court action brought against him or her because of this refusal, the threat of subpoenas may be enough to discourage the practice of using "unnamed" sources. It may also discourage these sources from openly revealing information to a reporter. Some predict that a 1978 Supreme Court ruling permitting police to search newspaper offices like any other business may further restrict investigative reporting efforts.

deadlines

Every reporter lives with deadlines. The ever-present deadline can make the difference between gaining an exclusive story or being "scooped" by a competitor, between being able to report all the facts or just some of them, between being able to use a story or being forced to hold it for lack of information. For news reporters, deadlines mean working under extreme pressure on a daily basis, pressure that forces them to spew forth their ideas, thoughts, and words at an often unsettling pace.

In the broadcast media, the pressure of deadlines is even more acute. Because radio and television can air news almost as it happens, deadlines literally come every minute. Of course, problems with accuracy arise when stories are broadcast too soon after a news event occurs. It takes time to gather news and prepare a story. Even when a story is reported live, there are many background details that cannot be reported without time and effort.

Deadlines and news reporting are always companions. To be a responsible consumer of news you need to know how they work together. When we read or hear news, we assume accuracy. We must, however, be alert to certain cues which may help us gauge the degree of this accuracy. Such phrases as *"at press time"* and *"at least one source"* alert us to missing gaps in a story or missing links in a chain of information.

personal and professional ethics

Assume you have just written a story for your newspaper about a local resident arrested on a charge of drunken driving. But as you are preparing to send the story to your editor, the owner of the paper walks in and kills your story because that particular resident had spent $50,000 in advertising last year. What would you do? Many reporters would quit immediately in disgust. Although economic concerns are undeniably important, the professional journalist cannot condone the suppression of newsworthy information, and his or her function is finding and publishing the truth. For the owner to have suggested compromising the newspaper's integrity for the sake of advertising would not only be considered poor journalism but also prostitution of the press and a request to participate deliberately in a breach of ethics. Or what would you do, if you opened your mail and found two free tickets to cover a local political rally? Marked "complimentary," the tickets are what journalists call *freebies*. Would accepting the tickets prejudice your coverage of the rally? Even if it would not, should you still accept them? What if buying the tickets was simply too expensive, and you had the choice of either accepting the tickets as freebies or not covering the rally? What if the competition accepted the tickets and covered the rally, gaining considerable reader or viewer interest in the report? Answers to these questions are not easy.

Freebies can range from tickets to a church supper to excursions to a foreign country, which also are called *junkets*. Some newspapers have a policy against accepting freebies. If the function is important and requires paid admission, then the newspaper will purchase admission passes. The policy against freebies tries to prevent any opportunity, regardless of how small, for biased reporting. The paper wants its readership to receive objective news coverage and does not want freebies to endanger that objectivity.

The author's own experiences in covering stories often have involved personal ethics. On one occasion, two fugitives from a mental institution stole a car and headed for the state line. After their capture, there was an opportunity to take pictures of them as they emerged from the squad car in police custody. However, the following day, when it came time to use the story, a superior made the decision not to use the names of the two fugitives or their pictures. The case fell into the realm of crimes committed by suicidal and mentally ill persons. The story that reached the public mentioned only that a stolen car had been recovered and that two escapees from the state correctional institution had been taken into custody.

About two months later, a similar incident forced another judgment of personal and professional ethics. On an early Sunday morning, the static on the police monitor was broken by a report of a sniper in a ravine shooting at police cars with a high-powered rifle. One officer whose car had been hit was keeping the man "pinned down" until assistance arrived. As the morning progressed, a number of other law enforcement officers arrived at the scene. It was determined that the sniper, who had escaped from the same state correctional hospital, had a high-powered rifle with a telescopic sight and ample ammunition. Unsuccessful attempts by law enforcement officials to entice the man to surrender prompted a decision that a group of officers, armed with rifles, form a human line and walk side by side toward the ravine, all the time requesting the man to surrender. Nightfall was rapidly approaching and many felt that in darkness it would be easy for the man to escape and threaten the lives of area residents. As the police line moved to a ridge above the ravine, the fugitive shot one of the officers in the stomach. Immediately, the line opened fire. The fugitive's body, riddled with holes, was a somewhat gruesome sight. Nevertheless, the same superior who had determined not to use the pictures or names of the fugitives who had stolen the car, made the decision to use pictures of the dead sniper as well as his name and all the details surrounding the event. Why that decision?

A number of personal and professional reasons were behind that decision. For one, the police officer died. In addition, this reporter's superior had been employed by a federal law enforcement agency before becoming a journalist. Moreover, the police officer had been a high-ranking official in one of the communities served by the news medium. The incident, unlike that of the stolen car, had occurred in broad daylight, and the standoff with police officers had lasted for almost eight hours. The activity also took place on the only main highway connecting two major communities. All traffic for an eight-hour period was either stopped or detoured. In short, it was an incident of which the public became very much aware, especially in an area in which events of this magnitude were not that common. Thus, the story captured more attention than it might have, had the event occurred in a high crime area.

Similar personal and professional decisions are made every day by gatekeepers responsible for reporting news to the public. Ask yourself what decisions you might have made had you been the news executive. Would you have used the story with the pictures? Would you have used film of the event if it had been available?

competition

Concern over the possibility of another medium nabbing a scoop story is typical of competition among the news media. This competition is inherent in a free press and usually fosters the reporting of more than one opinion or approach to a story. Competition also can nurture the growth of true investigative journalism. Media in competition will sometimes take the extra initiative to explore an issue in depth rather than be satisfied with superficial information.

Plain economics encourages competition in many areas. Larger markets, for instance, have the financial base to support more than one news medium; large metropolitan areas can support even more than one newspaper. Some smaller communities, however, face information control by a single news medium that may be biased on certain issues. In such cases, competition would have a positive effect on freeing the flow of information to the public. As we learned in chapter 2, concentration of media control in joint newspaper-broadcasting ownerships has been curtailed by the actions of the FCC. In some localities, direct orders by the FCC have blocked concentration of media owner-ship by requiring the sale of some properties by multi-media owners.

Negative aspects of media competition surface particularly in the electronic media, in which the ability to air news almost simultaneously as it occurs breeds frenzied competition. The result can be news distortion. For example, put your-self in the seat of a radio news cruiser that has just received a call to cover a labor dispute at a major industrial plant. Also enroute to the event is another news cruiser from a competing station. Both cruisers are equipped for live, on-the-scene broadcasts. Both of you, sensing the other's presence, begin live reports. You describe a group of men fighting and report that it is the result of another flareup at the picket line. After the broadcast, you get out of the news cruiser to learn some details. You discover the fight you were reporting was actually a rough and tumble football game. You are shocked. Had you not been quite as concerned about the competitive edge, you would have taken the time to investi-gate all the details. Your actions were inexcusable, to say nothing of being unprofessional and irresponsible. You may also have opened yourself and your station to a libel suit. Except under extreme crisis conditions, such as a natural disaster, the impression that listeners spend their time switching back and forth from one station to another just to see who airs the news first is a fallacy.

One of the nation's leading broadcast news consultants reacts negatively to the common practice among broadcast journalists of listening to the compe-tition's newscasts. Such a practice, he contends, is a waste of time and effort since the listeners or viewers who are tuned to your station will not know what the competition is scooping you on in the first place. Certainly, a news medium that consistently airs or prints information days after an event occurs will lose credibility. Yet, the continual dissemination of misinformation due to hasty overreaction to competition also will lose credibility.

Competition in itself is beneficial and safeguards a free press. It must, however, be taken in its proper perspective so that both a free and *responsible* press is the end result.

news value

The term news value is a relative term. It refers to the *value or importance of an event or the potential impact of an event in relation to other events or potential news stories*. For example, the news value of the story about the sniper who shot the police officer was very high. But it was high *in comparison* to other events that may have been happening simultaneously or that had happened on previous occasions in the community. Note the words "in the community." The geographical sphere of influence of the message also will affect its value. Again, the story of the sniper had its highest value on the community in which it occurred. Although it may have had enough value to be selected as news by a gatekeeper in a neighboring community, its relative value there might have been less.

Another factor influencing news value is the number of people affected by an event. For example, the sniper's actions caused many hundreds of people to be stopped or detoured from their normal route of travel. The fact that a high-ranking police officer was shot affected everyone in the community in which he worked. All the people affected by an event contribute indirectly to the news value of the story.

the news hole

The news hole is directly related to news value. To understand this concept, imagine a large auditorium full of students, each of whom wants to spend the day on a bused field trip. But only one bus load can go. When the instructor looks over the auditorium, everyone in the room tries to gain attention. Some shout. Others wave their hands and hold up signs. Still others become the object of attention by sheer accident, such as having a sign fall on their heads. Still, only a small percentage will be able to make the trip since space is limited. Now compare the students to all the events in society competing for the attention of the gatekeepers in the media. Some events may be deliberate attempts to gain attention, such as issuing a press release. Other events attract attention by accident, such as the sniper shooting. Certainly many of the events to which a gatekeeper is exposed can become news stories. But the news hole is only so big. There are only so many pages to a newspaper and so much time allotted to an evening television newscast.

The size of the news hole is also determined by the number and news value of events that attract the gatekeeper's attention. A busy news day may fill the news hole to capacity, leaving little room for press releases. We, the public, are exposed to only a fraction of the information that *could* be reported to us. What we do receive is determined by the *size* of the news hole in relation to the number and value of the messages that vie for attention in the limited space or time at the gatekeeper's disposal.

attention factors

Many things besides news value draw our attention to messages in the media. Although certain stories in themselves often command our attention, others may need help in the form of visual or aural stimuli. A story about a robbery, for example, might make the front page because an accompanying picture attracts attention to it. Audio actualities on radio and film or videotape on television all can attract attention to the newscast.

Although both the print and broadcast press have been accused of sensationalism, the use of pictures, newsfilm, and audio actualities do make a difference in which stories are reported as well as their location in the news hole. Certainly we should not assume that members of the press choose news only because of these added factors. If something important happens to a community, it will make news regardless of the visual or aural stimuli it contains. However, these factors *do make a difference* for stories with minimal or average news value. For example, if an editor has two stories about a beauty pageant and can only use one story, the one with the accompanying photograph of the queen may have an advantage.

As consumers of mass communication, we need constantly to keep in mind that these attention factors can make a difference. Ask yourself the next time you read a story on the front page of a newspaper or see the lead story on the evening newscast: Is it there because of its news value or because it had a picture, newsfilm, or audio actuality to accompany it?

peer group pressure

One effective means of peer group pressure is the increasing number of local newspaper columnists who keep an eye on the broadcast press through regular columns about radio and television. Items that have appeared in newspaper columns include analyses of internal hiring practices and broadcast employee qualifications. Some broadcasting stations have also aired programs critical of the work of newspaper journalists. Such peer group pressure among media personnel can make gatekeepers look seriously at their work and the implications it has for the public.

Numerous *journalism reviews* keep a watchful eye on members of the press. The nationally famous *Columbia Journalism Review* is one example, and there are other journalism reviews in large cities which treat the activities of the press in their own locale.

Lack of peer group pressure can have just the opposite effect. This condition, which exists especially in small communities, is reflected in an almost narrow-minded reporting of the issues. Consider the life of a newspaper reporter in a small town that has no local radio or television station. Also imagine that the reporter has no one else on the staff to assist with news gathering and reporting. What happens? Stated succinctly, the reporter can get into a rut, and the public suffers. Day in and day out, the reporter sees the same people and reports the same news, but at no time is his or her work scrutinized. The basic facts can be correct, but the stories reflect a narrow line of thought that pervades the limited number of news sources. Isolation and lack of peer group pressure thus have resulted in a daily diet of limited reporting.

Perhaps the reporter develops what is commonly called a "police complex," in which the only real news the community receives comes from the police blotter and the traffic fatality list. Meanwhile, the other issues affecting the community go unnoticed and unchecked. This kind of reporting could permit a slow takeover of corrupt government, it might even seem, with the tacit approval of the press.

reacting to feedback

Perhaps the most common form of feedback to the press is the letter to the editor. Although not necessarily representative of the general public, letters to the editor have been a traditional part of journalism since a free press began to flourish.

Some newspapers may even employ an ombudsman whose sole responsibility is to review feedback from the readership. Reaction to this feedback may prompt moderate changes such as a new emphasis on the coverage of a particular series of events. On the other hand, it may influence editorial comment or even necessitate special feature articles.

You should never discount the impact of reader or viewer feedback. Your own letter to the editor or the head of a major broadcasting complex can be a key indicator to personnel on what the public is thinking and why. One letter indicates to management that there are many other people who undoubtedly feel the same way but just did not take the time to write. One letter may be all it takes to prompt a reporter to question a news source, check an additional source, or conduct an in-depth interview that reveals a serious problem affecting the community.

PROCESSING NEWS UNDER CRISIS CONDITIONS

In recent years, increased attention is being given by both news organizations and the public to mass media news disseminated under crisis conditions. Such acts as terrorist campaigns, frequent world conflicts, and inevitable natural disasters all create abnormal conditions within the media. The work load becomes tremendous, and schedules are carried out under great tension. The media become a clearing house for information, both incoming and outgoing. There is also far more information processing than under noncrisis conditions. A radio station, for example, may typically schedule a newscast once every hour. During a crisis, however, that same radio station may switch its format to continuous all-news programming in order to serve its stricken community. The station's staff may also change roles in a crisis. The program and music directors may completely disregard their regular duties to aid the news staff. In addition, the news director will usually assume charge of all on-air programming.

Problems arising from these abnormal conditions vary. Two university professors, Galen Rarick, Dean of the School of Journalism at the University of Oregon, and James Harless of the School of Journalism at Ohio State University, investigated what happens to local radio stations and their personnel during a natural disaster. Under a grant from the National Association of Broadcasters, they investigated the operations of stations when faced with one of three different types of disasters—flood, blizzard, or tornado. They found a major problem for station personnel during a disaster was transportation. They found that four-wheel drive vehicles were almost indispensable. Without four-wheel drive, tire chains had to be used for many hours at a time, causing tires to "overheat and pop," leaving personnel stranded and unable to provide needed information to their community. Rarick and Harless also found that if reporters had two-way radios installed in their vehicles, they would not have to waste time searching for a telephone to relay their reports. Station personnel also felt that walkie-talkies would be beneficial, and , for stations that could afford it, auxiliary power and transmitting equipment. Management agreed that "if you are off-the-air, you are nothing."

In investigating the role of the station staff, the two professors discovered that at many stations, the staff was willing to work to the point of exhaustion. There were no interpersonal problems among the staff—they pulled together. Yet there were difficulties in the staff's ability to gather and process the news during the crisis. One reporter who was not accustomed to carrying a press pass had a hard time gaining access to an area that had been sealed off to prevent looting.

Rarick and Harless also found that news personnel had to be careful of whom they used as news sources. One reporter found the public to be no more than 80 percent accurate in reporting details of a snowstorm. In the case of tornados, people were so "frightened and shocked" after it hit that they could not remember what happened. Government agencies may be reliable sources for accurate information, but their helpfulness varies from town to town. A classic case cites a local official who could not even find the key to the courthouse! Rarick and Harless recommend that stations processing news and information during a crisis be prepared in advance. News personnel should have at their fingertips the names of the best news sources, and the station should become an integral part of its community disaster plan.

SUMMARY

This chapter dealt with mass media news. Two forces that have a significant effect on news processing are the gatekeeper group and the gatekeeper chain. The gatekeeper chain allows for little interpersonal communication between gatekeepers and consequently fosters a greater opportunity for distortion. The gatekeeper group, on the other hand, permits gatekeepers to check and recheck each other's decisions and therefore reduces the opportunity for distortion.

Closely related to the gatekeeper's responsibility is the process of news diffusion. News of high value will be diffused faster than news of little value. As in processing, rapid diffusion will increase the possibilities for distortion. In high intensity situations, we are more apt to communicate and to receive important news by word of mouth than from mass media.

The medium that disseminates the news also can affect how we perceive it. Because society is so attuned to television, it is generally accorded more credibility than other mass media in the face of conflicting news reports. Media credibility is, however, not an absolute, but a relative term. Each medium has its own forte, lending its superior credibility for a particular message and source.

Many factors work together to influence the selection and treatment of mass media news. These include (1) economics, which refers to the profit-loss structure of media operating as part of a free enterprise system; (2) regulations legislated by local, state, and federal governments to control the operations of the media and to ensure freedom of the press; (3) deadlines, which limit the time in which a gatekeeper can collect news before it is necessary to disseminate it; (4) personal and professional ethics, those forces on which gatekeepers often base decisions in selecting information to become news; (5) competition, the safeguard of a free press in a democracy; (6) news value, which signifies the importance of one event in relation to other events; (7) the news hole, which refers to the total amount of available space or time in which to present messages in order of decreasing value; (8) attention factors, visual or aural stimuli that enhance a story; (9) peer group pressure, those decisions that are influenced by colleagues; and (10) reaction to feedback, the communication received from the audience.

Under crisis conditions, different forces act upon the media and alter this news selection and dissemination process. Increased dissemination of news, demands on the media to provide information, and difficulty in gathering information are just some of the problems that can occur under crisis conditions.

OPPORTUNITIES FOR FURTHER LEARNING

BABB, LAURA LONGLEY, ed., *Of the Press, by the Press, for the Press and Others Too....* New York: Houghton Mifflin Company, 1976.

BEHRENS, JOHN C., *The Typewriter Guerrillas: Closeups of 20 Top Investigative Reporters*. Chicago: Nelson/Hall, 1977.

DOWNIE, LEONARD, *The New Muckrakers*. New York: Mentor Books, 1978.

DYGERT, J. H., *The Investigative Journalist: Folk Heroes of a New Era*. Englewood Cliffs, N.J.: Prentice-Hall, Inc., 1976.

ENGLISH, EARL, and CLARENCE HACH, *Scholastic Journalism*. Ames, Iowa: Iowa State University Press, 1978.

GANS, HERBERT J., *Deciding What's News: A Study of CBS Evening News, NBC Nightly News, Newsweek, and Time*. New York: Pantheon Books, 1979.

HAGE, GEORGE, and others, *New Strategies for Public Affairs Reporting: Investigation, Interpretation, and Research*. Englewood Cliffs, N.J.: Prentice-Hall, Inc., 1975.

HALBERSTAM, DAVID, *The Powers That Be*. New York: Alfred A. Knopf, Inc., 1979.

HULTENG, JOHN, *The News Media: What Makes Them Tick?* Englewood Cliffs, N.J.: Prentice-Hall, Inc., 1979.

JOHNSTONE, JOHN W. C., EDWARD J. SLAWSKI, and WILLIAM W. BOWMAN, *The News People: A Sociological Portrait of American Journalists and Their Work*. Urbana: University of Illinois Press, 1976.

KIRSCH, DONALD, *Finance and Economic Journalism: Analysis, Interpretation and Reporting*. New York: New York University Press, 1979.

McCOMBS, MAXWELL, DONALD LEWIS SHAW, and DAVID GREY, eds., *Handbook of Reporting Methods*. Boston: Houghton Mifflin Company, 1976.

MERRILL, JOHN C., *Existential Journalism*. New York: Hastings House, 1977.

METZLER, KEN, *Newsgathering*. Englewood Cliffs, N.J.: Prentice-Hall, Inc., 1978.

MEYER, PHILLIP, *Precision Journalism*. Bloomington, Ind.: Indiana University Press, 1973.

PICKETT, CALDER M., ed., *Voices of the Past: Key Documents in the History of American Journalism*. Columbus, Ohio: Grid, Inc., 1977.

POWERS, RON, *The Newscasters*. New York: St. Martins Press, 1978.

RUBIN, BERNARD, *Media Politics & Democracy*. New York: Oxford University Press, Inc., 1977.

SCHWOEBEL, JEAN, *Newsroom Democracy: The Case for Independence of the Press*. Iowa City: School of Journalism, University of Iowa, 1977.

WENDLAND, MICHAEL F., *The Arizona Project*. Mission, Kans.: Sheed Andrews & McMeel, Inc., 1977.

WICKER, TOM, *On Press*. New York: The Viking Press, 1978.

WILLIAMS, PAUL N., *Investigative Reporting and Editing*. Englewood Cliffs, N.J.: Prentice-Hall, Inc., 1978.

12

Media Delivery Systems:
cable, satellites, and computers

In studying mass communication, it would be easy to limit our investigation to the actual media and the audiences they serve. But by doing this, we would fail to understand the whole picture of how messages are processed by the media and how these messages reach us. New technology is constantly improving the process of mass communication. Satellites hovering in space beam television pictures across continents. No longer are live television pictures from abroad a novelty. No longer do we sit in amazement at computer predictions of national election outcomes when only a handful of votes are in.

The purpose of this chapter is to give a better understanding of this new technology, technology that has become part of our media delivery systems, helping both to process and distribute messages through mass communication.

CABLE

The only communities capable of financially supporting several television stations are large population centers. The residents of these large cities have thus long enjoyed good reception of all the major network programs as well as those produced by independent stations. During television's early years, however, people living far away from these centers had no recourse but to sit in front of their sets, watching distant signals blurred by interference. People began investing in every type of complex antenna system imaginable, and a maze of television antennas covered rooftops everywhere.

In the late 1940s, there was a breakthrough in the previously fruitless efforts to receive clear, interference-free television signals from distant stations. It was putting a large antenna on a hilltop high above the average terrain, from which the distant signals would be carried by shielded wires, called cables, directly into home television receivers (Figure 12-1). Thus began the development of *cable television*, also called *community antenna television* or CATV. Residents whose televisions were connected to a community antenna paid a monthly rental fee for the service. Others could, of course, still use their rooftop antenna but usually sacrificed good reception. It soon became evident, especially in outlying areas, that the way to receive quality television signals and have a wide selection of channels was to link onto the local cable system. With the development of color TV sets, which accentuate poor reception, cable television became even more helpful.

CATV refined its system even further, including the application of sophisticated transistorized electronic equipment and improvements in the construction of the cable. Both developments made it feasible to send many more channels via cable without having to eliminate intermediate channels because of interference. Instead of receiving about half a dozen programs on the VHF spectrum, a cable subscriber could receive all twelve channels if the cable system carried all twelve. Still other developments in cable expanded this twelve-

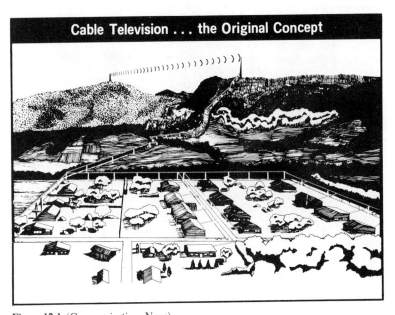

Figure 12-1 (*Communications News*)

channel capacity to carry as many as forty or fifty separate channels, and fiber optics (Figure 12-2) can handle as many as 1,000 channels.

The FCC now requires that CATV systems, depending on the number of subscribers, permit local access to one of their channels. This means that in many communities, a local organization or university may have access to one of the CATV channels and provide locally originated programming to subscribers. It also gives many systems the option of two-way transmission, something which, at least under current technology and development, broadcast systems cannot provide.

The new two-way systems, commonly called *broadband* communication, are opening up exciting media possibilities. One of the more fully developed two-way systems is the QUBE system in Columbus, Ohio. Although they pay a higher monthly fee, QUBE subscribers also have a wider selection of programs and services from which to choose. A special home terminal unit (Figure 12-3) operates on a thirty-channel capacity system in Columbus. When operating at full potential, the home terminal integrated with the two-way system permits subscribers to participate in interactive games, educational testing, and public opinion polling, in addition to receiving regular television programming. The potential for full scale use of broadband communications includes automatic reading of utility meters such as electric, water and gas, picture telephone systems facsimile data, and video and telephone.

How do subscribers receive this regular programming? Let's find out how CATV works.

Figure 12-2 Fiber-optic technology promises wide use of light-waves in communication, permitting hundreds of times more channel capacity than conventional coaxial cables of the same size. (Western Electric)

Figure 12-3 The Warner QUBE system permits two-way channel capacity using the home terminal pictured here, and lets the subscriber select from a number of different channels as well as take part in instantaneous public opinion polls. The QUBE system has been featured in such things as major network analysis of public opinion following a Presidential address. (Warner Cable of Columbus, Inc.)

components of a cable system

The basis of the CATV system is the *receiving antenna* (Figure 12-4). This, along with the amplifier, which retransmits signals to home subscribers, is called the *head end*. This term does not necessarily connote a specific location. Broadly speaking, it is *the human and hardware combination responsible for originating, controlling, and processing signals over the cable system.* In most cases, a separate antenna receives each individual signal; thus optimal reception is assured. In some instances, the head end will have the means to originate local programming. For example, it could contain a studio complex complete with a modest assortment of cameras and switching equipment. On other occasions, the studio may be at an adjacent site, such as a university campus or community center. In still other cases, the head end may include the local weather bureau which transmits emergency weather bulletins over the cable—for instance, small craft warnings.

The second major component of a cable system is its *distribution system.* As opposed to the head end, which originates, controls, and processes messages,

Basic Cable Television System

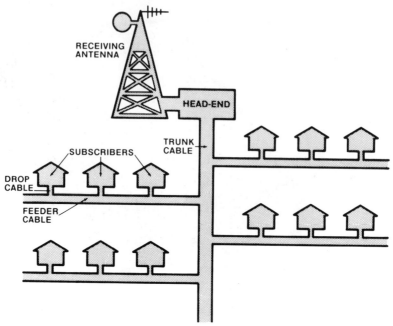

Figure 12-4 (NCTA)

the distribution system simply dispenses the system's messages. The most important component of the distribution system is the cable itself. The type of cable
most commonly used is called *coaxial cable* and consists of an inner wire core
surrounded by plastic, metal-webbed insulation and another coating of plastic.
Coaxial cable, because of its thickness and shielding, is capable of carrying
considerably more information than telephone lines can. It is strung out over a
community in much the same way that other utility lines are, usually connected
to utility poles or installed as underground cable. A special line from the main
cable then runs into a subscriber's home or office and connects directly to the
television set.

The entire cable system can be compared to a tree. The main transmission
line of the cable is called the *trunk* cable (Figure 12-4). Looking at a typical map,
the trunk would usually parallel a community's main traffic arteries. Branching
out from the trunk are feeder cables that convey the signal to outlying areas,
some only a few streets away, others possibly miles from the main trunk line.
Amplifiers are used at strategic locations to give the signal a boost when it gets too
far away from the head end. In some areas, the cable company owns or leases
microwave links for long distance transmission.

Another important part of the distribution system is the *drop cable*. The
drop is that section of cable that brings the signal from the trunk or subtrunk
directly to a subscriber's set. Usually about one to two hundred feet in length, it

connects directly to the back of the television set, making the use of any other external antenna unnecessary.

The third part of the system is the *home terminal*. There are basically two types—*one-way* and *two-way* terminals. One-way terminals are the typical home television receiver. Two-way terminals are the television receiver, which is used as a visual display terminal, and a control board capable of sending commands into the system.

uses and issues

Our discussion of one-way CATV systems already has mentioned some of the principal uses of this type of operation. One is the retransmission of television signals too weak for the average home antenna to pick up clearly. Another is the opportunity for universities to originate local programming, not only to train students preparing for careers in mass communication but also to broadcast convocations, recitals, and even academic courses to cable subscribers. Local civic meetings can also be televised by the cable.

Two-way cable, or broadband communication, has an almost unlimited, still largely untapped potential. Consider the heart patient who at present must remain in the hospital for continual monitoring. With two-way cable, this same patient can return home and connect himself or herself to a home two-way cable terminal. The terminal connects to a computer at the hospital that monitors the heartbeat for a short period each day and signals the patient if anything is wrong. It also will automatically notify the hospital staff if emergency care is needed.

Central computers hooked up to home terminals can provide services that may seem like pure science fiction—for example, performing complex mathematical formulas or giving you access to your checking account records. Mailing lists also can be sorted on the computer. If you had decided to send holiday greeting cards only to friends in your local community this year, you could ask the computer to sort those names from a master zip-code list. Additional tasks you can perform in your home via two-way cable include buying groceries, participating in group therapy sessions, and playing in chess tournaments.

First-run current movies can be part of your cable viewing. Instead of driving a date to the theater, you may want to stay at home to watch a movie. A channel on your two-way cable system will permit selection of any number of feature films. Using the two-way cable home terminal, you simply punch the code for the movie you want to watch.

policy concerns affecting cable

Although the subject of government control over cable television will be discussed in more detail in another chapter, we must raise several important issues here. One is the problem of public acceptance of new media. Over the past decades, we have become conditioned to resist such things as invasion of privacy, big government, corporate control, and similar factors that have an effect on our lives but over which we feel we have little or no control. History shows there has been similar resistance to new technology whenever it evolved. CATV did not suffer from excessive resistance since it was a logical extension of television. However, the concept of two-way cable is something entirely different. For many who do not understand the potential of the system, there is a feeling that "big brother" has arrived and should be stopped at all cost. A typical reaction toward two-way cable envisions a superspy electronic eye lurking in the living room. Although it is possible to develop such a system, that is not the current aim of two-way cable. But until public resistance to the new technology diminishes, it will continue to stifle two-way cable's growth possibilities.

Government control also affects the cable industry. The use of microwave transmission systems (Figure 12-5) placed cable companies under FCC regulation, whose jurisdiction spread to areas such as local access and eventually locally originated programming. However, unlike standard radio and television broadcasters, cable companies are also accountable to local and state government. This may mean government-controlled rate schedules or the adoption of guidelines for local access programming. Inevitably jurisdictional conflicts will arise among local, state, and federal regulatory agencies. In one community, even when the cable system owners were alleged to have violated federal laws and the FCC wanted to take action, local officials said that they had the authority to

Figure 12-5 Microwave relay permits long distance communication without the use of cables. (AT&T)

deal with the matter and that the FCC did not. Similar conflicts are undoubtedly going to occur whenever several governmental agencies have overlapping regulatory powers. We shall learn more about regulating cable in the following pages.

Pay cable will also become an increasingly contested issue. Pay cable refers to an amount paid over and above the monthly rental fee to see a particular program. With pay cable in your home, you can see such selected features as major concerts, sports events, plays, and other attractions. Opponents of pay cable argue that it discriminates against those who cannot afford this type of "luxury programming." Broadcasters are worried that it will take away from their viewing audience. Proponents of pay cable argue that admission prices to movies and theaters are already discriminatory and that pay cable will make available to the public a much greater variety of cultural and educational events. Obviously these arguments are not easily resolved.

The fact that your home terminal would be connected to a central computer creates widespread anxiety. Questions immediately asked are, How can the information I store in the computer remain confidential? What if the computer feeds me wrong information? If I am balancing my checkbook and someone finds out how much money I have in my checking account, what would prevent that person from making a computer withdrawal? If information about my heart condition is stored in the computer at the local hospital, what would prevent my employer from finding out about it and stopping my next promotion? These questions are obviously practical concerns that affect public acceptance of new media.

REGULATING CABLE

The barrage of rules and regulations that has evolved since cable television became a major carrier of media content boggles the mind. Federal legislation is almost equal in amount to the combined regulations governing commercial radio and television broadcasting, and when we add to this the maze of local and state regulations, we may stand back in amazement. At least with standard broadcasting stations, the federal government has the responsibility for making and enforcing the laws. Such is not the case with cable. Regulations enacted by local municipalities abound, establishing standards for the local cable operator on everything from fees to program content. They have legislated to which poles cables can be attached, where they must be underground, why cable operators cannot work on actual television sets, and numerous other regulations. Officials at all levels of the regulatory ladder have discovered the potential of cable systems, and state and FCC lawmakers also want a voice in controlling them. There are no clearly defined rules or court precedents giving the FCC *exclusive* jurisdiction. Thus, in many areas there are significant conflicts, if not confusion, over exactly who has jurisdiction over the case.

regulatory conflicts

At the local level, control stems from the communities' realization that the cable system has much more potential than merely bringing distant entertainment radio and television to the community. It can reach local school children with information about their schools. It can broadcast meetings of the city council and bring the workings of municipal government into living rooms with a realism that the local newscast or newspaper would find hard to match. With so many channels available to community groups, almost anyone can gain access to a local cable channel and disseminate a message to area cable subscribers. Moreover, there is the problem of categorizing cable in relation to other media. Legal precedent has suggested that the printed press and broadcast press are equal under the First Amendment rights of free speech and free press. However, is cablecasting the same as broadcasting? What would happen, for instance, if a cable company's news programs became justifiably critical of the city council, in a community in which the city council had control over the cable company's franchise? These and other questions have posed many regulatory quandaries. Simple answers are just not available.

When a municipality becomes involved in cablecasting, problems of jurisdiction among the three governmental levels are bound to occur. Whenever state and local laws conflict, the state law will almost always have the advantage in an appeal. Similarly, in a conflict between state and federal laws, the federal law will usually take precedent. Thus, to avoid problems with possible appeals, many states and localities have borrowed regulations that closely resemble federal legislation.

state control of cable

State laws governing cable fall into three categories—*full preempt statutes, appellate function statutes,* and *advisory statutes.* Of the three, the most encompassing is the full preempt statute. Here, the state assumes full control of licensing decisions and, in effect, "preempts" the municipalities' rights to determine licensing and programming. In other words, the state becomes the primary governing authority, and the loyalty of the cable operator is to the state. In the appellate function statutes, the state has the authority to review local decisions concerning cable operating and franchising. "State approval does *not* preempt federal review (before the FCC). However, state disapproval may effectively preempt ultimate municipal authority...."[1] Advisory statutes are the least encompassing, Massachusetts has a "pure" advisory statute. In other words, the state cannot normally regulate cable "in any way except when 10 percent of the system subscribers petition the State CATV Commission for review."[2]

Cable has significant potential. If trends toward specialized media continue, then cable has even more growth possibilities for carrying much of this specialized communication on its many channels. Two-way systems will add a new dimension to cable's future, and if suggested legislation frees the industry from some of its regulatory constraints, then more investment capital may be attracted to cable development.

SATELLITES

As we already have learned, various technological advancements throughout history have had a profound impact on our ability to communicate with each other. These included the printing press, radio, and television. Other developments increased the efficiency of these mass communication advancements; among them were the application of steam power to the printing press and the miniaturization of radio and television components. At the same time we were perfecting these developments, we also were gaining knowledge about the earth's orbital characteristics and jet propulsion. Jet propulsion permitted us to launch instruments into space which could facilitate mass communication worldwide. We had reached the age of *satellites*.

Perhaps no other technological advancement in our history had or will continue to have such a tremendous impact on our lives. We have already mentioned some applications of satellite technology that have revolutionized communication. Newspapers such as the *Wall Street Journal* are printed in regional distribution centers using satellite communication.

Wire service transmissions also can reach newspapers, as well as radio and television stations through satellite distribution. Earth stations (Figure 12-6) beam signals into space (Figure 12-7), and the satellites relay them back to earth. In addition to the wire services, broadcast stations receive both audio and video program services through satellite transmission.

Some "super" stations beam their signals directly to the satellites that, again, relay those signals back to earth thousands of miles away. Cable subscribers in Nebraska, for example, can receive television programming direct from Atlanta, Georgia. Ted Turner's WTBS-TV in Atlanta now reaches a nationwide cable audience that numbers well into the millions. Broadcasters everywhere are watching closely the impact the Atlanta superstation is having on both audience and the industry. If successful, if a favorable regulatory climate exists, and if advertisers support it, superstations could become the new networks of the future.

Sputnik through SYNCOM

When the Soviet Union launched Sputnik in 1957, it sent the world a message far more significant than "beep beep." It signaled the beginning of a new era in which we would have groups of satellites hovering in a global communication network as well as manned space flights. Compared to today's satellites, Sputnik was very rudimentary indeed. It did not have a ground system relaying messages to the satellite for return transmission. There was no real message broadcast, just

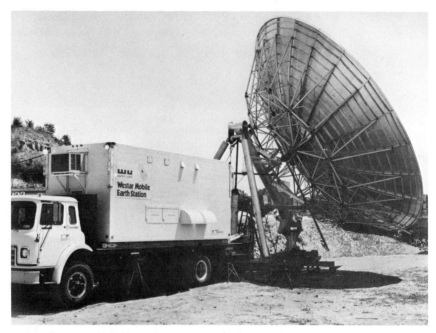

Figure 12-6 Satellite relay permits even greater flexibility to communicate over very long distances. The earth station can send and/or receive signals from a satellite in space, which in turn can relay signals to other earth stations thousands of miles away. (Western Union)

the continual, intermittent tones. Sputnik's antenna was not directed toward any particular part of space or earth; thus it could be heard only when it passed over that area of the earth containing a receiving antenna.

In 1958, the United States launched the SCORE satellite, the first to carry a taped message. SCORE was followed in 1960 by Echo I, which became the first *relay satellite* capable of bouncing messages back to earth. Satellite technology was now advancing rapidly. The United States' Courier 1-B, also placed into orbit in 1960, was the world's first *repeater satellite*. The repeater satellite differed from Echo I in that it was capable of receiving signals and then retransmitting them back to earth. With repeater satellites, it was now possible to send telephone and television signals by satellite.

The public's attention to satellite technology again was stirred in 1962 when a 170-pound satellite named *Telstar* relayed signals among the United States, England, and France. Powered by solar energy, it was the first display of television pictures by satellite, and it featured then Vice President Lyndon Johnson in the United States, Deputy Chief Engineer Captain Charles Booth in England, and Minister of Postal Services and Telecommunications Jacques M.

Maretts in France. Headlines greeted the event as a new era and a triumph for private industry.

But the real breakthrough was yet to come. For all practical purposes, satellite communication had two big liabilities. First, satellites were useful only when they passed over an earth station's repeating or transmitting antennas. That meant if the United States wished to send a satellite signal to England, it was necessary for the satellite to be within "eye shot" of the two countries. As soon as its orbit placed it over another land mass, it could no longer function. Second,

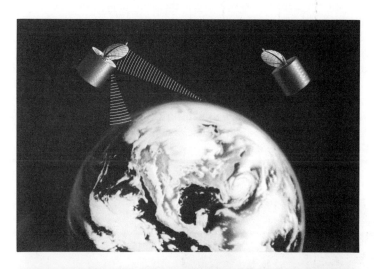

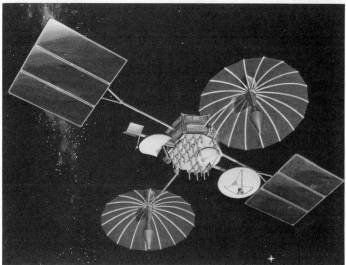

Figure 12-7 Two generations of Western Union satellites—two satellites of the Westar domestic satellite system and the Western Union-NASA tracking and data relay satellite. When completed, the tracking and data satellite system will consist of three synchronous orbit satellites plus an in-orbit spare, which will relay data between orbiting-user satellites and a ground terminal located in White Sands, New Mexico. (Western Union and TRW Defense and Space Systems Group)

satellites had short life spans. Since the *perigee*, the point closest to the earth during an orbit, was at very low altitude, gravity would pull the satellite into the earth's atmosphere, and it would burn up after relatively short use. The solution to the two problems was first to launch a satellite that could be positioned so that its orbit would remain at a given altitude, making the *apogee*, the orbiting point farthest away from the earth, equal to the perigee. The second step was to position the satellite so that its orbit at 22,300 miles above the earth would travel at the same speed in proportion to the earth's rotation, resulting in a synchronous or *geostationary* orbit. Although the satellite was orbiting at a faster rate than the earth because its circumference path was larger, the satellite appeared to remain stationary above the earth at a stationary point in space.

The feat was accomplished by Huges Aircraft Company engineers Harold Rosen, Donald Williams, and Tom Hudspeth. In July, 1963, crews at a ground station in Lakehurst, New Jersey and on board the Navy ship *Kingsport* stationed off the coast of Nigeria waited patiently for the launch. Then through the ship's speakers came a voice saying, *"Kingsport* this is Lakehurst; *Kingsport* this is Lakehurst; how do you read me?"* This crystal clear signal launched a new era of communication. It would also launch a new system of satellite development called the SYNCOM series, which stood for *synchronous orbit* satellite.

Figure 12-8 INTELSAT satellites ringing the earth. (Courtesy, Hughes Aircraft Company)

Following the development of synchronous orbit satellites, engineers developed a satellite antenna system that rotated freely from the base of the unit. This enabled a microwave antenna system to point in one stationary direction. It was like having a satellite stopped in space pointed at a given spot on earth.

COMSAT and INTELSAT

To provide some form of regulation and control over the new developments in satellite technology, in 1964, the International Telecommunication Satellite Consortium (INTELSAT) was formed. INTELSAT is composed of countries working together for the mutual cooperative development of satellite communication. The manager of INTELSAT is the United States Satellite Corporation called COMSAT. COMSAT was formed under the Communications Satellite Act of 1962, which provided for our commercial communication satellite system. Under the INTELSAT arrangements, there has been a systematic progression of satellite launches providing cooperative communication lines between nations. The INTELSAT series is capable of virtually all types of communication, including color television transmission (Figure 12-8). The first in the INTELSAT series was the Early Bird Satellite, which was then followed by INTELSAT II. INTELSAT II placed satellites over both the Pacific and Atlantic Oceans. The INTELSAT III series placed a satellite over the Indian Ocean, and the INTELSAT IV series greatly increased the circuit capability of the system as did INTELSAT V.

domestic satellite systems: Westar and Satcom

Along with the international satellite systems, a number of domestic satellite systems are in operation. In the United States, the Westar system, operated by Western Union, and the Satcom system, operated by RCA, provide numerous services for companies wishing to lease frequency space.

The RCA system was inaugurated in 1973 using leased channels from Canada's Anik II satellite and later Westar. Following initial operation of the system, RCA launched its own satellites: the Satcom series, Satcom I in 1975 and Satcom II in 1976.

Western Union's Westar system has two satellites and an extensive ground-based microwave interconnection system. A third satellite is planned. The ground-based system consists of five earth stations connecting such cities as New York, Atlanta, Georgia, Los Angeles, and Dallas. Earth station 1, outside New York City, is the main control point of the system. The earth station in Atlanta keeps the satellite antenna in position. The Westar system serves other companies besides Western Union. In fact, it is becoming increasingly popular as an alternative to expensive telephone facilities for transmitting such messages as network radio and television programming.

Americans are conditioned to the idea that the First Amendment to the Constitution is a universally held principle of law and morality—it is not. Its jurisdiction applies only within United States boundaries. When other countries become involved, as they immediately do with direct broadcast satellite communication, new issues of international law and understanding arise.

legalities and cultural integrity

These issues were summarized by Paul L. Laskin and Abram Chayes in an essay prepared under the auspices of the American Society of International Law and published by the Aspen Institute for Humanistic Studies.[3] In their summary, they contended that there is no way to ensure that television programs sent from direct broadcast satellites would remain inside national boundaries. For example, a nation surrounded by a ridge of high mountains may effectively keep within its boundaries television signals sent from land-based transmitters. However, signals from satellites do not respect such natural terrain and can spill over into bordering nations. Even new developments in satellite technology that permit signals to be directed within areas of approximately 100 miles in diameter still cannot provide directional coverage to match the irregular political boundaries. Most satellite coverage areas must be circular. When spillover does occur, it can easily threaten a nation's culture, integrity, or even its security.

There is also the fear that the superpowers may be in a position to dominate world development of satellite communication. Because the United States, for example, has the technology as well as the economic base to develop a worldwide system of satellite communication, other countries, especially the less developed ones, are resistant to American programming, especially programming from the major commercial networks. These nations also fear that bad American programs may drive out or keep out the good ones.[4]

Commercialism is another contested issue. Countries in which commercials are not a major part of the television fare are afraid that the influence of United States programming will ignite a commercial bombardment. There is also the fear that commercials of one country would tend to create a desire for goods of that country and, as a result, provide unfair competition to local industries. In addition, certain societies are apprehensive that commercial programming will create a thirst for consumer goods and portray consumer-oriented societies too positively. Such examples may disrupt national plans for orderly social and economic development.

international law

Added to these considerations is the difficulty of formulating any international law. Laskin and Chayes noted: "Where the Anglo-American countries, for example, proceed pragmatically, formulating the rules of legal behavior as they acquire experience, the civil law tradition tends to rely on the codification of rules in advance of action."[5] Such concepts become important when trying to establish systems in which agreements will *precede* the beginning of direct satellite communication into a country, or if the regulatory function is to begin *after* the broadcasts commerce, determining when there may be a need to control them.

Clearly, the solutions to these issues are not easy. In the United States, the only two documents that really reflect any attempt to govern satellite communication are the Communications Satellite Act of 1962 and the Communications Act of 1934 as amended. The 1962 legislation was concerned mainly with setting up COMSAT, creating a common channel of communication and control with other nations, and ultimately fixing the position of the United States with IN-TELSAT. The 1962 law followed precedents established by the 1934 legislation in that the FCC's responsibility for regulating television programming within the boundaries of the United States would logically carry over to programming beamed outside United States boundaries. Beyond this, however, control is vague if not nonexistent. This regulatory gap in American policy toward direct broadcast satellite communication is not necessarily negative. Premature control could place satellite communication in the same category as cable television, which both industry and government officials have contended is being stifled by overregulation. The incentive to develop new hardware and software systems stagnates when constant rewriting of government regulations leaves companies uncertain of definitive guidelines. To prevent this from happening to satellite communication, many of the issues and incentives for developing an international system of direct broadcast satellites have purposely been kept in the discussion stage.

COMPUTER TECHNOLOGY

When station KDKA broadcast the results of the Harding-Cox election returns in 1920, few people could have imagined that giant computers would someday predict with uncanny accuracy the outcome of national elections hours and sometimes days before all the votes were counted. The average citizen who sits in front of a television set and watches an election night broadcast is perhaps not aware of the full scope of the computer's power. For the publisher whose newspaper must go to press a short time after the polls close, however, with computer predictions there is far less chance of headline errors such as the famous boner made by the nation's major newspapers in predicting the outcome of the 1948 presidential election. Harry S. Truman went to bed listening to broadcast reports of his loss, only to awake the next morning as president-elect of the United States. The ability of the computer to analyze data from selected voting precincts, to use voting trends from previous years, to plot trends and probabilities, and to predict victories has given added credibility to all media.

Today's newspaper owes its greatly increased efficiency to computer technology. The ability of a major national newspaper to compose pages and advertisements, edit copy, set type, and effect regional distribution, all by computer, has become commonplace. Computers also have reduced errors in newspaper production. In the past, "scissors and paste" manuscripts were marked with pencil and passed through many different copy desks. With computers, the copy is now clean, and erasures and changes are edited electronically instead of manually. Type is set automatically through electrical impulse instead of by hand. Even the spacing of the lines and margins has been computerized.

operation and application

In most applications to mass communication, the basic operation of a computer is information storage and retrieval. The three major components of the computer are *input*, *processing*, and *output*. Data, usually in the form of numbers, are entered into the computer by one or more mathematical operations. The answer is then typed on a teleprinter or displayed on a visual display terminal. In our example of election night news coverage, information about previous voting trends first is stored in the computer. This might include the similarity in voting of key precincts to the total overall vote of a given area; how this has affected previous elections; and the percentage of voters eighteen to twenty-four years of age and how frequently they vote as their parents do. On election night when the votes are tabulated in the sample precincts, the information previously stored in the computer is combined with the new vote totals and then processed. The result is a prediction of voting results based on sample data collected in the current election as well as on information collected from previous elections.

A large midwestern newspaper that also owns broadcast and magazine interests has most of the company's financial data stored in its computer. Through sophisticated analysis, the company can consider such factors as expansion trends toward specialized media, annual billings, rate of inflation, printing costs, plant expansion, and countless others, then use the computer to project these same cost factors over the next decade. At a command, the company president can have at his fingertips what percentage of his operating costs printing will consume by the next decade, how much paper he should stock, and what the price of advertising will be in the years ahead. Management might then decide to purchase more broadcast stations and to sell some of its magazine interests, or just the opposite. Management might also decide that it needs to hire more employees to keep pace with the company's projected development over the next five or ten years. A composite sales chart can be developed by computer so that every person will know his or her quota. Perhaps, on the basis of cost data, management will even decide to move into other investments related to mass communication, such as purchasing a chain of movie theaters or starting a book publishing company.

Another use of the computer is to help mass media sales personnel sell advertising. If you were sitting in the office of a major advertiser selling a segment of network television programming, you would find the computer indispensable. Assume that the sale is in the neighborhood of $200,000 for a series of network commercials. You have just spent the past hour convincing the prospective advertiser how good your network programming is and how a commercial on your network will reach more prospective buyers than another network can deliver. Just then your client says, "OK, I'll buy *if* you can place all the commercials in a certain selection of afternoon programming, alternating them every other day and alternating programs as well, but with three commercials running every day in one very popular program." The complexity of the request may boggle your mind. Moreover, if the competing network's representative was outside in the waiting room, it could be even more serious. To return to your office, work out the schedule, and then call her back could mean the loss of $200,000, plus your commission. Her interest could dwindle after you left, and the competition could steal your sale. Instead, you simply call your office and ask the traffic director to check the time availabilities on the computer for the requested advertising schedule. In a matter of seconds, the computer feeds the information to the traffic director who tells you the requested time is free. The time slots you sell are then logged into the computer, and that action prevents another member of the sales force from selling them to another prospective advertiser. New developments in computer hardware also enable you to carry a miniature teleprinter in your briefcase. This teleprinter enables you to make direct contact with the computer by using the phone on the advertiser's desk, and both of you can watch the advertising schedule being printed right before your eyes.

The computer can also be used in broadcast engineering. For example, the chief engineer at a modern broadcasting complex can go directly to a visual display terminal (Figure 12-9) or can read computer printout data on the operation of the station's transmitter or automation system. In the past, the same engineer would have to spend much time each day walking around with a clipboard taking meter readings required by the FCC. Now, the computer receives data directly from the transmitter and translates this into a printout of the meter readings. The computer also stores these data for future reference. For example, by reviewing a list of the times the transmitter was off the air, the engineer can tell what the operating time of many key instruments is. He can then prepare for future equipment failures by replacing these instruments before they wear out.

New developments in computer technology have also been applied to radio and television production. A disc jockey can sit at the controls of a radio station and, with a keyboard and VDT nearby, automatically select the next song to be aired (Figure 12-10). A television program is recorded on magnetic videotape in much the same way that sound is recorded on magnetic audiotape. If a section of videotape needs to be edited, you find that portion of the tape and then electronically edit it. You may have two videotapes and want to blend video from both of them onto a third tape. You may want to dissolve or slowly change from one tape to another. Simply turn on the tape machines, and the computer will automatically edit, stop, and start the tapes exactly when you command it. Also, you might want to insert a sound effect at the moment a specific picture appears. By giving pre-edit commands to the computer, the exact picture and sound combination will occur automatically. The time segments on the computer are very detailed, down to tenths and even hundredths of a second. The ability to edit in such detailed segments permits almost error-free editing.

transition to computer technology

The integration of computer technology into mass communication did not occur overnight. There naturally has been some resistance to computers by segments of organized labor who see union jobs being eliminated or reduced. In many cases, these fears have been justified. Linotype operators who have spent their lives setting type face a bleak future as the linotype machine simply disappears.

Psychological adjustment also enters the picture. The reporter who has made a living pounding out stories on an old typewriter for the past twenty-five

Figure 12-9 Satellite control centers can select and transmit programming to any number of selected geographical regions.

Figure 12-10 Disc jockey Johnny Walker at radio station CKXL in Calgary, Canada uses a computer-based system to select records for airplay. (Moffat Communications photo)

years may be hesitant to give up the "friend" and replace it with an electronic keyboard and visual display terminal. In most cases, however, the remorse is only temporary, and after there has been ample opportunity to become accustomed to the new equipment, the changeover is welcomed. One newspaper made the transition to a computerized system by first installing electric typewriters. The feeling of the managing editor was that the electric typewriters were the real transition, not the electronic keyboards and visual display terminals. Most of the employees, therefore, easily made the adjustment to computers. However, one reporter did run into trouble when he wanted to use a slightly off-color word which had come into acceptable vogue. Programmed into the computer was a block system in which a list of certain words would not appear in printed type. When the reporter wanted to use the word as an adjective, the computer refused to print it. Incidents like this are common. At a major wire service bureau, it was discovered that the static electricity built up in the rug would, when an employee wore wool clothing, erase portions of completed stories from the visual display terminal. In both the above cases, some minor adjustments solved the problem.

SUMMARY

CATV, called cable or community antenna television, first was developed in the 1940s when large community antennas were shared by many people living far away from television stations. Later, cable developed as a two-way communication medium. Today, cable systems offer the potential for home hookups with central computers, medical monitoring, grocery shopping, and access to first-run movies. When public resistance to the new two-way cable systems begins to diminish, more opportunities for using the system will unfold.

Satellites have been important in fostering international mass communication. The first satellite in orbit was the Russian Sputnik. It was followed by the American SCORE satellite and then Echo-I, the first relay satellite. The United States's Courier 1-B was the first repeater satellite. The world body governing the development of satellite communication is the International Telecommunication Satellite Consortium called INTELSAT. The management of INTELSAT is under the United States's Communication Satellite Corporation (COMSAT). There are many policy issues still affecting the development and operation of satellites. Cultural invasion by television programs from other countries is one major concern.

Computers also are essential to mass communication. From the rapid tabulation of election-night results, to making management decisions, to sales assistance, computers are yet another example of hardware systems making the process of mass communication more efficient.

OPPORTUNITIES FOR FURTHER LEARNING

ADLER, RICHARD, and WALTER S. BAER, eds., *The Electronic Box Office: Humanities and Arts on the Cable.* New York: Praeger Publishers, Inc., 1974.

BABE, ROBERT E., *Cable Television and Telecommunications in Canada: An Economic Analysis.* East Lansing: Michigan State University Press, 1975.

GILLESPIE, GILBERT, *Public Access Cable Television in the United States and Canada.* New York: Praeger Publishers, Inc., 1975.

HALLMARK, CLAYTON L., *Lasers: The Light Fantastic.* Blue Ridge Summit, Pa. : TAB Books, 1979.

LEDUC, DON R., *Cable Television and the FCC: A Crisis in Media Control.* Philadelphia: Temple University Press, 1973.

PELTON, JOSEPH N., *Global Communications Satellite Policy.* Mt. Airy, Md.: Lomond Books, 1974.

PELTON, JOSEPH N., and MARCELLUS S. SNOW, eds., *Economic and Policy Problems in Satellite Communications.* New York: Praeger Publishers, Inc., 1977.

POLCYN, KENNETH A., *An Educator's Guide to Communication Satellite Technology.* Washington, D.C.: Academy for Educational Development, Inc., 1973.

SNOW, MARCELLUS, *International Commercial Satellite Communications.* New York: Praeger Publishers, Inc., 1976.

13

Wire Services, Syndicates, and Networks

Although the media themselves are key links in bringing communication to a mass public, they are supported by many other media services. This chapter examines three such services that support both the print and broadcast media. First, few newspapers could successfully gather regional and national news without the help of wire services. Broadcasters would have similar difficulties. Second, neither the comics nor single panel cartoons, among other features, would appear in most newspapers or magazines without the help of syndicates. Many radio and television programs also reach the airwaves through this syndicated service. Third, both radio and television stations would have a difficult time filling their programming schedules without the services of some type of network. Let us begin by discussing wire services.

THE WIRE SERVICE CONCEPT

CBS news commentator Walter Cronkite once described working in a wire service as being in the "hot seat" of journalism. His analogy is not far from the truth. Sometimes called *press associations* or *news services*, wire services are essential information support systems for many mass media. Radio and television stations, newspapers, and specialized publications such as news magazines all use wire services as a source for their presentations. The most familiar wire services are the Associated Press (AP), United Press International (UPI), and Reuters. Stop and listen carefully to a television or radio news program. You will hear many reporters introduce the news program with a reference to the wire service. The reporter may say, "and now from the wires of United Press International," or "the Associated Press stated today . . . ." What follows is a story originally sent to subscribing media through a system of leased telephone lines and teletypes or teleprinters. Much of the national and international news offered by radio and television stations or newspapers comes from the wire services. Even networks rely heavily on wire services. It is obviously impossible for every radio and television station or newspaper to have correspondents throughout the world. The wire service is an important link in providing information to these media and consequently to the public.

in the beginning: AP and Reuters

The modern concept of wire services began in 1848 in the office of the *New York Sun* where New York newspaper publishers met and formed a news gathering organization called the Associated Press. Dr. Alexander Hones directed AP until 1851 when Daniel Craig, who had started AP's first foreign bureau two years earlier in Nova Scotia, became head of the organization under the title of "general agent." Mass transportation systems not only increased the potential number of newspaper subscribers but also created a demand for news content beyond the provincial reporting that permeated local presses of the era. In the same decade, the telegraph had become a major communication link. It provided instant news to places that just a few years earlier had waited for months to learn of events happening a mere hundred miles away.

Reuter's pigeon service

At the same time Craig took over at AP, Paul Julius Reuter began his first full year of operating a European carrier pigeon service relaying economic news to bankers between Aachen, in what is now West Germany, and Brussels, Belgium. The distance between the two points, 100 miles, was a large gap in the already developed telegraph network, and Reuter was able to bridge this gap. Not long after, Reuter hired help to run his own pigeon service and moved to London to try to develop a stronger base for his operation and also to have access to the coming Atlantic Cable. Although the London stockbrokers were eager for economic news, the London newspapers were not. It was not until 1858, after Reuter had provided a free trial service to the newspapers, that they entered into an agreement allowing them to receive general news from Europe.

dissension in the AP ranks

In our own country, the AP was responsible for much of the news disseminated during the Civil War. The journalistic prowess and objective reporting of the AP even gave it exemption from censorship orders by the government. After the end of the war, the AP struggled with some organizational problems. Specifically, the Western Associated Press complained that it was not receiving enough quality news from the New York headquarters bureau, which was controlled by New York interests. The Western Associated Press claimed that when the New York press learned of a big story, instead of turning it into the wire service for distribution, they would simply hold on to it. Even today, if a major paper or a radio or television station wants to keep a scoop story from its competition, it may not immediately turn over the story to the wire service. Although the AP is legally entitled to all news gathered by its subscribers, there is no contractual agreement binding the subscriber to relay a major scoop immediately to the wire service.

The split between the two factions of AP temporarily healed, and the wire service expanded its operation with the development of its own leased lines for exclusive AP distribution. However, the split appeared again in 1891 when an investigative team of the western group went to New York and discovered that some of the key AP people were in a secret news trade agreement with and were shareholders in a rival organization called United Press. This United Press was no relationship to the later service that eventually evolved into UPI. The outcome of the investigation was the formation of the Associated Press of Illinois, which was incorporated as a nonprofit organization and became the foundation for the modern AP. AP of Illinois also entered into agreements with foreign press associations, including Reuter's, which increased its coverage of foreign news.

John Vandercook and United Press

In 1897, the old United Press went out of business and left the new AP without any real competition. At about the same time, a twenty-five-year-old New York correspondent with the Scripps-McRae newspapers was beginning his career as a foreign correspondent and pursuing the opportunity to develop and enlarge the international wing of the Scripps-McRae Press Association. His name was John Vandercook. Seven years after his successful foreign assignment, he walked into his boss's office and asked E. W. Scripps for a promotion. He got it and began a fifteen-month position as editor of the *Cincinnati Post*. Not satisfied with being an editor, Vandercook again approached Scripps with an ever weightier proposition. Since the end of the old United Press in 1897, the Scripps papers had not fared well. Their own Scripps-McRae Press Association was no match for AP, but membership in the rival wire service was not an attractive prospect. Vandercook proposed consolidating the Scripps-McRae Press Association with the East Coast Publishers Association and the Scripps News Association, which served the West Coast members of the Scripps chain. Scripps bought the idea, and the three merged into a new press association called United Press. United Press prospered even after Vandercook's death a year later in 1907. In 1958, it merged with the International News Service to form United Press International. During the years between its founding and the merger, it also became the first major supplier of news to broadcasting stations and gave the broadcast media equal status with newspapers in helping to determine wire service policies. It also launched UPI Audio to provide radio stations with audio actualities, correspondent reports, and regularly scheduled newscasts. AP began a similar audio service in 1974 called AP Radio.

Meanwhile, Reuters was developing its own sizeable list of subscribers in the United States and especially in Europe. It continues to support many individual European bureaus that specialize in news services for specific countries. In 1967, it terminated agreements with AP and has since made great strides on its own, including the development of general and specialized services for the news media and such financial institutions as the Reuters Financial Report, Reuters Commodity Report, Reuters Money Report, and Reuters Metals Report.

USING A WIRE SERVICE

To understand how wire services function and how they are used by individual media, let's eavesdrop on a conversation at a local radio station. We are standing in the news room as the news director walks in. It is 6:00 A.M., and part of the news team is already sitting around having coffee. The "sitting around" will stop shortly; the coffee will remain a constant friend throughout the day.

News Director: What's it look like today, gang?

Reporter: We've had a big night. The jury on the Simpson case didn't get in until 1:30 this morning.

News Director: Did you get the story finished?

Reporter: I roughed out a draft and called it in to the wire service. They sent out a story on the morning split. They included some background information that we had overlooked. I had forgotten that Simpson had also been involved in that bank holdup five years ago.

News Director: Anything else breaking?

Reporter: Yea. Remember the hustler on the loan fraud case in Gainesville? Well, the wire says he tried it again last night and picked an undercover state trooper for his customer.

News Director: Call the state police headquarters and see if you can interview the trooper. We'll use it as an audio actuality.

Reporter: Already did that. Also there are some stories on the wire about the boy scout troop that uncovered the Indian ruins. It has some local interest for scouts in this area. There is even a good kicker story on the wire which should make you think about stopping your smoking, boss.

News Director: What's that?

Reporter: Some guy was out riding with his girlfriend in his convertible last night. She was driving and he was sitting in the passenger seat smoking a cigarette. The wind hit the cigarette ashes and burned a hole in his pants. He jumped up in the open convertible just as his girlfriend took a sharp S-curve. He fell out of the car and is in the hospital with a concussion.

From our conversation, let's examine the uses of a wire service. Keep in mind that a similar conversation could have taken place in a television station or a newspaper news room.

backgrounding stories

From the wire, the news team acquired additional information about local stories. Although the reporter had the information about the jury in the Simpson trial, the wire service filled in the details that gave greater depth to the story. The wire service also added another dimension to the station's news programming, an *audio actuality*, the recording of the "actual" sounds in the news. A portion of the station's interview with the state trooper will be used in the local newscast as an audio actuality. A television station or newspaper could accomplish the same thing with videotape. Our radio reporter also used the wire service as a source of new information—the story about the boy scout troop uncovering the Indian ruins. The wire even had a *kicker* story. This refers to the closing story of a newscast, which is in many cases a humorous anecdote, such as that about the fellow who fell out of his convertible.

We also heard some newsroom jargon during the conversation. For example, the word *split* was used to refer to a given news report sent over the wire. In wire service terminology, there are state splits, regional splits, morning splits, evening splits, and so forth. A split is simply a feature newscast on a particular region or a specialized interest, such as business, agriculture, weather, or sports.

audio services

Along with the printed copy, a wire service also offers audio feeds to subscribers. The audio feed is sent via telephone lines to local radio stations where it is either recorded or aired live. Audio feeds can be a single story or a complete newscast, such as UPI Audio or AP Radio provide. When your local radio station airs an interview with an international leader, the chances are that the interview was recorded first on location, then sent to the wire service headquarters by telephone where it was recorded and added to an "audio file" with other prerecorded stories. At a given time, all of the prerecorded stories in the wire service's audio file are sent to all subscribing stations through leased telephone lines. If you were responsible for preparing a radio newscast, you would learn which prerecorded stories were available by checking the wire service audio *billboard* which periodically clears the teletype.

picture wires

Many of the pictures you see in the newspaper are also prepared by the wire services. Most newspapers subscribe to a *picture wire*. The next time you read the newspaper or look at a news magazine, examine the photographs. Probably under one of them will be the words AP WIRE PHOTO or UPI WIRE PHOTO. In each case, the picture was transmitted through a special photo transmission system to the newspaper or magazine. New developments in wire photo transmission have made it possible to transmit photos of almost lifelike quality. Using a process similar to color television, color pictures also can be transmitted.

video feeds

Television stations also can benefit from wire service photographs. For example, video systems make it possible for television stations to receive daily video feeds of both still and motion pictures from the wire service. These are recorded on the station's videotape recorders and are later used in television newscasts.

THE BUREAU'S ROLE IN GATHERING NEWS

The major wire services have bureaus throughout the world staffed with experienced reporters, photographers, and editors all responsible for gathering and disseminating news to subscribers (Figure 13-1). In the United States, wire service bureaus are located in state capitals and metropolitan centers. Many of the major bureaus are responsible for disseminating world news that they receive from other wire service bureaus. In wire services, then, we have one of the most important gatekeepers of mass communication. In any given twenty-four hour period, wire service bureaus determine the news that billions of people will hear, see, and read.

reporters, photographers, and technicians

When a major story breaks, a wire service bureau may dispatch a reporter, photographer, and technician to cover the event. In many cases, one person performs all of these tasks. The nature of the wire service as news supplier to subscribers over a wide region requires that it carry the big stories and leave less important or local interest stories for individual broadcast stations and newspapers to carry. When major news does break, wire service reporters are under considerable pressure to get as much accurate information over the wire as soon as possible. After all, these reporters are actually doing the leg work for a large group of professional journalists who are dependent on their first hand reports. Added to this is the pressure of competition among rival wire services.

Figure 13-1 Large wire service bureaus process millions of words of news copy every day and distribute it throughout the world. Once primarily the workhorse of the newspaper industry, wire service bureaus now serve broadcast and cable clients as well. (United Press International)

covering major events

An example of one enterprising wire service reporter in action is the account of UPI reporter, John Gregory, now assigned to the Chicago Bureau. Late one afternoon when Gregory was still with UPI's Indianapolis Bureau, a passenger jet collided with a small plane above the Indianapolis airport, and both planes crashed, killing all aboard. It was one of the country's largest air disasters. Gregory left the office, and, in the process of driving to the scene of the event, pulled into a service station to ask directions. There he encountered a student on a school bus who had been an eyewitness to the event. Gregory directed the student to a telephone at the gas station, called UPI Audio headquarters in New York, and instructed the student to tell the wire service audio bureau about his eyewitness account of the crash. The New York bureau recorded the student's remarks. Continuing on his way to the scene, Gregory again stopped to ask for directions, this time at a nearby farmhouse. He was met at the door by a lady who had been picking vegetables outside when the crash occurred and had therefore been another eyewitness. In a few moments, Gregory had placed another call to UPI Audio in New York, and the woman was giving her eyewitness account of the event. Subscribers to UPI Audio thus had access to eyewitness interviews ready for airing on their evening newscasts, something that most other stations could not match. Gregory followed up the story that night with data on casualties, flight plans of the aircraft, and background information on the personal lives of passengers who never reached their destination. It was an example of what working at a wire service and being on the "hot seat" is like.

THE SUBSCRIBERS' ROLE IN GATHERING NEWS

Not all the work in gathering news falls on the shoulders of the wire service. It would be simply impossible for a wire service bureau to cover every news item in its assigned area. So they count on their subscribers to tip them off to major stories and to provide in-depth coverage of others. It is this willingness on the part of subscribers to contribute news to the wire service that improves the quantity and quality of news sent to all subscribers and, consequently, to the public. For example, AP is organized as a news cooperative and is entitled to all of the news that its subscribers gather. UPI is not automatically entitled to news that subscribers gather but does not operate at a disadvantage to AP. Both arrangements work equally well. AP simply puts into contractual terms what UPI has in an unwritten agreement. In some instances, subscribers are paid a nominal fee for their efforts. This token payment does not buy subscriber loyalty, however. The wire service's ability to provide a significant amount of important, accurate news on a regular basis is what keeps a subscriber renewing his or her contract.

Theoretically, the more subscribers a wire service has, the more information that can be fed back to the wire service from local areas and distributed to all other subscribers. In some states, the dominance of one wire service has created a lopsided situation, resulting in that wire service disseminating more stories of better quality.

SPECIALIZED WIRE SERVICES

Our discussion of wire services has centered on the major wire services of AP, UPI, and Reuters. There are also many specialized wire services serving specific news markets. We have already mentioned those furnished by Reuters. Another example is the Commodity News Service headquartered in Chicago and Kansas City. The Commodity News Service provides a series of specialized market analysis wire services of specific types of information. For example, it offers the Lumber Instant News (LIN), carrying such information to the lumber industry as daily cash prices of plywood, forest ranger reports, construction trends, and mortgage and financial information. This information is not only of interest to the mass media located in the heart of the lumber country but also provides an important service for the lumber industry, a subscriber to the LIN wire. Commodity News Service also offers the Farm Radio News (FRN) and Grain Information News (GIN), both offering crop reports, market quotations for the United States and Canada, and information on planting conditions. Also available are the Activity Commodity Trading News (ACT), Livestock Feed and Market News (LFM), and Poultry and Egg News (PEN).

Another example of a specialized wire service is the Public Relations Wire.

It is for the exclusive use of companies or other institutions and individuals who want to disseminate press releases through a wire service rather than to send them through the mail. Sending a press release over a wire service provides an aura of importance and urgency that the mail cannot convey. The income for the wire comes from two sources—subscribers, such as newspapers, broadcasting stations, and networks; and the companies which pay a fee to have their news releases distributed.

At first you might ask, "Why would any medium want to subscribe to a public relations wire?" The answer lies in its content and in the speed of distribution. Certainly much of the information received from such a source is biased in favor of the company or institution that distributes it. On the other hand, special feature information from a particular company or institution—discussing a major industrial development, executive transfers, or quarterly earnings—may be of interest to a specific public. Highly competitive media, such as the networks or media that carry a significant amount of financial news find the wire informative and rely on it for information a day or two in advance of the mails—and therefore well ahead of the competing media.

WIRE SERVICES AND NEW TECHNOLOGY

New technology has greatly increased the efficiency of the wire service. For instance, it is now possible to transmit wire photos through the process of *electrostatic transmission*. Using specially prepared paper, this system processes pictures to subscribers as glossy prints on dry paper ready for printing. Before the electrostatic process, subscribers still had to develop wire photos for printing. The new system, pioneered by UPI, not only facilitates the work of the photo editor on a major newspaper but also makes it possible to use photos received only minutes before press time.

The computer also has been important to wire service operation and is now responsible for the storage and retrieval of most copy disseminated from wire service bureaus worldwide. No longer is the typewriter the standard piece of equipment in the wire service bureau. It has been replaced by the visual display terminal. As noted earlier, the VDT is a television screen with a keyboard on which are typed the stories to be sent to subscribers. The stories are then edited and stored in a computer until ready for transmission. At any point during the transmission process, an editor can call forth on the VDT a list of stories currently stored in the computer and then determine which stories are to be sent and in which order.

access to stories

There are tremendous advantages to a computerized wire service system. Besides speed and efficiency, local news editors have *access* to stories formerly available only to national wire service editors. An editor in Iowa, for example, might want a feature article on harvest conditions in other parts of the world. Previously, the national wire service editor would control the dissemination of such features. Now the Iowa editor can scan the list of wire service stories on file in New York and call forth to his or her own VDT a completed story about harvesting. If the Iowa editor likes the story, a command to the computer will order that complete story automatically typed on the local teletype, ready for printing.

Even the teletype is succumbing to new technology and is being replaced by the quiet, compact teleprinter. Used in many bureaus and news rooms throughout the world, the teleprinter eliminates the familiar drumming sound of the teletypes associated with radio newscasts for decades. The small, boxlike machine sitting on a stylish base joins the silent VDTs in news rooms where the only sounds are those of conversation, not of pounding typewriters and clicking teletypes.

increased channel capacity

Channel capacity is another important consideration of wire services. By channel capacity, we mean *the number of words a wire service can transmit during a given time period*. In effect, this determines the amount of information a subscriber can receive. In the past, the channel capacity of standard teletype systems with information transmitted over telephone lines was limited to approximately 66 words per minute. However, new developments in technology, including high-speed teleprinters and cable systems, have the potential channel capacity of 70,000 words per second. Although the average news room will not ever receive that much news, developments such as these allow subscribers to receive an almost unlimited amount of news in any twenty-four hour period.

The future of wire services depends on their ability to remain free and independent suppliers of news. Currently, they are facing serious price squeezes because of increased costs for leased lines. If they can survive this era financially intact, and there is every indication that they will, new technology such as satellite communication may aid in disseminating the news to their subscribers much more economically.

FEATURE SYNDICATES

The next time you read the comics or your favorite feature column in the newspaper, notice in the corner of one of the panels or columns the small print reference to the copyright of a syndicate. The small print with the name King Features Syndicate, United Features Syndicate, National Newspaper Syndicate, or a similar reference spells the story behind one of the most important information systems for the newspaper and magazine industries. These publishers subscribe to syndicates in the same way they subscribe to wire services. In the past seventy years, the role of the syndicates has steadily increased in size and importance. Moreover, newspapers long ago learned that the features they carry often determine the size and loyalty of their readers. Although people turn to the newspaper for news, they also depend on the newspaper for entertainment—

entertainment that is just as important to the lifeblood of the newspaper as programming is to radio and television. It is mostly for this that the syndicates, sometimes called *feature* or *press syndicates*, operate.

Even books can become an important part of syndicate publication. Many times a syndicate will purchase the rights to a book and release it piecemeal before the complete publication is made available to the public. Along with providing good reading material for many magazines, the author and publisher also receive beneficial promotion. Records of special events are also syndicated. Many of the Apollo astronauts syndicatd the stories of their adventures in space as have famous explorers.

SYNDICATED COMICS

Of all the syndicated features, perhaps none reflects the concept more than the comics. Throughout this century, comic strips have reflected virtually every segment of life and have stereotyped such characters as the fighting soldier and the kid down the street. Every family with children can identify with such strips as *Dennis the Menace, Blondie,* and *Tiger.* The world of law enforcement has been accorded its share of attention through decades of *Dick Tracy.* We have watched this world-famous police officer tackle criminals with such crime fighting devices as two-way wrist radios and later two-way wrist television. The universal experience of romance has been captured in such popular strips as *Juliet Jones* and *Mary Worth.*

Although not new, direct social commentary has become acceptable comic material and has gained popularity and loyalty among comic enthusiasts. One of the most successful is the strip *Doonesbury,* created by a twenty-five-year-old Yale student named Gary Trudeau. The strip, an outgrowth of the turbulent late 1960s, first appeared in the *Yale Daily News* before being discovered and syndicated by Universal Press Syndicate. This comic has taken an almost no-holds-barred approach to current issues. In fact, some newspapers have refused to run certain episodes that pertain, by name, to some of the highest officials in government. Treatment of issues such as the energy crisis, protest marches, hippies, drugs, communal living, and life at the White House is common. Current estimates by Universal list the readership at eighteen million.

Syndicated artists and writers have emerged from some strange and unrelated backgrounds. Not atypical are the personal backgrounds represented by employees of King Features Syndicate. According to the Syndicate, Otto Soglow, who created *The Little King,* was a dishwasher, shipping clerk, and switchboard operator; the creator of *Prince Valiant,* Hal Foster, worked as a trapper, hunter, and boxer; Chic Young, who created *Blondie,* was once a mailcarrier; and Roy Crane, who created *Buz Sawyer,* claimed to have once been a hobo. But before you decide immediately to become a feature syndicate writer or artist, keep in mind that on the average, only about 1 in 10,000 attempted features ever reaches publication.

the readership

Of those that do reach publication, the impact and readership are astounding. In comparison, syndicate publications hold their own among such media systems as the networks and wire services. Unofficial estimates for the comics alone range in the vicinity of 100 million readers per day. The comic strip characters have also traveled beyond the pages of newspapers. Major radio serials have been developed around various comic strip personalities as have special radio and television programs. For example, Charlie Brown is not only a favorite among newspaper comic readers everywhere but has also starred in several prime-time television specials. In addition, his dog Snoopy adorns the dormitory rooms of countless students as a cuddly stuffed pillow dog, a perky poster, or in the form of countless other knickknacks. The character Ziggy, created by Tom Wilson of American Greetings Corporation and syndicated by Universal Press Syndicate, is also seen in stores as the little statue with the funny sayings inscribed on its base which seem to say anything you want about this charming little underdog.

panel cartoons

Panel cartoons are also popular syndicate features. These are cartoons contained in a single frame instead of a series of frames. Popular single frame cartoons include *Dennis the Menace, Marmaduke, Grin and Bear It*, and *Dunagin's People*. Editorial panel cartoons are syndicated in virtually every major newspaper in the free world.

As long as people continue to enjoy the escape to identification with characters whose experiences and life styles are similar, so will syndicate publications continue to thrive. With the ability to adapt to changing moods, issues, and experiences, the features of a syndicate can live almost indefinitely, appealing to generation after generation. Although the high cost of newsprint and other expenses associated with newspaper production have cut many pages from the print medium, the loyalty of readers to the comics and other features has been too steadfast for editors and publishers to gamble with removing some of the most popular characters of our daily lives.

EARLY SYNDICATE DEVELOPMENT

The beginning of the syndicate can be traced back to the late nineteenth century when Joseph Pulitzer published in the Sunday editions of his newspapers a comic character created by cartoonist Richard F. Outcault. But Pulitzer did not keep Outcault very long. The cartoonist soon began working for William Randolph Hearst and created his cartoon character, the "Yellow Kid," as mentioned in chapter 2. The success of the syndicated features became apparent as newspapers realized there was more to attracting readers than just publicizing hard news.

Following the Yellow Kid, the Katzenjammer Kids were born, and they were joined in the early 1900s by such strips as "Mutt and Jeff" and in 1917 by "The Gumps."

Hearst and King Features

Hearst also guided the founding of King Features Syndicate which was responsible for producing comic strips and other features for the Hearst newspapers as well as for subscribers. "Happy Hooligan" and "Bringing up Father" appeared along with book reviews, fashion features, and reproductions of art. M. Koenigsberg became the first president of King, and some of his early writers included George Bernard Shaw and William Jennings Bryan. Today, King is responsible not only for its printed features but also for the production of radio features and cooperative ventures into motion pictures, such as the film *The Yellow Submarine*.

John Dille and Buck Rogers

Another syndicate pioneer, John Flint Dille, founded the National Newspaper Syndicate in 1916. Dille, who had an interest in science and the intellect, combined these qualities in 1929 to create the popular "Buck Rogers in the 25th Century." The series was the forerunner of science fiction. One of the characters in the series, the famed Dr. Huer, differed from the usual athletic hero. He was an intellectual who was responsible for applying the discoveries of science to the imagination and creating mind-expanding adventures. He planted in many young readers of the era a hunger for scientific knowledge which undoubtedly influenced many of their professional careers. Along with becoming a successful and profitable entrepreneur, Dille wanted to give some social significance to his enterprise. So at a time when the word "psychology" still belonged to the realm of skepticism and suspicion, Dille launched the feature called "Let's Explore Your Mind," written by Dr. Albert Edward Wiggam. Dille's son, Robert C. Dille, now heads National.

Many other feature syndicates developed concurrently. The principal wire services also entered the feature syndication field. Many major newspapers have syndicated their best writers and artists, including the *Washington Post*, *Chicago Tribune*, *New York Times*, *Los Angeles Times*, and *Denver Post*. Individual writers and artists also have independently syndicated their material for distribution.

SCOPE OF SYNDICATES: GOLF TO GALL BLADDERS

The scope of content found in contemporary syndicate features is as broad as the tastes of the readership they serve. For example, our preoccupation with the sport of golf has prompted the syndicated "golf tips" of such sports immortals as Arnold Palmer, Gary Player, Sam Snead, Cary Middlecoff, Jack Nicklaus, and many others. "Mark Trail's Outdoor Tips" and the Publisher Hall Syndicate's "Jimmy 'The Greek' Snyder," plus many other sports cartoons, are further examples. Syndicated columnists themselves are popular with many readers. Jack Anderson has become a journalistic legend with his inside scoops on happenings in government. Other syndicated political columnists included on editorial pages include Rowland Evans, Robert Novak, and Carl Rowan. In some areas, regional columnists are also popular.

In addition, such specialized features as "Ann Landers" have gained tremendous loyalty among readers. Victor Reisel writes about the labor movement and has a wide following in areas in which a significant percentage of the readership are union members or come from union families. Hobbies have always been popular syndicated subjects, and many run on a seasonal basis, such as those dealing with gardening and landscaping. Medicine is also a popular feature, and the number of famous doctors writing syndicated columns has increased steadily. One of the most famous is Dr. Spock, the "baby doctor," whose column is found not only in newspapers but in magazines as well. Dr. Brady's health advice was syndicated by the National Newspaper Syndicate for over fifty years. National also syndicated the column by Dr. Lindsay Curtis entitled "For Women Only," which deals exclusively with women's health problems.

SYNDICATED BROADCAST PROGRAMMING

While feature syndicates provide newspapers and magazines with much of the material that reaches readers, syndication is also becoming a big business for broadcast programming. For example, some shows run a successful schedule on the network and are then syndicated, that is, sold directly to individual television stations for local programming and sponsorship. Shows such as *Bonanza, Ironside, Star Trek, The Mary Tyler Moore Show, Gunsmoke,* and countless others have not only made a successful run on network television but are now reaping additional income through syndication. In certain instances, production companies, the organizations that first produce the shows, place programs directly in syndication instead of first in network television. An example of this type of "first-run" or "original" syndication was Independent Television Corporation's *Space 1999.*

One of the most famous and successful programs to go directly into syndication was *Mary Hartman, Mary Hartman.* Having been turned down by networks for his program, creator Norman Lear resorted to this direct syndication approach. His success startled even the networks. The program dealt with formerly taboo social issues. Sex therapy and pot smoking, which had previously been left to late-night documentary fare, were discussed openly in *Mary*

Hartman, Mary Hartman. Understandably, some areas of the country protested bringing these subjects daily into their living rooms.

Although the program did not have a lengthy air life, *Mary Hartman, Mary Hartman* had long-range effects on television. The major networks' local television affiliates had been increasingly dissatisfied with the type of programming coming from network hoppers. Although other programs had had success on the syndication circuit, *Mary Hartman, Mary Hartman* was a first in the amount of attention and popularity that a program had captured going *directly* into syndication. Television station managers suddenly realized that perhaps the networks' distribution system might not always produce programming that suited their individual market. What is appropriate fare for Portland might not be appropriate to Paducah. Why should each city have to suffer with the other's programming? If the Portland television station manager can negotiate programming for Portland directly with production companies and syndicators, why make major commitments to the networks? Although it may be a while before the basic structure of the television networks changes and each individual station manager programs his or her own station much as radio now programs, this possibility is not escaping either the network or local station management.

HOW NETWORKS OPERATE

Most television stations operate on a profit. They derive their income from advertising, and their expenditures are primarily personnel salaries. But paying the number of people necessary to produce eighteen hours of daily local programming would bankrupt the average television station. To produce a full day of local programming would require numerous sets, production crews, and theater and film crews, just to name a few. And because of the limited number of people a local station is capable of reaching, it cannot charge enough for advertising to offset the cost of all that production. Thus, the network provides its affiliate stations with high-quality programming. Most stations need only to supplement this programming with two or three local shows per day, usually news programs. Since a network can charge more for advertising because of the large national audience it reaches, it can afford to provide programming with the talent capable of attracting and keeping sizable audiences.

Networks also act as a distribution system for commercials as well as for entertainment, news, and other types of programming. A national advertiser, usually through an advertising agency, can purchase advertising time on a network and reach millions of people without having to contract with each individual station. The three major commercial networks all are in competition for a share of the total national television viewing audience. The number of viewers a network is able to capture, measured in ratings, determines how much money it can charge for a segment of advertising. Certain special audience characteristics, such as the age and income of the audience, also will affect charges for network advertising. For example, a certain type of sports programming may appeal to a special type of audience, such as a predominantly male viewership with an average income of over $15,000 a year. Obviously, this type of listener is much more capable of purchasing sponsors' products than is an audience of equal size but with little buying power, such as a group of preschoolers. Thus, advertising on this type of programming will be more expensive.

The local television station is bound by an *affiliate contract* with the network but is not obligated to carry all of the available network programming. Naturally, it is a rare occasion when a local affiliate will not carry network programming, although it does happen. It is the local station and not the network that is responsible to the FCC for meeting the needs of the station's local community. Thus, when a local station feels that some type of programming may be objectionable to its audience, it may decide not to air the program or to shift it to another time period.

The networks must keep attuned to the needs and desires of their local affiliates. A network could not survive if its affiliates objected to its programming and refused to broadcast it, because sponsors could no longer be guaranteed a specific audience for commercials. Some advertisers might also object to sponsoring programs distasteful to the public. Thus, it is easy to see that in the long run the networks, although competing with each other, still must program shows that appeal to the great majority of the national audiences.

NETWORKS AND OTHER BUSINESSES

Up to now, our discussion has centered on the networks as systems used to supply programming and information to affiliate broadcasting stations. We should, however, be aware that the overall corporate structure of the parent corporations of most major networks includes other business enterprises, which have a broader financial base than the networks alone would have. Often a common theme, such as ABC's entertainment basis, runs through all the ventures. Along with the ABC television and radio networks, ABC also owns a group of seven AM and seven FM radio stations. The seven AM stations include such famous call letters in broadcasting as WABC in New York, WXYZ in Detroit, KABC in Los Angeles, KGO in San Francisco, KQV in Pittsburgh, KXYZ in Houston, and WLS in Chicago. Its profitable chain of theaters also gives ABC financial flexibility. There is no limit to the number of theaters a corporation can own, but the FCC limits to fourteen the number of AM and FM (seven of each) stations under single ownership.

All three of the major networks are involved in major publishing operations, including books, magazines, and specialty publications. CBS (Figure 13-2), for example, owns both Holt, Rinehart & Winston and W. B. Saunders Company, which publishes specialty material in the health sciences field. CBS Consumer Publishing Division publishes *Field and Stream, Road and Track,*

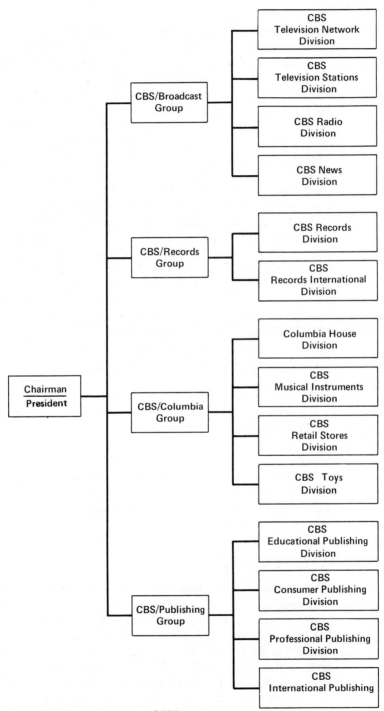

Figure 13-2 Corporate structure of CBS.

World Tennis, and *Cycle World*. ABC Publications include more specialized magazines, such as the *Wisconsin Agriculturist* and *Prairie Farmer*. RCA, of which NBC is a part, is involved in publishing through its subsidiary company, Random House. Allied publishing interests also are common, such as BFA Educational Media products, part of CBS, and RCA's Random House Enterprises, designed to compete in direct-mail sales.

One of the enterprises most closely allied to broadcasting is the recording business, in which both ABC and CBS have substantial interests. CBS's purchase of Columbia records in 1938 signaled the beginning of a lasting interest in the recording industry. Today, the CBS Records Group includes not only manufacturing and distribution but also talent scouting. Stars such as those of the early 1940s were the first on a long list of recording artists that includes some of the most popular contemporary singers associated with all different types of music both here and abroad. Mounting interest in tapes has also helped the industry. Closely aligned to CBS's recording interests is the CBS Retail Stores Division. Headquartered in California, the division includes Pacific Stereo, a group of stores selling high fidelity and stereo components, and Discount Records, a chain of retail record stores. ABC also has a major records division, contracting many important recording stars. Its purchase of Duke/Peacock Records now permits ABC Records to produce its own black gospel recordings. Group-owned stations, theaters, publishing houses, and recording companies are just some of the many diversified interests with which the major networks are associated.

THE NETWORK-AFFILIATE RELATIONSHIP

A broadcast network is basically as strong as its affiliate stations. Remember that without the affiliates there would be no network. To understand the network-affiliate relationship, it first is necessary to understand the communication occurring between the two. The key element is *feedback*, feedback from the affiliate to the network management.

commercial networks

Affiliates make their opinions known to network management through a group of delegates, usually certain station managers of the network's affiliate stations. If local stations have complaints or opinions they wish expressed to the network, they tell their delegates, who in turn meet with the network's management. Although no network will act on isolated complaints, when affiliate feedback on an issue becomes substantial and is well represented geographically and demographically, then the networks will make efforts to remedy the situation.

Another method of feedback to commercial networks is provided through the *clearance ratio*. If a network plans to broadcast material of questionable taste, it will notify all the affiliates well in advance of the forthcoming program and then air it on closed circuit to all network stations for their perusal. If enough of the stations decide they do not want to air the program, then the network will realize that it will suffer from the low ratings the program will undoubtedly receive. It is then up to the network to decide: (1) to air the program at all; (2) to reschedule it for another time period; (3) to permit local affiliates to videotape the program, then air it at a later hour; or (4) to cancel the program entirely.

How do the affiliates make their programming decisions? They do so by being responsive to the feedback they receive from their viewing audience. By carefully monitoring this feedback, broadcast management can determine what is suitable or unsuitable to local audience consumption. However, communicating their preferences to local broadcast management is the public's responsibility. Only when individuals take time to communicate their reactions to the local broadcaster can the local broadcaster, in turn, relay that feedback to the networks.

public broadcasting

In the Public Broadcasting Service, feedback has a much different form from that originating from commercial affiliates. This feedback comes mainly from what is called the Station Program Cooperative (SPC). The SPC utilizes direct feedback in the form of financial commitment from affiliate stations to determine which programs will make up approximately one-third of the programming distributed by PBS.

Essentially, the SPC operates in the following manner. As the person responsible for determining what program will be funded under the SPC system, you first will develop a set of national program needs using all of the feedback information mentioned above. Based on these needs, you will solicit proposals from program producers. From this information, you then will prepare a catalogue of the program proposals for use by the individual public broadcasting system's licensees in planning their next season's programming.

This selection process by the individual licensees initiates a direct feedback procedure that eventually determines which program will be funded and which program will be dropped from further consideration. The first step in this feedback process is a *bidding round* in which the licensees indicate their interest in specific programs. At this point, there is no financial commitment by the licensee. From this information, the SPC official then determines which programs are the top contenders for selection by affiliate stations. After a second bidding round, during which the stations begin to commit themselves financially, some programs are tentatively accepted, and others are dropped from the list. The final step, a *purchase round*, involves stations making final commitments and programs being selected.

Feedback is one of the most important steps in the decision-making process of a public broadcasting station. Public broadcasting, by its very nature, must monitor more detailed feedback at every level of the management chain. The interests of the local audience become feedback to the affiliates, and these data are in turn utilized by the PBS network. PBS programming is generally the result of a much more "participatory process" than occurs with other forms of mass communication, a type of feedback in which you, as a consumer, can become personally involved.

REGIONAL, INFORMAL, AND SALES NETWORKS

Along with the major radio and television networks, other types of networks affect the flow of information to the public. These are the regional, informal, and sales networks.

Regional networks provide programming and information to specific geographic areas. They are incorporated into the regular programming of the station in much the same way as national network programming is. The regionals' supplemental programming, especially news, figures importantly in attracting local audiences. An audience in Maine, for instance, is more interested in news of Maine and New England than in news of Alabama. With the advent of CATV, regional networks have become increasingly important to individual stations. CATV takes the station's signal beyond its primary broadcast contours into many outlying communities. Since for most broadcasting stations the cost of sending reporters to cover all these surrounding areas is prohibitive, the regional network solves the problem.

Informal networks are news networks created by a professional group of radio or television news personnel. There is no contract or written document spelling out services or agreements. Such networks are in existence everywhere and are a big help to participating stations.

Let's assume that you are working as a radio reporter in a large city and want to carry news of three surrounding cities. To do so, you develop an association with news personnel at a station in each of the three surrounding cities and call on them whenever you need information about a story in their community. The advantage of this informal network is that because the desired story is important local news, the originating station will probably cover it in depth and can provide additional background information that other networks, including a wire service, might not have. Usually called *co-ops*, these informal networks can consist of two to as many as fifteen or more newspersons who exchange news on a fairly regular basis.

Sales networks are designed principally for advertising. Although participating stations may occasionally receive programming material, this is not the network's main purpose. A sales network is usually a group of stations linked together through some common bond to benefit all member stations financially. As with informal networks, this bond can be aided by a permanent communications system, such as teletypes or leased transmission lines. The networks are often formed by advertising agencies or broadcast station representatives.

For example, there might be one such network in an area noted for its vacation opportunities or tourist attractions. Let us assume that this area consists of three states and that you are responsible for buying advertising for a chain of restaurants in the three-state area. You decide to purchase commercials on different radio and television stations in the area and are looking for an inexpensive group rate. However, since the stations do not often voluntarily cooperate—mostly because they are competing businesses and are perhaps miles apart—an advertising agency in the area might contact the group of stations and ask if they would like to join together in, for example, a "tourist network." The advertising agency or station representative then would sell commercials for all member stations, taking a commission from the total price of the commercials. All stations would benefit from the sale as would you, the advertiser, who would receive a group purchase discount. The difference between this type of a network and the others is that dissemination of information is not the primary service provided by the network; its benefits come from group purchasing power.

SUMMARY

In this chapter we have studied wire services, syndicates, and networks. Wire services are responsible for supplying the bulk of news to the mass media, which in turn disseminate it to the public through broadcast and printed news reports. Specialized wire services carry news designed for specialized audiences such as the agricultural and business communities.

The concept of a wire service actually found its first application in the nineteenth century with carrier pigeon service between towns not connected by telegraph. The first modern wire service was Associated Press, which did not acquire its present form until a dispute between its western and eastern factions resulted in the formation of the Associated Press of Illinois. United Press International became the first supplier of news to broadcast stations. Reuters, AP, and UPI are the three major wire services.

Syndicates are another principal source of information for mass media, especially newspapers. The syndicate concept, which dates back to the end of the last century, has now been applied to everything from books to cartoons. Based on this same syndicate principle, many broadcasting stations are also using syndicated programming.

Broadcast networks, especially television networks, are responsible for providing much of the programming that affiliate stations air. These networks also are associated with other businesses through their parent companies. The ownership of motion picture theaters, radio and television stations, book and magazine publishing houses, and retail stores forms a broad base of financial support for the networks. In commercial broadcasting, networks are made aware of the concerns of their affiliates through affiliate representatives and organizations. In public broadcasting, affiliates directly participate in what becomes network programming through the station program cooperative.

OPPORTUNITIES FOR FURTHER LEARNING

BERGER, ASA, *The Comic-Stripped American*. Baltimore: Penguin Books, 1974.

CAMPBELL, ROBERT, *The Golden Years of Broadcasting: A Celebration of the First 50 Years of Radio and TV on NBC*. New York: Simon and Schuster, Inc., 1976.

DREHER, CARL, *Sarnoff: An American Success*. New York: Quadrangle/The New York Times Book Co., Inc., 1977.

EPSTEIN, EDWARD J., *News from Nowhere*. New York: Vintage Books, 1974.

ESTREN, JAMES, *A History of Underground Comics*. New York: Quick Fox, Inc., 1974.

FRIENDLY, FRED W., *Due to Circumstances beyond Our Control . . .* New York: Random House, Inc., 1977.

HORN, MAURICE, ed., *The World Encyclopedia of Comics*. New York: Chelsea House, 1976.

LEE, STAN, *Origins of Marvel Comics*. New York: Simon and Schuster, Inc., 1974.

MACY, JOHN W., *To Irrigate a Wasteland, the Struggle to Shape a Public Television System in the United States*. Berkeley: University of California Press, 1974.

NELSON, ROY PAUL, *Cartooning*. Chicago: Henry Regnery Co., 1975.

PALEY, WILLIAM S., *As It Happened*. New York: Doubleday & Co., Inc., 1979.

QUINLAN, STERLING, *Inside ABC*. New York: Hastings House Publishers, 1979.

ROBINSON, JERRY, *The Comics: An Illustrated History of Comic Strip Art*. New York: G. P. Putnam's Sons, 1974.

ST. HILL, THOMAS NAST, *Thomas Nast: Cartoons and Illustrations*. New York: Dover Publications, Inc., 1974.

WEINER, RICHARD, *Syndicated Columnists*. New York: Richard Weiner, Inc., 1976.

14

Regulatory Control of Mass Communication

Freedom from regulatory control of American mass media is guaranteed by the Constitution. In other countries, legislation either guarantees the free flow of information via the media or establishes very strict controls over such messages. However, because space on the electromagnetic spectrum is limited, American electronic media operate *under* government control, originating from such agencies as the Federal Communications Commission on a national level, to the International Telecommunications Union (ITU) on an international level. To understand control of mass communication, we shall begin by examining a theoretical model of control. Keep in mind as we examine the model of control that different media have different regulatory needs. Broadcasting, because it is a limited resource, has more regulations than magazines do. And although magazines are not regulated by a federal agency as such, they are affected by a complex array of postal regulations. In different countries, the control of media varies, and the limitations of the print or broadcast media in one country can be entirely different in another.

A MODEL OF CONTROL

One way to view control of mass communication is through a model developed by Osmo Wiio, professor and director of the Helsinki Research Institute for

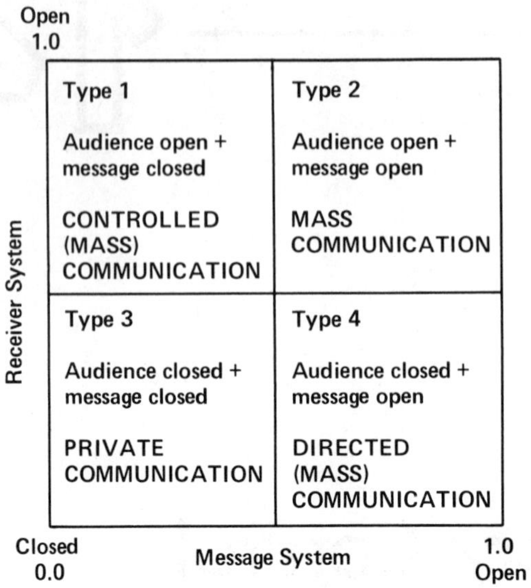

Open
1.0

	Type 1	Type 2
Receiver System	Audience open + message closed CONTROLLED (MASS) COMMUNICATION	Audience open + message open MASS COMMUNICATION
	Type 3 Audience closed + message closed PRIVATE COMMUNICATION	**Type 4** Audience closed + message open DIRECTED (MASS) COMMUNICATION

Closed   1.0
0.0   Message System   Open

Figure 14-1 Wiio's model of mass communication.

Business Economics.[1] In Wiio's model, mass communication is viewed on a two-dimensional, open-closed continuum of the receiver system (the audience) and the message system (the media) as shown in Figure 14-1. The left vertical line of the model represents the audience, and the bottom horizontal line represents the message system. A numerical range of 0.0 to 1.0 is used to characterize the degree of control, with 1.0 representing the most open system, and 0.0 representing the most closed system. Thus, the most *closed* system, for example, a Type 3 private telephone system, is actually private communication, not mass communication at all. Type 2, uncontrolled mass communication, which directs its messages to anyone who can hear them, represents the other end of the spectrum, a completely *open* mass communication system.

Each medium operates under varying amounts of control and for an audience at some position on the open-closed continuum. For example, a company magazine is more closed both in terms of message and audience than is a major metropolitan newspaper. Certain messages within the same medium may also be more closed than others. Consider the local television cable system that provides a fairly wide range of programs for its viewers. Some channels, however, may be accessible only to those viewers who pay an additional fee to the cable system. In this case, the system itself represents a more open position on the model, and a given cable channel represents a more closed position. It is important to realize that the model is not meant to be a tidy classification of media. It is presented to help you conceptualize the various dimensions of control that affect mass communication. As you read about the specific agencies and regulations, consider how they would interrelate with the model we have just discussed. In addition, remember that many of these "controls" are not controls in the traditional sense but are actually safeguards to ensure our system's "openness."

EARLY RADIO LEGISLATION

The twentieth century had barely begun when it became clear that Marconi's invention was quickly getting out of hand. Interference, jamming, and crowded frequencies were just some of the conditions that resulted in the United States bringing radio under government control.

the Wireless Ship Act of 1910

The Wireless Ship Act of 1910 was the first piece of legislation to affect directly the new "wireless" communication that later became known as radio. Basically, the law made it illegal for any "ocean-going steamer" carrying more than fifty persons to leave a United States port for a trip of more than two hundred miles without ship-to-ship and ship-to-shore communication equipment (Figure 14-2) operated by a trained technician. Enforcement of this regulation was the duty of the Secretary of Commerce and Labor, who had the authority to arrest the "master" of any ship violating the order. The courts were authorized to slap a maximum $5000 fine on the "master" for that violation. The act accomplished three things: (1) it provided an impetus for the beginnings of the radio industry;

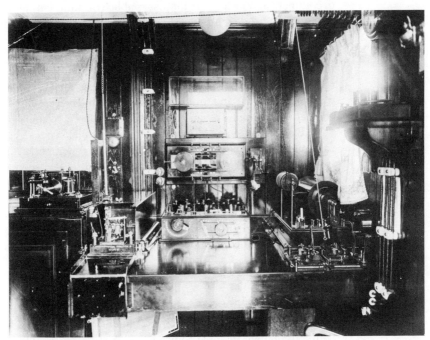

Figure 14-2 Shipboard wireless. Typical Marconi-equipped facility was this wireless room aboard the *Lusitania*. (The Marconi Company Limited, Marconi House, Chelmsford, Essex)

(2) it was evidence that Congress recognized the potential of the new medium; and (3) it sparked research and development of wireless communication for improving long-distance radio service.

the Radio Act of 1912

It was not long after the 1910 act, however, that Congress realized that it would be necessary to keep track of who owned and controlled the two-way communication equipment so the President of the United States could gain control of it during wartime, should that become necessary. Thus, two years later, Congress passed a second piece of legislation, the Radio Act of 1912. In the 1912 act, Congress effectively legislated that anyone operating a radio transmitter first had to have a license; that the only people who could obtain a license were citizens of the United States and Puerto Rico or corporations chartered in either the United States or Puerto Rico; that the owners and location of the equipment be identified; and that there be some estimate of the distance over which the transmitter could send messages. The act also provided for separation between the frequencies of stations to eliminate interference, but it left these decisions more up to the owners of the transmitters than to the government.

Yet the 1912 act really had no practical way of controlling the development of commercial broadcasting for mass public consumption, for radio was far more than shipping and commerce. Experimental stations began testing the air waves. The 1920s arrived with KDKA broadcasting the Harding-Cox election and WGN carrying Chicago Cubs and White Sox baseball, Big Ten Football, and the Indy 500. Radio was suddenly everywhere. Broadcasters also realized that with an audience of this size they could charge for messages sent over the air waves. Excitement and turmoil within the industry were mounting. To fight off competition, stations began to operate with more and more power.

By the 1920s, the air waves were in complete chaos. Yet the courts overruled the Department of Commerce and Labor's attempts at control. Secretary of Commerce and Labor Herbert Hoover (Figure 14-3) then called a series of National Radio Conferences to try to develop legislative proposals that if passed, might solve some of radio's crowding problems. The conferences brought together everyone from the military, to private owners of broadcasting stations, to amateur radio operators. Finally, after a number of false starts with inadequate legislative proposals, Congress responded to the problem by passing the Radio Act of 1927.

the Radio Act of 1927

The Radio Act of 1927 recognized for the first time the need for broadcasting to be in "the public interest, convenience, and necessity," although in 1927 programming was not the issue it is today. Legislators also paid heed, both legal and political, to the fact that the airwaves, unlike the print media, were limited in

Figure 14-3 Herbert Hoover. (AT&T)

their capacity to transmit messages at any one time. Only so much of the electromagnetic spectrum could be efficiently used for broadcasting; this scarce resource thus needed to be controlled.

The 1927 legislation also established the first governmental body to control broadcasting—the Federal Radio Commission—a five-member group appointed by the President. The Act of 1927 contained some significant legislation that still applies to broadcasting today. It established a system of call letters for radio stations, a systematic method of license renewal and equipment modification, and qualifications for station operators. It also gave government the power to revoke licenses, to provide for inspection of station apparatus, and to assign frequency and power limits to stations while retaining the regulatory provisions of the 1912 legislation on communication for ships at sea.

the Communications Act of 1934

The Radio Act of 1927 remained in force until 1934 when Congress, on the recommendation of President Franklin D. Roosevelt, passed the Communications Act of 1934. This act identified broadcasting as a separate entity apart from both the "utility" or "power" concept and apart from "transportation." The act replaced the Federal Radio Commission with the Federal Communications Commission and became the main piece of legislation, as later amended, under which the American system of broadcasting now operates.

THE FEDERAL COMMUNICATIONS COMMISSION

Of all governmental agencies, the FCC is second to none in its direct and profound effect on the lives of virtually everyone. The FCC is, whether directly or indirectly, the governmental body responsible for regulating relatively all of the messages millions of people see and hear every day through the broadcast media. Although the commission has no broad power to censor the content of broadcasting, it does have the power to ensure that those in broadcasting are responsible and consider the public "interest, convenience, and necessity." By one sweep of the regulatory hand or even by the suggestion of a major policy statement, it can affect the content of prime-time television, give networks second thoughts about children's television programming, give a politician equal air time, and affect the daily operation of every local broadcasting operation in the country, which in turn affects each citizen.

organizational structure and effectiveness

The commission consists of seven FCC commissioners appointed by the President with the advice and consent of the Senate (Figure 14-4). In recent years their appointment has come under close scrutiny in confirmation hearings, a sign of the importance of mass communication to our society in general and the

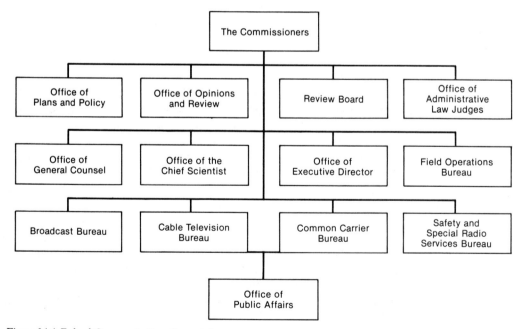

Figure 14-4 Federal Communications Commission.

326

control of that communication in particular. The Communications Act prohibits the commissioners from having any conflicting interests while serving on the commission. It also sets their terms for seven years and limits to four the members from any one political party.

There are arguments on both sides of the fence as to how effective the FCC is. On the one hand, the commission has been criticized for being too lenient in broadcast programming regulation and allowing the networks, the broadcasting industry, and the politicians the upper hand. Others have argued that although the FCC is in fact a regulatory agency, it can very easily come into conflict with the First Amendment to the Constitution. Over the years, the commission has increased in size to more than 2,000 employees, a development indicative of the trend toward government bureaucracy. However, the FCC does patrol the operation of thousands of commercial broadcasting stations and many times that number of two-way radio stations operated by citizens, local governments, and municipalities. The surge of interest in citizens' band radio has also increased the commission's workload.

As with any governmental agency, many commission actions and decisions take their cue from developments within the industry. This is because in order to regulate an industry effectively and fairly, one first needs to know how that industry works. To obtain this feedback, the FCC initiates a system of "opinion filings" in which broadcasters file with the commission their opinions on pending rules and regulations. The FCC, in turn, weighs these opinions, because significant industry opposition to a proposed regulation might result in more law suits than in compliance, once it is passed.

Many of the decisions the FCC makes are not popular with the industry, and many should not be. But the commission is caught between regulating an industry that must operate in the public interest and being the instrument of a political process that is ultimately accountable to Congress. The commission can even face pressures from the industry directed at members of Congress. Comments from broadcasters are not ignored in Congress, and a high level of criticism against any governmental agency can cause everything from investigative inquiries to budget hassles.

policing the industry

Despite the pros and cons of FCC regulation, the average broadcaster views the commission as a very visible "police" force. Public interest groups often view it as an ineffective "paper tiger." A network of FCC field offices does send out inspectors to make periodic, unannounced visits to stations to scrutinize various aspects of station operation. They check logs to determine if commercial messages are recorded as aired and billed to the sponsor; they check the station's public file to see if documents open to the public are in order; they inspect equipment; and they monitor the programming of the station. Any perusal of the back pages of

Broadcasting will document the violations and penalty fines resulting from these inspections. At license renewal time, each station makes a complete accounting to the FCC of its operating procedures and promises of service to the community.

complaints to the FCC

Although it is usually more effective to deal directly with a local station when complaining about some aspect of broadcast communication, everyone has a right to complain directly to the FCC. If you are not satisfied with the action taken by the local broadcaster to resolve your complaint, then the FCC may be your only recourse. When this procedure is used, the Broadcast Procedural Manual of the FCC outlines specific guidelines which you should follow:

> Submit your complaint promptly after the event to which it relates. Include at least the following information in your letter of complaint: The full name and address of the complainant. The call letters and location of the station. The name of any program to which the complaint relates and the date and time of its broadcast. A statement of what the station has done or failed to do which causes you to file a complaint. Be as specific as possible. Furnish names, dates, places and other details. A statement setting forth what you want the station and/or the Commission to do. A copy of any previous correspondence between you and the station concerning the subject of the complaint. Try to appreciate that the person reviewing your complaint must make rapid judgments regarding the gravity of the matters related and the action to be taken. There are a number of simple things you can do to make his job easier and to aid your own cause: State the facts fully and at the beginning. Subject to fully stating the facts, be as brief as possible. If the facts are self-explanatory, avoid argument; let the facts speak for themselves. Avoid repetition or exaggeration. If you think a specific law or regulation has been violated, tell us what it is. If possible, use a typewriter, but if you do write by hand, take special pains to write legibly.

These guidelines are both to make the job of the FCC easier and to process your complaint more efficiently. If you do file a complaint to the FCC, you will be one of almost 25,000 people who do so every year. With this volume of feedback to assimilate, it is easy to see why step-by-step guidelines are a necessity. It is also easy to see why the best method is first to contact the local station and try to resolve the issue at that level.

It is wise to learn something about broadcast regulations before filing such a complaint. Some people are under the impression that the FCC has the power to demand that certain programs be aired or taken off the air. *It does not.* Also, some people are under the mistaken impression that news programming is fair game for complaints. Although anyone is entitled to file a complaint about the operation of a broadcast station's news department, strong safeguards assure freedom of the press, which in many ways exempts the news department from any control, including that of station management.

Despite these precautions, the person who contributes responsible feedback to the media advances the democratic process in a free society. The commercial broadcasting industry, because its licensees have the "privilege" of operating a station, is particularly sensitive to feedback from its audience and is prepared to react to this in a responsible manner.

input to FCC rule making

Complaints are not the only reason to contact the commission. The FCC welcomes input from the public when it is considering issues affecting the operation of broadcasting stations or other areas of its jurisdiction. In such cases, your letter should state precisely the issue to which you are responding, the FCC file or docket number assigned to the issue, and what background you have that may make you particularly qualified to respond. The FCC distributes regular *Action Alerts* (Figure 14-5) memoranda that explain in lay terms the issues being considered. Broadcasters and interested citizens groups are on its mailing list, and many libraries receive them. Single copies of *Action Alert* can be obtained by writing the FCC in Washington.

As with any governmental agency, the FCC must be flexible in the face of pressures from both the industry it regulates and the public it serves. The future is going to bring many more difficult decisions by the commission. As new

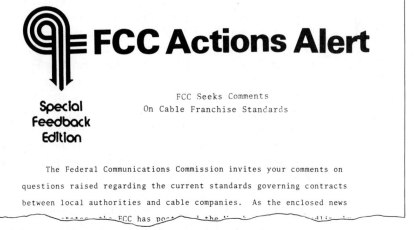

Figure 14-5 FCC Actions Alert soliciting public feedback.

technology continues to affect our lives, and as Congress continues to define its regulation of electronic mass communication, the work of this regulatory body will become significantly more important.

SECTION 315

Of those sections found within the Communications Act of 1934, perhaps none has been more discussed than Section 315. It has had a profound effect on the operations of political broadcasting. Section 315 concerns the ability of political candidates to gain access to the airwaves during political campaigns. It states:

> If any licensee shall permit any person who is a legally qualified candidate for any public office to use a broadcasting station, he shall afford equal opportunity to all other such candidates for that office in the use of such broadcasting station: *Providing,* that such license shall have no power of censorship over the material broadcast under the provisions of this section.

pros and cons of access

Section 315 has received serious criticism from candidates and broadcasters alike. To understand these feelings, imagine that you have just filed candidacy for your city council and plan to make arrangements to purchase advertising time on one of the radio stations in your community. You make an appointment with the sales manager to discuss the amount of money you have to spend and the type of political announcement you will make. You look at the station's rate card and discover that by purchasing 100 commercials, you will obtain a discount. You are not sure you can afford 100 commercials and are relieved to hear the sales manager say that you can purchase a lesser number of commercials and still receive the discount rate. He explains that under Section 315, you are entitled to the "lowest unit charge" and therefore will receive the station's "discount rate" for purchasing 100 commercials even though you will only purchase 50 commercials. The discount rate for 100 commercials is $5.00 per commercial. You can afford to purchase 50 commercials for a total of $250.00 You agree to the contract and then explain that you want to use the station's facilities to produce your commercials. The sales manager quotes you a per-hour rate for the use of the facilities. Returning the next day to produce your commercials, you tie up the facilities for about two hours. Finally with the help of the program director, you produce an acceptable commercial. After you leave, the sales manager goes in to talk with the general manager.

Sales Manager: Well, that job is finished. We tied up the main studio for two hours and all for $250 in advertising. I could have used the same time to produce a commercial for the hardware store worth $500 in advertising.

General Manager: Yes, I know. This Section 315 is getting to be a real headache. We haven't heard the end of it, either. You know that when the opponent hears that commercial, she'll be in here wanting to buy time, and we'll be faced with the same tied-up facilities and low sales that we were on this one. What do you think? Would it be a good idea simply to refuse to sell political advertising next year and instead offer free time to all the candidates?

Sales Manager: Do you have any idea how many people are running for city council? This place would be like a zoo. We would have every candidate in here who wanted to state a case. This way, the cost of purchasing commercials at least keeps the crowd down.

General Manager: Yes. It also keeps our profits down.

The conversation between the sales manager and the general manager illustrates just one of the issues surrounding Section 315—money. A station does not realize much profit from political commercials. In addition, because a station is required to permit all candidates for any one office to purchase time, every candidate is assured equal access and equal rates. Besides this, since a radio station is allowed to program only so many minutes per hour of commercials, and since Section 315 says stations must grant candidates access to these minutes, many other advertisers who would pay more for commercials and who may be long-term, good customers may have to be pushed off the air to accommodate political advertisements. But remember the positive side of Section 315. Without it, candidates with smaller campaign budgets might not be able to use the broadcast media to bring their campaign to the public.

exempting news programming

One area that is exempt from the provisions of the law is news programming. Section 315 states that the equal time provisions do not apply to

1. bona fide newscasts;
2. bona fide news interviews;
3. bona fide news documentaries (if the appearance of the candidate is incidental to the presentation of the subject or subjects covered by the news documentary); or
4. on-the-spot coverage of bona fide news events (including but not limited to political conventions and activities incidental thereto). [A 1975 ruling by the FCC added press conferences and political debates broadcast live in their entirety to this exemption.]

If you interviewed a candidate and aired his or her remarks in a newscast, it would be up to you whether or not to air the comments of the opposing candidate. Although you would want to exercise your responsibility to seek out both sides of an issue, the opponents could not demand equal time based on Section 315. An example of this exemption occurred with the *CBS Morning News*, which covered a story about an ex-convict running for sheriff in the state of Virginia. The story showed the candidate campaigning, interviewed him, and told of his background, which had included time served at a number of prisons for felony convictions. When the report was broadcast, there was even a campaign poster behind Hughes Rudd, the CBS news commentator, which said "vote for" and the name of the candidate. Although the man was an officially declared candidate, the news about his campaigning came under the exemption provisions of Section 315.

A station, of course, cannot completely refuse access to candidates and close itself off from its community. For instance, it cannot refuse free time and also refuse to sell political advertising. That would be denying "reasonable opportunity for the discussion of conflicting views on issues of public importance." The main purpose of Section 315 is to assure minority candidates and candidates with limited funds at least a minimal access to the broadcast media. Although there is continued criticism of the law, so far it is the best measure the FCC has to assure candidates an opportunity to be heard.

THE FAIRNESS DOCTRINE

The Fairness Doctrine goes beyond political broadcasting to the overall treatment of controversial issues. The issues are not limited to politics as codified in Section 315 but go beyond them to include other issues deemed important to the community served by the broadcasting station.

the fairness doctrine is issued

In the spring of 1948, the FCC began a series of hearings on the subject of editorializing by the broadcast media.[2] Out of these hearings arose the Fairness Doctrine, which pertains to the responsibility of every broadcaster to provide station facilities for the expression of controversial issues and all sides of those issues.[3] In a statement on the matter, the commission noted on June 1, 1949, that editorializing was "consistent with the licensee's duty to operate in the public interest." The commission went on to emphasize the responsibility of the licensee to seek out opposing views on controversial issues, commonly referred to as the "seek out" rule. The 1949 report also charged the licensee with the responsibility to "play a conscious and positive role in bringing about a balanced presentation of opposing viewpoints."

Since 1949, the FCC has periodically issued a series of statements on the interpretations of the Fairness Doctrine. Among these is the "personal attack" rule requiring notification and offers of equal time to people verbally attacked on the air.

the 1974 report

Reopened hearings on the Doctrine in 1974 led to the FCC issuing the "Fairness Doctrine Report: 1974." That report specifically exempted product advertisements from the Doctrine's jurisdiction. The 1974 report also attempted to create an atmosphere of flexibility in interpreting the Doctrine. What the FCC, the broadcasters, and the public had been concerned over was that there were no guidelines for any of the groups to follow in defining such important concepts as "a controversial issue" or "reasonable opportunity for contrasting viewpoints." The commission summed up its feelings on these matters as follows:

> The Fairness Doctrine will not ensure perfect balance and debate, and each station is not required to provide an "equal" opportunity for opposing views. Furthermore, since the Fairness Doctrine does not require balance in individual programs or a series of programs, but only in a station's overall programming, there is no assurance that a listener who hears an initial presentation will also hear a rebuttal. However, if all stations presenting programming relating to a controversial issue of public importance make an effort to round out their coverage with contrasting viewpoints, these various points of view will receive a much wider public dissemination.

The 1974 report has not reduced the debate over the Fairness Doctrine. When cable television systems fully utilize their multi-channel capacity and when citizen groups take advantage of their opportunities to help determine programming on these channels, then the restricted broadcasting "spectrum" will expand as will its potential for disseminating information. Perhaps there will come a time, then, when both the implied and stated controls that comprise the Fairness Doctrine may be unnecessary.

reconsidering the fairness doctrine: 1976

The commission decided to reconsider the Fairness Doctrine in 1976 after citizens' groups wanted more access to broadcasting. The FCC generally reaffirmed its decisions in the 1974 report. It felt that the Doctrine should continue to be applied to advertisements that pertain to public issues, not to specific products. It agreed that broadcast editorials should come under the Doctrine's aegis and reaffirmed the right of the broadcaster to decide how the Doctrine should be applied on a local basis. In the case in which the FCC did have to intervene, it felt that the probable action would be simply to require the station to provide time for opposing viewpoints.

UPS AND DOWNS OF THE REWRITE ISSUE

The impetus for a major rewrite of the Communications Act of 1934 came out of congressional hearings held in 1976 on the proposed Consumer Communications Reform Act, which would have overhauled telephone regulation. Commonly called the "Bell Bill," the proposed legislation went into hearings before the U.S. House of Representatives' Communications Subcommittee under the chairmanship of Lionel Van Deerlin, a California Democrat. Cable television also received close scrutiny by Van Deerlin that year. In October of 1976, Van Deerlin announced a full-scale inquiry into rewriting communications legislation after concluding during the hearings that, among other things, the 1934 legislation was insufficient to regulate the new technology that had been developed since its passage—technology that included satellites, microwave, cable, fiber optics, citizens band radio, radar, land mobile communication, and light wave or laser beam communication.

After a series of hearings on the subject, Van Deerlin's subcommittee released the first draft of the proposed changes in the spring of 1978 and another draft in 1979. In addition, other bills rewriting the act were also introduced. But none managed much success in committees, and even Van Deerlin dropped the broadcast provisions.

The future of a major legislative overhaul of the communications act will depend on Congress, and although broadcasters recognize the problems with the current system, they fear that changing it would only create more problems. More enthusiastic about a change are cable operators, citizens groups, and minorities, although most realize that they, in some way, must compromise with broadcasters in order to exert a successful lobbying force on Congress.

COPYRIGHT

In 1976, a complete revision of United States copyright statutes took place, with most of the new statutes taking effect on January 1, 1978. The new law was much more extensive than the old 1909 legislation, taking into account photocopy technology, cable television, and other changes that had evolved in the sale and distribution of copyrighted material.

For example, libraries received some measure of protection in reproducing copyrighted works with their photocopy equipment, a practice common to every college and university. Although the new law did not absolve the person desiring to make the copy from penalties, it gave libraries some immunity if they posted a public notice next to the photocopy machines stating that the use of the machine to reproduce material may be governed by copyright law.

This new law also clearly spelled out the fair use of copyright material. In particular, material used by reporters, critics, scholars, or teachers for noncommercial purposes became somewhat exempt from copyright restrictions. The key test of copyright infringement was whether someone other than the copyright holder used the reproduced documents for *profitable gain* and whether such reproductions *reduced the demand* for the original copyrighted work. The new law also extended copyright protection for life plus fifty years for authors and seventy-five years for copyright holders.

Certain activities of the broadcasting industry also came under this new law. Users of instructional television programs gained more jurisdiction to use copyrighted material without clearance and payment of fees if the taping and showing of the program was directly related to the teaching function. Negotiations began immediately after the law was passed to establish the rates that public broadcasters would pay for the use of copyrighted musical works licensed under the performance rights societies, such as ASCAP, BMI, and SESAC. SESAC did not wait for the other two to arrive at rates and instead sent public broadcasters a licensing agreement that many signed and returned with the requested licensing fee. Other stations waited to see what ASCAP and BMI would do. Professional organizations even joined together to resist payment of the licensing fees. A copyright royalty tribunal was formed under the law with jurisdiction to establish terms of the royalty payments to performers and fees to broadcasters,

As for cable television systems, the copyright law permits them to obtain a compulsory license and pay a single fee for both the license and rebroadcasting signals not only from FCC licensed stations but also from similarly licensed stations in Canada and Mexico. Cable systems also can carry other signals that FCC rules permit them to carry. Locally originated programming, however, is separate from the compulsory license, and carrying it subjects the cable system to certain copyright fees similar to those paid by commercial broadcasters for airing copyrighted works.

As with all new legislation, this copyright law will undergo numerous court tests to become defined precisely. But it is a welcome relief to all media and related industries to have updated guidelines to a very complicated issue.

NATIONAL TELECOMMUNICATIONS AND INFORMATION ADMINISTRATION

In 1978, President Jimmy Carter signed an executive order creating the National Telecommunications and Information Administration (NTIA) in the U.S. Department of Commerce. The idea was not new. It evolved in 1970 when President Richard Nixon coordinated the advisory functions on telecommunication, including both domestic and international radio and television and other electronic communication services, under the Office of Telecommunications Policy (OTP) in the Office of the President. He concurrently created the Office of Telecommunications (OT) in the Department of Commerce. The OTP's purpose first was to advise the president. The OT's purpose was to *conduct research* in order to make intelligent recommendations for telecommunications policy.

Both the OT and OTP worked closely, in theory but not always in politics, with other agencies of government. For example, they consulted with the FCC about frequency assignments and policy affecting domestic broadcasting stations.

They worked with the State Department on relations with other countries concerning such issues as satellite communication and mutually cooperative efforts to establish communication systems abroad. They also worked with the Office of Management and Budget to gain insights into and policy recommendations for the fiscal aspects of a national telecommunication policy. In addition, they worked with the Defense Department on the role of telecommunications in wartime and in peacetime defense policy.

Unfortunately, both the OTP and the OT came in less than ideal political times. First, Nixon's first vice president, Spiro Agnew, lashed out at the media in a speech made in Des Moines, Iowa in 1969, criticizing the supposed concentrated power and news bias in the three commercial television networks. The speech received wide publicity and alerted the networks that the White House was jumping into the communications policy arena. Then the OTP's first director, Clay Whitehead, delivered a famous speech to a group of journalists in Indianapolis, implying that radio and television stations could improve their chances for a five-year license renewal if management took an active interest in how their news departments functioned. Implied pressure from the executive branch over the license renewals of Florida television stations combined with the criminal implications of the Watergate scandal sent the Nixon administration to a low ebb among much of the public and the media establishment. President Carter, realizing the political liability of having the OTP located in the Office of the President and sensing the need for better cooperation between the OTP and other agencies of government, instituted the executive order creating the NTIA.

Specifically, the order initiated five actions:

1. Transferred all functions of the Office of Telecommunications Policy to the Department of Commerce.
2. Abolished the Office of Telecommunications Policy.
3. Abolished the Office of Telecommunications.
4. Established an assistant secretary for communications and information in the Department of Commerce.
5. Formed the National Telecommunications and Information Administration with the assistant secretary for communications and information as the NTIA director.

President Carter appointed Henry Geller (Figure 14-6) as the first head of the agency. Geller was a former deputy general counsel and general counsel of the FCC under two presidents and served with the Rand Corporation and later the Aspen Institute Program on Communications and Society.

Although the NTIA's charge is still one of advising the president and is still an executive branch agency, moving it out of the Office of the President has at least presented the appearance of detachment and has opened the potential for better cooperation with other agencies of government. How effective that cooperation will be remains to be seen.

Similar in many ways to the old Office of Telecommunications, the NTIA has four primary functions, or *program elements*, as NTIA calls them. The first is

Figure 14-6 Henry Geller, first head of the National Telecommunications and Information Administration.

Policy Analysis and Development, which includes analyzing the issues surrounding common carrier industries such as telephone communication, options for deregulating cable and broadcasting, international telecommunications, and protection of privacy in data communications. A second element is *Telecommunications Applications*, which includes such concerns as improving telecommunications in rural areas, stimulating minority ownership in broadcasting and cable TV stations, coordinating local and state telecommunications policy, and working on user-industry cooperation in developing satellite systems for public service activities. A third element is *Federal Systems and Spectrum Management*, which includes assessing the federal use of the electromagnetic spectrum and evaluating the procurement plans of other federal agencies. A fourth element is *Telecommunications Sciences*, the research arm of NTIA, which studies climatic effects on radio waves, studies various direct-broadcast systems for public service use, and develops user-oriented standards for federal data communication systems.

The elements we have been discussing are just *some* of those perceived by NTIA at its inception. Only the future will determine what road the new agency will take, how much it will become involved in politics, and how effective it will be in formulating policy and dealing with other federal agencies.

ADVERTISING AND THE FTC

We need only look at a collection of bygone advertisements to see why current advertising controls exist. A perusal of old medicine ads, for example, would

MODICON* Tablets

IMPORTANT NOTE—This information is a BRIEF SUMMARY of the complete prescribing information provided with the product and therefore should not be used as the basis for prescribing the product. This summary was prepared by deleting from the complete prescribing information certain text, tables, and references. The physician should be thoroughly familiar with the complete prescribing information and patient information before prescribing the product.

INDICATION: CONTRACEPTION. The pregnancy rate in women using conventional combination oral contraceptives (containing 35 mcg or more of ethinyl estradiol or 50 mcg or more of mestranol) is generally reported as less than one pregnancy per 100 woman-years of use. Slightly higher rates (somewhat more than one pregnancy per 100 woman-years of use) are reported for some combination products containing 35 mcg or less of ethinyl estradiol, and rates on the order of three pregnancies per 100 woman-years are reported for the progestogen-only oral contraceptives. Table 1 gives ranges of pregnancy rates reported in the literature for other means of contraception. The efficacy of these means of contraception (except the IUD) depends upon the degree of adherence to the method.
Table 1: Pregnancies Per 100 Women-Years. IUD, less than 1-6; Diaphragm with spermicidal product (creams or jellies), 2-20; Condom, 3-36; Aerosol foams, 2-29; Jellies and creams, 4-36; Periodic abstinence (rhythm) all types, less than 1-47; 1. Calendar method, 14-47; 2. Temperature method, 1-20; 3. Temperature method—intercourse only in postovulatory phase, less than 1-7; 4. Mucus method, 1-25; No contraception, 60-80. **DOSE-RELATED RISK OF THROMBOEMBOLISM FROM ORAL CONTRACEPTIVES:** Two studies have shown a positive association between the dose of estrogens in oral contraceptives and the risk of thromboembolism. For this reason, it is prudent and in keeping with good principles of therapeutics to minimize exposure to estrogen. The oral contraceptive product prescribed for any given patient should be that product which contains the least amount of estrogen that is compatible with an acceptable pregnancy rate and patient acceptance. It is recommended that new acceptors of oral contraceptives be started on preparations containing .05 mg or less of estrogen. **CONTRAINDICATIONS:** Oral contraceptives should not be used in women with any of the following conditions: 1. Thrombophlebitis or thromboembolic disorders. 2. A past history of deep vein thrombophlebitis or thromboembolic disorders. 3. Cerebral vascular or coronary artery disease. 4. Known or suspected carcinoma of the breast. 5. Known or suspected estrogen-dependent neoplasia. 6. Undiagnosed, abnormal genital bleeding. 7. Known or suspected pregnancy (see WARNINGS, No. 5).

WARNINGS

Cigarette smoking increases the risk of serious cardiovascular side effects from oral contraceptive use. This risk increases with age and with heavy smoking (15 or more cigarettes per day) and is quite marked in women over 35 years of age. Women who use oral contraceptives should be strongly advised not to smoke.
The use of oral contraceptives is associated with increased risk of several serious conditions including thromboembolism, stroke, myocardial infarction, hepatic adenoma, gallbladder disease, hypertension. Practitioners prescribing oral contraceptives should be familiar with the following information relating to these risks.

1. THROMBOEMBOLIC DISORDERS AND OTHER VASCULAR PROBLEMS. An increased risk of thromboembolic and thrombotic disease associated with the use of oral contraceptives is well established. Four principal studies in Great Britain and three in the United States have demonstrated an increased risk of fatal and nonfatal venous thromboembolism and stroke, both hemorrhagic and thrombotic. These studies estimate that users of oral contraceptives are 4 to 11 times more likely than nonusers to develop these diseases without evident cause. Overall excess mortality due to pulmonary embolism or stroke is on the order of 1.0 to 3.5 deaths annually per 100,000 users and increases with age. **CEREBROVASCULAR DISORDERS:** In a collaborative American study of cerebrovascular disorders in women with and without predisposing causes, it was estimated that the risk of hemorrhagic stroke was 2.0 times greater in users than in nonusers and the risk of thrombotic stroke was 4.0 to 9.5 times greater in users than in nonusers.
MYOCARDIAL INFARCTION: An increased risk of myocardial infarction associated with the use of oral contraceptives has been reported confirming a previously suspected association. These studies, conducted in the United Kingdom, found, as expected, that the greater the number of underlying risk factors for coronary artery disease (cigarette smoking, hypertension, hypercholesterolemia, obesity, diabetes, history of preeclamptic toxemia), the higher the risk of developing myocardial infarction, regardless of whether the patient was an oral contraceptive user or not. Oral contraceptives, however, were found to be a clear additional risk factor. The annual excess case rate (increased risk) of myocardial infarction (fatal and nonfatal) in oral contraceptive users was estimated to be approximately 7 cases per 100,000 women users in the 30-39 age group and 67 cases per 100,000 women users in the 40-44 age group. In terms of relative risk, it has been estimated that oral contraceptive users who do not smoke (smoking is considered a major predisposing condition to myocardial infarction) are about twice as likely to have a fatal myocardial infarction as nonusers who do not smoke. Oral contraceptive users who are also smokers have about a 5-fold increased risk of fatal infarction compared to users who do not smoke, but about a 10-to 12-fold increased risk compared to nonusers who do not smoke. Furthermore, the amount of smoking is also an important factor. In determining the importance of these relative risks, however, the baseline rates for various age groups must be given serious consideration. The importance of other predisposing conditions mentioned above in determining relative and absolute risks has not as yet been quantified; it is quite likely that the same synergistic action exists, but perhaps to a lesser extent. **Risk of Dose:** In an analysis of data derived from several national adverse reaction reporting systems, British investigators concluded that the risk of thromboembolism including coronary thrombosis is directly related to the dose of estrogen used in oral contraceptives. Preparations containing 100 mcg or more of estrogen were associated with a higher risk of thromboembolism than those containing 50-80 mcg of estrogen. Their analysis did suggest, however, that the quantity of estrogen may not be the sole factor involved. This finding has been confirmed in the United States. Careful epidemiological studies to determine the degree of thromboembolic risk associated with progestogen-only oral contraceptives have not been performed. Cases of thromboembolic disease have been reported in women using these products, and they should not be presumed to be free of excess risk. The risk of thromboembolic and thrombotic disorders, in both users and nonusers of oral contraceptives, increases with age. Oral contraceptives are, however, an independent risk factor for these events. **ESTIMATE OF EXCESS MORTALITY FROM CIRCULATORY DISEASES:** A large prospective study carried out in the United Kingdom estimated the mortality rate per 100,000 women per year from diseases of the circulatory system for users and nonusers of oral contraceptives according to age, smoking habits, and duration of use. The overall excess death rate annually from circulatory diseases for oral contraceptive users was estimated to be 20 per 100,000 (ages 15-34—5/100,000; ages 35-44—33/100,000; ages 45-49—140/100,000), the risk being concentrated in older women, in those with a long duration of use, and in cigarette smokers. It was not possible, however, to examine the interrelationships of age, smoking, and duration of use, nor to compare the effects of continuous versus intermittent use. Although the study showed a 10-fold increase in death due to circulatory diseases in users for five or more years, all of these deaths occurred in women 35 or older. Until larger numbers of women under 35 with continuous use for five or more years are available, it is not possible to assess the magnitude of the relative risk for this younger age group. This study reports that the increased risk of circulatory diseases may persist after the pill is discontinued. Another study published at the same time confirms a previously reported increase of mortality in pill users from cardiovascular disease. The available data from a variety of sources have been analyzed to estimate the risk of death associated with various methods of contraception. The estimates of risk of death for each method include the combined risk of the contraceptive method (e.g., thromboembolic and thrombotic disease in the case of oral contraceptives) plus the risk attributable to pregnancy or abortion in the event of method failure. This latter risk varies with the effectiveness of the contraceptive method. The findings of this analysis are shown in Figure 1 below. The study concluded that the mortality associated with all methods of birth control is low and below that associated with childbirth, with the exception of oral contraceptives in women over 40 who smoke. (The rates given for pill only/smokers for each age group are for smokers as a class. For "heavy" smokers [more than 15 cigarettes a day], the rates given would be about double; for "light" smokers [less than 15 cigarettes a day], about 50 percent.) The mortality associated with oral contraceptive use in nonsmokers over 40 is higher than with any other method of contraception in that age group. The lowest mortality is associated with the condom or diaphragm backed up by early abortion. The risk of thromboembolic and thrombotic disease associated with oral contraceptives increases with age after approximately age 30 and, for myocardial infarction, is further increased by hypertension, hypercholesterolemia, obesity, diabetes, or history of preeclamptic toxemia and especially by cigarette smoking. The risk of myocardial infarction in oral contraceptive users is substantially increased in women age 40 and over, especially those with other risk factors. The use of oral contraceptives in women in this age group is not recommended. Based on the data currently available, the following chart gives a gross estimate of the risk of death from circulatory disorders associated with the use of oral contraceptives:

SMOKING HABITS AND OTHER PREDISPOSING CONDITIONS—RISK ASSOCIATED WITH USE OF ORAL CONTRACEPTIVES

Age	Below 30	30-39	40+	
Heavy smokers	C	B	A	A—Use associated with very high risk.
Light smokers	D	C	B	B—Use associated with high risk.
Nonsmokers (no predisposing conditions)	D	C,D	C	C—Use associated with moderate risk.
Nonsmokers (other predisposing conditions)	C	C,B	B,A	D—Use associated with low risk.

The physician and the patient should be alert to the earliest manifestations of thromboembolic and thrombotic disorders (e.g., thrombophlebitis, pulmonary embolism, cerebrovascular insufficiency, coronary occlusion, retinal thrombosis, and mesenteric thrombosis). Should any of these occur or be suspected, the drug should be discontinued immediately. A four- to six-fold increased risk of postsurgery thromboembolic complications has been reported in oral contraceptive users. If feasible, oral contraceptives should be discontinued at least four weeks before surgery of a type associated with an increased risk of thromboembolism or prolonged immobilization. 2. OCULAR LESIONS. There have been reports of neuro-ocular lesions such as optic neuritis or retinal thrombosis associated with the use of oral contraceptives. Discontinue oral contraceptive medication if there is unexplained, sudden or gradual, partial or complete loss of vision; onset of proptosis or diplopia; papilledema; or retinal vascular lesions and institute appropriate diagnostic and therapeutic measures. 3. CARCINOMA. Long-term continuous administration of either natural or synthetic estrogen in certain animal species increases the frequency of carcinoma of the breast, cervix, vagina, and liver. Certain synthetic progestogens, none currently contained in oral contraceptives, have been noted to increase the incidence of mammary nodules, benign and malignant, in dogs. In humans, three case control studies have reported an increased risk of endometrial carcinoma associated with the prolonged use of exogenous estrogen in postmenopausal women. One publication reported on the first 21 cases submitted by physicians to a registry of cases of adenocarcinoma of the endometrium in women under 40 on oral contraceptives. Of the cases found in women without predisposing risk factors for adenocarcinoma of the endometrium (e.g., irregular bleeding at the time oral contraceptives were first given, polycystic ovaries), nearly all occurred in women who had used a sequential oral contraceptive. These products are no longer marketed. No evidence has been reported suggesting an increased risk of endometrial cancer in users of conventional combination or progestogen-only oral contraceptives. Several studies have found no increases in breast cancer in women taking oral contraceptives or estrogens. One study, however, while also noting no overall increased risk of breast cancer in women treated with oral contraceptives, found an excess risk in the subgroups of oral contraceptive users with documented benign breast disease. A reduced occurrence of benign breast tumors in users of oral contraceptives has been well-documented. In summary, there is at present no confirmed evidence from human studies of an increased risk of cancer associated with oral contraceptives. Close clinical surveillance of all women taking oral contraceptives is, nevertheless, essential. In all cases of undiagnosed persistent or recurrent abnormal vaginal bleeding, appropriate diagnostic measures should be taken to rule out malignancy. Women with a strong family history of breast cancer or who have breast nodules, fibrocystic disease or abnormal mammograms should be monitored with particular care if they elect to use oral contraceptives instead of other methods of contraception.

Figure 1. Estimated annual number of deaths associated with control of fertility and no control per 100,000 nonsterile women, by regimen of control and age of woman.

	15-19	20-24	25-29	30-34	35-39	40-44
No method	5.5	5.2	7.1	14.0	19.3	21.9
Abortion only	2.3	2.5	2.5	5.2	9.8	6.6
Pill only-nonsmokers	1.3	1.4	1.4	2.2	4.5	3.1
Pill only-smokers	1.5	1.6	1.6	10.8	13.4	58.9
IUDs only	1.1	1.2	1.2	1.4	1.6	1.4
Traditional contraception only	1.1	1.4	1.9	3.7	4.7	4.0
Traditional contraception and abortion	0.3	0.4	0.4	0.8	1.4	0.8

4. HEPATIC TUMORS. Benign hepatic adenomas have been found to be associated with the use of oral contraceptives. One study showed that oral contraceptive formulations with high hormonal potency were associated with a higher risk than lower potency formulations. Although benign, hepatic adenomas may rupture and may cause death through intra-abdominal hemorrhage. This has been reported in short-term as well as long-term users of oral contraceptives. Two studies relate risk with duration of use of the contraceptive, the risk being much greater after four or more years of oral contraceptive use. While hepatic adenoma is a rare lesion, it should be considered in women presenting abdominal pain and tenderness, abdominal mass or shock. A few cases of hepatocellular carcinoma have been reported in women taking oral contraceptives. The relationship of these drugs to this type of malignancy is not known at this time. 5. USE IN OR IMMEDIATELY PRECEDING PREGNANCY, BIRTH DEFECTS IN OFFSPRING, AND MALIGNANCY IN FEMALE OFFSPRING. The use of female sex hormones—both estrogenic and progestational agents—during early pregnancy may seriously damage the offspring. It has been shown that females exposed in utero to diethylstilbestrol, a nonsteroidal estrogen, have an increased risk of developing in later life a form of vaginal or cervical cancer that is ordinarily extremely rare. This risk has been estimated to be on the order of 1 to 4 in 1000 exposures. Although there is no evidence at the present time that oral contraceptives further enhance the risk of developing this type of malignancy, such patients should be monitored with particular care if they elect to use oral contraceptives instead of other methods of contraception. Furthermore, a high percentage of such exposed women (from 30 to 90%) have been found to have epithelial changes of the vagina and cervix. Although these changes are histologically benign, it is not known whether this condition is a precursor of vaginal malignancy. Male children so exposed may develop abnormalities of the urogenital tract. Although similar data are not available with the use of other estrogens, it cannot be presumed that they would not induce similar changes. An increased risk of congenital anomalies, including heart defects and limb defects, has been reported with the use of sex hormones, including oral contraceptives, in pregnancy. One case control study has estimated a 4.7-fold increase in risk of limb-reduction defects in infants exposed in utero to sex hormones (oral contraceptives, hormonal withdrawal tests for pregnancy or attempted treatment for threatened abortion). Some of these exposures were very short and involved only a few days of treatment. The data suggest that the risk of limb-reduction defects in exposed fetuses is somewhat less than one in 1,000 live births. In the past, female sex hormones have been used during pregnancy in an attempt to treat threatened or habitual abortion. There is considerable evidence that estrogens are ineffective for these indications, and there is no evidence from well-controlled studies that progestogens are effective for these uses. There is some evidence that triploidy and possibly other types of polyploidy are increased among abortuses from women who become pregnant soon after ceasing oral contraceptives. Embryos with these anomalies are virtually always aborted spontaneously. Whether there is an overall increase in spontaneous abortion of pregnancies conceived soon after stopping oral contraceptives is unknown. Pregnancy should be ruled out before initiating or continuing the contraceptive regimen. Pregnancy should always be considered if withdrawal bleeding does not occur. If pregnancy is confirmed, the patient should be apprised of the potential risks to the fetus and the advisability of continuation of the pregnancy should be discussed in the light of these risks. It is also recommended that women who discontinue oral contraceptives with the intent of becoming pregnant use an alternate form of contraception for a period of time before attempting to conceive. Many clinicians recommend three months although no precise information is available on which to base this recommendation. The administration of progestogen-only or progestogen-estrogen combinations to induce withdrawal bleeding should not be used as a test of pregnancy. 6. GALLBLADDER DISEASE. Studies report an increased risk of surgically confirmed gallbladder disease in users of oral contraceptives and estrogens. In one study, an increased risk appeared after two years of use and doubled after four or five years of use. In one of the other studies, an increased risk was apparent between six and twelve months of use. 7. CARBOHYDRATE AND LIPID METABOLIC EFFECTS. A decrease in glucose tolerance has been observed in a significant percentage of patients on oral contraceptives. For this reason, prediabetic and diabetic patients should be carefully observed while receiving oral contraceptives. An increase in triglycerides and total phospholipids has been observed in patients receiving oral contraceptives. 8. ELEVATED BLOOD PRESSURE. An increase in blood pressure has been reported in patients receiving oral contraceptives. In some women hypertension may occur within a few months of beginning oral contraceptive use. In the first year of use, the prevalence of women with hypertension is low in users and may be no higher than that of a comparable group of nonusers. The prevalence in users increases, however, with longer exposure, and in the fifth year of use is two and a half to three times the reported prevalence in the first year. Age is also strongly correlated with the development of hypertension in oral contraceptive users. Women who previously have had hypertension during pregnancy may be more likely to develop elevation of blood pressure when given oral contraceptives. Hypertension that develops as a result of taking oral contraceptives usually returns to normal after discontinuing the drug. 9. HEADACHE. The onset or exacerbation of migraine or development of headache of a new pattern which is recurrent, persistent, or severe, requires discontinuation of oral contraceptives and evaluation of the cause. 10. BLEEDING IRREGULARITIES. Breakthrough bleeding, spotting, and amenorrhea are frequent reasons for patients discontinuing oral contraceptives. In breakthrough bleeding, as in all cases of irregular bleeding from the vagina, nonfunctional causes should be borne in mind. In undiagnosed persistent or recurrent abnormal bleeding from the vagina, adequate diagnostic measures are indicated to rule out pregnancy or malignancy. If pathology has been excluded, time or a change to another formulation may solve the problem. Changing to an oral contraceptive with a higher estrogen content, while potentially useful in minimizing menstrual irregularity, should be done only if necessary since this may increase the risk of thromboembolic disease. Women with a past history of oligomenorrhea or secondary amenorrhea or young women without regular cycles may have a tendency to remain anovulatory or to become amenorrheic after discontinuation of oral contraceptives. Women with these preexisting problems should be advised of this possibility and encouraged to use other contraceptive methods. Postuse anovulation, possibly prolonged, may also occur in women without previous irregularities. 11. ECTOPIC PREGNANCY. Ectopic as well as intrauterine pregnancy may occur in contraceptive failures. 12. BREAST FEEDING. Oral contraceptives given in the postpartum period may interfere with lactation. There may be a decrease in the quantity and quality of the breast milk. Furthermore, a small fraction of the hormonal agents in oral contraceptives has been identified in the milk of mothers receiving these drugs. The effects, if any, on the breast-fed child have not been determined. If feasible, the use of oral contraceptives should be deferred until the infant has been weaned. **PRECAUTIONS: General:** 1. A complete medical and family history should be taken prior to the initiation of oral contraceptives. The pretreatment and periodic physical examinations should include special reference to blood pressure, breasts, abdomen and pelvic organs, including Papanicolaou smear and relevant laboratory tests. As a general rule, oral contraceptives should not be prescribed for longer than one year without another physical examination being performed. 2. Under the influence of estrogen-progestogen preparations, preexisting uterine leiomyomata may increase in size. 3. Patients with a history of psychic depression should be carefully observed and the drug discontinued if depression recurs to a serious degree. Patients becoming significantly depressed while taking oral contraceptives should stop the medication and use an alternate method of contraception in an attempt to determine whether the symptom is drug-related. 4. Oral contraceptives may cause some degree of fluid retention. They should be prescribed with caution, and only with careful monitoring, in patients with conditions which might be aggravated by fluid retention, such as convulsive disorders, migraine syndrome, asthma, or cardiac or renal insufficiency. 5. Patients with a past history of jaundice during pregnancy have an increased risk of recurrence of jaundice while receiving oral contraceptive therapy. If jaundice develops in any patient receiving such drugs, the medication should be discontinued. 6. Steroid hormones may be poorly metabolized in patients with impaired liver function and should be administered with caution in such patients. 7. Oral contraceptive users may have disturbances in normal tryptophan metabolism which may result in a relative pyridoxine deficiency. 8. Serum folate levels may be depressed by oral contraceptive therapy. Since the pregnant woman is predisposed to the development of folate deficiency and the incidence of folate deficiency increases with increasing gestation, it is possible that if a woman becomes pregnant shortly after stopping oral contraceptives, she may have a greater chance of developing folate deficiency and complications attributed to this deficiency. 9. The pathologist should be advised of oral contraceptive therapy when relevant specimens are submitted. 10. Certain endocrine and liver function tests and blood components may be affected by estrogen-containing oral contraceptives: a. Increased sulfobromophthalein retention. b. Increased prothrombin and factors VII, VIII, IX, and X; decreased antithrombin 3; increased norepinephrine-induced platelet aggregability. c. Increased thyroid-binding globulin (TBG) leading to increased circulating total thyroid hormone, as measured by protein-bound iodine (PBI), T4 by column, or T4 by radioimmunoassay. Free T3 resin uptake is decreased, reflecting the elevated TBG, free T4 concentration is unaltered. d. Decreased pregnanediol excretion. e. Reduced response to metyrapone test. **INFORMATION FOR THE PATIENT: (See Patient Package Insert). DRUG INTERACTIONS:** Reduced efficacy and increased incidence of breakthrough bleeding have been associated with concomitant use of rifampin. A similar association has been suggested with barbiturates, phenylbutazone, phenytoin sodium, and ampicillin. **CARCINOGENESIS, PREGNANCY, NURSING MOTHERS: See CONTRAINDICATIONS and WARNINGS. ADVERSE REACTIONS:** An increased risk of the following serious adverse reactions has been associated with the use of oral contraceptives (see WARNINGS): Thrombophlebitis. Pulmonary embolism. Coronary thrombosis. Cerebral thrombosis. Cerebral hemorrhage. Hypertension. Gallbladder disease. Liver tumors. Congenital anomalies. There is evidence of an association between the following conditions and the use of oral contraceptives, although additional confirmatory studies are needed: Mesenteric thrombosis. Neuro-ocular lesions, e.g., retinal thrombosis and optic neuritis. The following adverse reactions have been reported in patients receiving oral contraceptives and are believed to be drug-related: Nausea, usually the most common adverse reaction. Vomiting, occurs in approximately 10% or less of patients during the first cycle. Other reactions, as a general rule, are seen much less frequently or only occasionally. Gastrointestinal symptoms (such as abdominal cramps and bloating). Breakthrough bleeding. Spotting. Change in menstrual flow. Dysmenorrhea. Amenorrhea during and after treatment. Temporary infertility after discontinuance of treatment. Edema. Chloasma or melasma which may persist. Breast changes: tenderness, enlargement, and secretion. Change in weight (increase or decrease). Change in cervical erosion and cervical secretion. Possible diminution in lactation when given immediately postpartum. Cholestatic jaundice. Migraine. Increase in size of uterine leiomyomata. Rash (allergic). Mental depression. Reduced tolerance to carbohydrates. Vaginal candidiasis. Change in corneal curvature (steepening). Intolerance to contact lenses. The following adverse reactions have been reported in users of oral contraceptives, and the association has been neither confirmed nor refuted: Premenstrual-like syndrome. Cataracts. Changes in libido. Chorea. Changes in appetite. Cystitis-like syndrome. Headache. Nervousness. Dizziness. Hirsutism. Loss of scalp hair. Erythema multiforme. Erythema nodosum. Hemorrhagic eruption. Vaginitis. Porphyria. Impaired renal function. (ORTHO-NOVUM 1/50□21 and ORTHO-NOVUM 1/50□28 contain tartrazine. Allergic reactions have been reported with the ingestion of this dye in some patients.) **ACUTE OVERDOSE:** Serious ill effects have not been reported following acute ingestion of large doses of oral contraceptives by young children. Overdosage may cause nausea, and withdrawal bleeding may occur in females.

*Trademark

Ortho Pharmaceutical Corporation • Raritan, N.J. 08869

Figure 14-7 The extensive information accompanying this ad shows the extent of disclosure required in food and drug advertising. (Ortho Pharmaceutical Corporation)

bring to view labels for everything from horse liniment to castor oil, all capable of curing everything that could possibly ail man, woman, or beast. Their claims to cure were outdone only by those to prevent, claims that, figuratively speaking, promised the fountain of youth overnight—or in three doses! When the medicine wagon rolled through the frontier West, there was not much concern over the outlandish claims that the barker made. However, when the twentieth century saw mass circulation magazines roll off the presses, when it heard radio commercials jingling their way across the countryside, and when television began to assure "miracle" results, advertising was due for some regulation (Figure 14-7).

criticism and compliance

When the Federal Trade Commission was formed in 1914, its first duties did not center on advertising regulations. It was mainly concerned with guarding against corporate monopolies. In later years, however, the FTC became deeply involved in controlling deceptive advertising. The agency has had its share of ups and downs over the years, and in 1969 and 1970, both consumer advocate Ralph Nader and the American Bar Association criticized the agency's performance. The FTC consequently undertook a major reorganization, establishing a separate division to handle food and drug advertising within the FTC's Bureau of Consumer Protection. The agency's enforcement powers range from simple letters reprimanding those who the FTC feels have violated its rules to the stronger "cease-and-desist" orders. Through regular press releases to nationwide news media, the FTC notifies the public of its actions, the dates, times, and places of agency hearings, the companies involved, and any final action taken by the FTC or by the judges hearing appeals on FTC decisions. It was not until consumer awareness developed that FTC press releases received such extensive news coverage. Now, however, with an increase in the number of "special reporters" and consumer watchdogs, virtually no development in this area goes unnoticed.

celebrity endorsements

The FTC has been especially careful in recent years to scrutinize the use of celebrities in advertising. For one, the FTC expects celebrities who use their name or picture with a product to use the product. Also, in some cases, the FTC has gone so far as to hold celebrities responsible for the quality of the products or services they advertise. Stringent controls such as these can make manufacturers, advertising agencies, and celebrities alike be careful of what products they represent and what they say about the products.

INTERNATIONAL TELECOMMUNICATION UNION

The International Telecommunication Union is a United Nations organization responsible for coordinating the use of telecommunication between nations.[4] It does not have the enforcement powers of the Federal Communications Commission. Rather, it is a collective body of sovereign states and is only as strong as is the willingness of the sovereign states to abide by its treaties. In other words, if a country violates an ITU agreement, no "field office" will revoke licenses or impose forfeitures. ITU's sovereign states view it not so much as an independent agency but as an arena in which to negotiate the uses of telecommunications.[5] And as that arena, it has been effective.

The principal functions of the ITU include:

1. Effective allocations of the radio frequency spectrum and registration of radio frequency assignments;
2. Coordinating efforts to eliminate harmful interference between radio stations of different countries and to improve the use made of the radio frequency spectrum.
3. Fostering collaboration with respect to the establishment of the lowest possible rates;
4. Fostering the creation, development, and improvement of telecommunication equipment and networks in new or developing countries by every means at its disposal, especially its partiticipation in the appropriate programs of the United Nations;
5. Promoting the adoption of measures for ensuring the safety of life through the cooperation of telecommunication services;
6. Undertaking studies, making regulations, adopting resolutions, formulating recommendations and opinions, and collecting and publishing information concerning telecommunications matters benefiting all Members and Associate Members.[6]

SUMMARY

Our chapter began with a discussion of different theories of control over mass communication, pointing out that controls differ among print and broadcast media, and among countries. The electronic media that have evolved in the course of the twentieth century are a far cry from the colonial presses that the founding fathers had in mind when they wrote the constitution. In the public interest, therefore, Congress sought more definitive controls to regulate the new media and accordingly formulated such legislation as the Wireless Ship Act of 1910, the Radio Act of 1912, the Radio Act of 1927, and the Communications Act of 1934. From this legislation, the 1934 law created the Federal Communications Commission, the governmental body responsible for the control of electronic communication. The commission is under the direction of seven FCC commissioners, each serving a seven-year term.

Two of the most familiar regulations of standard radio and television programming are Section 315 of the Communications Act of 1934 and the Fairness Doctrine, a special 1949 ruling of the FCC. Section 315 covers political broadcasting, and the Fairness Doctrine sets up guidelines for unbiased treatment of controversial issues.

The newest regulatory agency of government is the National Telecommunications and Information Administration. Formed under an Executive reorganization order in March 1978, this agency of the executive branch combines the duties of the former Office of Telecommunication Policy in the Office of the President with the former Office of Telecommunications in the Department of Commerce. The four program elements or functions of the NTIA are policy analysis and development, telecommunications applications, federal systems and spectrum management, and telecommunications sciences.

The Federal Trade Commission continues to police advertising. Its powers range from requesting information to major cease-and-desist orders which it may institute after an advertising review process takes place.

The International Telecommunication Union operates on the international level. Formed in 1865 to control telegraph communication, it has evolved to its current status as part of the United Nations. The ITU's areas of concern range from international spectrum allocations, to satellite development, to broadcasting in developing nations.

OPPORTUNITIES FOR FURTHER LEARNING

Applicability of the Fairness Doctrine in the Handling of Controversial Issues of Public Importance. Washington, D.C.: Federal Communications Commission, 1964 (FCC 64-611).

BOSMAJIAN, HAIG A., *Obscenity and Freedom of Expression.* New York: Burt Franklin & Co., 1976.

BOTEIN, MICHAEL, *Legal Restrictions on Ownership of the Mass Media.* New York: Seminars, Inc., 1977.

GINSBURG, DOUGLAS H., *Regulation of Broadcasting: Law and Policy Towards Radio, Television and Cable Communications.* St. Paul, Minn.: West Publishing Co., 1979.

HYMAN, ALLEN, and M. BRUCE JOHNSON, eds., *Advertising and Free Speech.* Lexington, Mass.: Lexington Books/D.C. Heath, 1977.

JOHN and MARY MARKLE FOUNDATION and the TWENTIETH CENTURY FUND, eds., *Global Communications in the Space Age: Toward a New ITU.* New York: Markle Foundation and Twentieth Century Fund, 1972.

KAHN, FRANK J., ed., *Documents of American Broadcasting* (3rd ed.). Englewood Cliffs, N.J., Prentice-Hall, Inc., 1978.

KRASNOW, ERWIN G., and LAWRENCE D. LONGLEY, *The Politics of Broadcast Regulation.* New York: St. Martin's Press, Inc., 1978.

LEDUC, DON R., *Cable Television and the FCC.* Philadelphia: Temple University Press, 1973.

MOSCO, VINCENT, *The Regulation of Broadcasting in the United States: A Comparative Analysis.* Cambridge, Mass.: Harvard University Program on Information Technologies, 1975.

NOLL, ROGER G., MERTON J. PECK, and JOHN J. McGOWAN, *Economic Aspects of Television Regulation.* Washington, D.C.: The Brookings Institution, 1973.

PALETZ, DAVID L., ROBERTA E. PEARSON, and DONALD L. WILLIS, *Politics in Public Service Advertising on Television.* New York: Praeger Publishers, Inc., 1977.

RIVERS, WILLIAM L. and MICHAEL J. NYHAN, eds., *Aspen Notebook on Government and the Media.* New York: Praeger Publishers, Inc., 1975.

WALLESTEIN, G. D., *International Telecommunication Agreements.* Dobbs Ferry, N.Y.: Oceana Publications, 1977.

WILL, THOMAS E., *Telecommunication Structure and Management in The Executive Branch of Government: 1900-1970.* Dedham, Mass.: Horizon House and Thomas E. Will, 1978.

15

Legal Issues and The Working Press

As we learned in chapter 1, mass communication does not occur in a vacuum. Many different controls affect the final message the public receives—government regulations, codes of ethics, and court orders, among others. This chapter examines some of the controls that both safeguard and in some ways hamper the working press.

First, however, we shall attempt to place these various controls in a broader perspective by studying four theories of how the press functions in society.

FOUR THEORIES OF THE PRESS

In their classic book, *Four Theories of the Press*, Fred S. Siebert, Theodore Peterson, and Wilbur Schramm outline four theories which have characterized the operation of the press in society. The oldest of these is the authoritarian theory.

authoritarian theory

The authoritarian theory evolved in the sixteenth and seventeenth centuries, spreading throughout Europe with the invention of the printing press. It was associated with such reigning families as the Tudors in England, the Bourbons in France, and the Hapsburgs in Spain. In modern society, it has at various times found its way into the governments of Japan, Imperial Russia, Germany, and Spain, as well as some Asian and South American countries.

The authoritarian theory views humans as subservient to the state and as instruments of the state's natural, if not divine, right to maintain order and further the state's existence. The press in such a society is viewed as an instrument for disseminating the state's position to the populace, informing the populace what is right and wrong based on the state's interpretations of issues, and providing official policy statements of the ruling elite. The state, after determining its objectives, uses the press as a means of obtaining those objectives. The press becomes a means to an end rather than an instrument of criticism of either means or ends. In writing about the authoritarian theory, Siebert points out that in its early stages, the state used the press negatively by making sure that the press did not interfere with the attainment of national ends. Later the press, and for that matter the mass media in general, was used positively as an instrument for helping the state achieve its ends.

Who owned the press was of equal importance under the authoritarian theory as how the press was used. In early England, the private sector was permitted to own the press, but that sector contained only wealthy friends of the Crown who did not abuse their ownership priviledge by criticizing it. Later, government use of the media spawned various official journals that echoed the government line. Eventually, these government media were joined by other private media. Herein was the difficulty of the authoritarian theory—how to control the private press.

The control took various forms. We already discussed the permits to publish that were granted by the government to the privileged few. This "patent" system existed for about 200 years in England. Then in the seventeenth century, the system began to collapse because of the success of the competing private press. So the government next decided to limit the number of journeymen trained as apprentices for the monopolists. But this method soon disintegrated. Because ownership of the press was limited, the apprentices found that they could not get jobs when they reached the journeyman stage and instead began to operate their own presses illegally. A third method of control was outright censorship, requiring state approval of the content of selected works. Yet censoring proved so unpopular that it also did not succeed. A fourth method, again rather unsuccessful, was trying a person under the laws of treason or sedition for printing material unfavorable to the state.

In the United States, the transition from authoritarian to libertarian press occurred more abruptly than in some other countries. The signing of the Declaration of Independence set forth new principles for freedom of expression. Indicative of this transition was the change in the *Virginia Gazette* published in Williamsburg, Virginia in 1776 (Figure 15-1). The masthead of May 10, 1776 reflects British dominance with its coat of arms. A week later, the masthead took

MAY 10, 1776.   T H E   NUMBER 67.

VIRGINIA GAZETTE.

ALWAYS FOR LIBERTY,   AND THE PUBLICK GOOD.

ALEXANDER PURDIE, PRINTER.

MAY 17, 1776.   T H E   NUMBER 68.

VIRGINIA GAZETTE.

THIRTEEN UNITED COLONIES.

United, we stand—Divided, we fall.

ALWAYS FOR LIBERTY,   AND THE PUBLICK GOOD.

JUNE 7, 1776.   T H E   NUMBER 71.

VIRGINIA GAZETTE.

ALWAYS FOR LIBERTY,   AND THE PUBLICK GOOD.

High HEAVEN *to* GRACIOUS ENDS *directs the* STORM!

Figure 15-1 Three different mastheads of the *Virginia Gazette* showing the growing spirit of independence and the change from the authoritarian to the libertarian press. (*The Printer in 18th-Century Williamsburg.* Williamsburg, Va.: Colonial Williamsburg, 1955)

on the revolutionary spirit, replacing the coat of arms with the words "THIRTEEN UNITIED COLONIES" and the slogan, "United, we stand—divided, we fall." By June 7, 1776, independence was declared with a new coat of arms and the slogan, "Don't Tread on Me."

Today, the authoritarian system of the press is still in operation in many parts of the world. In Communist countries, in nations under dictatorial control, and in some sections of Africa, a free press is little more than a theory without practice.

libertarian theory

The libertarian theory developed slowly in the sixteenth century, being refined in the eighteenth century as libertarian principles found their way into nations' constitutional framework. In theory a libertarian press is the exact opposite of an authoritarian press. Libertarianism places the individual above the state, not below it, and humans are viewed as rational animals who, although imperfect as individuals, will collectively arrive at the best decision for the general welfare of society.

Fred Siebert, in discussing the development of libertarianism, credits its transition from authoritarianism to the efforts of four men: John Milton in the seventeenth century, John Erskine and Thomas Jefferson in the eighteenth century, and John Stuart Mill in the nineteenth century. Milton (Figure 15-2) argued that people had the capacity to distinguish between right and wrong and good and bad. As a result, to make decisions, people should have "unlimited access to the ideas and thoughts of other men." Erskine argued that people seeking to enlighten others, and not intending to mislead, should be able to address the universal reason of a whole nation on what is believed to be true. John Stuart Mill felt that people had the right to think and act as they pleased if they did not infringe on the rights of others. Jefferson, borrowing from Milton's

Figure 5-2 John Milton.

ideas, felt that the collective aggregate of a people, if intelligent and informed, could arrive at sound decisions. The press was the instrument to inform the people and therefore had to be free of control. In 1774 when Jefferson published his *Summary View of the Rights of British America* (Figure 15-3), it set the stage for the libertarian press.

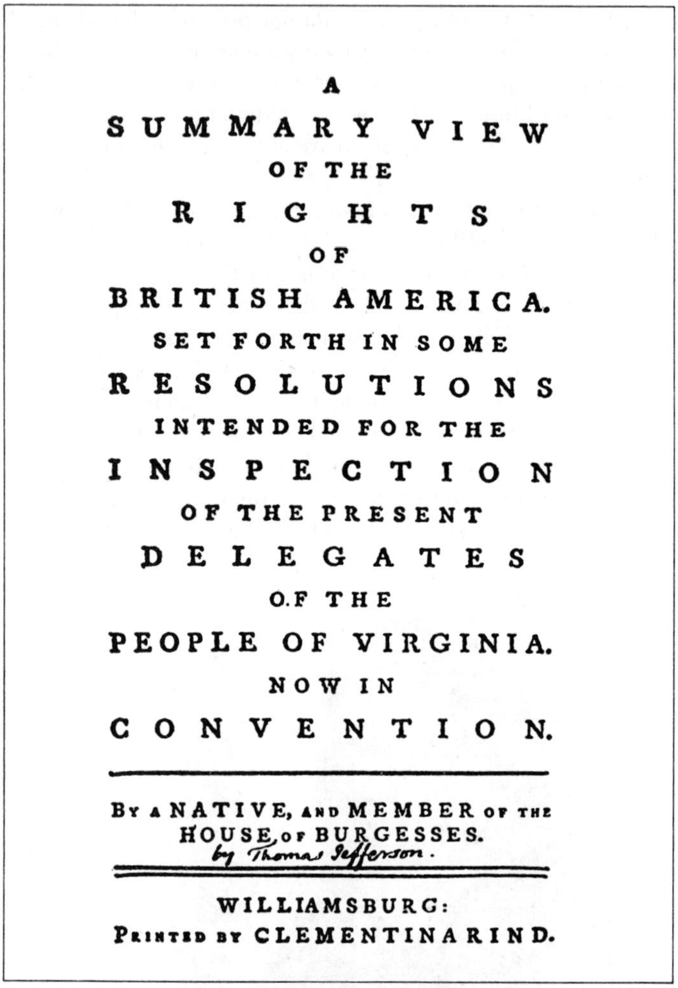

A

SUMMARY VIEW

OF THE

RIGHTS

OF

BRITISH AMERICA.

SET FORTH IN SOME

RESOLUTIONS

INTENDED FOR THE

INSPECTION

OF THE PRESENT

DELEGATES

O.F THE

PEOPLE OF VIRGINIA.

NOW IN

CONVENTION.

By a NATIVE, and MEMBER of the HOUSE, of BURGESSES.
by Thomas Jefferson.

WILLIAMSBURG:

Printed by CLEMENTINA RIND.

Figure 15-3 Published by Thomas Jefferson as a pamphlet in 1774, this piece is credited with giving Jefferson the stature that resulted in his being selected to write the Declaration of Independence. The pamphlet is a classic example of the beginnings of the libertarian press in America. (*The Printer in 18th-Century Williamsburg.* Williamsburg, Va.: Colonial Williamsburg, 1955)

Gradually, the rights of the press and libertarianism began to gain ground. The road started in the courts where charges of seditious libel, or publishing language that incites rebellion against the state, were continually overthrown, since the jury had the right to determine if a person was guilty of printing the allegedly libelous piece. Since the jury was interested more in independence from the Crown than in supporting the decisions of Crown-appointed judges, even when a judge ruled material libelous, more often than not the jury simply claimed that the accused did not print the piece and therefore was not responsible for its dissemination. Eventually, libertarianism, with its freedom of the press, became part of the constitutional doctrine both in the United States and later in England.

social responsibility theory

By the twentieth century, the printed press had been through the era of yellow journalism and was beginning to see the first glimpses of radio and motion pictures. Political ideas could persuade from such platforms as the airwaves and the giant screen.

In this atmosphere of the industrial revolution and a multimedia society developed a theory of a *free but responsible* press. It held that a press has the right to criticize government and institutions but also has certain basic responsibilities to maintain the stability of society. Nurturing this theory is the rise of professional associations associated with journalism—the American Society of Newspaper Editors and the Society of Professional Journalists—Sigma Delta Chi, among others. Both started near the turn of the twentieth century, and both have codes of ethics encouraging responsible actions by their members. Furthermore, the Communications Act of 1934, by which broadcasting is governed, is built upon the phrase, "in the public interest, convenience, and necessity."

We see open criticism of the press in many journalism reviews and books. Theodore Peterson, writing about the social responsibility theory, points out that this criticism has its roots in Will Irwin's series on the press which appeared in *Colliers* magazine as early as 1911; in Upton Sinclair's book, *The Brass Check*, appearing in 1919; and in George Seldes book, *Freedom of the Press*, written in 1935. All based their criticisms on dangers inherent in the increased reliance on advertising by the press. For even though the press is expected to be commercially independent of government control, profits achieved at the expense of public service are taboo. This concept permeates everything from the monopolistic practices blamed on the film industry in the 1930s to the cross-ownership controversy of newspaper and broadcasting properties in the 1970s. Within the framework of open and free press criticism, codes of ethics or government regulation, and guidelines for responsible action on the part of members of the press, lies the social responsibility theory.

In *Four Theories of the Press*, Wilbur Schramm writes about the Soviet-Communist theory of the press, aptly beginning his discussion by noting that when a reporter from the United States and one from the Soviet Union get together, "The talk is apt to be both amusing and frustrating. . . ." Their different frames of reference are simply incompatible. The American loathes the Soviet reporter's life with a government-controlled press. The Soviet reporter loathes the American's association with a "corrupt," "venal," "irresponsible," press "controlled by special interests."

To understand the Soviet-Communist theory of the press, one must examine not only the basic Soviet political implications as derived from Marxist doctrine but also the Soviet interpretation of the word freedom. You may be surprised to learn that the Soviet Constitution guarantees both free speech and a

Figure 15-4 *PRAVDA*, official newspaper of the Communist Party of the Soviet Union. The headline in the upper right says, "The Five Year Plan, Second Year." To the left of that headline is the slogan, "Proletarians of All Countries Unite." *PRAVDA* was founded in 1912 by Lenin.

Figure 15-5 Inside *PRAVDA*. (Courtesy, MTV Finland—from the documentary on *PRAVDA*)

free press. In addition, the principle tenet of Soviet political life is one of unity. The rise of the working class, the revolution, was a movement of unity within Soviet society. This joining together of the people into a classless society has become the philosophy of the Soviet state. Thus, freedom from the Soviet point of view is freedom from the oppression of a class—upper, middle, lower—society.

Schramm explains that mass communication in the Soviet-Communist theory is an instrument of the state. The two large Soviet newspapers, *Pravda* (Figures 15-4 and 15-5) and *Izvestiya*, are the best examples. International propaganda publications such as *Soviet Life* magazine reflect the Soviet-Communist theory. In *Four Theories of the Press*, Schramm writes: "The point is, that Soviet mass communication do not have integrity of their own. Their integrity, such as it is, is that of the state. They are 'kept' instruments, and they follow humbly and nimbly the gyrations of the Party line and the state directives." Mass communication is integrated with other instruments of the state, such as schools, the police, and even assemblies as instruments protecting the Communist philosophy. Yet while the press is considered an instrument of unity, it is also considered an instrument of revelation to provide enlightenment and to prepare the masses for unity and eventually revolution. The press is an "agitator, propagandist, and organizer."

Broadcasting (Figure 15-6) under the Soviet-Communist theory likewise is designed not so much to serve the public but to inform it. Programming is again

Figure 15-6 Inside Soviet television. (Courtesy, Radio Moscow)

the instrument of the state, and the medium is important to it because of the large numbers of people that broadcasting can reach.

Our discussion of the four theories of the press should be viewed not so much as categories in which various mass media can be placed but rather as different variations of media systems. These systems can apply to different media across different countries or even different media within one country. They represent the roots of not only the press in society but of mass communication in general. Keep this in mind as we now turn our attention to more specific legal issues and to the working press.

FREEDOM OF THE PRESS: THE CONSTITUTION

The association of the working press with the Constitution is closest to the First Amendment: "Congress shall make no law abridging the freedom of speech, or of the press." To give some assurance that a state could not completely negate the U.S. Constitution, the Fourteenth Amendment was passed, stating "No State shall make or enforce any law which shall abridge the privileges or immunities of citizens of the United States nor shall any state deprive any person of life, liberty, or property, without due process of law." The Fourteenth Amendment was not affirmed by the courts until 1925, in the case of *Gitlow* v. *New York*. Gitlow was the business manager of a newspaper that had published a "Manifesto" supporting Communist revolution in the United States. In this case, the Supreme Court declared: "For present purposes we may and do assume that freedom of speech and of the press—which are protected by the First Amendment from abridgement by Congress—are among the fundamental personal rights and liberties protected by the due process clause of the Fourteenth Amendment from impairment by the states."[1]

Yet the Constitution has not stopped the states from passing countless laws affecting the confidentiality of sources for both print and broadcast journalists, from passing laws affecting the right of access to public meetings or cameras in the courtroom, nor from passing laws governing cable television. Continually, in broadcasting, the twentieth-century concept of the electromagnetic spectrum as a limited resource has been used as a basis for more legislation and interpretation, although not without criticism. Former CBS commentator Eric Sevareid, addressing a meeting of the National Association of Broadcasters, remarked, "I could never understand why so basic a right as the First Amendment could be diluted or abridged simply because of technological change in the dissemination and reception of information and ideas."[2]

The broadcast press has had to fight continually for its rights as an equal partner with the print media under the First Amendment. This fight has entailed visible lobbying efforts by the National Association of Broadcastors (NAB), such as its Declaration of Broadcast Freedoms (Figure 15-7) passed as a resolution by NAB's Board on June 17, 1976. The declaration states that broadcasters "will increase our vigilance in defending our rights to stand equal to the written press. . . ." The NAB even published a mock newspaper (Figure 15-7) publicizing "future" government control of the newspaper industry. Spokespersons for the broadcasting industry have been equally as vocal. CBS's William S. Paley remarked that the First Amendment freedom "presupposes, in us as broadcasters, a greater sense of responsibility. If we fail to see the dimensions of that responsibility and to measure up to them, we are in for constant threats of restrictions and policing."[3]

Figure 15-7 National Association of Broadcasters.

With the rhetoric has come some judicial support for the First Amendment's application to broadcasting. In the case of *CBS* v. *the Democratic National Committee,* Justice William O. Douglas wrote:

> My conclusion is that the TV and radio stand in the same protected position under the First Amendment as do newspapers and magazines. The philosophy of the First Amendment requires that result, for the fear that Madison and Jefferson had of government intrusion is perhaps even more relevant to TV and radio than it is to newspapers and other like publications.[4]

A panel of five justices of the New York State Supreme Court affirmed the right of WABC-TV to show a documentary about conditions in a children's home.[5] Presiding Justice Harold A. Stevens wrote:

> While the protection of freedom of the press is not absolute, the burden of demonstrating a condition which warrants a prior restraint is indeed a heavy one. Television broadcasting falls under the umbrella of protection afforded the press, for it too, in matters such as the subject under review, is engaged in the dissemination of information of public concern.[6]

Ironically, while affirming the right to show the documentary, the court stopped the broadcast for five days to give the children's home time to appeal.

The spirit of the First Amendment is inherent in other laws, one example being the Communications Act of 1934 and its amendments. Section 326 of the Communications Act of 1934 states: "Nothing in this Act shall be understood or construed to give the Commission the power of censorship over the radio communications. . . shall interfere with the right of free speech by means of radio communication."

Although the U.S. Constitution remains the umbrella document under which legal theory functions in America, it is only a small part of the total regulatory scheme affecting the working press.

REPORTERS' SHIELD LAWS

Reporters' shield laws are designed to protect the anonymity of a reporter's sources of information. The laws received great attention in the early 1970s when the courts with interesting frequency began jailing journalists for not divulging their sources of information. One of the most publicized cases involved *Los Angeles Times* reporter William Farr, who refused to divulge the source of information he had received from an attorney during a murder trial. Farr served some time in jail. As a result of several other similar cases, a number of states began realizing that the Constitution did not give journalists sufficient protection and that there was a real need either to legislate new reporters' shield laws or to strengthen old ones. By 1980, more than twenty states had shield laws. Two states whose legislatures instituted typical changes were Indiana and Oregon. Indiana had had a shield law on the books since 1941, but it had become outdated. This, accompanied by the reasons mentioned above, prompted the legislature to change the law in 1971 and 1973. Below is the new law. The portion crossed out belongs to the 1941 law.

> Section 1. IC 1971, 34-3-5-1 is amended to read as follows: Sec. 1. Any person connected with, or any person who has been so connected with or employed by, a weekly, semiweekly, triweekly, or daily newspaper that conforms to postal regulations, which shall have been published for five (5) consecutive years in the same city or town and which has a paid circulation of two per cent (2%) of the population of the county in which it is published, newspaper or other periodical issued at regular intervals and having a general circulation or a recognized press association; a wire service as a bona fide owner, editorial or reportorial employee, who receives or has received his or her principal income from legitimate gathering, writing, editing and interpretation of news, and any person connected with a commercially licensed radio or television station as owner, official, or as an editorial or reportorial employee who received or has received his or her principal income from legitimate gathering, writing, editing, interpreting, announcing or broadcasting of news, shall not be compelled to disclose in any legal proceedings or elsewhere the source of any information procured or obtained in the course of his employment or representation of such newspaper, periodical, press association, radio station, or television station, or wire service, whether published or not published in the newspaper or periodical, or by the press association or wire service or broadcast or not broadcast by the radio station or television station by which he is employed.

Although Indiana's 1941 shield law may seem rather shortsighted by today's standards, it was felt conclusive enough for that era. Today, however, there are many other considerations. Technology and judical precedent have created a need for more inclusive shield laws.

An example of this inclusiveness is the Oregon shield law. In the Oregon law, the scope of the media covered under the statute is much broader than in the Indiana law. Although a court might interpret the Indiana law as being just as broad, the Oregon law specifically states that: "Medium of communication has its ordinary meaning and includes, but is not limited to, any newspaper, magazine or other periodical, book, pamphlet, news service, wire service, news or feature syndicate, broadcast station or network, or cable television system . . . ."

Laws as encompassing as Oregon's are rare. Not all states are explicit in their definition of media, and reporters working for magazines or writing books are not always protected as fully as newspaper journalists are. Although judicial precedent has firmly established radio and television as being "press" in the traditional sense, there still are many legal frontiers to be conquered before shield laws can be said to have universal application.

Reporters are also faced with the fact that orderly judicial procedures must be followed when a court order demands that a reporter reveal confidential sources of information. Courts also have ruled that reporters are not exempt from appearing and testifying before grand juries. Even the strongest shield laws may not prevent a judge from issuing a contempt order, and although a reporter may win a case on appeal, he or she may in the meantime spend considerable time in jail and be faced with huge legal fees.

FREEDOM OF INFORMATION LAWS

Closely related to reporters' shield laws are freedom of information laws. Both are designed to help guarantee the ability of the news media to disseminate truthful, accurate, and complete information. Freedom of information laws attempt to assure the press access to (1) meetings of governmental bodies and (2) documents that are classified or are part of public officials' files and reflect possible corrupt activities in government. These laws exist not only on a national level, as was so vividly brought to the public's attention during the Vietnam War and the Watergate era, but also on the state level.

For the news media, the most common contact with freedom of information laws is in the area of open meetings. Investigative journalism is, of course, concerned with open records legislation, but the average reporter preparing information for daily public consumption is also concerned with whether or not he or she will be admitted to the local meeting of the city council or whether the executive meeting of the zoning board is going to shut the door to the news media. A report written by Dr. John Adams of the University of North Carolina and funded by the American Newspaper Publishers Association listed eleven different classifications of open meetings laws.[7]

1. Include a statement of public policy in support of openness,
2. Provide for an open legislature,
3. Provide for open legislative committees,
4. Provide for open meetings of state agencies or bodies,
5. Provide for open meetings of agencies and bodies of the political subdivisions of the state,
6. Provide for open County Boards,
7. Provide for open City Councils (or their equivalent),
8. Forbid closed executive sessions,
9. Provide legal recourse to halt secrecy,
10. Declare actions taken in meetings which violate the law to be null and void,
11. Provide for penalties for those who violate the law.

Of all the classifications, the four most common types of open meetings legislation currently in operation include open state agencies, open county-local agencies, open county boards, and open city councils. For the average reporter, these are the most common types of governmental bodies to which he or she would need access.

Two other key areas in which the press would like to see open information laws enforced are executive sessions and actions taken in meetings that violate the law. When important desicions must be made before they can be voted on in public, many governmental bodies may call executive sessions. The problem with these closed sessions is that they can easily become a habit. When such issues as budgets, firing employeees, planning raises, and similar items arise, public reaction and concern can be significant. Voting and deciding behind closed doors and then merely "rubber stamping" the decisions at the public meetings of these agencies deprives the public of the information they need as constituents of elected officials.

The real teeth in open meetings laws are found in points 10 and 11. Any law is only as good as its ability to be enforced. Laws are strong when they void any action taken in closed session and even stronger when they provide penalties for those who violate the law. When the news media have this type of legislation protecting their ability to report, the free flow of information to the public is much more open.

CAMERAS IN THE COURTROOM

In 1935 when Bruno Richard Hauptmann was tried for the kidnapping of the son of famed aviator Charles Lindbergh, the courtroom resembled more a county fair than a judicial proceeding. Reporters were falling over reporters, vendors were selling souvenirs, and when the judge barred cameras from the courtroom, one reporter still managed to sneak a camera into court and snap a picture that bannered in papers across the country.

The American Bar Association approved its famous Canon 35 two years after the Lindbergh trial. Amended in 1963 to include television, Canon 35 forbade either taking photographs of or broadcasting court proceedings. Individual states were quick to affirm Canon 35's principles and to place it in statutes affecting court proceedings. The Federal Rules of Criminal Procedures, specifically Rule 53, carries the prohibition of cameras to federal courts. A special committee of the Judicial Conference of the United States reaffirmed Canon 35 in 1968, calling for prohibition of " . . . radio or television broadcasting from the courtroom or its environs, during the progress of or connection with judicial proceedings. . . . " Clearly, from the standpoint of the courts and many lawyers, there is popular support for the Sixth Amendment's position guaranteeing a fair trial.

Such claims for constitutional priority are not founded in merely supposition or conjecture. The annals of case law are filled with overturned verdicts, appeals, and charges of biased juries, because the news media have been less than restrained in their coverage. Cases that stand out include *Rideau* v. *Louisiana*.[8] In this case, the suspect was interviewed by a country sheriff, and the interview was filmed and played on local television. The suspect's confessions made during the interview and the subsequent televising of those confessions prompted the defense attorney to request a change of venue. A denial and subsequent guilty verdict were all that was needed for the United States Supreme Court to reverse the conviction and state that the jury should have been drawn from a community whose residents had not seen the televised interview.

The case of Texas businessman Billie Sol Estes added fuel to this constitutional fire. Estes was tried and convicted of swindling. An appeals court affirmed the conviction, but when the case reached the United States Supreme Court in 1965 in *Estes* v. *State of Texas*, the conviction was reversed.[9] Massive national publicity surrounded the trial, and when it first went to court, the trial judge permitted television coverage of portions of the trial. In fact, the initial hearings were carried live. The scene was described by Justice Clark, who delivered the opinion in the case:

> Indeed, at least 12 cameramen were engaged in the courtroom throughout the hearing taking motion and still pictures and televising the proceedings. Cables and wires were snaked across the courtroom floor, three microphones were on the judge's bench, and others were beamed at the jury box and the counsel table. It is conceded that the activities of the television crews and news photographers led to considerable disruption of the hearings.

Justice Clark summarized four areas in which television could potentially interfere with a trial: (1) Television can have an impact on the jury. The mere announcement of a televised trial can alert the community to "all the morbid details surrounding" the trial. "Every juror carries with him into the jury box those solemn facts and thus increases the chance of prejudice that is present in every criminal case." (2) Television can impair the quality of testimony. "The impact upon a witness of the knowledge that he is being viewed by a vast audience is simply incalculable. Some may be demoralized and frightened, some cocky and given to overstatement; memories may falter. . . . " (3) Television places additional responsibilities on the trial judge. Along with other supervisory duties, the judge must also supervise television. The job of the judge, "is to make certain that the accused receives a fair trial. This most difficult task requires his undivided attention." (4) On the defendant, television "is a form of mental if not physical harrassment, resembling a police line-up or the third degree. The inevitable close ups of his gestures and expressions during the ordeal of his trial might well transgress his personal sensibilities, his dignity, and his ability to concentrate. . . . "

The Supreme Court's decision, however, did not stop the courtroom access of omnipresent television cameras. Breakthroughs did occur in 1972 when the American Bar Association's House of Delegates approved a Code of Professional Responsibility, permitting the use of television in the courtroom for such activities as prerecording testimony and playing back the videotape to present evidence. Another breakthrough came in 1974 when the Washington State Supreme Court instructed a county superior to select a trial and to experiment, for "educational" purposes, with televising it. The experiment was generally successful.[10] In Las Vegas, Nevada, the fall of 1976 saw KLAS-TV televise in color a criminal court trial. Sixty hours of courtroom activity, including interviews with the defendant, jury, and attorneys, were videotaped and edited for a three-part, prime-time special. And one of the most publicized trials took place in Florida in 1977 when a teenager was accused of murder (Figure 15-8). The trial was televised, and segments appeared regularly on network television, calling national attention to the camera-courtroom issue. A few weeks later, when the verdict was read in an Indiana kidnapping case, cameras were again present, and the courtroom once again made national television.

In 1976, a Montgomery, Alabama courtroom opened its doors to a reporter from the Montgomery *Advertiser Journal.* Using the Alabama Supreme Court ruling that permitted pictures to be taken during court proceedings when judges permit it, the photographer captured a ten-year-old deaf-mute girl identifying the defendant in a case. The child testified in sign language and her testimony was translated for the jury by a teacher. Judge Richard Emmet, who presided over the case, was quoted by Associated Press as saying that taking of pictures in court was

Figure 15-8 (George Chase and WPBT-TV)

Figure 15-9 Arguing a point in the trial of Patty Hearst. The scene is the work of NBC courtroom artist Walt Stewart of KRON-TV in San Francisco. (Walt Stewart)

not in any way disruptive. He felt that the trial went very well and that the camera did not disrupt the courtroom.

The future of camera coverage of court proceedings will depend on the willingness of the courts to recognize the public's right of access to trials, their permission in court for the apparatus necessary to capture the actual sounds and sights of the court in session, and the willingness of the press to use restraint and the highest professional attitude and activity while covering a trial. Certainly, not all of the courts across the country are going to open their doors to cameras overnight. The process will be slow and gradual, and many trials will remain closed at the request of the parties involved. Meanwhile, the familiar and talented courtroom artists will continue their craft of capturing on sketch pad (Figure 15-9) the activity barred from the eyes of the news cameras.

TELEVISION AND LEGISLATIVE PROCEEDINGS

While many broadcasters have been fighting to gain access to the courtrooms, others have been lobbying for access into legislative chambers, especially on the state level. One reason for this effort is to offset the lopsided coverage that the executive branch of government always receives. Another reason is the public's right to know. Critics argue that the legislature is where the real coverage should take place, since this is where an informed public needs to exert its opinions through its elected representatives. Although the U.S. House of Representatives voted in 1977 to permit television cameras in its chambers for certain proceedings, many state bodies have lagged behind.

Two factors have continually snarled the full-scale coverage: (1) the necessity to garner enough votes to pass a full-coverage measure and (2) the inability to muster a plan for the coverage. Sticky points include whether or not cameras should show all of the chamber. Can the gallery be seen? Do the cameras need to be in fixed positions? Who will determine what will and will not be televised? Will the charismatic representatives steal the show from their less "polished" counterparts? Will politicians play to the cameras instead of doing their job?

Nevertheless, the broadcast press is making progress. After court pressure was brought by a Chicago station, the Illinois Commerce Commission opened up its sessions to television coverage in 1977. Temporary guidelines were issued pending the adoption of permanent ones. Those guidelines restricted cameras and recording equipment to a designated area in the back of the hearing room. Television lights could not be set up outside the designated area; camera persons could have access to other areas of the room before the conference was called to order; and microphones could not be placed on the staff tables at the front of the room nor on the commissioner's bench. Photo journalists had similar restrictions placed upon them and were prohibited from using flash bulbs during the conference.

Such specially called conferences are just a brick on the road to unrestricted coverage of the day-to-day business of the legislative process. But again, as with the courts, as television cameras become smaller and less conspicious, and as broadcast journalists act more responsibly, there are bound to be greater opportunities for legislative coverage.

GAG RULES

In their attempts to assure a fair trial and to secure the "dignity" of the court, some judges have placed restraints on the press by keeping them from reporting those aspects of the trial that the judges feel might interfere with the judicial process. Such actions are commonly called "gag rules" and create a direct conflict between the news media and the judiciary in the issue of free press versus fair trial. Gag rules have ranged from attempts to keep all news media from reporting any and all aspects of a trial, to orders stifling just one particular reporter. In many cases, reporters have been held in contempt of court for publishing or broadcasting information the judge has deemed unacceptable for public consumption via the news media.

scope of gag rules

In recent years, gag rules have become increasingly common. Although there seems to be little constitutional foundation to such rules and they are almost always voided when appealed, this has not hampered their frequent issuance. For instance, in California, Superior Court Judge J. A. Leetham barred journalists from reporting the identity of witnesses in a murder case. The same gags were placed on defendants, documents, and exhibits. The gag rule was eventually struck down by an appeals court.[11] An Ontario, California judge issued a gag rule against publication of the names of certain witnesses, also in a murder trial. A well-publicized gag rule resulted when a Baton Rouge, Louisiana judge, Gordon E. West, prohibited reporting news of a pretrial hearing involving a civil rights worker. Two reporters, Gibbs Adams of the *Morning Advocate* and Larry Dickinson of the *State Times*, defied the gag rule and were consequently fined and held in contempt of court. The rule was overturned by an appeals court, but the contempt citation was upheld, leaving the clear directive that, although a gag order may later be struck down in an appeal, it should be obeyed until that appeal has been completed.[12] In Texarkana, Arkansas, an editor was found in contempt of court for reporting the verdict in a rape case. That decision also was overturned by a higher court.[13]

the judicial dilemma

Although these judicial decisions may seem arbitrary to you, place yourself behind the bench for a few moments and consider what might go through your own mind. You are considering a controversial murder case which has received considerable publicity. You, as a judge, have the responsibility to guide the attorneys in the search for truth. It is your responsibility to secure the defendant a fair trial and to see that everyone is equally represented in the case. You know from previous decisions that if you do not adhere to the rules of the court, the final decision in the case will be appealed, and your own actions will be held accountable in the appeal. If there is considerable pretrial publicity and an appeals court rules that the defendant is entitled to a new trial, then this reflects on the operation of your own courtroom, especially if during the trial the defendant's attorney requested a change of venue for the trial based on that very pretrial publicity. Perhaps you are an elected judge and are caught between giving the press complete freedom to do and say what they please and thus risk the dignity of your court, or attempt to gag them and thus incur their ire which could have an effect on your chances in the next election. Even if the press is responsible in your community, you may still wrestle with the question of what should be done and how it will affect your political career. On the other hand, you may be asking yourself, "If I issue a gag rule and in my opinion protect the dignity of the court, then when the gag rule is subsequently struck down, what does that action create?" In trying to protect the dignity of the court and the due process of law under one constitutional amendment, you successfully nullify the effect of another one. Thus, from behind the bench, it is a real dilemma, one which is not easily solved.

Now place yourself in the shoes of the reporter assigned to cover the case. From the morning that the case first appeared on the police log, you have worked to provide complete and impartial information about it. You have based your activities not only on the fact that you have a job to do but also that the public has a right to know. As a journalist, you have the responsibility to report the activities of the government and the courts and to point out any deficiencies which might exist. Now comes the day of the trial. The judge issues you an order to not publish any information about the case. You are faced with some rather unpleasant alternatives. You can defy the judge and publish the story. You can also land in jail and be fined in the process. On the other hand, you can abide by the judge's ruling and tell your peers back at the office why you sold out. Suppose you decide at least to take the issue to a higher court to try and have the gag rule reversed. Chances are you will be successful, but in the meantime, you will have missed the story. At the very least, you will have spent valuable time and money and may face the situation again when the judge decides to issue another gag rule. There is no easy solution to your dilemma any more than there is an easy solution to the judge's dilemma.

voluntary cooperation

Occasionally, the press has agreed to voluntary silence arrangements with the judge. For example, in Cartersville, Georgia, Judge Jefferson L. Davis simply calls a conference with the reporters whenever he wants information withheld from publication. He explains why, and the arrangement seems to work.[14] Yet Cartersville is not Los Angeles or New York, and what may work in a small Georgia community may not prove feasible in a major city. Moreover, many journalists would claim it should not work. That is not the job of a journalist.

In an article in *Time* magazine, the following incident was reported. When two persons accused of murder were brought to trial in Pennsylvania, the judge informed the press that the cases for the two defendants had been separated, and each was to receive a separate trial. The press agreed to withhold reporting the first trial so as not to prejudice the second trial. The news media, including radio and television stations as well as newspapers, went along with the judge and not only failed to cover the proceedings but even omitted any public mention of the trial. When it was all over, the press was divided on whether or not they had made the right decision.[15]

The problem of ensuring a free press but at the same time according a defendant a fair trial is a dilemma far from nearing a solution. Gag rules will probably continue to be issued, and journalists will probably continue to defy them, as will judges persist in citing members of the news media for contempt.

This is one of those gray areas in regulatory posture that places law, journalism, and the Constitution right in the middle.

RIGHTS OF THE STUDENT PRESS

The courts' continued support of First Amendment principles as they apply to the student press depends on the responsible actions of student reporters. Although the legal issues are complex, generally the college press is afforded somewhat more freedom than the high school press. One reason for this greater freedom is because college students are usually of legal adult age, over eighteen in most states, and can therefore assume some of the responsibility for their actions that the school district must assume for high school journalists.

Any school system typically finds itself in the awkward position of being an instrument of the state, supported by taxpayers' dollars. As a result, schools can exercise control over the student press when the content of the press directly and specifically affects the maintenance of the school system. In other words, calls for revolution in a school newspaper, especially in a high school newspaper, can be a sticky legal issue. For example, in one case the Supreme Court ruled, "the First Amendment can be abridged by state officials if their protection of legitimate state interests necessitates an invasion of free speech."[16] This does not, however, sanction blanket authority to censor anything disagreeable to a school administration. Specific actions affecting the control of a student press must be based on evidence. Moreover, money, once appropriated, cannot be withdrawn or threatened to be withdrawn as a means of controlling press content. Firing a student editor can be just as touchy, especially if it is done under the guise of an infraction of school rules.

As a result of the obscure legal issues, many student newspapers have tried to become independent of their parent institution. Yet how independent a student newspaper is from the school usually does not matter until the newspaper becomes involved in a libel suit. Attorneys can be rather disinterested in "independent" status and can be quick to name the school as a defendant, regardless of how independent the paper claims it is. Court arguments purporting to show this association can center on such factors as the newspaper being widely publicized in school literature, from admissions brochures to school catalogues; articles written in journalism classes under faculty direction finding their way into print; the college or university handling some of the newspaper bookkeeping; facilities of the college or university being used to house the newspaper; and endowments administered through the school directly benefiting the student newspaper.

Most student journalists have the opportunity in a high school or college curriculum to experience both responsible reporting and the exercise of free press. Taking advantage of both opportunities can be a valuable training ground for a professional career or for better understanding and critical evaluation of the press. Most of the student publications operate under faculty advisors. Students who fail to take advantage of these advisors or who look upon them as potential censors instead of as colleagues concerned about a responsible press are failing to tap a valuable resource which can pay off in later years.

LIBEL AND SLANDER

Although the First Amendment gives reporters the ability to pursue truth, criticize government, and generally take a no-holds-barred attitude toward the exercise of a free press, there are certain legal safeguards against irresponsible journalism that may libel a person, institution, business, or other identifiable entity.

definition

Libel is defined as *the publication of material that identifies and defames a person, resulting in that person's exposure to hatred, contempt, ridicule, and causes him or her to be shunned or avoided.* Closely related to libel is *slander,* which can apply to broadcasting, and is the *voicing of defamatory statements about someone to another person.* Libel and slander are in some ways interchangeable. For example, someone who is libeled on a radio newscast may also be slandered, inasmuch as the actual "publishing" of the news story was in the form of an oral presentation. A test to determine whether or not something is libelous has three parts: publication, defamation, and identification. If a person is written about in a newspaper or mentioned during a broadcast and that mention defames the person, then publication, defamation, and identification have occurred and the person may have been libeled.

avoiding libel

It is as important to understand libel as it is to avoid it. Most reporters have some knowledge of mass communication law, and although every case is different and every jury and judge can make a different interpretation of that law, there are guidelines for staying out of libel court. Of these, nothing is more important than to *avoid mediocre reporting practices.* Journalism is extremely serious business. A name misspelled, a false association with the scene of a crime, or an implied immoral act may wind up as a law suit in the millions of dollars. There is no substitute for sacrificing accuracy, regardless of how big the story or how tight the deadline. Second, truth, although a defense against libel, may not hold up in court unless the *truth can be proved.* Simply saying that something is fact, yet not being able to prove it in court may not be enough. A reporter cannot *assume* something is true simply because someone says it is. Regardless of how close to the truth a source may seem to be, documents may be necessary to defend a libel suit. A third way to avoid libel is to *make sure the story is objective.* Words often can bring on a libel suit. If a reporter writes that someone is a swindler, that reporter had better be sure the person has been tried in court and convicted of swindling before using the noun in print. Even then it is safer to say that the person was "found guilty" in a court of law rather than using the word "swindler." Quotations can be particularly difficult. A reporter may accurately report a quotation. However, if the quotation is an untrue statement, regardless of how accurately it is reported, the reporter and his or her respective medium are open to charges of libel. Finally, if an error is made and a libelous statement is reported, a *full and complete retraction* should be made. Although only a few states make it a complete defense against libel, a retraction can nevertheless reduce the damages.

libel per quod, libel per se

Courts can award two types of damages in libel cases. One type results from what is termed libel *per quod* and the other from libel *per se*. Libel per quod refers to libel from association. For example, a newspaper gossip column reports that two public school teachers, Mr. Smith and Miss Jones, are going to make it legal and get married next week. The comment merely refers to their upcoming wedding but could infer that they have been living together, which a conservative school board might not consider the best publicity for their teachers. Smith and Jones might decide to sue for libel. If they did, it would be considered libel per quod. On the other hand, if the paper reported that Mr. Smith, who happens to be happily married, is getting a divorce to marry Miss Jones, when in fact it is not the case, Smith might decide to sue on grounds of libel per se, that the words themselves are libelous.

defense against libel

When the press does find itself in libel court, it has three primary defenses. The first is *truth*. In some states, truth is an absolute defense against libel. In other words, regardless of how defamatory a statement or story is, if it can be proved true, then the plaintiff has little recourse but to live with the consequences without receiving any damages. The second defense is *reporters' privilege*. For example, comments made by politicians in a governmental forum, such as a legislature, are primarily immune from libel actions. Statements made by witnesses, judges, and lawyers in open court are also poor arguments in a libel case. In addition, comments made by heads of governmental agencies in the official discharge of their duties also can be freely reported on as long as the reporter does not show malice in reporting them.

A third defense is *fair comment*: comment about books, artistic works, and performers and others in the public light. However, recent Supreme Court decisions have greatly narrowed this privilege by narrowing the definition of a public figure. Simply putting someone in the news does not make him or her a public figure. When fair comment is employed, malice cannot be the motive and the statements must be opinions, not statements about what the reporter believes to be *fact*. Other defenses also exist beyond the three primary ones stated. For example, having permission to report something can be a defense. It must be proved, however. Consent in writing is much better than someone's verbal consent. Permitting the person to reply is another defense, and if the statute of limitations has expired, the person libeled has little recourse.

In recent years, libel suits have increased in frequency, and the press is not always held in high esteem among juries. So despite a defense of free press, truth, a retraction, or reporters' privilege, the reporter and the medium can find themselves paying significant damages. In fact, the problem is becoming so serious that some insurance companies are considering discontinuing libel insurance. Those companies that still have the insurance have raised their premiums so high that they are almost prohibitive for many small newspapers and broadcast stations. Yet the risk of libel judgments running into the millions of dollars can lead only to bankruptcy. The result is the need, more than ever, for responsible journalists.

INVASION OF PRIVACY

In its search for truth, the press deals daily with the issue of invasion of privacy. How far can the press go to gather information without infringing on the rights of others, specifically the right of privacy? Both statutes and judicial precedent have established parameters within which reporters must work to gain information. Going outside these parameters can result in actions against the press for invasion of privacy and, depending on what is reported, libel or slander. Generally, four areas must be avoided to avoid an invasion of privacy action.[17]

These include: (1) *physical intrusion*—breaking into someone's office or home is clearly off limits, although if the police raid the office or home and you accompany them, you would at least be on safer grounds. Good taste still can be considered. If the police arrest the occupant and drag him nude into the street and you film that and show him nude on the evening news, you may find yourself in court for invasion of privacy. Similarly, bugging a telephone or using a telephoto lens can get a reporter into the same kind of trouble, especially if a private citizen is involved and no crime has been committed. But even if a crime has been committed, publishing the picture or the results of the wiretap can be extremely serious and good cause for legal action. (2) *Appropriation*—showing a person's picture or using a person's name for commercial purposes without his or her permission can also be costly. Although this type of privacy invasion mostly concerns the advertising department of a newspaper or broadcasting station, the reporter taking the photograph or providing it to the commercial department for use can be named a defendant. (3) *Public disclosure*—exposing private, embarrassing facts about an individual can provoke legal action against the reporter. A patient hospitalized for obesity would have a case if a reporter took a picture of the individual in the hospital and published the photo without the person's permission. (4) *Placing a person in false light*—file photos can be particularly troublesome in this area. Publishing a picture of a policeman in conjunction with a story about a police corruption probe when the policeman in the photo is in no way connected with the probe would definitely be cause for legal action.

Much like libel, responsible reporting is the best insurance against an invasion of privacy suit.

SEARCH AND SEIZURE

In 1978, the Supreme Court ruled that police could search for criminal evidence believed in possession of a third party. The decision arose from a case concerning the *Stanford Daily* at Stanford University. Some say the ruling has frightening implications for a free press. At the extreme, it means that a corrupt government can use police action to secure documents from reporters who may be trying to expose that corruption. At the very least, it threatens every reporter who has ever worked on a story that may have criminal implications. If all police forces were without the taint of corruption and every officer of the law carried the banner of a free press, perhaps the ruling would not be as serious. But they are not. It was not surprising that the press was concerned about the ruling, and trade publications were quick to point out its dangers. *Broadcasting* magazine, in an editorial, noted: "It will be a public-spirited cop indeed who chances upon evidence of a journalistic investigation of the local police and keeps it secret."

The threat of a search warrant rests in the fact that it is a surprise document thrust in the front door and not subject to challenge. Instead of issuing a subpoena and having it challenged in court, a police officer can show up at the front door of a newspaper and, as one network executive commented, "break the door down." Moreover, when the warrant is requested from the judge, no one from the press will be there to argue against its issuance. Although the Supreme Court suggested that judges be careful of protecting First Amendment concerns when issuing warrants, the press found little solace in this, pointing out that local officials on the magistrate level will likely be less than cognizant of First Amendment principles, especially when police officers and prosecutors are standing in front of them demanding a search warrant in the name of law and order.

ALTERNATIVE CONTROLS: THE NATIONAL NEWS COUNCIL

It was at the height of the Watergate era, when news reporters were being jailed and the administration of former President Richard Nixon was protesting the press coverage it was receiving, that the National News Council became a reality. Supported by a grant from the nonprofit Twentieth Century Fund, the council was charged with the responsibility of considering the accuracy and fairness of news disseminated by national news-gathering organizations. Anyone can bring a complaint before the council as long as he or she waives filed legal proceedings against the news-gathering agency in regard to the complaint.

After some well-publicized criticism, the council finally became a reality in early 1973 and in July of that year formally announced its fifteen members, representing people from a wide range of backgrounds. William B. Arthur, a former editor of *Look*, was named executive director. Roger J. Traynor, a former chief justice of the California Supreme Court, became chairman, and the former city editor of WCBS-TV, Ned Schnurman, was named associate director. Three years later, the council increased its size to eighteen members, permitting two additional representatives from the media and one from the general public.

Ironically, Richard Nixon's criticism of the press coverage of his administration was not handled by the news council, mostly because it could not gain the cooperation of the Nixon administration officials to substantiate the charges.

Other cases have come before the council. A CBS television documentary about the life of former President Franklin Delano Roosevelt was criticized for misleading the viewers into assuming that troops had killed marchers during a Washington, D.C. protest in 1932. The council said the complaint brought against CBS was warranted. The *Washington Post* also received council scrutiny when the *Post* edited a UPI story and thus, the council claimed, changed the reported thrust of a speech by a woman's rights advocate.

In 1976, the scope of the council expanded beyond the national press to include press that may not be national in initial circulation but that deals with issues of a national concern or concern for journalists. Certainly the future of such a body will be dependent on the ability of the council to obtain three things—money, public support, and media support. Without any one of these, it cannot succeed. The thought by some that the council might turn into a type of hatchet body was not justified. While criticizing some media, it found that other complaints were not warranted. Currently, the council operates much like a watchdog without teeth. It can investigate and comment, but it cannot take action against the media, short of attempting to publicize its findings.

SUMMARY

Our discussion of legal issues and the working press began by examining four theories of the press as discussed by Siebert, Peterson, and Schramm. Of these theories, the authoritarian theory is the oldest and is based on the assumption that the individual is subordinate to the state. The press functions as an instrument of the state under this theory, with limited private control of the press for selected individuals who will publish the state's position on issues affecting society. As the authoritarian theory began to deteriorate, it was gradually replaced by the libertarian theory, which espouses a free press. Libertarianism envisions a society in which the individual is the concern of society, and society's goal is the achievement of the greatest happiness possible for the largest number of people. In the twentieth century, partly based on criticism of the role of advertising in the press, arose the social responsibility theory of the press. This theory suggests that while a free press exists, it must operate within certain safeguards to ensure that it will be both a free and responsible press. The Soviet-Communist theory is an example of a press that is not only an instrument of the state but one that is integrated with other instruments to maintain the theory of unity in Soviet society.

The basic legal document affecting the press in America is the First Amendment of the U.S. Constitution. Even when the federal government becomes directly involved in regulating mass media, the free press—free speech concept applies. Indicative of this is the Communications Act of 1934, which prohibits direct censorship of the media by government.

Our chapter also discussed reporters' shield laws, those laws protecting the confidentiality of reporters' news sources. Because of the lack of specificity of the Constitution with regard to safeguarding the confidentiality of news sources, individual states have enacted shield laws to strengthen their own commitment to freedom of the press. Closely related to shield laws are freedom of information laws which guard against the secrecy of governmental record keeping and meetings. Measures that control the press in the coverage of judicial proceedings include Canon 35 of the American Bar Association and gag rules. Canon 35 was designed to prevent cameras in the courtroom but is slowly being revoked by both courts and forward-thinking judges. Gag rules are issued by judges to thwart journalists from reporting news of court proceedings.

The student press enjoys many of the same rights as other media. There are, however, some restrictions placed on high school newspapers, and the student press that receives funds from a tax-supported college or university retains the somewhat precarious position of being an extension of the state. Whatever the relationship to the funding source, a student press provides an opportunity for students to learn from responsible advisors and to gain experience in reporting practices which can be beneficial in later professional careers.

Libel laws are among those safeguards that ensure a responsible press. Publication, identification, and defamation are three facts that can spell libel and a court suit for reporters. Similarly, invading someone else's privacy can also cause legal difficulties. Recent Supreme Court rulings have lifted the press's immunity from police search and seizure tactics. Placed in the same category as other businesses, the press is concerned about the possible abuse of this search and seizure privilege and the use of warrants to silence any record of possible criminal activity.

Alternatives to legal controls on the working press can be found in the activities of the National News Council. Operable in 1973, the council operates mainly as a watchdog.

BERN, WALTER, *The First Amendment and the Future of American Democracy.* New York: Basic Books, Inc., Publishers, 1976.

DEVOL, KENNETH S., *Mass Media and the Supreme Court: The Legacy of the Warren Years.* New York: Hastings House, 1976.

FRANKLIN, MARC A., *Cases and Materials on Mass Media Law.* Mineola, N.Y.: The Foundation Press, Inc., 1977.

GILLMOR, DONALD M., and JEROME A. BARRON, *Mass Communication Law* (3rd ed.). St. Paul: West Publishing Co., 1979.

JOHNSTON, DONALD F., *Copyright Handbook.* New York: R. R. Bowker Company, 1978.

PEMBER, DONALD, *Mass Media Law.* Dubuque, Iowa: William C. Brown Co., Publishers, 1977.

POWERS, RON, *The Newscasters.* New York: St. Martin's Press, Inc., 1977.

REDDICK, DEWITT, *The Mass Media and the School Newspaper.* Belmont, Calif.: Wadsworth Publishing Co., Inc., 1976.

RUCKELSHAUS, WILLIAM, and ELIE ABEL, eds., *Freedom of the Press.* Washington, D.C.: American Enterprise Institute for Public Policy Research, 1976.

SANFORD, BRUCE W., *Synopsis of the Law of Libel and the Right of Privacy.* Cleveland: Baker Hostetler & Patterson, 1977.

SIEBERT, FRED S., THEODORE PETERSON, and WILBUR SCHRAMM, *Four Theories of the Press.* Urbana: University of Illinois Press, 1956.

SIMONS, HOWARD, and JOSEPH A. CALIFANO, JR., eds., *The Media and the Law.* New York: Praeger Special Studies, 1976.

TRAGER, ROBERT, and DONNA L. DICKERSON, *College Student Press Law.* Athens: School of Journalism, Ohio University and ERIC, 1977.

ZUCKMAN, HARVEY L., and MARTIN J. GAYNES, *Mass Communications Law in a Nutshell.* St. Paul: West Publishing Co., 1977.

16

Audience and Effects of Mass Communication

Ever since the press began to exert an influence in society, people have been concerned about the effects of the press. Today that concern ranges far beyond the press. Scan the topics in an evening newspaper, listen to radio or television, or read a news magazine, and you will realize why there is concern about the effects of mass media on our lives. The impact of editorials on the election process, the influence of televised violence in contributing to or in alleviating real-life violence and teenage delinquency, and the effect of comic books—all of these have entered the discussions of legislators, parent-teacher associations, and academicians.

The purpose of this chapter is to examine the effects of mass communication on our lives. Before doing this, however, it is necessary also to understand the audience for mass communication. We shall learn how we view the audience in terms of its demographic and psychographic characteristics and then shall discuss some of the pitfalls in studying the audience and effects.

AUDIENCE DEMOGRAPHICS

With a mass audience, it is often difficult to find certain segments of the population to which specific mass media messages are to be directed. For example, a successful advertising campaign for a Rolls Royce must first select an audience whose income level is high enough to afford it. As a result, media buyers must rely on demographics to categorize the population. *Demographic characteristics are the basic statistical data on such things as age, sex, education level, income, and ethnic background.* They are used more often than any other method to pinpoint a certain mass audience and thus to determine such things as how much an advertiser will be charged for airing a commercial during a particular television program at a specified time.

Demographics can be applied to local media that serve a given geographic area as well as to national media. For instance, your local radio station reaches a specific portion of the total community listeners, which again can be identified as a group because of its demographic characteristics. If you were to walk into the manager's office at the local station and ask him what the characteristics of his station's audience are, he might reply, "We reach the upper-income, middle-aged male." Further investigation might reveal that his station programs a lot of play-by-play sports which attract this type of sudience.

Similarly, if you were to walk into the office of a network executive and ask what type of audience her network prime-time programming reaches on Wednesday nights, she might say, "the middle-income individual whose median age is thirty-four." In each case, both media executives identified their audience by demographic characteristics.

Now for comparison, let's examine what would happen if you walked into the office of a media manager who was responsible for publishing a magazine called *Skiers.* The publisher would certainly be able to tell you the demographic characteristics of her audience. However, this would not be the only important quality of the audience. Of equal importance would be their interest in skiing. They would be joined, not so much because of their demographic characteristics, but because they liked to ski. Advertisers, although wanting to know the average income of the audience, would be mainly interested in them because of this skiing interest. It would be an ideal place to advertise ski apparel, ski equipment, and ski resorts. On the other hand, if an advertiser wanted to reach an audience predominantly in their mid-twenties, all hobbies or other interests aside, he would want to find another mass medium that would accurately reflect this demographic feature. Perhaps network television or radio would be a better medium in this instance.

As a result of certain demographic characteristics, media specialists and resarchers have become very proficient in determining media habits of the mass audience. Although new research techniques are being developed to supplement audience demographics, demographics still remain the foundation for categorizing the mass audience.

AUDIENCE PSYCHOGRAPHICS

One of the new research frontiers that scrutinizes the mass audience is called psychographics. Psychographics attempts to define and to distinguish the psychological characteristics of the mass audience. Examples are attitudes, opinions, values, or self-esteem.

Psychographics come into play when the traditional demographic characteristics are not sufficient to plan a media buy or to explain our reaction to media messages. For instance, age and income may very well help to determine attitudes toward welfare payments. However, if these were the only characteristics you considered when planning a media persuasion campaign to revise the welfare system, you would have little success. Many other characteristics of the mass audience help determine attitudes toward welfare, and it is imperative for the media buyer to look directly at those attitudes, disregarding, for the moment, demographic characteristics.

After sampling audience attitudes, you may discover that unfavorable attitudes toward the current welfare system are held by middle-income people. Based on psychographic information about these individuals, you plan your media campaign to reach them. Had you assumed that the attitudes of all income groups were alike, your media campaign would have been needlessly expensive. Moreover, had you assumed that certain attitudes toward welfare followed directly from membership in specific age and income groups and had not investigated these attitudes, your media campaign would have failed miserably. Based on the information you have received, you may also discover that you will need to use different media to reach these middle-income individuals. Perhaps they watch more television than other income groups do, or read certain consumer magazines. Your media campaign will then have the greatest chances for success if advertisements are placed in these media.

RESEARCHING THE AUDIENCE AND EFFECTS: SOME PITFALLS

What we know about the characteristics of the mass audience and the effects that mass communication has on this audience is the result of about four decades of research, a short span of time when we consider how long, for example, the print media have been with us. There is still much to learn.

methodology and theory

For instance, in chapter 1 we learned there were three basic types of communication—intrapersonal, interpersonal, and mass communication. Research in each of these three areas has proceeded from a different methodological base. In intrapersonal communication, highly controlled laboratory experiments have employed sensitive electronic measurements of such physiological processes as brain waves and galvanic skin response. Interpersonal communication research has been mostly under closely controlled laboratory conditions, frequently in the college classroom. In many cases, this research has consisted of students receiving some type of message and then being tested for attitude change. Mass communication research, on the other hand, has consisted of mostly field or survey research, in which the sample population responds either to a question-naire or to a home interview.

experimental vs. survey methodologies

When people have tried to structure a theoretical base for all types of communi-cation from these three very different types of data, results have been less than ideal. Psychologist Carl Hovland, in discussing the subject of attitude change, summarized the differences in results obtained through research using experi-mental and survey methodologies.[1] Among these differences were such things as the *length of the message* used to test attitude change, the *influence of experimen-ters*, the *difference in interpersonal reaction*, and the *elapsed time after exposure to the message*. These differences, among others, reflect some of the difficulties in researching the mass audience and studying the effects of mass communica-tion.

Imagine that you are a reseacher hired to test viewers' reactions to a new television commercial for a certain brand of soap. You arrange for a group of people not currently using that brand of soap to gather in a classroom, sit quietly, and watch the commercial. You then elicit their opinions about new soap. Their answers suggest they have changed their opinion about their current brand of soap and will try the new one. You are excited; your commercial works. But does it? You select a community in your area, purchase time on a local television station, and wait for sales to go up. But they do not. What happened?

To answer the question, review some of the carefully controlled conditions of your "laboratory." Recall first that your group watched the entire commercial from start to finish. But what happened outside the laboratory? Many people only saw part of the commercial. They may have headed for the refrigerator at the very instant the commercial appeared. This limited exposure naturally affected their reaction to the commercial. Second, when your group entered the classroom setting, they perceived your wishes and reacted accordingly. This influence was not present in the home environment. Third, you also asked your group to sit quietly. They were not permitted to talk to each other. Yet when viewers saw the commercial in their home environment, the situation was entirely different. They would interact freely, and their reactions may have been exactly opposite to those expressed in the classroom. Perhaps one member of the family told the rest that the brand of soap featured in the commercial was not any good, and the rest of the family believed her. When you showed the commercial in the classroom, you tested for attitude change immediately after the airing. But after waiting a few weeks to compile the results of your mass communication campaign, you discovered what you could not find out from the interpersonal, classroom setting—that after a few weeks, people's preferences for soap returned to what they had been before the commercial.

Of course, there are many other factors, all making the results of your research misleading. These four conditions are just some of the ones that make researching the mass audience a difficult process. Although you wanted to obtain as truthful and as valid results from your research as you could, moving research out of the laboratory made it possible for many unknown variables to interfere with the results.

In the following pages, keep in mind that the results of research can vary with different methodologies. Human communication is a very complex phenomenon. It is not easily defined, let alone completely understood.

EARLY APPROACHES TO UNDERSTANDING EFFECTS: THE BULLET THEORY

Early theories held that the mass audience was an unidentifiable group of people with separate life styles, who were individually affected by the various mass media with which they came in contact. Reaction to mass media was thus seen as an individual rather than a collective experience. This approval to understanding the effects of mass communication was termed the *hypodermic* or *bullet* theory. Two assumptions that can easily be drawn from such an approach are (1) people receive information directly from the mass media and not through an intermediary, and (2) that reaction is individual, not based on how other people might influence them.

REVISING THE BULLET THEORY

As psychologists and sociologists began to work with the bullet theory, it just did not seem to explain why people reacted the way they did to messages from the mass media. Gradually, the idea of *subgroups* began to emerge.

subgroups

This concept of a subgroup, a "mass within a mass," provided new insights into how we, as members of a mass audience, both receive information from the mass media and react to that information. For example, we can receive information directly by watching television, listening to the radio, reading a newspaper, leafing through a magazine, or some other form of direct contact with the media. On the other hand, some of our knowledge is derived from *other people* who have been exposed to the media and who have, in turn, relayed the message to us. In a sense, these people who relay the message to us play the role of gatekeeper. And, just as the gatekeeper working in the media both expands and restricts our informational environment, so the person delivering interpersonal communication may both expand and restrict our informational environment.

To understand this concept, let's imagine an executive of a large fertilizer company is sitting at lunch reading the financial page of the local newspaper.

That afternoon he leaves the office and on the way out meets the office manager. They stop to chat for a moment, and in the course of their conversation, the executive suggests that the office manager consider purchasing agribusiness stocks as an excellent personal investment. The office manager mulls over the advice of the executive. She has heard about a number of the agribusiness stocks and feels that they might make a good investment. However, until now, she has never been influenced to the point of buying. Her conversation with the executive changed all that. She values his advice. He has made many successful investments in the stock market. She also knows that he reads a large number of financial magazines, the financial page of the local newspaper, and specialized economic publications that offer tips on potential investments. Based on the executive's advice she decides to purchase the agribusiness stocks.

opinion leaders and the two-step flow

The above example illustrated two important concepts in understanding the mass audience—the *two-step flow* and *opinion leaders*. First, let us study the two-step flow. This theory was posited by three researchers, Paul Lazarsfeld, Bernard Berelson, and Hazel Gaudet, who studied the 1940 American presidential campaign.[2] In the process of interviewing people about the election, they found that much of the voters' information about the campaign came from other people. This concept has been expanded upon since that time, but the primary hypothesis remains essentially the same—that much of the information disseminated by mass media comes to the individual's attention secondhand from people who relay their interpretation of it. The case of the executive reading the financial news in the newspaper and then suggesting that the office manager buy stock was an example of the two-step flow.

In addition, the executive *influenced* the office manager's opinion of the stocks—he was an opinion leader. This concept, which also evolved from the research of Lazarsfeld, Berelson, and Gaudet,[3] hypothesizes that relayers of information from mass media can also influence the attitudes and/or decisions of the receivers.

interpersonal influence

We all are acquainted with someone we respect for his or her opinions on world affairs. This other person is usually very much attuned to the mass media and may read more than one newspaper per day, some news magazines, and also listen to a number of radio and television news presentations. We may thus tend to rely on this person's judgments of world affairs. Type of medium may also determine how and with what influence an opinion leader functions. For example, some opinion leaders are attuned to more specialized media which give them an authoritative stance on specific subjects. You, as students, are in class to learn about mass communication. You rely on your instructor to provide you with recent and authoritative information. Your instructor, because of his or her interest in mass communication, most likely reads scholarly journals on the subject, journalism reviews, radio-television columns in the local newspaper, and probably watches television programs on issues surrounding mass media in society. Because your instructor is so attuned to the mass media, especially when it concerns his or her area of expertise, you rely on this person as an opinion leader.

Now imagine for a moment that you cut class and miss a lecture in which the instructor relates new research findings that he or she read about in a scholarly journal. You know you probably will be penalized when it comes time for an examination, so you borrow another student's class notes. When you choose the student, you pick someone that you feel took good notes and could relay to you an accurate interpretation of the instructor's remarks. You were again seeking someone who, for you, would be an opinion leader. Notice that more than one person was involved in relaying information to you from the mass media—in this case, the scholarly journal. Both the instructor and your fellow student became opinion leaders. Thus, *although this process is still referred to as the two-step flow, it may involve more than just one relay person.*

In addition to the indirect communication we receive via the two-step flow, we may turn directly to the media either to receive more information, to reinforce an opinion presented to us by an opinion leader, or to form our own opinions. For instance, assume that the information about new research published in the scholarly journal seems strange to you. You feel that despite the authoritative posture of both your teacher and your friend, you just cannot accept it as valid. Instead, you decide to refer to the journal and read the article yourself. In this case, you use media as a *check* and *reinforcement* for the information that you received from the opinion leader. What actually occurred was an interrelationship between the media and the opinion leader, an interrelationship that ultimately determined how you were informed and influenced by media content.

UNDERSTANDING REACTION TO MEDIA MESSAGES

If we accept the idea that different individuals and groups affect how we react to messages from the mass media, we can begin to understand the different approaches to explaining these reactions. These approaches can be grouped into the individual differences, categories, and social relationships approaches.

individual differences approach

The *individual differences* approach proposes that each of us has unique qualities that result in our *reacting differently* to media messages. Professors Melvin De Fleur and Sandra Ball-Rokeach in their book, *Theories of Mass Communication*, state:

Individual differences perspective implies that media messages contain particular stimulus attributes that have differential interaction with personality characteristics of audience members. Since there are individual differences in personality characteristics among such members, it is natural to assume that there will be variations in effect which correspond to these individual differences.[4]

Variables in these differing effects are partially caused by the audience's *exposure, perception*, and *rentention* of media content, which we shall discuss later in this chapter.

Although at first the individual differences approach may seem like the bullet theory, it is more complex and takes into consideration the differences among individuals in accounting for different reactions to the same message.

categories approach

Another approach to the mass audience and the effects of media content is the *category* approach.[5] Its origin stems from the needs of advertisers to reach more specialized audiences. Although the simplest way to group an audience into categories is by demographics—sex, age, etc.—researchers are looking more and more at the physiographic—values, beliefs, attitudes, lifestyles—components of the audience. Looking at the audience through categories can be much more complex than the old bullet theory. Notice we said, *can be*. For the ad buyer wanting to reach eighteen-to twenty-one-year-old females, the application of the theory becomes mechanical. But for social scientists wanting to know how categories of people think and how they interact with other categories of people, the approach becomes much more involved. Moreover, if we want to use these interrelationships to understand how people react to mass communication, the process becomes even more sophisticated. Buying an ad to reach the homemaker is one thing; buying an ad to reach the homemaker who *interacts* with another homemaker viewing a competing commercial is something else.

social relationships approach

Concentrating on this interaction and the people taking part in it would describe the *social relationships* approach to studying the audience and media effects. The importance of interpersonal communication becomes evident in the social relationships approach, as does the realization that although the media can help disseminate the initial message, how it is retransmitted, discussed, and rediscussed among audience members will significantly determine the effect of the message.

After considering the different approaches to studying the audience and the effects of mass communication on an audience, we readily can see that not only do the three approaches overlap, but that in some ways, all come into play in the communicative process. It is much like viewing that process through different colored glasses. A psychologist concerned with an individual's behavior might feel more comfortable with an individual differences approach, although that same psychologist would be foolish to ignore the other approaches. Similarly, an advertiser wanting to reach a specific type of audience might be concerned with categories but cannot ignore the interrelationships among people that demand the attention of the social relationships approach.

SELECTIVE EXPOSURE, PERCEPTION, AND RETENTION

In discussing the individual differences approach, we talked about exposure, perception, and retention. Each influences our interaction with the media and how they affect us. For instance, research has taught us that we selectively expose ourselves to certain types of programming, the process being called *selective exposure*. If a politician is delivering a televised address, you might tune in the program because you agree or disagree with the politician. For either reason, you selectively exposed yourself to the program.

Second, the perceptions you hold prior to watching the televised address will also affect your reaction to it. If you are extremely loyal to the politician, you might agree with everything she says regardless of *what* she says, so much so that if her opponent said the same thing, you might completely disagree with him. You would be guilty of *selective perception*. It is not a serious crime, but one that can considerably distort how you react to messages.

Third, because of your selective perception, you may retain only those portions of the address with which you agree. If you perceive the entire address as favorable, you may remember all of it. If you perceive it as unfavorable, you may wipe it entirely from your mind. If parts of the address affect you positively, those may be the portions that you remember while forgetting the negative elements. Or the negative elements may be the very ones you remember. Either way, how you originally perceived the address determines what you retain, a process called *selective retention*.

THE FUNCTIONAL USE OF MEDIA

For the most part, our discussion has been in the context of how the media influence the audience or how the mass audience reacts to the media content. Our study has been primarily one-sided, and we have so far failed to consider the *interactive* qualities of our media-audience relationship. We have been asking the question, "What do the media do *to* people?" instead of "What do people do *with* media?" This same myopic approach was noted by well-known media researcher and scholar Elihu Katz, who stressed that much media research proceeded from a "bookkeeping" outlook indicative of the first question, rather than to a "functional" or "uses and gratification" approach, indicative of the second question.[6] Let's look at this "functional" concept in more detail so that we can become aware of how the mass audience interrelates with the mass media.

film: highbrow, middlebrow, lowbrow, postbrow

One of the ways that we can study this concept is through film audiences. The motion picture has become an established medium of mass communication. Over the past sixty years, it has touched on virtually every segment of society, has dealt with every subject, and has reached every audience. Yet for these audiences, it has had many different meanings and has performed many different functions.

Louis M. Savary and J. Paul Carrico, in writing about motion pictures and their audiences, divide the film audience into three distinct groups—*highbrows, middlebrows,* and *lowbrows.*[7] For each audience, film performs a different function and has a different meaning. For example, the highbrows look at the medium as an artistic expression and derive intellectual satisfaction from a well executed film. They may attend a movie more than once, not necessarily because they like the plot or the actors, but because they want to study the work of a famous director or review the camera techniques. For the lowbrow audience, the experience is entirely different; perhaps it is an excuse to get out or an escape from life's daily routine. Between these two groups are the middlebrows, somewhat knowledgeable in what a good motion picture consists of and able at least to differentiate between a really good and really bad film.

Savary and Carrico typify the current audience for films as belonging to none of the three types previously mentioned. Still predominantly in their late teen and young adult years, they are more sophisticated than past generations. Having taken courses in film, they have a much deeper understanding of the medium and its social implications. Savary and Carrico have labeled this knowledgeable generation the "postbrow" or "no-brow" audience.

Stephenson's play theory

Using a data gathering procedure called Q-sort, William Stephenson did extensive research on how different types of audiences, expressed as typical individuals, feel about the media. From this research has evolved Stephenson's play theory, which suggests that we use the media as a means of escaping into a world of "play" not accessible at other times.[8] Those researchers familiar with Stephenson's data gathering methods have given considerable support to Stephenson's theory as well as to his methodologies. Others have been severely critical, like Professor David Chaney who contends that "Stephenson . . . fails to move beyond an individualistic level of description. While the importance of audience commitment is understood, his concern with finding a methodological demonstration of his argument leads his audience to be conceived as only a conglomeration of individuals."⁹

Professor Deanna Robinson of the University of Oregon provides a more generous view of Stephenson's methodologies. Conducting research on the uses of television and film by upper-middle class professionals, she suggested that Stephenson's technique could be used for a direct examination of people's attitudes toward media and be able to demonstrate "(1) that within any single, demographically defined audience group, several attitude or 'taste' groups exist and (2) that similar taste groups exist within other classes."¹⁰ Further support for Stephenson has been offered by Wilbur Schramm who generalized that Stephenson, with a style of writing like McLuhan's, could have been the guru of modern media.¹¹

uses and gratifications

Moving from the specific to the general, Stephenson's play theory is part of a wider body of research and theory centering on what *uses* we make of media and what *gratifications* we gain from exposing ourselves to media. Research of these uses and gratifications has been conducted in populations ranging from farmers in less developed countries to American homemakers. The research has not escaped vigorous debate, however, not only on the different types of uses and gratifications but also on the very methodologies that attempt to identify them.

Part of the debate is a conflict between the individual differences approach and the social categories approach to the study of media effects. Consider a television program. We could argue that a soap opera provides certain role models for homemakers or college students. We also could contend that reaction to soap operas cannot be classified in demographic terms but, rather, in psychographic terms. Soap operas have certain *uses* for people possessing specific motivations or certain psychological characteristics. Or we could argue that even this approach is unsatisfactory since each individual is different, and many different individuals may have many different uses for the same soap opera. How we learn what uses these many different people or groups of people make of the media is still another dilemma. Do we individually test them in tightly controlled laboratory situations, psychologically wiring them up to get at the depths of their thought processes?

What has the research told us about uses and gratifications? Sampling a few of these studies, Professor Deanna Robinson studied upper-middle class professionals. She discovered the presence of "information absorbers," people who passively absorb information from television without actively interpreting it. Another group she labeled "analytical artists" who use television to increase their understanding of themselves, other people, and the world. Researcher Neil A. Weintraub suggested that radio gives teenagers awareness, makes their day pass more quickly, and also tells them what is happening.¹² Researcher Lawrence

Wenner examined the elderly and found that one use of television among this group was companionship.[13]

One of the earliest studies on the uses of the media was conducted by Herta Herzog who examined the reasons that people listen to radio soap operas. Conducting in-depth interviews, Herzog found three reasons: compensation, wish fulfillment, and advice.[14]

Consider the area of *compensation through identification.* As members of society, we assume certain roles and must make decisions based on these roles. Naturally, we seek to receive approval or recognition for what we do. Direct approval comes from someone telling us that we are doing the right thing. Indirect approval comes from our knowledge or assumption that others are doing the same things that we are. The soap opera thus provides a form of indirect approval. The person watching sees other people experiencing the same relationships, trials, and tribulations that he or she experiences. It may be meeting a new neighbor, having a love affair, splurging for a new coat, or whatever. The important thing is that there are, even though only portrayed on the television screen, people living similar lives and having experiences similar to our own.

The person who views soap operas as a means of *wish fulfillment* has a different functional relationship with the medium. This individual wishes that those things taking place on the screen were happening to her or him but is not actually experiencing them. In this situation, the audience uses the program to fantasize about the lives of other people. Perhaps their environment is unpleasant, drab, or routine, and they have neither the ability nor the real desire to change their life style. Yet simply by exposing themselves to the soap opera, these viewers are given the opportunity to fantasize.

Anyone who has ever watched any soap opera will notice the development of a series of plots and subplots that represent human relations problems to be solved; for example, an in-law spending too much time at her married child's home, a member of the family suffering from alcoholism, or a neighbor with marital problems. The viewer is faced with the question of how to deal with these situations. The soap opera provides the answers. This type of viewer is seeking *advice* on what he or she should do in his or her own life when faced with similar situations.

Television news has also been found to have uses and gratifications for viewers. Researcher Mark R. Levy categorized five different areas of uses and gratifications based on statements by viewers of television news.[15] One category defined by Levy is *surveillance-reassurance.* The surveillance-reassurance category is exemplified by such viewer statements as: "TV news makes me realize that my life is not so bad after all," "I watch TV news so I won't be surprised by higher prices," and "TV news helps me keep track of what is happening to people like myself." Another category is *cognitive orientation.* In this category, Levy grouped viewer statements such as: "I like to compare my ideas to what the commentators say" and "Watching TV news keeps me in touch with the world." Levy's third category is *dissatisfactions*. Statements in this category include: "The TV news programs try to make things seem more dramatic than they really are" and "By the time I see the TV news at night, I've already read or heard about most of the headline items." The fourth category Levy labels *affective orientation*, characterized by such statements as: "After a hard day, watching the TV news helps me relax"; "I feel sorry for the newscasters when they make mistakes"; and "Television news is sometimes very exciting." Levy's fifth category of uses and gratifications is *diversion*, characterized by such viewer statements as: "When the newscasters joke around with each other, it makes the news easier to take"; "TV news satisfies my sense of curiosity"; and "I enjoy hearing funny, different, or strange things on the news."

Stop and consider your own uses and gratifications of the messages you receive from mass media. What do television soap operas mean to you? Why do you watch television news? What meanings do films have for you?

agenda-setting function

With the advent of sophisticated means of measuring the relationship between mass media and media audiences has come the development of preliminary theoretical concepts, which state that media not only inform us but also influence us as to what is important to know.[16] In other words, the media create an *agenda* for our thoughts and influence us in what seems important. For example, if the media in a local community provide considerable coverage of a local bond issue, the residents of the community may very well perceive the bond issue as being of great importance to the community, even if it is not. The media coverage of issues in a political campaign may help us to perceive certain issues as being more important than others and consequently influence our decisions about candidates based on how they address themselves to those issues.

Major research on the agenda-setting function of the mass media is now being conducted at a number of universities. There are some problems associated with this research, however. One of the most troublesome is monitoring all media that affect an individual and then determining how they actually do affect the person. For instance, a major market may have upwards of fifty different media channels bombarding a population. Keeping track of all of these media messages is an awesome task. By first determining which media are important to certain population groups and then concentrating on these media, the control of intervening variables has permitted at least a preliminary theoretical base for the agenda-setting function.

the broad context of functional use

The uses and gratification, or functional relationships, described here are only a few of the many ways a person attuned to the various mass media can interact with them. The importance of these functional relationships is in the context of the mass audience, and it is on this level that they will affect societal development. For instance, if you personally need a new dress and cannot find one you like in the store, you may order one from a catalogue. The catalogue, a medium directed to a specialized audience, has a very identifiable use—to order merchandise—and each individual purchaser's decision will affect only that person. On the other hand, the content of television and film affects millions. Yet we have seen that researching the mass audience is difficult. When we do understand more about our functional relationship to the mass media, we will undoubtedly have a far greater insight into how we use media, instead of how media use us.

This emphasis on future research is important. Some of the criticism of media has been that media give us exactly what we want to consume, and as we consume, media managers and planners provide us with more of the same. If we are, in the broader sense of an entire society, interrelating with media in a functional sense, then we need to know more about this relationship. We need to know such things as how media affect our political system, how our attitudes and values are formed, and what effect media have on this formation. Answers to these questions will come from more than just a "bookkeeping" approach to mass media research. Perhaps as students of mass communication, you can help find these answers.

SOCIALIZATION

Closely related to how we use media is their effect on our social development in acquiring culture and social norms. Although a significant amount of research centers on media, especially broadcasting's effects on the socialization of children, we know that socialization continues throughout our lives. As with other approaches to studying effects, the content of messages can mean different things to different people. For example, the effect of a violent television program on a group of male adults can be in sharp contrast to the effect of that same program on a group of small children, whose world and ideas are just being formed and whose socialization process is much less developed than that of the adults. The adult might go to bed thinking how great John Wayne was as the hero. The child may have frightful nightmares about evil forces affecting his or her ability to survive in the world.

Here again, research has opened up a plethora of debate. And here again, different methodologies are used. As responsible consumers of mass communication, we should recognize these. Since socialization does not occur simply by being exposed to a single message, we must draw from a wide body of research across many disciplines to begin to theorize exactly how media affect our socialization process. Moreover, that data must be drawn over time. Few studies examine socialization over time. Most ask a given group of individuals what meaning mass media has for them and then group the results under the heading of socialization or uses and gratifications research. Although studying the research on these different audiences is valuable, studying the *same* individuals over a *longer* time period is much more desirable.

stages in studying effects on socialization

Socialization research has three stages. First, numerous studies have examined the "content" of media messages. Such elements as the image of women in advertisements, hero figures in movies, and acts of violence on television have told us much about what we see or hear. The second stage of this research tells us if people exposed to the message actually perceive or recognize it. Were the children who saw a given television program able to recognize examples of good behavior and prosocial messages? The third stage of investigation must determine what effect the messages have once they are received.

studying the results

From socialization research, we have learned that children can identify certain prosocial content themes. For example, CBS has actively supported various research projects on this issue. Even though beneficial from a public relations standpoint, the research has been conducted under responsible scrutiny.[17] Examining the program *Fat Albert and the Cosby Kids*, research in three cities—Cleveland, Philadelphia, and Memphis—revealed that close to nine out of ten children who had seen an episode of *Fat Albert* received one or more messages of social value. Some of the prosocial messages reported being received included, "Take care of younger children," "Father's job is important," "Support a friend in trouble," "Be honest," and "Be friendly; don't be rude, nasty, jealous, or mean."

Similar research by CBS showed that older children were more likely to receive more abstract messages than younger children were. For example, in studying the program *Shazam*, about a Superman figure, about half the seven to eight year olds received the message "obey your parents," whereas about three-fourths of the ten to eleven year olds and the thirteen to fourteen year olds received that message. Only 4 percent of the seven to eight year olds received the message "be independent," whereas eleven percent of the ten to eleven year olds and 25 percent of the thirteen to fourteen year olds received the message. Examining the program *Isis*, about a superhuman female figure, the research discovered that girls were more likely than boys to comment on Isis's concern for others and her beauty, while boys mentioned her superhuman qualities as often as did girls.

Analyzing the effects of broadcasting on socialization, we can conclude that parents can have responsibility in the relationship and should not permit television to become a surrogate parent.[18] Watching television with very young children, then discussing the results while referring to the prosocial lessons that may appear is one positive use of the medium. This same process was common in pretelevision times as parents read storybooks to children, then discussed the content of the books. Children apparently learn from television, and such broadcasting practices as stereotyping the roles of certain classes of people therefore can become a child's perception of reality.

The amount of television and when and how it becomes part of children's lives can also influence how they relate to their environment. Studying three towns in Australia that had three different availabilities of television, researchers found that the content viewed was directly related to the context in which it was viewed.[19] When television experience was restricted to mostly an informative-educational context, children perceived it to be far more than just entertainment. When high levels of television viewing tended initially to decrease the involvement in such outside activities as sports, the involvement returned to normal levels after the novelty wore off.

There also are content and context variables in research on the political socialization of children. Political knowledge, news discussion, public affairs interest, and seeking information about news events were investigated by Professors Charles K. Atkin and Walter Gantz.[20] They found that the amount of news viewing to be associated mildly with children's political awareness, with the highest correlations being among older children. The amount of exposure to television news has some relationship to children's knowledge of politics, but more so among middle-class youngsters than among working-class youngsters. Many children in the research reported being stimulated to seek further information after watching television news, and to some degree this desire for more information increased with the amount of news exposure.

Advertising also can influence the socialization process. For example, one study showed children three different eyeglass advertisements with a woman giving a testimonial.[21] One advertisement showed her dressed as a court judge, another as a computer programmer, and the third as a television technician. The children who saw that woman in a particular role were more apt to choose that occupation as appropriate for women.

There is still a great deal to be learned about mass media's relationship to the socialization process. Because socialization among children centers on the broadcast media, broadcasting has been singled out as the basis for research. However, we need to understand the influences of other media in the socialization process. Even though children may not be able to read yet, what images are being formed and what behavior patterns are being developed by children leafing through a magazine and seeing the pictures? What indirect socialization may occur as parents discuss the content of media in the presence of children? How do newspapers affect the socialization process when children are exposed to special inserts designed for younger readers? What influence do comics have among children old enough to consume comics? These questions need to be investigated and answered before we can make intelligent conclusions about how the media affect our lives and the learning process.

VIOLENCE ON TELEVISION

Violence in media can be traced back to ancient pictographics which displayed such sacrificial acts as carving a heart out of a person's chest, ceremonial torture methods used to bestow adulthood on children reaching puberty, and other activities that by today's standards, if shown, would never make late night television. Awareness of the effects of violent programming in general and on television in particular began in 1952 during television's formative years when Senator Estes Kefauver's subcommittee investigated juvenile delinquency. Testimony by authorities charged television with being responsible not only for showing violence but also for prompting juveniles to imitate it. The issue might have vanished from public attention except for that afternoon in 1963 when a sniper's bullets killed President John F. Kennedy. Ironically, it was television that brought three days of national mourning into American living rooms in what was hailed as the medium's finest hours. That same medium would later be blamed by its critics for causing the warped minds that were responsible for similar events.

the surgeon general's report

The bloodshed was not over. Black leader Martin Luther King was next to fall to an assassin's bullet. Then another assassin killed Senator Robert Kennedy as he was celebrating with hundreds of campaign workers his victory in the 1968 California presidential primary. The entire era had been spiced with dinnertime detail of the Vietnam War, plus political protests at the 1968 Democratic presidential convention. What many saw as inevitable finally occurred as the American government examined the issue of violence on television and committed $1 million to a study, with additional funds for administrative and publishing costs. The project, titled "The Surgeon General's Study of Television and Social Behavior," involved leading social scientists and produced a multi-volume work which, when completed, posed as many questions as it had answered. The summary report of the study stated:

> There is a convergence of the fairly substantial experimental evidence for short-run causation of aggression among some children by viewing violence on the screen and the much less certain evidence from field studies that extensive violence viewing precedes some long-run manifestations of aggressive behavior. This convergence of the two types of evidence constitutes some preliminary evidence of a causal relationship.

From this statement, it is easy to see how the press and critics jumped on the report with varying interpretations. The reactions ran from the *New York Times's* headline of "TV Violence Held Unharmful to Youth," to then FCC Commissioner Nicholas Johnson's comparing the network executives responsible for programming to child molesters.

Since the report was released and the public's attention was drawn to the issue, the press has been filled with reference to television's causal relationship to violent behavior. To examine what trends do exist in the research on this subject, we'll center our discussion on learning theory.

effects of televised violence: the role of learning theory

Four theories predominate in the violence-media relationship. The *catharsis theory* suggests that we build up frustrations in our daily lives which are released vicariously by watching violent behavior. This theory claims that there are actual benefits gained from televised violence. This theory is the least supported of the four, although the results of some studies have provided limited support for the idea.[22] The *aggressive cues theory* suggests that exposure to violence on television will raise the level of excitement in the viewer, forming a catalyst to trigger already learned behavior resulting in violent acts being repeated in a real-life setting.[23] Closely aligned to the aggressive cues theory is the *reinforcement theory*, suggesting that televised violence will reinforce behavior already exsisting in an individual.[24] Inherent in such a theory is the probability that the violent person, because of violent tendencies, perceives violent behavior as a real-life experience, whereas the nonviolent person may perceive the violent program as entertainment without becoming psychologically involved with the program. The *observational learning theory* suggests that we can *learn* violent behavior from watching violent programs.[25]

Clearly all of the theories have merit, and none should be discounted. Moreover, research is examining new variations of these four principal approaches. The observational learning theory, for example, could apply more strongly to very young children who are in their formative years of growth when their environment has a significant effect on what they learn. In essence, if television becomes a surrogate parent, it could certainly teach behavior. Later in the child's life, with the behavior well manifested, violence learned in the formative years could be reinforced. For a child who is hyperactive or easily excitable, the aggressive cues theory might be used to explain easily heightened emotions from exposure to televised violence. Even the catharsis theory could apply to the business executive who uses television to unwind and vicariously vent his or her frustrations through the actions of others.

We immediately begin to see all sides of the violence debate surfacing. Current research is concentrating primarily on children, partly because of funding for such research and partly because of a general feeling that children may very well be the most affected by television violence. In this arena, the violence debate is becoming public with considerable pressure and visibility from citizens' groups.

Along with suggesting the casual relationship of televised violence to aggression, the widely quoted research of George Gerbner, Director of the Annenberg School of Communication at the University of Pennsylvania, is used to support the arguments. For more than a decade, Gerbner and his associates have compared violence on television among the major networks, then plotted their data over time, providing a running record of the number of violent acts representative of each new television season. Two often discussed measures are Gerbner's Violence Index, measuring the actual acts of violence, and the Risk Ratio, describing the risk of encountering violence. The index is used mainly to count violent acts on television; the ratio is a bit more complex. It measures the aggressors and the victims, dividing the larger into the smaller with the final figure preceded by a plus sign if aggressors exceed victims and a minus sign if victims exceed aggressors. CBS employs a different violence measuring device, prompting continuing debate over which measure is more accurate and representative of actual violence.[26]

effects of portrayal on aggressive behavior

The research on televised violence in now voluminous, with more studies on the way. What the research is telling us about the relationship between the portrayal of violence and aggressive behavior was summarized by Professor George Comstock in the *Journal of Communication*. He stated that the evidence suggests:

1. Cartoon as well as live portrayals of violence can lead to aggressive performance on the part of the viewer.
2. Repeated exposure to cartoon and live portrayals of violence does not eliminate the possibility that new exposure will increase the likelihood of aggressive performance.
3. Aggressive performance is not dependent on a typical frustration, although frustration facilitates aggressive performance.
4. Although the "effect" in some experiments may be aggressive but not antisocial play, implications in regard to the contribution of television violence to antisocial aggression remain.
5. In ordinary language, the factors in a portrayal which increase the likelihood of aggressive performance are the suggestion that aggression is justified, socially acceptable, motivated by malice, or pays off; a realistic depiction; highly exciting material. The presentation of conditions similar to those experienced by the young viewer, including a perpetrator similar to the viewer and circumstances like those of his environment, such as a target, implements, or gives other cues resembling those of the real-life milieu.
6. Although there is no evidence that prior repeated exposure to violent portrayals totally immunizes the young viewer against any influence on aggressive performance, exposure to television portrayals may desensitize young persons to responding to violence in their environment.[27]

In concluding our discussion of televised violence, we should reemember that accompanying the issue are numerous policy decisions that can affect the future of television programming. If a casual link is established and if legislators feel that something should be done to curtail the violence, then major First Amendment issues of free speech will arise. Yet this curtailment may have legal precedent. A recent court decision giving the FCC the authority to control programming that airs when children may be present indicates a shift toward some type of control over entertainment programming, control that in the past had been limited to the vagueness of the Fairness Doctrine and indecent programming.

DIFFUSION OF INNOVATIONS

As consumers of mass communication, we are constantly exposed to material that both informs and persuades: information about new discoveries in technology, products designed to make our life easier, inventions, and other innovative procedures. The importance of mass communication in convincing us of the worthiness and benefits of various innovations has been under research and investigation for some time.[28] There are *no concise formulas* to express the importance of mass communication in convincing us to acquire these products, because each of us is unique, as is each product and each situation. But some general trends are discernible and can aid in our understanding of this process.

To understand the process, imagine that you are considering purchasing a new portable electric typewriter. Your old manual typewriter just does not work well anymore, and you *need* a new one. While reading a magazine, you happen to stumble across an ad for such a typewriter, and the ad catches your eye. The new electric portable has a cartridge ribbon system, which means you do not have to change ribbons, and also has a separate cartridge from which to make erasures. You glance at all the features the ad presents and then flip to another article in the magazine.

The next day you happen to be watching television, and a commercial appears that shows the typewriter you first became *aware* of while reading the magazine. Now you are really *interested*. There it is in living color with all of its new features. You then decide to discuss the machine with some of your friends who also have similar portable electric typewriters. While you are discussing it, you are constantly *evaluating* its features. Next, you make a trip to the office supply store and further investigate the typewriter. There you encounter the sales clerk who explains the features to you and asks you if you would like to borrow the typewriter on a *trial* basis until you make up your mind. You think that idea is great, bring the typewriter back to your room, and begin using it in your school work. Finally, after about two weeks of trying it out, you decide you like the typewriter and *acquire* it. Of course, you could have decided to reject the typewriter in favor of a different model.

The process that led up to your decision to buy the typewriter had several steps. First, you had a *need* to purchase the typewriter. Your old typewriter just was not satisfactory. Second, you became *aware* of the new typewriter. Your accidental encounter with it in the magazine alerted you to its many features. Your second exposure to the typewriter, this time on the television commercial, created an *interest* sufficient to discuss it with your fellow students. These discussions helped you *evaluate* the typewriter in comparison to your old one and others on the market. Then you made the decision to go one step farther. You made arrangements at the office supply store to take the typewriter on a *trial* basis. After the trial period, you then decided to *acquire* the typewriter.

SUMMARY

There are many variables in researching the audience and the effects of mass communication. As a result, it has become difficult to develop a theoretical base for studying them and to provide a link with research in intrapersonal and interpersonal communication.

Early explanations centered on the bullet theory that stated that people were individually affected by mass media. Gradually, though, we became aware that subgroups influenced how we consumed mass media. Research began to tell us that messages reached us not only from the media but also from other people. In fact, these other people could influence us even more than the media could. How we reacted to messages began to be explained in three different but interrelated theoretical frameworks: individual differences, categories, and social relationships. How we react to messages can also be explained by how we selectively expose ourselves to media as well as how we perceive and retain that to which we are exposed.

Although we need to know how we react to media, we also need to understand how we use media. Our discussion centered on such concepts as the lowbrow, middlebrow, and highbrow film audiences; Stephenson's play theory's uses and gratifications; and the agenda-setting function of media. How we learn and how our behaviors develop from media messages is called the socialization process. Although television and children are the major emphases of current media research, we also need to examine other media audiences and their effects. Violence on television is one of the most visible issues on the effects of mass communication. Current studies of learning theory have shown that there may be some trends that link aggressive behavior with viewing televised violence.

Mass communication also is important to the diffusion of innovations. From products found in commercial advertising to new innovations in developing countries, we are learning more about how the media influence our decisions to accept new products and services.

OPPORTUNITIES FOR FURTHER LEARNING

BLUMLER, JAY G., and ELIHU KATZ, eds., *The Uses of Mass Communications: Current Perspectives on Gratifications Research*. Beverly Hills, Calif.: Sage Publications, Inc., 1974.

CATER, DOUGLASS, and STEPHEN STRICKLAND, *TV Violence and the Child*. New York: Russell Sage Foundation, 1975.

CBS Office of Social Research, *Communicating with Children through Television*. New York: CBS, 1977.

CHAFFEE, STEVEN H., ed., *Political Communication: Issues and Strategies for Research*. Beverly Hills, Calif.: Sage Publications, Inc., 1975.

CHANEY, DAVID, *Processes of Mass Communication*. London: The Macmillan Press Ltd., 1972.

COMSTOCK, GEORGE, STEVEN CHAFFEE, NATAN KATZMAN, MAXWELL McCOMBS, and DON ROBERTS, *Television and Human Behavior*. New York: Columbia University Press, 1979.

KATZ, ELIHU, *Social Research on Broadcasting: Proposals for Further Development*. London: BBC, 1977.

KRAUS, SIDNEY, and DENNIS DAVIS, *The Effects of Mass Communication on Political Behavior*. University Park: Pennsylvania State University Press, 1976.

LESSER, GERALD S., *Children and Television: Lessons from Sesame Street*. New York: Random House, Inc., 1974.

MILGRAM, STANLEY, and R. LANCE SHOTLAND, *Television and Antisocial Behavior: Field Experiments*. New York: Academic Press, Inc., 1973.

PIEPE, ANTHONY, MILES EMERSON, and JUDY LANNON, *Television and the Working Class*. Lexington, Mass.: Lexington Books/D.C. Heath, 1975.

ROGERS, EVERETT M., and F. FLOYD SHOEMAKER, *Communication of Innovations: A Cross Cultural Approach* (2nd ed.). New York: The Free Press, 1971.

RUBIN, BERNARD, *Political Television*. Belmont, Calif.: Wadsworth Publishing Co., Inc., 1967.

SCHRAMM, WILBUR, and DONALD F. ROBERTS, eds., *The Process and Effects of Mass Communication* (2nd ed.). Urbana: University of Illinois Press, 1971.

SHAW, DONALD, and MAXWELL E, McCOMBS, eds., *The Emergency of American Political Issues*. St. Paul: West Publishing Co., 1977.

SHERIF, CAROLYN W., MUZAFER SHERIF, and ROGER E. NEBERGALL, *Attitude and Attitude Change: The Social Judgement—Involvement Approach*. Philadelphia: W. B. Saunders Company, 1965.

Sveriges Radio, *Uses and Gratifications Studies: Theory and Methods*. Stockholm: Sveriges Radio, 1974.

WINICK, CHARLES, ed., *Deviance and Mass Media*. Beverly Hills: SAGE Publications, Inc., 1978.

WINICK, MARIANN P., and CHARLES WINICK, *The Television Experience: What Children See*. Beverly Hills: SAGE Publications, Inc., 1979.

17

Media Ethics
and Social Issues

Any technological or social force that reaches down to affect the majority of society's members is bound to produce a number of controversial topics. Although there are many issues that directly confront the role of media in contemporary society, only some have been singled out for treatment in this chapter. Each discussion is not an answer or solution to these issues. Rather, it is hoped that the reader will reflect on the problems, perhaps discuss them with fellow students, and possibly even fill in pieces of the puzzle with which he or she may be familiar from past experiences or reading. We will begin with media ethics and conclude with a more philosophical approach to the future of mass communication as espoused in the writings of Marshall McLuhan.

ETHICS AND THE PRESS

A student reporter sits at his desk finishing a story for the next day's edition of the campus newspaper. By-lining the story that has taken a week to compile, he decides at the last minute to use a quotation from a professor's lecture, feeling that it will add to the story. He neither tells the professor that the quotation will be published in the campus newspaper nor does he make any attempt to inter-

394

view him about other points of view he may have. He also quotes other people from information he has received secondhand. Even a damaging opinion about a campus administrator is attributed to an "unnamed," high-ranking military official who happens to be stationed at the school's ROTC detachment. The next day, the professor, in another class lecture, gives the other side of the issue about which the student was reporting. But there is no reason to print excerpts from that lecture because the material does not fit the slant of the student reporter's story. Besides, the newspaper already has gone to press. No follow-up story is ever printed.

A few weeks later, the colonel who heads the ROTC detachment is relieved of his command, the resignation of the professor is called for in an editorial in the local paper, and the president of the school receives angry calls from members of the state legislature. A year later, when a multi-million dollar libel suit is filed against the campus newspaper by the professor and the colonel, the real facts of the story come out. The "unnamed," high-ranking military official turns out to have been the student reporter's roommate who is a cadet captain in the ROTC. The court also hears how the professor's lectures were quoted out of context. The student testifying under oath speaks in his defense and says that he did not realize that what he was doing was wrong. Along with awarding damages to the plaintiffs, the judge also sentences the student reporter to take some courses in ethics. The example of the student reporter is fictitious.

specific cases

Another example is not fictitious. Consider the case of the *Indianapolis Star,* which during the 1968 presidential primary in Indiana, published an editorial from the *New York Times,* deleting, however, a section unfavorable to Indiana's favorite son candidate, then Governor Roger Branigan. The resulting editorial was a critical stance toward former Senator Robert Kennedy, a candidate and later victor in the Indiana primary, but a rather uncritical review of Branigan. Jules Whitcover, a reporter for the Newhouse News Service, brought the matter to the attention of the profession with an article in the *Columbia Journalism Review* that examined the reporting quality of Indianapolis newspapers during the campaign.[1] Whitcover's analysis was not favorable and cited other questionable reporting practices by the same newspaper.

The version of the editorial that had been published in the *Times* referred to candidate Branigan as "the leader of the state party organization which controls thousands of patronage jobs and which still engages in the ancient and disreputable practice of levying a 2 percent party tax on the salaries of state employees." When the *Indianapolis Star* reprinted the editorial from the *Times,* that passage was omitted. The editorial reprinted on the front page of the *Star* carried the headline, "Is Indiana For Sale? Asks the New York Times." Whitcover quoted the *Times's* editorial page editor, John B. Oakes, as characterizing the *Star's* action as "reprehensible, unethical and the kind of newspaper practice that blackens the reputation of American journalism." Kennedy won the primary.

It is important to point out, however, that not everything that happens in one area of a newspaper necessarily reflects on the rest of the staff. Almost seven years later, a team of tough investigative reporters for the *Indianapolis Star* went to work on a major police corruption story inside the Indianapolis police department. Having battled several lawsuits, they emerged with a series of stories that not only brought them a major share of journalism awards in the state but national awards as well, including the coveted Pulitzer Prize.

The broadcast media also have not been immune from such ethical quandaries. The well-known and criticized Chicago "pot party" staged by WBBM-TV drew fire from a number of critics. The station's purpose was to show that there were young people who, with some regularity, were smoking pot in Chicago. The station filmed people smoking marijuana and telling why they smoked it. The problem was that the pot party had been prearranged for the television cameras. The questions are whether or not this was the only way that the medium could show what was taking place, was it an accurate reflection of what these people were experiencing, and was it a breach of ethics to stage the party?

Not every questionable ethical practice occurs in the reporting functions of media. A case in point occurred with the now defunct *National Observer*. The *Observer*, which had done a front-page article on the subject of journalism ethics three months earlier in July of 1975, found itself in a very embarrassing situation caused by a readership survey questionnaire that had been sent to 3,000 of its subscribers. The eight-page questionnaire asked everything from what they liked in the *Observer* to what their income was and what jewelry they owned. The questionnaire and its results would have become a quiet part of the *Observer's* research files until a University of Wisconsin professor happened to put the questionnaire under ultraviolet light and found an identifying code number in the upper lefthand corner of the questionnaire. It meant that the questionnaire could be traced back to its sender. When the editor of the *Observer*, Henry Gemmill, received a letter from the professor who had uncovered the hidden code number, Gemmill was appalled and brought the whole issue to the attention of the public in a full-page explanation entitled, "The Invisible-Ink Caper." It covered the back page of the November 1, 1975 issue. Gemmill assured those who had filled out the questionnaire that he believed they would suffer no harm from the incident and in the process was candid about his personal feelings of distaste for the entire matter.

public response

Generally, however, the public does not strike back against what it feels are unethical practices. Public inaction can be attributed to two factors: on the one hand, people may be unaware of the unethical conduct; on the other, they may feel powerless against the press or the red tape of media business in general.

Although there are national news councils to which people and organizations can complain about unethical activities, proportionately few have taken their complaints to these bodies. Others have used a different retaliatory approach.

One such instance was an advertisement purchased in a number of major newspapers by the Mobil Oil Corporation. Capitalizing on the *Jaws* motion picture phenomenon that had swept the country, Mobil placed an ad under its trademarked "Observation" series that claimed that the profits of Mobil Oil had been inaccurately reported by columnist Jack Anderson. In bold-faced type at the top of the first paragraph was the word "Shark-bait." The article went on to describe how Mobil could sympathize with "owners of beach cottages, hotels and water-ski shops who suffered from the 'Jaws' exaggerations." The second paragraph detailed a specific charge of alleged inaccurate reporting by Anderson and was bold-faced with the words, "We were 'jawed' by Jack Anderson." Four other paragraphs highlighted Mobil's case. Regardless of the accuracy of either Anderson's or Mobil's claims, Mobil felt it had received the brunt of unfair reporting and attempted to show the other side, even if it meant buying advertising to do it.

Cases of questionable conduct are common in many media circles. Stories of a reporter identifying police detectives to a group of civil protesters, reporters on the payroll of a government agency threatening the agency with bad publicity if their raises did not come through, reporters working for politicians while also being active members of the press—these sagas are all too common. They have provoked a serious crisis in media ethics which has created a major credibility gap with the public. Why do they happen?

ETHICS AND DECISION MAKING

There has been considerable speculation about the credibility gap among academicians and working media professionals alike. Yet most of the discussion centers on excuses for the failure of moral leadership rather than on solutions to the problem. Some suggest that unethical journalism is a combination of circumstances and forces. The college student reporter, for example, without proper training and proper advisement, reads professional newspapers that liberally use such phrases as "unnamed sources" or "reliable sources" whose "truth is self-evident." Without any background in the ethical responsibilities attached to professional reporting, certain campus reporters try to impress their peers by adopting those same reporting methods for local stories, using every Tom, Dick, and Harry who has an opinion on any subject as an "unnamed" source. This is not to suggest that all campus news media are suggestible and irresponsible or, conversely, that those reporters who work at leading newspapers or broadcast complexes throughout the nation are immune to breaches of ethical conduct. It simply points out how the public becomes the loser in these cases.

Many forces taken singly or together can precipitate unethical conduct. For example, if a small media outlet does not or cannot afford to pay its staff a decent wage, employees are usually forced to seek additional employment. Such employment can provide the potential for conflict of interest. There is many a journalist who could not be objective about reporting a boss's arrest for fraud, especially when the reporter needs the money to keep his or her family in food. Although many journalism veterans would not hesitate to ban such reporters from the profession, these same veterans probably have not faced a similar situation and would be the first to tell a new journalism graduate to take a job at any small newspaper or broadcast outlet just to gain experience, regardless of the pay.

Some very tough journalistic decisions also require ethical considerations. For instance, the necessity to publish information about a terminally ill cancer patient as her relatives fight for permission to remove her from life-support machines may not be pleasant for anyone concerned. It may also be a very private family matter, which makes it even more difficult to have the responsibility of calling it to the attention of the public. The decision of an editor not to publish the name of a suicide victim is another ethical question. If the person had been a public figure, the editor's feelings on the matter might have been different. Those feelings might also have been different if the person had taken his or her life in a public place, such as jumping off a well-traveled highway bridge. The problems that face the press covering human activities become even more complex if the people are prominent in government, education, or industry. Here, still other forces act upon the media, creating conflicting goals and decision-making perplexities.

Such ethical dilemmas were put into perspective by a professor of sociology at the University of Texas, Gideon Sjoberg. Professor Sjoberg contended that ". . . the major ethical orientation of most people in the modern world is that of system loyalty or system maintenance. Indeed, commitment to the nation-state has been the basic ethical orientation during the past century and a half of most politicians, citizens, and scholars of the West. In contradistinction to this system ethic, we need one that transcends any given social system.[2] Professor Sjoberg warned of the dangers in a system-specific ethic ". . . wherein loyalty to the system is the dominant concern, . . ." these dangers ". . . loom ever more serious with the proliferation of large-scale organizations."

He cautioned that all ". . . large-scale bureaucracies seem to generate a secret side, and part of that secret tends to become a dark side where a great deal of manipulation takes place." Much of this manipulation, Sjoberg declared, maintains the bureaucracies for those who hold power. It is in this area that many investigative journalists circulate and function. The crux of the problem, however, is that by working within this secret side and developing overt or covert relationships with inside sources, journalists can lose their ethical perspective. For instance, a journalist can find himself or herself becoming so sucked into the system, that he or she fails to be objective and thereby perpetuates its secret purposes.

Communication researcher and anthropologist Alfred G. Smith noted:

"An ethic that stresses compatibility among the parts of a system, conservation of the system, limited change, and control, may lead it to control the system to its own advantage.[3] Such journalists become purveyors and communicators of only positive information about the system.

Consider the journalist who travels the police beat, reporting the daily activities of the department. To obtain this information, the reporter usually must develop a close association with the police. They become friends, associates, "buddies," and even godfathers or godmothers to each other's children. When one of these "close friends" becomes involved in a police corruption scandal, what happens? Can the reporter dislodge himself or herself from the system-specific ethic to report the corruption? Will he or she be commended by the police department for reporting this or be chastised, as Professor Sjoberg described, for "disrupting the social order." Stop and consider your own ethics. What if it were necessary for you to work in this situation? Would you be able to report corruption in the police department if you had become close friends with the officers? Would you be able to report police bribery if you were working on an investigative story in which you needed the police as sources? What if you were dating a police officer? Would you be able to report corruption in the department if you were married to the police chief?

The answers to these questions grow increasingly complex. The role of any gatekeeper is not one of easy solutions to simple problems. He or she sits among a multitude of events with the awesome responsibility of determining which event will reach the public with consequences of untold impact.

PRESS CODES

The press, because of its foundation in the First Amendment, has been the least controlled of any American institution of mass communication. Although certain regulations have been placed on broadcast journalism through the Communications Act of 1934, the news media generally have operated with only conscience as a guide. Unfortunately, some journalists are less scrupulous than others, and in many cases this laissez-faire atmosphere has resulted in journalism of less than good taste. Yet there is an attempt by some professional organizations to encourage responsible journalism practices, more through social and professional sanctions than through concerted attempts at enforcement. Three codes among many that reflect these thoughts are the Code of Ethics of the Society of Professional Journalists, Sigma Delta Chi; the Code of Broadcast News Ethics of the Radio/Television News Directors Association (RTNDA); and the Code of Ethics of the American Society of Newspaper Editors.

the society of professional journalists, sigma delta chi

The Society's code charges journalists to exercise boldness in reporting the news but cautions them to do so responsibly. This particular code was cited fequently during the Nixon era when journalists were facing jail sentences for refusing to divulge their sources of information. The code is divided into six areas: (1) responsibility, (2) freedom of the press, (3) ethics, (4) accuracy and objectivity, (5) fair play, and (6) pledge.

Under *responsibility*, the code reminds the journalist of two forces. These are in the "mission of the mass media," which is based on the public's right to know, and the great trust that the public places in the news media. *Freedom of the press* is expressed as the "right of people in a free society." The code endorses journalists' "responsibility to discuss, question, and challenge actions and utter-ances" of government and institutions, both public and private. The *ethics* section is concerned with such things as journalists' refusing freebies, moonlight-ing, and personal life styles that might reflect negatively on the profession. News judgment, overcoming obstacles in gathering news, and protecting the confiden-tiality of sources also are covered. The *accuracy and objectivity* section stresses "truth" as the ultimate goal and charges journalists to distinguish between news and opinions, to recognize editorializing, to keep informed, and to label clearly their "own conclusions and interpretations." *Fair play* treats the right to reply, invasion of privacy, handling details of vice and crime, correcting errors, and accountability to the public. Compliance with the code is entirely voluntary, being signified by a *pledge* charging journalists to "censure and prevent violations of these standards."

radio/television news directors association (RTNDA)

The RTNDA is composed mainly of men and women whose responsibility it is to direct the news operation of a broadcasting station. Membership dues are based on the size of the station's news staff, and associate memberships are available to educators and other practicing broadcast news professionals. The Code of Broadcast News Ethics of RTNDA has ten articles, within which are found the major issues affecting most working broadcast journalists. Many of these articles parallel those of the Code of the Society of Professional Journalists. For instance, there are similarities in the areas of rights of privacy, overcoming obstacles, keeping informed, confidentiality of sources, and censuring other professionals who violate the code. The RTNDA's unique qualities surface in such areas as broadcasting court proceedings. This section calls for journalists to "conduct themselves with dignity" when covering such proceedings, as do the NAB's Standards for Broadcasting Public Proceedings. Other articles within the RTNDA Code cover the individual's right to a fair trial, the use and abuse of news bulletins, and guarding against sensationalism.

american society of newspaper editors

Similar to both the codes of Sigma Delta Chi and RTNDA is the Code of Ethics of the American Society of Newspaper Editors. It stresses: "A journalist who uses his power for any selfish or otherwise unworthy purpose is faithless to a high trust." Two other sections pertain to freedom of the press and the independence of the press. The latter states: "Promotion of any private interest contrary to the general welfare, for whatever reason, is not compatible with honest journalism." Editorialism also is discussed when the code warns that ". . . editorial comment which knowingly departs from the truth does violence to the best spirit of American journalism; in the news columns it is subversive of a fundamental principle of the profession." Other concepts include the use of headlines and fair play— the opportunity for the accused to be heard.

code enforcement

The Achilles' heel of every journalism code is, of course, the actual ability to enforce sanctions on violaters. With protection of the press well established in law, there are few ways to force reporters to make public the "secrets," "confidential sources," and other "protected" information that may be necessary to investigate some aspect of a journalist's ethical conduct. The journalism profession is full of stories, some rumor and unfortunately some fact, of serious breaches of professional ethics despite the professional organizations' noble guidelines. Fear of retaliation, lack of concern, and desire to avoid publicity for the competition, all combine to make direct attack or censure by one medium on another rare occurrence.

CENSORSHIP

The issue of censorship will always be in the forefront of any discussion of mass media. The forces that act toward greater control of media content and those that act against it are present in all societies. We tend to think of censorship as something negative, but we have yet to define this phenomenon that spans all media and all types of media content.

Earlier in this text, we learned how colonial governments virtually controlled the fledgling publishing industry in early America. Today we would have little difficulty in defining such control as a form of censorship. If an eighteenth century newspaper wanted to publish articles critical of the government, the owner would usually find himself out of work; his government subsidy would be cut off, his presses might be confiscated, and there was always the possibility that he would be deported to England. In retrospect, we can see that it took the American Revolution to free the press from its shackles. Yet, if there had been no government control over the press during its formative years, would the republic have survived and prospered as much as it did? Did our republic need a period of time simply to gain a foundation and population, even if it was the recipient of a daily diet of censored news? If the American Revolution had occurred earlier than it did, would the country have had the solidarity to conquer suppression?

These rhetorical questions could be debated for hours. Yet when India's Prime Minister Indira Ghandi censored the press during nationwide upheavals in 1975, many gasped in amazement at how such a dictatorial attitude could be displayed. An ambassador to India appearing on a television news program was not nearly as taken back by the action, commenting that in the early stages of a democracy when certain political forces could actually harm it, censorship was necessary.

During the War between the States, we again saw the press shackled, this time by generals who were unhappy with the newspaper coverage they were receiving. In other wars in which Americans took part, notably World War II, the press voluntarily complied with government orders to withhold news from the public. In such cases, are the members of the press guilty of censorship just as much or more than the officials who order the news embargo? Are such embargoes ever justified? Would you comply with such an embargo if you were a reporter covering the battlefront?

We already have learned about shield laws that protect the confidentiality of news sources and freedom of information laws that guarantee the press and public access to public records. What about laws against censorship? What about the reporter who is subpoenaed before a grand jury to identify his or her source of information for a story? Can a zealous prosecutor use this same threat of subpoena to wrest this information from a reporter before the journalist is even called before the grand jury? Having been through this experience, will the reporter tend in the future to avoid the hassle represented by such a threat by shunning controversial stories? Is the prosecutor then, with this threat of subpoena, guilty of news censorship? Is the judge who issues a gag order preventing or trying to prevent pretrial publicity guilty of censorship?

The molders of our Constitution could not have foreseen the advent of electronic media. When these media did make their impact felt, government found itself as an umpire in assigning portions of the electromagnetic spectrum to specific radio and television stations. The FCC and its regulatory actions came about by necessity. When sex-talk shows scintillated the airwaves, the FCC let explicit on-air discussion of sexual activities go only so far. It then decreed that continuing such programming could provoke action against the licensee.

In 1978, the Supreme Court upheld the FCC's decision to take action against a New York radio station that broadcast comedian George Carlin's album about seven words you cannot say on television. Court cases and rulings such as the Fairness Doctrine have now established a legal precedent for determining the content of broadcast programming. Yet, there has been little solid legal ground on which to justify similar controls in the print media. Consider the broadcast manager who operates a station in a large city where there are ample opportunities for the public to obtain diversified programming. The FCC can admonish the manager that he or she has certain programming guidelines to follow. But, wait a moment—is this government control any different from the control placed on the prerevolutionary press? Are the actions of the FCC a form of censorship?

What about the small newspaper that receives a sizeable share of its advertising from a large business in the community? Can the threat of withdrawing that advertising make an editor think twice about giving the big business unfavorable publicity? Is this form of economic censorship any different from what the early colonial printer faced when he printed news unfavorable to the politicians subsidizing his enterprise?

What about the student press? At many colleges and universities, the campus newspaper as well as the campus radio and television station receive subsidies from the parent institution. What happens when these media grow critical of the college or university administration? The loss of such subsidies, especially when the broadcast media are noncommercial and prohibited by law from selling commercials to raise money, can become instantly crippling.

Other censorship issues focus on the internal operations of mass media. Take a labor dispute, for example. Perhaps the labor union strikes after newspaper management refuses to consider a union-proposed wage package. As negotiations progress, it is clear that nonunion labor will be called in to run the presses. Thus, on the day before the strike, the presses are "accidentally" damaged beyond immediate repair and cannot operate. Is this action a form of censorship? Is it a means of stopping the free flow of information to the public? Does censorship exist when the purpose of an action is not directly to inhibit the free flow of information but to protect workers' rights?

None of these answers is easy. Remember, censorship can be obvious. It can be the court order that keeps a newspaper story from being published. It can be the network executive's decision to scrap an evening television show that the executive views as too sexually explicit for a home viewing audience. Yet even these rather obvious forms of censorship can be seen as decisions in the public interest, actions that protect other constitutionally guaranteed freedoms. In this "in between" area lie many of the cases involving censorship. Continued discussion of individual situations as well as a reasonable definition of the issues are necessary to make sure that decision makers do not stray too far in either restricting our freedoms or ruining our social order.

MEDIA AS "BIG BROTHER"

Sitting in your room, you reach over to switch the channel on the television set from the instructional television program you have been watching as a class assignment. You feel that you know the material being shown in the program and are ready to be tested on it in class. As you turn the dial to another channel, a warning light flashes on a master control console in the basement of a building at the other end of the campus. There, a lab assistant quickly traces the source of the alarm light to your room and, in a special notebook, records a check next to your name. It is not the first time you have changed channels in the middle of a televised course assignment. At the end of the semester, you receive a lower grade than the one you expected. In a consultation with the instructor, you are told you did not watch the assigned programs and made fun of the course to friends who would stop by your room. That is why your grade was lowered. You discover that a two-way interactive cable system was hooked to your television set which made it possible for the master control to monitor what channels you watched and also to listen in to conversations in your room. You are shocked and file a lawsuit claiming that your privacy has been invaded.

Our example brings to light some of the concerns that recent technological capabilities have placed in the minds of the public. Many people feel we are no longer "secure" in our homes as guaranteed by the Fourth Amendment to the Constitution. We have become the watched instead of the watchers, the invaded instead of the invaders. The thought of an unseen, unknown, ever-present "big brother" looms over us as we become pawns to a technological society. Although the example in the preceding paragraph was fictitious, it is well within the confines of technology at this very moment. Increasingly, we are faced with policy decisions that affect our rights to privacy and our ability to maintain confidential such items as our medical records, financial statements, and educational transcripts.

Among the media under fire in this issue, cable television perhaps more than any other has captured the limelight, mostly because of its two-way operability. Already the hardware exists to monitor when television sets are on or off and to what channel a set is tuned. Hooked to central computers, these systems can be used for opinion polling and similar data-gathering exercises. Obviously, one of the first concerns of the public is how to control such a system. The federal government, the logical governing body, has in recent years discredited itself with news of snooping into citizens' private affairs and violating the same safeguards that it has been charged with protecting. Reports from Washington reveal that the CIA, in the name of national security, has actively participated in opening mail—approximately a quarter-million letters—and the National Security Agency (NSA) has even monitored messages sent via overseas telephone and cable in attempts to find people suspected of being involved in political dissent. Computers at NSA were programmed to activate on such key words as "assassination" and to identify the sender and receiver of such messages. Certain communication companies have been charged with routinely turning some messages sent through company facilities over to government officials. Such massive surveillance measures create a gloomy picture for those who feel that technology has already invaded our privacy and shows no signs of retreating.

MEDIA'S PORTRAYAL OF WOMEN

The women's rights movement has been responsible for much more than merely identifying women as a target audience (Figure 17-1). It has produced a groundswell of attention on how the media portray women. The National Associa-

TODAY'S WORKING WOMAN:

VERY SPECIAL CONSUMER...

VERY SPECIAL NEW NSI CATEGORY

The working woman of today is *different*. She has a higher household income, she's better educated and she's more style-conscious. In short, she's a prime target for products such as clothing, cosmetics, convenience foods, home furnishings and leisure-time goods and services, to mention only an obvious few.

But her television viewing habits are different too. Her preferences frequently differ from her non-working counterpart. The key to reaching her efficiently is in knowing *what* she watches.

NSI provides that key in the form of a "working woman" category in all three report sections—Program Audience, Time Period and Day Part. This Fall, use NSI to give this very special consumer some very special consideration in your spot buying.

nsi NIELSEN STATION INDEX
A SERVICE OF A.C. NIELSEN COMPANY

NEW YORK • CHICAGO • HOLLYWOOD • MENLO PARK, CA. • DALLAS
(212) 956-2500   (312) 828-1170   (213) 466-4391   (415) 321-7700   (214) 620-0225

Figure 17-1

tion of Broadcasters even revised its codes to prohibit sex discrimination in radio and television programming. Similar action has taken place in other media.

The major controversy over the portrayal of women in mass media has tended to concentrate on television, most obviously because of the dominance of the medium but also because other media, such as specialty magazines, do treat women as competent professionals, since this is the target audience the magazine reaches.

women in television

Although any study can be criticized on methodological grounds, research has shown some definite trends in television's projection of women. Professors Alice

E. Courtney and Thomas W. Whipple of York University in Toronto, Canada, summarized four research projects investigating the image of women in television commercials.[4] One of the four studies was done in Canada, the others in the United States. Results were fairly consistent. The first of these applied to the *appearance* of males and females in television commercials. Results showed that "... men were overwhelmingly present as voice-overs, the announcing or authority figures employed..." in television commercials. A positive point was found in the proportion of males and females as product representatives in television commercials; three studies investigated this concept and found a fairly equal balance between males and females. Three research studies investigated occupational data. Courtney and Whipple's survey showed that females were "over-represented in family/home occupations while males dominate the media/celebrity and business/sales/management occupations. Furthermore, women are still seen in a more limited variety of occupational roles than they actually perform." Courtney and Whipple did state, though, that this imbalance seems to be changing. Researchers William J. O'Donnell and Karen J. O'Donnell examined the roles of men and women in prime-time television commercials.[5] Their research concluded that an equal number of men and women appeared as visible product representatives, but women were more likely to represent domestic products. Men were more likely to represent nondomestic products and women were three times as likely as men to appear as product representatives in a home setting. Men were almost three times as likely to appear in settings outside the home. They concluded, "The picture presented by television commercials is unchanged—the home is the woman's domain."

women in the print media

Despite the publicity that television has received in this area, other media have also come under criticism for their portrayal of females. At the University of Illinois, Cheris Kramer directed research that investigated the stereotypes of women's speech found in cartoons published in the *New Yorker, Playboy, Cosmopolitan,* and the *Ladies Home Journal.*[7] Students who analyzed the speech of women in the cartoon captions found it to be "ineffective and restricted." It could not "deal forthrightly with a number of topics, such as finance and politics...." Kramer went on to report that students "... in writing about how they determined the sex of the speaker of the captions characterized the stereotyped women's speech as being stupid, naive, gossipy, emotional, passive, confused, concerned, wordy, and insipid."

ms., miss, or mrs.

Even journalism has had many problems in accurately reflecting the new title of "Ms." when covering a story. One editor of a major paper summed up the use of Ms. by saying that it was mostly common sense. If you were aware that a person did not like the title Ms., then you did not use it. If the person was a senior citizen, then usually the term Miss or Mrs. was more appropriate. Many women in the news found themselves referred to by their last names on second reference just as their male counterparts were. A resolution passed by the 7,000-member Women in Communication, Inc., called on the wire services to "eliminate the use of courtesy or social titles for newsmakers who happen to be female or extend such usage to newsmakers who happen to be male, and . . . to adopt the practice of identifying all newsmakers by gender and marital status directly and only when pertinent to the story . . . ."

How media will portray women in the future will be determined by how many changes media planners make on their own, how much pressure is placed on them by women and men, and what economic indicators suggest about the profit or loss of changing portrayals. Although economic indicators may seem like a poor excuse for discouraging changes, it is indeed a powerful motivation and one to be reckoned with, especially when dealing with media decision makers.

MEDIA AND THE ELDERLY

Only in recent years has there been a serious and detailed study of the relationship of the elderly to mass media. The fruits of those labors, both in scholarly circles and within media organizations, have finally recognized the traditional stereotype of the elderly as just that. For as a group, the elderly are not necessarily a depressed, socially isolated burden of society. The media, however, have not paid serious attention to this group of people; one reason being simply that they did not represent the affluent middle-aged consumers of society and were therefore neglected by media whose main concern was reaching the affluent.

media portrayal of the elderly

Their portrayal in the mass media was characterized by such spoofs as the *Over The Hill Gang* on the late night television movie or public service announcements asking for "young" volunteers to work with the "old" people in society.

Craig Aronoff examined the portrayal of the elderly in prime-time television and found a relationship between the way the media portrayed its characters and the age of those characters.[7] The research reported that the older a male character was, the more he was apt to be portrayed as a "bad guy" (Figure 17-2). The older a female character was, the more apt she was to be portrayed in a role that implied failure (Figure 17-3). There is evidence to indicate some minor changes in these trends. The elderly are beginning to be portrayed as authoritative figures dispensing "wisdom" on a subject. Not atypical is the commercial for Sominex, a substance advertised as helping people to fall asleep. The commercial shows two generations portrayed by a mother and daughter both having

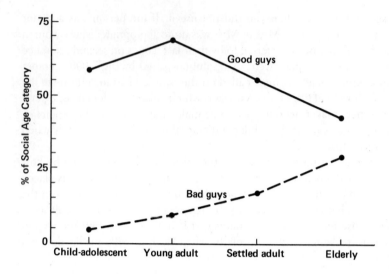

Figure 17-2 Frequency of "good guys" and "bad guys" among social age categories for major male non-cartoon characters.

trouble falling asleep at night. The daughter learned about the product because her mother told her how effective it was. A commercial showing an elderly figure expounding the good taste of "Country Time" lemonade-flavored drink is another example of the elderly being the authority.

There has also been an effort to call attention to the plight and "portrayed plight" of the elderly, especially in radio and television fare. One organization that actively supports fair treatment of the elderly in media is the Gray Panthers. They appeared before the Television Code Review Board of the National Association of Broadcasters to lobby for a change in the NAB Television Code that would alert broadcasters to be sensitive to portrayal of the aged. Whereas the code

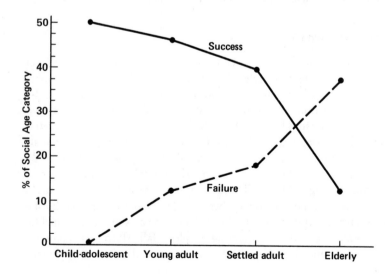

Figure 17-3 Frequency distribution of success and failure among major non-cartoon female characters.

had previously alerted the broadcasters to material dealing with sex, race, creed, religion, or ethnic background, the word *age* now has been added. The board itself said the inclusion was directed not only toward the elderly but to all ages.

special features and functional uses

Scholarly research has made a systematic investigation of the ways in which the elderly use media.[8] Many newspapers are now beginning to carry special syndicated features as well as local news and special sections devoted to the elderly. The content of these publications varies greatly, but most have common themes of activities for the elderly and programs in which the elderly are participating. There also are special consumer tips for the elderly, such as advice on money management and nutrition as well as medical information. More publications are now directed exclusively toward the elderly, such as the magazine *Retirement Living*. Many are official journals of organizations whose membership mainly consists of the elderly. Such publications also provide an avenue for advertisers to reach this target audience at what is usually a more efficient cost per thousand than through other media.

There are also many functional uses of media for the elderly. For instance, soap operas permit the elderly to identify with characters with whom, because of their own life style, they have little real contact. Such identity can help reduce the feeling of isolation that often occurs when one lives alone.[9]

The real groundwork for a beneficial relationship between the elderly and the media will be laid when media content reflects the true characteristics of this audience and portrays them realistically rather than stereotypically. Untapped frontiers are available for cable television to "involve" the elderly with media. Such factors as a special broadcast seminar permitting two-way interaction among shut-ins can help alleviate the loneliness that some elderly persons face and can actually stimulate a "neighborly" environment for them, thus creating new and vital interpersonal relationships.

MASS MEDIA PAST, PRESENT, AND FUTURE: MCLUHAN'S PERSPECTIVES

In the early 1960s, a Canadian professor of English literature with a background in science and technology began offering a perspective on the role of media in society. For ten years, between 1962 and 1972, Marshall McLuhan's writings and articles written about him filled everything from discussions by the street cultures in San Francisco to pages of the *New York Times*. He was the subject of serious broadcast interview programs and popular comedy routines. He was adored, idolized, and discarded. Critics called him everything from the greatest original thinker in centuries to a charlatan of intellectual thought. He reached the peak of his popularity in 1967. Shortly thereafter, the media movement gave way to the environmental movement, campus unrest, and the Vietnam War.

Although theories attributed to him stirred great scholarly debate at the beginning of the 1970s, the excitement soon died down. In its place, a concerted effort toward professional education developed and a concern over the individual's ability to survive economically, as opposed to the view that one could live on ideas and "happenings." Nevertheless, McLuhan did have some important ideas. Whether they have failed to achieve the limelight in recent years as a result of a passé attitude toward his philosophy, or whether we are in a transitional state waiting for his predictions to come true, we should still take a few moments to view the very broad subject of mass communication, the media, and civilization from his perspective. His influence in initiating the testing of hypotheses and attempting to coordinate such hypotheses into a composite theory about people and technology can profit today's student of mass communication.

the ages of technological determinism

Certainly anthropology, if not archeology, has long since known that human beings were not always the creatures they are today. The newness in McLuhan's thinking lies in the way he relates human evolution to the senses.

McLuhan supports the contention that we have been the product of technological determinism—technology forcing us into our future. In the preliterate era of our development, we used all of our senses equally to relate to our environment. We were just as apt to react to touch as we were to sight, sound, or smell. There was no order or priority among our senses, and they were, for the most part, in balance with one another. We could, therefore, absorb the total experience of our environment. We were part of a tribal culture in a global village.

The second era of McLuhanistic development occurred as we left the preliterate state and moved into the era of communication symbols, from the pictographics on the walls of caves to the development of the alphabet. This transition into the first stage of human communicative technology caused a serious disruption in what had been a well-balanced relationship. For one thing, the very presence of the alphabet brought about an imbalance in the human perceptual system, a shift toward a predominantly visual orientation. We began to evolve along unidimensional lines—our thinking became linear, our advancement became linear, and we began to use the linear technology of the alphabet as a means of securing and making other discoveries. The tribal group culture of the preliterate era was replaced with an individualized culture of the linear-visual period. We could participate in communicative acts without the presence of other people.

The next great invention was the printing press. Now, although humans were still oriented to the visual dimension, communication began on a mass scale. For a time, the new technology disrupted the status quo, as thoughts and ideas penetrated all levels of society on a scale and with an impact much greater than in the past. Print media became the "goggles" of society through which we viewed and learned about our world experience. Yet these "goggles" also perpetuated our one-dimensional perpective. We all know, for example, that although many profound words define love, nothing in print successfully captures the actual feeling of love. This discrepancy between the printed word and a life experience was a theme running through McLuhan's work and probably one of the chief reasons for his popularity. Members of the street cultures read and studied his philosophy and searched for a more sensual experience in life.

To McLuhan, print at its best was communicative but suppressive. It hindered more than helped and thrust us into a technological world and later a revolution. We could store ideas, compute ideas, and express ideas in print. As the new print technology spread, an almost competitive neurosis developed alongside an uncontrollable nationalism. Our visual culture spawned more visual culture; our technological determinism spawned more technological determinism. What had begun with pictographics and was immeasurably accelerated by the printing press, served merely to increase our linear world perspective and to spur the general process of industrial development. McLuhan contends that assembly line factories were the result.

The most disruptive age that we have encountered, according to McLuhan, is the new electronic age. In it, humankind was propelled into many new communication processes, both in media and in systems. These systems included the telegraph and ocean cables, especially the Atlantic Cable which linked the United States and Great Britain. The new media—radio, television, and the computer—connected countries and cultures massively and instantaneously. We now have come full circle, in a sense—we are once again a global village in which everyone is connected and attuned to the same "tribal" drums.

media hot and cool

Media in this electronic age, McLuhan contends, are basically of two types—hot and cool. Cool media demand the active, tactile participation of the individual. Although at first glance this might convey the idea that "touching" and turning the knobs on a radio is experiencing a cool medium, while sitting and watching television would be experiencing a hot one, just the opposite is the case. If we grant McLuhan's hypothesis that our culture is primarily visual, and since, as we learned earlier, it is necessary for our eyes and brain to assimilate the actual picture on a television from the lines and dots, then we are mentally "touching" television and it is thus a cool medium. Radio, on the other hand, is a hot medium. It does not demand as much of our senses or our involvement as television does. The same is true with newspapers or magazines. They all are hot because they are unidimensional.

McLuhan also contends that there can be serious conflicts when the wrong medium is matched with the wrong message. A hot message on a cool medium will be less favorable than matching a cool medium with a cool message. As an example, McLuhan predicted the end of the Vietnam War because the public would be so tired of seeing a hot message (the war) on a cool medium (television), that they would finally react and demand an end to it. He also credited the 1960 loss of the American presidency to Richard Nixon because in the great television debates with John Kennedy, Nixon was clearly a hot personality on a cool medium. Later, observing Nixon on an evening variety show playing the piano in a casual, impromptu manner, McLuhan contended that his image could be favorably transmitted to the viewers and the voters.

criticism of McLuhan

The majority of McLuhan's most publicized thoughts about media came during the 1960s. They appeared in such profusion within such a short time period that his ideas almost seem to be expressed first and pondered later. Attention to them decreased in the early seventies, but they recently have received renewed interest.

Some basic conflicts in his theory development can be argued. For example, McLuhan criticized radio as a serious intrusion into minority cultures. However, research shows it has been a significant educational medium for such cultures. In addition, although McLuhan describes television as a cool medium because it forces us to use our brain and eyes to complete the picture before us, he criticizes movies for being a hot medium. Yet the procession of rapidly moving motion picture frames passing before our eyes necessitates a similar "visually tactile" experience.

Many of McLuhan's published works have been criticized for being unclear. His defense in some cases has been to claim that he was limited by the single dimension of the print medium in expressing thoughts that were part of a much larger experience of the senses. McLuhan uses the term "rear view mirror" to express our involvement with our senses and society. Yet, we could apply this same criticism to his "rear view" thinking, grounding much of his thoughts on the historical foundation of the past.

McLuhan and the future

Our encounter with McLuhan would have little relevance if we did not at least offer some perspective on the future validity of his contentions. McLuhan said that as one medium arrives, it creates disruption; the medium overtaken then becomes an art form. History has generally tended to confirm this. Scrolls from biblical times have now become priceless art treasures, as have the books printed on the first printing presses. History has also recorded that when the new print media did arrive, there was in fact a disruption of society.

The age of electronics has created an equal concern and disruption at all levels of society. The telegraph, for example, accelerated our decision making. No longer were economic market quotations received days late. We suddenly had "instant" decisions and predictions available for immediate analysis. Life in our industrial society thus moved faster and became more competitive. The telegraph became what McLuhan called the central nervous system of our com-munication network. But voice transmission and the advent of radio soon eclipsed dots and dashes. This new medium created further disruption as it paved the way for the truly electronic media. Newspaper "extras" ceased to be sold on the street corner. They became the instant news bulletins of radio. Parents shuddered in horror as teenagers seemed to care about little except having a transister radio glued to their ears. The masses either tuned to the rhetoric of acid rock, or brought claims that the medium responsible for disseminating these unnatural sounds resulted in all sorts of ills among young adults. In retrospect, we see that an art form is already taking shape among the electronic media. Telegraph apparatus is an artifact of antique stores, and the radio drama of the 1930s became part of the nostalgia of the 1970s. Reproductions of early radios fill department stores, and one can even purchase a working replica of the large, "church steeple" radio of the 1940s.

Television caused a similar disruption. A scant decade after its debut, government commissions conducted full-scale hearings on how television af-fected violent behavior, how it affected childhood development, how it corrupted our morals, and countless other "disruptions" in our society. It is ironic that the debate on those issues goes on simultaneously as television is being considered a serious art form. Experimental video centers are using television as a medium of artistic expression for everything from multimedia "experiences" to video feed-back, in which a television camera takes a picture of its own monitor (Figure 17-4). Video cassettes and video discs, capturing the nostalgia of early television

Figure 17-4 Marshall McLuhan.
(Photo by Robert Lansdale)

programs, are available much like recordings of early radio. Some programs, such as the famed "Mickey Mouse Club," even returned to television after having appeared as nationally popular programs twenty or so years ago. If television is becoming an art form, then what medium will supersede it? Computers?

Computers have brought with them the same disruption and acceleration in pace that accompanied the entry of other media into general usage. Already they are used as systems of communication, and the wired-city concept, in which everyone will have access to a central computer, opens up even broader avenues of communication for this medium. Yet we have resisted the advent of computer technology. At the very least, we regard it as a common nuisance; at most, we fear being taken over by it.

It is important, however, to focus on the future. What if McLuhan was correct? How will this technological determinism affect us in the last quarter of the twentieth century? Consider the ever increasing velocity of technological development that we have observed so far. The time between the introduction and the demise of new media has continually shrunk, until we are now living in an era of overlapping media. What effect is this having on our lives, and what new media are yet to appear? What will happen to the media that currently exist? How great will be the disruption? Will we be overtaken by media? Certainly questions such as these are much easier to ask than to answer. Our lives are, however, totally interrelated with mass media. Perhaps nothing has affected our past or will affect our future as much as this tremendous capability to communicate all sorts of information across cultures almost instantaneously. We must begin now to prepare ourselves to develop a satisfactory relationship with the media, based on fulfilling human needs and goals.

SUMMARY

Chapter 17 looked at the ethics and social issues confronting mass media. On the subject of media ethics we saw how questionable actions occurred within both the print and broadcast media. We also saw that within any single medium lies the potential for responsible professional and ethical practices or a blatant violation of those principles. Assisting in guiding the actions of the press are codes of ethics, such as the codes of the Society of Professional Journalists (Sigma Delta Chi), the Radio Television News Directors Association, and the American Society of Newspaper Editors. Within any code, however, there is a potential weakness in its ability to be enforced, and in the end, the real responsibility for ethical conduct rests with the individual.

Censorship of the media is an age-old philosophical issue. Procensorship arguments champion the need to protect social order, while anticensorship arguments argue the necessity for the free flow of information in a democracy. Media as big brother is another issue constantly facing us. Although this fear has been particularly applicable to two-way television, other types of technology, such as computers, are also a perceived threat to many people. Policy making on such issues often comes to a stalemate when the need for government control is pitted against the necessity to prevent abuse of that control.

Content of the media has also become an important social issue. For example, women and the elderly are two groups that have been portrayed as possessing negative qualities which are not accurate or reflective of women or the elderly in society. Although these images are changing, there needs to be considerable improvement.

Canadian philosopher Marshall McLuhan speculated on the development of media in society and advanced the theory that we are caught in a process of technological determinism that has seen the preliterate era give way, in turn, to the era of visual dominance, the era of the printing press, and the era of electronic media. McLuhan looks at media as being either hot or cool and stresses the importance of matching the proper message with the proper medium. Many of McLuhan's perspectives on mass media, regardless of the controversy surrounding them, seem to have some validity as we view the future of mass media in society.

OPPORTUNITIES FOR FURTHER LEARNING

BABB, LAURA LONGLEY, ed., *Of the Press, by the Press, for the Press, and Others Too....* New York: Houghton Mifflin Company, 1976.

BROWN, LEE, *The Reluctant Reformation.* New York: David McKay Co., Inc., 1974.

FRIEDMAN, LESLIE J., *Sex Role Stereotyping in the Mass Media: An Annotated Bibliography.* New York: Garland Publishing, 1977.

GALNOOR, ITZHAK, ed., *Government Secrecy in Democracies.* New York: Harper & Row, Publishers, Inc., 1977.

HOCKMAN, SANDRA, and SYBIL WONG, *Satellite Spies: The Frightening Impact of a New Technology.* Indianapolis: The Bobbs-Merrill Co., Inc., 1976.

HULTENG, JOHN L., *The Messenger's Motives: Ethical Problems of The News Media.* Englewood Cliffs, N.J.: Prentice-Hall, Inc., 1976.

LAUDON, KENNETH C., *Communication Technology and Democratic Participation.* New York: Praeger Special Studies, 1977.

MERRILL, JOHN C., and RALPH D. BARNEY, eds., *Ethics and The Press.* New York: Hastings House, 1975.

ROSHCO, BERNARD, *Newsmaking.* Chicago: University of Chicago Press, 1975.

Glossary of Media Terms

A.A.A.A. American Association of Advertising Agencies.

Action line a service of a newspaper or magazine that offers readers a forum in which to complain about some product, service, or company. The publication usually tries to help the complainant.

Advocacy advertising stresses issues of public concern that usually arise as the result of by-products of illegal activities (for example, crime as a result of drug abuse).

AEJ Association for Education in Journalism.

Affiliate a broadcasting station bound by contract to associate with a particular broadcasting network or wire service.

AM amplitude modulation.

Annual billings money billed advertisers for commercials carried in a medium over a one-year period.

ANPA American Newspaper Publishers Association.

Apogee that point in a satellite's orbit farthest away from earth.

ASCAP American Society of Composers, Authors, and Publishers.

Audio actuality the recording of the "actual sounds" in the news for incorporation into radio newscasts.

Authoritarian   characterized by media that are either "private or public" and "are chiefly instruments for effecting government policy, though not necessarily government owned."

AWRT   American Women in Radio and Television.

BEA   Broadcast Education Association.

Billboard   (1) a wire service feed listing all the prerecorded stories in the wire service's current audio file; (2) a major publication of the recording industry; (3) a slang term for outdoor advertising bulletin.

Blue box   slang term for the interactive earth terminal used for direct broadcast statellite communication.

BMI   Broadcast Music Incorporated.

Bulletin   (1) important news usually disseminated as an interruption in normal broadcast programming; (2) wire service (audio or video) feed to subscribers.

Capital intensive   when maximum costs occur immediately after an investment.

CATV   community antenna television, or cable TV.

Coaxial cable   heavy cable consisting of an inner wire core surrounded by a layer of plastic, metal-webbed insulation, and a third layer of plastic.

Cold type   various typesetting processes not including casting type from molten metal. The newest cold-type process is computer composition.

Contour   the geographic area covered by a broadcast station's signal.

Co-ops   also called *informal networks*, (1) broadcast news networks created by a group of radio or TV news personnel; (2) trade-out advertising agreements between advertisers and the individual advertising outlet.

Corrective advertising   advertising that rectifies, usually because of regulatory orders, false or misleading advertising.

Counter-advertising   advertising directed against a product or service.

CPB   Corporation for Public Broadcasting.

Cume   (or cumulative audience) the number of different persons or households that watch or listen to a given station or program during a certain time period.

Daytimers   radio stations required by the FCC to sign off at sunset.

Demographics   data on such things as age, sex, education level, income, and ethnic background.

Demo session   a preliminary recording session.

Diary   method of broadcast rating measurement in which viewers or listeners keep a record of the programs and stations they tune in at periodic intervals.

Directional antennas   a group of strategically placed broadcast antennas whose purpose is to transmit the signal in specific directions in order to achieve an irregular rather than a circular contour.

Directional stations   radio stations, primarily in the AM band, that utilize directional antennas to keep their signals from interfering with those of other stations.

Direct-wave propagation   radio wave pattern in which signals travel through direct line-of-sight transmission.

Drop   that section of a cable that brings the signal from the trunk or subtrunk directly into a subscriber's home receiver.

Electromagnetic spectrum   an atmospheric yardstick used to measure varying levels of electromagnetic energy, called frequency.

Electromagnetic waves   electrical impulses traveling through space at the speed of light. Used to transmit radio and television signals.

Electrostatic transmission   a system used to transmit wire service pictures. Subscribers receive glossy prints on dry paper ready for printing, thereby eliminating the need for the subscriber to develop the photo himself or herself.

ERI   Electronic Response Indicator.

ETV   educational television.

Feedback   reactions of a receiver to a message from a sender.

FM   frequency modulation.

Freebies   ranging from excursions to foreign countries to tickets to a church supper, these complimentary offerings are designed to entice journalists to cover a story.

Frequency   (1) broadcast rating term to indicate how often a viewer has tuned to a given station; (2) position on the electromagnetic spectrum.

Gatekeeper   any individual directly involved in the relay or transfer of information from one individual to another through the use of a mass medium.

Gatekeeper chain   chain of gatekeepers where little interaction can take place and ample opportunities for distortion exist.

Gatekeeper group   a group of gatekeepers among whom there is the opportunity for interaction to take place.

Gazetta   the Italian coin used as an admission price to hear a reader announce the day's news events.

Geostationary   or *synchronous*, an orbiting satellite that travels at the same speed in proportion to the earth's rotation and thus appears to remain stationary over one point of the earth.

GH2   Gigahertz. 1-billion hertz or 1-billion cycles per second.

Head end   the human and hardware combination responsible for originating, controlling, and processing signals over the cable system.

Hertz   last name of Heinrich Rudolph Hertz commonly used as abbreviation for "cycles per second" in referring to electromagnetic waves.

Home terminal   receiving set for cable TV transmissions that can be either one-way or two-way.

Horizontal publication   a category of business publications aimed at a certain level of employee across several different industries.

Hot type   typesetting process using linotype machines to cast letters and sentences into type from molten metal.

Households using television (HUT)   a term used in broadcast ratings to describe every household using television.

House organ   a direct-mail piece in the form of a newsletter or company magazine that is sent to all members of a certain organization.

Hypoing   sometimes called "*hyping*," heavily promoting something, usually to increase sales or ratings.

ICA   International Communication Association.

Image advertising   advertising designed to enhance a corporation's standing in the eyes of the consumer.

Impressions   the number of times a person is reached by an advertisement.

Industrial magazines   a type of business publication directed toward a specific industry, such as masonry.

Informal networks   broadcast news networks created by a professional group of radio or TV news personnel. These networks are also called co-ops.

In-house agencies   advertising agencies operating within a company solely to promote its products.

Institutional magazines   a type of business publication directed toward a specific institution.

In-the-can films   movies that have already been seen in movie theaters but whose income is assured through re-releases and release to television.

ITV   instructional television, programming specifically designed for direct or supplemental teaching.

Junkets   excursions for journalists, compliments of someone seeking news coverage of an event.

KHz   Kilohertz. 1000 hertz or 1000 cycles per second.

Kicker   closing story of a newscast, often a humorous anecdote.

Kinetoscope   forerunner of the motion picture developed by Thomas Edison, it was a crude device with a peephole through which a viewer could see pictures move.

Libertarian   describes a press privately owned and providing a check on government in addition to meeting other needs of society.

Mailgram   Western Union trade-marked system to send a message via computer and regular postal service mail delivery.

Market research   research, usually conducted by advertising agencies, into the potential market for products.

Mass communication   process by which messages are communicated by a mass medium to a large number of people.

Master control console   heart of a television control room operation through which both the audio and video images are fed, joined together, and improved, perhaps through special effects for the "on-air" image.

Master record   the master session is recorded on this record, from which additional records are pressed.

Master session   the final recording session in which a song is put onto tape. Costing many thousands of dollars, this uses full orchestration, a major control console, and a recording engineer.

Media brokers   persons in the business of selling media properties.

Media credibility   the effect that various media have on how mass communication messages are perceived.

Message intensity   the value or importance of an event or its potential impact in relation to other events or potential news stories.

Meter method   a broadcast ratings measurement in which a monitoring device installed on TV sets is connected to a central computer, which then records channel selection at different times of the day.

MHz   Megahertz. 1-million hertz or 1-million cycles per second.

Microwave   a very short wave frequency located above the area on the electromagnetic spectrum where standard broadcast transmission takes place.

MPA   Magazine Publishers' Association.

MPAA   Motion Picture Association of America.

NAEB   National Association of Educational Broadcasters.

News dissemination   the process by which news is diffused to the receiving public.

Noise   something that interferes with the communication process.

Offset   a printing process in which typeset copy is reproduced on a photographic, smooth-surfaced plate; the image is transferred to paper through a series of steps *not* using a plate with raised typefaces.

Ombudsman   personnel who accept feedback from readers on any issue, from suggestions to complaints.

Opinion leaders   people who influence thinking on a particular subject(s) because their opinions are respected.

Pass-around rate   the number of people who read a single copy of a publication.

Pay cable   a system in which cable subscribers pay an additional amount beyond the standard monthly rental fee in order to receive special programming.

PBS   Public Broadcasting Service.

Perigee   the closest point to the earth of a satellite's orbit.

Personalized book   composed and printed by a computer, these gift items can be programmed to incorporate specific names and places directly relevant to the recipient.

Picture wire   wire services through which photo transmission takes place.

Pilots   sample broadcasting programs produced either by networks or production companies for possible programming adoption.

Pirated tapes   illegally recorded music sold in violation of copyright and contractual agreements with artists.

Playlists   form of feedback for the recording industry in which individual radio stations list the songs popular in their listening area for a given time period.

Production companies   commonly called production houses, these businesses produce broadcasting programs for adoption either by networks or by individual stations via syndication.

Product research   research, usually instigated by advertising agencies, into a company and its product.

Professional magazines   a type of business publication directed at readers in a specific profession, such as law.

Projection   an estimate of the characteristics of a total universe based on a sample of that universe.

Psychographics   study of the psychological characteristics of the mass audience.

Public broadcasting   the operation of the various noncommercial radio and television stations in the United States.

Public service advertising   PSAs are designed to support a nonprofit cause or organization. Most of the time or space for this advertising is provided free as a service to the public by the print or broadcast media.

Random sample   a selection in which every item in a universe has an equal chance of being chosen.

Rating   a percentage of the total number of households or persons tuned to a station or program during a certain time period.

Reader profiles   research surveys designed to ascertain both the demographic and the psychographic characteristics of specialized audiences.

Reader service card   a device that gives magazine readers an opportunity to request additional literature and information about an advertiser's products by circling a corresponding number on a reply card.

Readership survey   detailed analysis of a newspaper's audience.

Regional networks   a system that provides broadcast programming and information to specific geographic regions of the country.

Relay satellite   Echo I became the first artificial device capable of bouncing messages back to earth.

Repeater satellite   the United States' Courier 1-B became the first of a series of satellites that could both receive and retransmit signals back to earth.

Research service   businesses that specialize in providing research on current topics for subscribers, primarily newspapers and broadcast executives.

RTNDA   Radio Television News Directors Association

Sales networks   a group of broadcasting stations linked together by a financial agreement to benefit all member stations by offering advertisers a joint rate.

Sampling   the process of examining a small portion of something to estimate what the larger portion is like.

Saturation   the percentage of the total number of households that subscribe to a given medium.

SCA   Speech Communication Association.

Schematic diagrams   blueprints for electronic circuitry.

Seditious libel   criminal libel against the government.

Semantic noise   interference with the communication process because of a misunderstanding caused by a cliché or slang.

Share   a percentage of households using television or people listening to radio who are tuned to a particular station or program during a certain time period.

Sky wave propagation   radio-wave transmission pattern in which the signals travel up, bounce off the ionosphere, and rebound from the earth in a continuing process.

SNAP   Society of National Association Publications.

Social responsibility   theory espousing privately owned media "unless the government has to take over to ensure public service."

Social responsibility advertising   publicity that warns consumers to be responsible to things that can hurt them.

Soviet communist theory   system of state-owned media functioning as a propaganda instrument of the government.

Speculators   people who buy a media property and hold it for a short time while heavily promoting it to increase sales.

SPJ, SDX   Society of Professional Journalists, Sigma Delta Chi.

Split   a given news report compiled by a wire service.

Standard advertising   its motive is to sell and to create in the consumer a feeling of need and desire for a product or service.

Station program cooperative (SPC)   concept in public broadcasting that utilizes direct feedback in the form of financial commitment from affiliate stations to determine which programs will compose about one-third of the programming distributed by PBS.

Subgroups   the "mass within a mass" on which the concept of the mass audience is based.

Sub-trunk   secondary cables branching out from the main trunk in a cable TV system to carry the signal to outlying areas.

Synchronous   or *geostationary*, a satellite that travels at the same speed in proportion to the earth's rotation and thus appears to remain stationary over one point of the earth.

Syndicates   companies whose business it is to promote and sell comics, columns, and other special features to newspapers.

Target audience   any group of persons who have a common bond, that bond being shared demographic and/or psychographic characteristics.

Television household   a broadcast rating term used to describe any home with a television set, as distinguished from a household using television.

Trade magazines   a type of business publication directed to specific businesses, such as hardware stores.

Trade-out   an exchange of merchandise for a service; for example, in advertising, a merchant will trade the use of a product for an equivalent amount of advertising in print or broadcast media.

Translators   television transmitting antennas, usually located on high natural terrain.

Trunk   main line of a cable system.

Two-step flow   process by which information disseminated by mass media is (1) received by a direct audience and then (2) relayed to other persons secondhand.

Universe   the whole from which a sample is chosen; in broadcast ratings, this can be the sample area, metro area, or rating area.

Value structures   a normative, conceptual standard of the desirable that predispositionally influences individuals in choosing among personally perceived alternatives of behavior.

VDT   visual display terminals. Data from electronic keyboards and computers appear on a device similar to a television screen.

Vertical publications   a category of business publications designed to reach people at all levels within a given profession.

Weekly carriage report   a local station's broadcast schedule.

White space   that portion of a printed advertisement devoid of printing or illustrations, that is, blank space.

WICI   Women in Communication, Inc.

Wireless   term used to describe early radio.

Notes

CHAPTER 1

[1]Richard Maisel, "The Decline of Mass Media," *Public Opinion Quarterly*, 37 (Summer 1973), 159–70.

CHAPTER 2

[1]Eric W. Allen, "International Origins of the Newspaper: The Establishment of Periodicity in Print," *Journalism Quarterly*, 7 (December 1930), 309–19.

[2]William M. Glenn, *The Sigma Delta Chi Story* (Choral Gables, Fla.: The Glade House, 1949).

[3]Jon G. Udell, *Economic Trends in the Daily Newspaper Business, 1946 to 1970.* (Madison, Wisconsin: Bureau of Business Research and Service, 1970), p. 9. See also: *Facts about Newspapers 1978*, American Newspaper Publishers Association.

[4]Jon G. Udell, *Future Newsprint Demand 1970–1980* (Madison, Wisconsin: Bureau of Business Research and Service, 1971).

[5]Jon G. Udell, *The U. S. Economy and Newspaper Growth: 1963–1973 and the Future Outlook*, ANPA Newsprint and Traffic Bulletin, no. 31, October 24, 1974.

[6]Gerald L. Grotta, "Prosperous Newspaper Industry May be Heading for Decline," *Journalism Quarterly*, 51 (Autumn 1974) 498–502.

CHAPTER 3

[1]Frank Luther Mott, *A History of American Magazines 1965–1885*, vol. 3 (Cambridge, Mass.: Harvard University Press, 1938), p. 5.

²Theodore Peterson, *Magazines in the Twentieth Century* (Urbana: University of Illinois Press, 1964), p. 23.

³Ibid., p. 23.

CHAPTER 4

¹Two publications contributed significantly to the discussion of book publishing in colonial America: *The Printer in Eighteenth Century Williamsburg* (Williamsburg, Va.: Colonial Williamsburg, 1974); and *The Bookbinder in Colonial Williamsburg* (Williamsburg, Va.: Colonial Williamsburg, 1973). For the reader with the opportunity to visit Williamsburg, the authentic recreation based on sound historical documentation of early printing and bookbinding processes is part of Colonial Williamsburg.

²See F. L. Shick, *The Paper Bound Book in America* (New York: R. R. Bowker Company, 1958).

CHAPTER 5

¹*Columbine*, 2 (April/May, 1974).

²Ibid.

³John Fink, *WGN: A Pictorial History* (Chicago: WGN, INC., 196 1), p.11.

⁴Wilbur Schramm, "Reading and Listening Patterns of American University Students," *Journalism Quarterly*, 22 (March 1945), 23–33.

⁵*Welcome South Brother* (Atlanta: WSB Radio, 1974), p. 17.

⁶"Annual Report of Research in Progress," Institute for Communication Research, Stanford University, 1972–73.

CHAPTER 6

¹Excerpt from "Preface," p. vii, in *Public Television: A Program for Action, The Report and Recommendations of the Carnegie Commission on Educational Television* (New York: Harper & Row, Publishers, Inc., 1967).

²Ibid.

CHAPTER 7

¹Edwin Emery and Michael Emery, *The Press and America*, 4th ed. (Englewood Cliffs, N.J.: Prentice-Hall, Inc., 1978), p. 365–66.

²"Alfred Eisenstaedt," *Studio Photography*, (February 1979), p. 27.

CHAPTER 9

¹The author is indebted to the Recording Industry Association of America for furnishing significant information used in this chapter. Other sources that proved particularly useful included: Harry Dichter and Elliott Shapiro, *Handbook of Early American Sheet Music 1768–1889* (New York: Dover Publications, Inc., 1977). Material for the section on the prerecording era is found in this source. Also especially useful in preparing this chapter were: Oliver Read and Walter L. Welch, *From Tin Foil to Stereo* (Indianapolis: Howard W. Sams and Co., Inc.; The Bobbs-Merrill Co., Inc., 1976); Ronald Gelatt, *The Fabulous Phonograph* (Philadelphia: J. B. Lippincott Company, 1955).

CHAPTER 10

¹Andrew Kershaw, "The Next Ordeal or the Biggest Problem of the Next Ten Years." Speech delivered to the annual meeting of the Association of National Advertisers, Hot Springs, Virginia, October 1974.

[2]James T. Lull, "Counter Advertising: Persuasability of the Anti-Bayer TV Spot,"*Journal of Broadcasting*, 18 (Summer 1974), 353–60.

[3]Walter L. Thomas, *A Manual for the Differential-Value Profile* (Ann Arbor, Mich., Educational Service Company, 1966). p. 6.

CHAPTER 12

[1]Frederick W. Ford and Lee G. Lovett, "State Regulation of Cable Television, Part 1: Current Statutes," *Broadcast Management/Engineering*, 10 (June 1974), 18, 21, 50.

[2]Ibid.

[3]Paul L. Laskin and Abram Chayes, "A Brief History of the Issues," *Control of the Direct Broadcast Satellite: Values in Conflict* (Palo Alto, Calif.: Aspen Institute Program on Communications and Society, 1974), pp. 3–14.

[4]Ibid.

[5]Ibid.

CHAPTER 14

[1]Osmo A. Wiio, "System Models of Information, Communication and Mass Communication: Reevaluation of Some Basic Concepts of Communication." Paper presented at the annual meeting of the International Communication Association, Montreal, 1973. See also Osmo A. Wiio and Leif Aberg, "Open and Closed Mass Media Systems." *Paper presented at the annual meeting of the International Communication Association, Chicago, 1975; and Osmo A. Wiio, Systems of Information, Communication, and Organization* (Helsinki, Finland: Helsinki Research Institute for Business Economics, 1975).

[2]*In the Matter of the Mayflower Broadcasting Corporation and the Yankee Network, Inc.* (WAAB), 8 FCC 33, 338, January 16, 1941.

[3]*In the Matter of Editorializing by Broadcast Licensees*, 13 FCC 1246, June 1, 1949.

[4]David M. Leive, *International Telecommunications and International Law: The Regulation of the Radion Spectrum* (Dobbs Ferry, N.Y.: A. W. Sijthoff, Leyden, and Oceana Publications, Inc., 1971); John and Mary Markle Foundation and the Twentieth Century Fund, eds., *Global Communications in the Space Age: Toward a New ITU* (New York: John and Mary R. Markle Foundation and the Twentieth Century Fund, 1972).

[5]Harold K. Jacobson, "The International Telecommunication Union: ITU's Structures and Functions, in *Global Communications in the Space Age: Toward a New ITU*, ed. John and Mary R. Markle Foundation and the Twentieth Century Fund, 1972, P. 40.

[6]Final Protocol, Documents of the Berlin Preliminary Conference (1903), pp. 83–85, as cited in Leive, *International Telecommunications*. The essence of the protocol agreement is carried throughout contemporary broadcast regulation.

CHAPTER 15

[1]*Gitlow* v. *New York* 268 U.S. 652, 666 (1925). The reference was a "casual statement not necessary to the decision." See: Donald M. Gillmor and Jerome A. Barron. *Mass Communication Law* (St. Paul: West Publishing Co., 1974.) p. 1.

[2]Eric Sevareid. Speech delivered at the "First Amendment Confrontation" during the fifty-fifth annual convention of the National Association of Broadcasters, March 28, 1977.

[3]Paley's remark was quoted by Archibald Cox, Carl Miloeb University Professor at Harvard University during a speech by Cox to the Anti-Defamation League of B'nai B'rith on the occasion of Paley receiving the First Amendment Freedoms Award, December 7, 1976, in New York City.

[4]*CBS* v. *Democratic National Committee*, 412 U.S. 94 (1973), William Small, "The First Amendment/Radio and Television: Treated Like Distant Cousins," *The Quill*, 64 (September 1976), 32.

[5]"State Court Holds Free-Press Rights Are Applicable to Broadcasting," *Broadcasting*, 45 (April 12, 1976), 59.

[6]Ibid.

[7]John B. Adams, *State Open Meeting Laws: An Overview* (Columbia, Mo.: Freedom of Information Foundation, 1974).

[8]*Rideau* v. *Louisiana*, 373 U.S. 723, 10 L. Ed. 2d 663, 83 S. Ct. 1417 (1963).

[9]*Estes* v. *State of Texas*, 381 U.S. 532, 85 S. Ct. 1628, 14 L. Ed. 2d 543 (1965).

[10]"Cameras in the Courtroom," *The Quill*, 63 (April 1975), 25.

[11]Roger M. Grace, "The Courts v. the News Media: Is the Conflict Necessary?" *Case and Comment*, 79 (March/April 1974), 3–10.

[12]Stan Crock, "A Flurry of Gag Rules," *The Quill*, 62 (March 1974), 21. *United States* v. *Dickinson*, 465 F. 2d 496 (5th Cir. 1972).

[13]Grace, "The Courts v. the News Media."

[14]Ibid.

[15]"York's Strange Silence," *Time*, November 18, 1974, pp. 88–89.

[16]*Dennis* v. *United States*, 341 U.S. 494, 510 (1951).

[17]See: *NAB Highlights* October 31, 1977, p. 3; Donald M. Gillmor and Jerome A. Barron, *Mass Communication Law* (St. Paul: West Publishing Company, 1974), 287–88.

CHAPTER 16

[1]Carl I. Hovland, "Reconciling Conflicting Results Derived from Experimental and Survey Studies of Attitude Change," in *The Process and Effects of Mass Communication*, ed. Wilbur Schramm and Donald F. Roberts (Urbana: University of Illinois Press, 1971), pp. 493–515.

[2]Paul Lazarsfeld, Bernard Berelson, and H. Gaudet, *The People's Choice*. (New York: Columbia University Press, 1948).

[3]Ibid.

[4]Melvin DeFleur and Sandra Ball-Rokeach, *Theories of Mass Communication* (New York: David McKay Co., Inc., 1975, p. 205.

[5]A discussion of how the categories approach evolved from the bullett theory and how it fits into current communication theory is found in Wilbur Schramm and Donald Roberts, *The Process and Effects of Mass Communication* (Urbana: University of Illinois Press, 1971), pp. 4–53.

[6]Elihu Katz, "Mass Communications Research and the Study of Popular Culture," *Studies in Public Communication*, vol. 2 (1959), as discussed in David Chaney, *Process of Mass Commuication* (London: The Macmillan Press, Ltd., 1972), pp. 11–36.

[7]Louis M. Savary and J. Paul Carrico, eds., *Contemporary Film and the New Generation* (New York: Association Press, 1971), pp. 15–19.

[8]William Stephenson, *The Play Theory of Mass Communication* (Chicago: University of Chicago Press, 1967).

[9]Chaney, pp. 20–21.

[10]Deanna Campbell Robinson, "Television/Film Attitudes of Upper-Middle Class Professionals," *Journal of Broadcasting*, 19 (Spring 1975), 196. Also discussed under the text subheading "Uses and Gratifications."

[11]Wilbur Schramm, *Men, Messages, and Media: A Look at Human Communication* (New York: Harper & Row, Publishers, Inc., 1973).

[12]Neil T. Weintraub, "Some Meanings Radio Has for Teenagers," *Journal of Broadcasting*, 2 (Spring 1971), 147–52.

[13]Lawrence Wenner, "Functional Analyses of TV Viewing for Older Adults," *Journal of Broadcasting*, 20 (Winter 1976), 77–88.

[14]Herta Herzog, "What Do We Really Know about Daytime Serial Listeners," in *Radio Research, 1942–1943*, ed. Paul. F. Lazarsfeld and Frank Stanton (New York: Duell, Sloan and Pearce, 1944).

[15]Mark R. Levy "The Audience Experience with Television News,' *Journalism Monographs*, no. 55 (April 1978).

[16]Bernard C. Cohen, *The Press and Foreign Policy* (Princeton, N.J.: Princeton University Press, 1963). See also: Maxwell McCombs and Donald Shaw, "The Agenda-Setting Function of Mass Media," *Public Opinion Quarterly*, 36 (1972), 176–87.

[17]CBS Office of Social Research, *Communicating with Children through Television* (New York: CBS. 1977).

[18]For example: Charles R. Corder-Bolz, "Television Content and Children's Social Attitudes," *Progress Report to the Office of Child Development* (Washington, D.C.: Department of Health, Education, and Welfare, 1976).

[19]John P. Murray and Susan Kippax, "Children's Social Behavior in Three Towns with Differing Television Experience," *Journal of Communication*, 28 (Winter 1978), 19–29).

[20]Charles K. Atkin and Walter Gantz, "The Role of Television News in the Political Socialization of Children." Paper presented at the meeting of the International Communication Association, Chicago, April 1975.

[21]Charles Atkin and Mark Miller, "The Effects of Television Advertising on Children: Experimental Evidence." Paper presented at the 1975 meeting of the International Communication Association, A review of recent research on television and advertising can be found in the *Journal of Communication*, 27 (Winter 1977).

[22]Seymour Feshbach, "The Stimulating vs. Cathartic Effects of a Vicarious Aggressive Experience," *Journal of Abnormal and Social Psychology* 63 (1961), 381–85.

[23]Leonard Berkowitz, *Aggression: A Social Psychological Analysis* (New York: McGraw-Hill Book Company, 1962).

[24]Joseph Klapper, *The Effects of Mass Communication* (New York: The Free Press, 1960).

[25]Albert Bandura and Richard Walters, *Social Learning and Personality Development* (New York: Holt, Rinehart & Winston, 1963).

[26]The *Journal of Broadcasting*, 21 (Summer 1977) features a discussion of Gerbner's methodology, CBS's criticism, and Gerbner's response.

[27]George Comstock, "Types of Portrayal and Aggressive Behavior," *Journal of Communication*, 27 (Summer 1977), 189–98.

[28]Everett M. Rogers and F. Floyd Shoemaker, *Communication of Innovations: A Cross Cultural Approach*, 2nd ed. (New York: The Free Press, 1971).

CHAPTER 17

[1]Jules Whitcover, "The Indiana Primary and the Indianapolis Newspapers—A Report in Detail," *Columbia Journalism Review*, (Summer 1968), 11–17.

[2]The quotation from Gideon Sjoberg was delivered at a conference on "Ethics and Communication" at the University of Texas at Austin, March 5, 1975, sponsored jointly by the University of Texas Center for Communication Research and the Shell Companies Foundation Incorporated.

[3]Alfred G. Smith, "The Ethic of the Relay Men," in *Communication: Ethical and Moral Issues*, ed. Lee Thayer (London: Gordon and Broach Science Publishers London, 1973), pp. 313–24.

[4]Alice E. Courtney and Thomas W. Whipple, "Women in TV Commercials," *Journal of Communication*, 24 (Spring 1974), 110–18.

[5]William J. O'Donnell and Karen J. O'Donnell, "Update: Sex-Role Messages in TV Commercials," *Journal of Communication*, 28 (Winter 1978), 156–58.

[6]Cheris Kramer, "Stereotypes of Women's Speech: The Word from Cartoons." Paper presented at the annual meeting of the Speech Communication Association, Chicago, Illinois, December 1974.

[7]Craig Aronoff, "Old Age in Prime Time," *Journal of Communication*, 24 (Autumn 1974), 86–87.

[8]For a source of articles and references on the subject, consult the *Journal of Communication*, 24 (Autumn 1974).

[9]James A. Peterson, "Guide to TV Viewing," *Modern Maturity*, (April—May 1974), 44–46.

Index

a

Aaker, David A., 259
ABC (American Broadcasting Company), 14, 51, 126, 314
Abel, Elie, 371
Aberg, Leif, 427n
A. C. Nielsen Company, 137
Acta Diurna, 19
Action for Children's Television (ACT), 126
Actions Alert, 332
Activity Commodity Trading News (ACT), 306
Adams, Gibbs, 362
Adams, Dr. John B., 356, 428n
Adams, President John Quincy, 149
Adler, Richard, 298
The Adventures of Dollie, 164
Advertising Council, 244
Advertising Journal, 359
Aeropagitica, 21
Agnew, Spiro, 336
Airport, 197; *Airport 1975*, 198
Aitken, Hugh G. J., 116
Alexanderson, Ernst, 98
Allegheny College, 31
Allen, Eric W., 425n
Alphabets, 2

American Association of Advertising Agencies (A.A.A.A.), 255
American Gas Association, 257
American Society of Composers, Authors, and Publishers (ASCAP), 223, 335
Anderson, Jack, 397
Annie, 199
Applause, 179
Archer, Frederick Scott, 144
Armour, Richard, 94
Armstrong, Edwin, 107
Aronoff, Craig, 429n
The Arrival of a Train, 161
Arsenal, 175
Arthur, William B., 369
Aspen Institute for Humanistic Studies, 292
Aspen Institute Program on Communications and Society, 336
Associated Press (AP), 38
Astaire, Fred, 183
AT&T (American Telephone and Telegraph Company), 102, 284
Atkin, Charles K., 387, 429n
Atlanta Constitution, 36
Atlanta Journal, 109
Atlantic cable, effect on newspapers, 25–26, 78
Audience, specialized, 13

Audio actuality, 303
Audion tube, 98
Austin-Lett, Genelle, 17

b

Babb, Laura Longley, 276, 415
Babe, Robert E., 298
Baer, Walter S., 298
Baker, Nicolas, 94
Ball-Rokeach, Sandra, 378, 428n
Bambi, 181
Bandura, Albert, 429n
The Bank Dick, 182
Bantam Books, 91
Barasch, Kenneth L., 259
The Barbarian, 183
Barbarella, 196
Bardan, A. M., 259
Barney, Ralph D., 415
Barnouw, Erik, 116, 140
Barron, Jerome A., 371, 428n
*Barron's National Business Financial
    Weekly*, 51
Barrymore, Lionel, 178
The Bastard, book cover, 87
Beach Party, 194
Beadle's dime novel, *illus.*, 85
Beadle, E. F., 93
The Beat Generation, 190
Beatles, The, 220
Becker, Lee B., 17
Becquerel, Alexandre Edmond, 117
Beef, 68; *illus.*, 70
Behrens, John C., 277
Bell, Chichester, 210
Belle de Jour, 197
Ben Hur, 170, 189
Benchley, Peter, 198
Benjamin, Curtis G., 94
Benny, Jack, 105, 108
Berelson, Bernard, 377
Berger, Asa, 320
Berkowitz, Leonard, 429n
Berliner, Emile, 212; *photo*, 213
Bern, Walter, 371
Bernard, T. N., 148, 149
Bicentennial Series, 85–86
Billboard, 225, 228
Billy Jack, 192
Billy Jack Goes to Washington, 194
Birds, The, 185
Birghden, Johann von den, 20
The Birth of a Nation, 165–167, 197
Bittner, Denise A., 116
Bittner, John R., 116

Black press, 28–32
Blackboard Jungle, 189
Blake, G. E., 206
Blodgett, Richard, 158
The Blonde Venus, 183
Blondie, 309
Bloom, Paul N., 259
Blow Up, 195
The Blue Angel, 183
Blumler, Jay G., 392
Bly, Nellie, 32
Bob and Carol and Ted and Alice, 196
Bogart, Humphrey, 183
Bohn, Thomas W., 201
Bollier, David, 54
Bond, Donovan H., 54
Bondanella, Peter, 201
Bonnie and Clyde, 196
Born Reckless, 190
Bosmajian, Haig A., 342
Boston News-Letter, 23
Botein, Michael, 342
Boudinot, Elias, 29
Bourke-White, Margaret, 155
Brady, Mathew, 149, 157
The Brass Check, 349
Brend, Thomas, 83
Bringing Up Father, 311
Broadcast Management and Engineering, 69
Broadcast Music, Inc. (BMI), 223, 335
Broadcasting, 69
Broadway Melody 1938, 183
Brown, David, 198
Brown, James, 197
Brown, Lee, 415
Brown, Roscoe Lee, 197
Bruccoli, Matthew, 94
Bryan, William Jennings, 108, 311
Buenhogar, 66
Bullet, 196
Burke, James Henry, 94
Burns, George, 108
Business Week, 61
Butch Cassidy and the Sundance Kid, 192
Buz Sawyer, 309
Bwana Devil, 188

c

The Cabinet of Dr. Caligari, 173
Cable, 14
Cagney, James, 183
Califano, Joseph A., 371
Calotype (photography), 144
Camille, 183
Campbell, Robert, 320

Carnal Knowledge, 197
Carnegie Commission for Educational Television, 106
Carnegie Commission on the Future of Public Broadcasting, 136
Carrico, J. Paul, 381
Carter, President Jimmy, 125
Caruso, Enrico, 219
Cat on a Hot Tin Roof, 189
Cater, Douglass, 393
Cathcart, Robert, 17
The Catholic Voice, 71
Cavallo, Robert M., 158
Caxton Press, 92
Caxton, William, 21
CBS (Columbia Broadcasting System), 120, 122, 299
Century Magazine, 147
Chaffee, Steven, 140, 393
Chaney, David, 381, 393
Channel capacity, wire service, 308
Chaplin, Charlie, 167–169; *photo*, 168
Chapple, Steve, 231
Charlie Chan, 173
Chase, Cochrane, 259
Chayes, Abram, 292, 427n
Cherokee Phoenix, illus., 31
Chess Fever, 175
Chicago Business, 65
Chicago, rock group, 229
Chicago Tribune, 311
Chief Crazy Horse, 190
Cincinnati Gazette, 33
Cinemascope, 188
Cinematographe, 161
Cinerama, 187
Citizen Kane, 38; *illus.*, 186
Citrus and Vegetable Magazine, 68
City magazine, 69
City Woman, 13–14
CKXL, 297
Clark, Dick, 231
Clark, E. E. Frazer, Jr., 94
Clark, Garry E., 232
Claude, Barbara Hall, 116
Clearance ratio, 316
Cleopatra, 189
A *Clockwork Orange*, 194
Close Encounters of the Third Kind, 199
Coaxial cable, 282
Cochran, Wendell, 94
Coe, Brian, 158
Coffy, 197
Cohen, Bernard C., 429n
Cohen, Marshall, 202
Colgate-Palmolive Company, 125
Collier's Weekly, 59, 148

Color television, *photo of first sets*, 121
Colorado Springs Gazette, 19
Columbia Journalism Review, 273
Commodity News Service, 306
Communication model, 7
Communications Satellite Act of 1962, 293
Comstock, George, 140, 390, 393, 429n
Cooper, Gary, 183
Coquette, 171
Corantos, 21
Corder-Bolz, Charles R., 429n
Cornish, Reverend Samuel, 28
Corporation for Public Broadcasting (CPB), 106, 132, 136
Cosmopolitan, 64, 406; Spanish edition, 65
Costello, Delores, 178
Costello, Helene, 178
Country Gentleman, 58
Courtney, Alice E., 406, 429n
Cox Broadcasting Corporation, 108
Craig, Daniel, 300
Crawford, Joan, 183
Creature from the Black Lagoon, 188; *illus.*, 188
Crock, Stan, 428n
Cronkite, Walter, 299
Cros, Charles, 209
Crowd estimation, 263
Csida, Joseph, 232
Current, Karen, 158
Curtis, Dr. Lindsay, 312
Curtis Publishing Company, 58
Custer's Last Fight, 171

d

Daguerre, Louis, 143
Daguerreotype camera, 144
Daily Courant, 22
Daily Graphic, 153
Daily Mirror, 153
Daily Pilot, 50
Dairy Herd Management, 68
Dallas Times Herald, 50
Darrow, Clarence, 108
Davis, Clive, 232
Davis, Dennis, 393
Davis, Jefferson, 33, 149, 363
Davis, Phil, 158
Day, Benjamin, 27
Dean, James, 190; *photo*, 190
DeFleur, Melvin, 378, 428n
De Forest, Lee, 98; *photo*, 99; *photo with sound motion picture camera*, 176
DeLozier, Wayne M., 17, 259
DelPolito, Carolyn M., 17
DeMille, Cecil B., 171

Demographic Networks (ABC radio), 104
Denisoff, R. Serge, 232
Dennis the Menace, 309, 310
Denver Post, 311
Dessauer, John P., 94
Destiny, 174
Destry, 190
Detroit News, 100
The Devil in Miss Jones, 197
The Devil is a Woman, 183
Devol, Kenneth S., 371
Dichter, Harry, 232
Dick Tracy, 309
Dickinson, Larry, 362
Dickson, William, 160, 176
Dickstein, Morris, 201
Dietrich, Marlene, 183
Direct mail, 255
Dirty Harry, 196
Disney, Walt, 180–182
Distilled Spirits Council of the United States,
   Inc., 244, 249
Documerica, *photo*, 156
Don Juan, 177
Doonesbury, 309
Douglas, William O., 354
Dovzhenko, Alexander, 175
Dow Jones Books, 51
Dow Jones–Bunker Ramo News Retrieval Ser-
   vice, Inc., 51
Downie, Leonard, 54, 277
Dreyer, Carl, 116, 175, 320
Drop cable, 282
Duck Soup, 183
Dumbo, 182
Dunagin's People, 310
Dunlap, Orrin, 116
Dunn, Lloyd, 232
Dunn, S. W., 259
Dygert, J. H., 277

e

Earthquake, 197
Eastman Dry Plate Company, 145
Eastman, George, 144, 160
Eastman Kodak Company, 144–145
Easy Rider, 194
Edey, Maitland, 158
Edison, Thomas, 160, 161, 176, 207
Edon, Clifton C., 158
Eidsvik, Charles, 201
Eisenstaedt, Alfred, 156
Electronic News Gathering (ENG), 129; *photos*,
   130–131
Emerson, Miles, 393

Emery, Edwin, 54, 152, 426n
Emery, Michael, 54, 152, 426n
Emmet, Richard, 359
English, Earl, 277
Epstein, Edward J., 320
Erskine, John, 347
Estes, Billie Sol, 358
Estren, James, 320
Ewen, Stuart, 259
Exorcist, 195

f

Fairbanks, Douglas, 171, 183
Fairness Doctrine, 246
Falana, Lola, 197
Fang, Irving E., 116
Fantasia, illus., 181
The Far Country, 190
Farm Radio News, 306
The Farmer Takes a Wife, 173
Farnsworth, Philo, 119
Farr, William, 354
"Fat Albert and the Cosby Kids," 386
FCC (Federal Communications Commission),
   107, 120, 128, 230, 247, 271, 280, 284, 285,
   326–330, 402; *illus.*, 326
FCC Report on Chain Broadcasting, 103
Febure, Lucien, 94
Federal Radio Commission, 325
Federal Trade Commission (FTC), 247, 248
Feedback, 11
Feeding Baby, 161
Fellini Satyricon, 195
Feshbach, Seymour, 429n
Fessenden, Reginald A., 98
Fiber optics, 280
Fields, W. C., 182
Filler, Louis, 54
Fleming, J. Ambrose, 98
Flesh and the Devil, 170
Foolish Wives, 171
Forbes, 70
Ford Foundation, 132
Ford, Frederick W., 427n
Fortune, 70
Fotonovel, *illus. of store display*, 89
Four Theories of the Press, 344
Fourzon, Pamela, 201
Fowles, J., 259
Fox, Walter, 54
Foxy Brown, 197
Frank Leslie's Illustrated News, 146
Franklin, Marc A., 371
Freebies, 269–270
Freedom's Journal, illus., 29

The French Connection, 195
The Freshman, 169
Friedman, Leslie J., 415
Friendly, Fred, 320
Fry, Ron, 201

g

Gable, Clark, *photo*, 185
Galnoor, Itzhak, 415
Gannett, 49
Gans, Herbert J., 277
Gantz, Walter, 387, 429n
Garbo, Greta, 183
Garland, Judy, 183
Garofalo, Reebee, 231
Gatekeeper, 10–11
Gaudet, Hazel, 377
Gaynes, Martin J., 371
Gelatt, Roland, 232
Georgia Gazette, 19
Geostationary satellite, 290
Gerbner, George, 389
Giannetti, Louis D., 165, 201
Gilbert, John, 170
Gillespie, Gilbert, 298
Gillmor, Donald M., 371, 428
Girls Town, 190
Gobright, Lawrence A., 33
The Godfather, 195
Goldmark, Peter C., *photo*, 217
Gold syndicates, 312
Gone With the Wind, 185–187; *photo*, 185, 189
Good Housekeeping, Spanish edition
  (*Buenhogar*), 66
Gould, Lewis L., 158
Grace, Roger M., 428n
The Graduate, 194
Grain Information News, 306
Grant, Barry K., 201
Graphophone, 210
The Great Train Robbery, *illus.*, 163
Greb, Gordon B., 100
Greed, 171
Greeley, Horace, 33
Green/Associates Advertising, Inc., 258
Green, Beverly, 258
Greffe, Richard, 158
Gregory, John, 305
Grey, David, 277
Grier, Pamela, 197
Griffith, David Wark, 164–167
Grin and Bear It, 310
Groth, Otto, 19, 22
Grotta, Gerald L., 425n

A *Guide for the Married Man*, 196
Gumpert, Gary, 17

h

Hach, C., 277
Hackett, Alice Payne, 94
Hage, George, 277
Halberstam, David, 277
Haley, Bill, 219, 221
Halftone, *illus.*, 151
Hallelujah!, 179
Hallmark, Clayton L., 298
Hamblin, Dora Jane, 77
Hamilton, Andrew, 24
Hanneman, Gerhard J., 17
Happy Hooligan, 311
Hardware Retailer, 68
Hardware Retailing, 74
Hardy, Oliver, 169–170; *photo*, 170
Harless, Jim, 275
Harlow, Jean, 183
Harper's Weekly, 146
Harris, Benjamin, 22
Harris, Morgan, 259
Hauptmann, Bruno Richard, 357
Hawks, Howard, 183; *photo*, 184
Hearst, William Randolph, 36, 37, 310
Hello Dolly, 192
Hell's Hinges, 171
Henderson, William, 232
Herrold, Charles, *photo*, 100
Hertz, Heinrich, 97
Herzog, Herta, 383, 429n
Heston, Charlton, 198
Hindenburg, 198
Hit Parade, The, 15
Hitchcock, Alfred, 183, 195; *photo*, 184
Hockman, Sandra, 415
Hohenberg, John, 55
Holiday, Billie, 197
Home terminal, 283
Hones, Alexander, 300
Hood, Stuart, 116
Horn, Maurice, 320
Hotel–Motel News, 69
Hottelet, Richard C., 105
House Beautiful, 258
House of Wax, 188
Hovland, Carl, 375, 428n
Howard, Roy, 39
"Howdy Doody," 122; *photo*, 123
Hubbard, Gardner, 209
Hulteng, John L., 277, 415
The Hunchback of Notre Dame, 170
The Huntress, 31

Hyde, Stuart W., 140
Hyman, Allen, 342

i

I Am Curious Yellow, 197
"I Love Lucy," 122
Illustrated Daily News, 153
Indian pictographics, 2
Indian press, 29–30
Indianapolis Star, 396
Industrial TV, *photo*, 138
Informer, 183
International Telecommunications Union
    (ITU), 321, 341
Interpersonal communication, 7, 9–10
In the Heat of the Night, 197
Intolerance, 165–167; *illus.*, 166
Intrapersonal communication, 7, 8–9
Irma La Douce, 197
It Came From Outer Space, 188
It Happened One Night, 183
ITT Continental Baking Company, 247
Ives, Frederic E., 150
Izvestiya, 351

j

Jacobson, Harold K., 427
Jakes, John, 85–87; *illus.*, 86
Jaws, 198
The Jazz Singer, 177
Jefferson, Thomas, 83, 347
Joe Kidd, 196
Johnson, Eldridge, 214
Johnson, George W., 219
Johnston, Donald F., 371
Johnstone, John W. C., 277
Jolson, Al, 177
Jones, James Earl, 197
Julian, Joseph, 116
Juliet Jones, 309
Juliet of the Spirits, 195
Junkets ("freebies"), 269–270
Jupiter, *photos of surface*, 6
"Juvenile Jury," 122

k

Kahan, Stuart, 158
Kahn, Frank J., 343
Kaltenborn, H. V., 105
Karp, Patti, 259
Katz, Elihu, 380, 392, 428n
Katzenjammer Kids, 311

Katzman, Natan, 140, 393
KCBS, 100
KDKA, 101, 293, 324
Keaton, Buster, 169–170, 178
Kefauver, Estes, 388
Keimer, Samuel, 23
Keith, Brian, 199
Kelley, Jerome E., 77
Kennedy, George, 197
Kennedy, President John F., 124
Kennedy, Senator Robert, 124
Kershaw, Andrew, 241, 242, 426n
Kesten, Paul, 105
KGO, 314
Kicker story, 303
Kimbrough, Marvin, 77
Kinetograph, 160
Kinetoscope, 160
King Features Syndicate, 308, 311
King, Martin Luther, 388
Kippax, Susan, 429n
Kirsch, Donald, 277
KISS, 221
Klapper, Joseph, 429n
KLAS-TV, 359
Koster's and Bial's Music Hall, 162
KQV, 314
Kramer, Cheris, 429n
Krasilovsky, William, 232
Krasnow, Erwin G., 343
Kraus, Sidney, 393
Krauss, Werner, 173
KRON-TV, 360
Kubrick, Stanley, 194
KUHT, 133
"Kukla, Fran and Ollie," 122
KXYZ, 314
KYW, 102

l

La Dolce Vita, 195
Ladies' Home Journal, 406
Landau, Martin, 199
Landis, Cullen, 178
Lane, Allen, 88
Lang, Fritz, 174
Langford, Michael, 158
L'Arroseur Arrose, 161
Laskin, Paul L., 292, 427n
The Last Picture Show, 196
Last Tango in Paris, 197
Laswell, Harold D., 17
Latham loop, 162
Laudon, Kenneth C., 415
Laugh-O-Grams, 180
Laurel, Stan, 169–170; *photo*, 170

Lazarsfeld, Paul, 377
Leaving the Lumiere Factory, 161
LeDuc, Don R., 298, 343
Lee, Stan, 320
Leese, Elizabeth, 201
Leetham, J. A., 362
Leigh, Vivien, *photo*, 185
Leive, David M., 343, 427n
LeRoy, Mervyn, 189
Lesser, Gerald S., 393
Levy, Mark R., 383, 384, 429n
Lewis, Alfred Allan, 55
Lewis, Fulton Jr., 106
Leymore, Varda Langholz, 259
Libel, seditious, 24
Lichty, Lawrence W., 116
Life, 57, 58; *cover illus.*, 155
The Life of an American Fireman, 163
The Lights of New York, 178
Lillies of the Field, 197
Lincoln, Abraham, 33, 149
Lindbergh, Charles, 357
Listerine, 247
Little King, The, 309
Little Lord Fauntleroy, 171
Littlefield, James E., 260
Livestock Feed and Market News, 306
Loevinger, Lee, 427n
London, Mel, 201
The Lone Ranger, 108
Longley, Lawrence D., 343
Look, 57, 58, 369
Los Angeles Times, 50, 311
Louisville Journal–Courier, 36
Lovett, Lee G., 427n
Loy, Myrna, 183
Luce, Henry R., 154
Lujac, Larry, 112
Luks, George B., 37
Lull, James T., 427n
Lumber Instant News, 306
Lumiere, Louis, 160
Lupinski, Lucian, *photo*, 59

m

Macy, John W., 320
Mad Love, 183
Maddox, Richard L., 144
Magazines, as network businesses, 316
Magnum Force, 196
Maisel, Richard, 15, 425n
Malden, Karl, 199
Man Who Knew Too Much, The, 185
Marconi, Guglielmo, 96, 97; *illus. of early transmitter*, 96
Marettes, Jacques M., 288

The Mark of Zorro, 171
Marmaduke, 310
Martin, Dean, 197
Martin, Henri Jean, 94
Marx, Chico, 182
Marx, Groucho, 182
Marx, Harpo, 182
"The Mary Tyler Moore Show," 125
Mary Worth, 309
Maryland Gazette, 23
Marzolf, Marion, 55
M.A.S.H., 192
Mast, Gerald, 202
Mate, Rudolph, 175
Maxfield, Joseph P., 215
McCable, John, 202
McCarthy, Senator Joseph, 124
McClure's magazine, 31
McCombs, Maxwell E., 17, 140, 393, 277
McCormick, Robert, 108
McCue, George, 232
McEwen, William J., 17
McGowan, John J., 343
McGuffy Reader, *illus.*, 84
McGuffey, William Holmes, 83
McLuhan, Marshall, 126
Melies, Georges, 162
Merrill, John C., 277, 415
Metropolis, 174
Metropolitan, 173
Metzler, Ken, 277
Meyer, Phillip, 277
Meyer, Susan E., 77
"Mickey Mouse Club," 122, 123
Midnight Cowboy, 194
Milgram, Stanley, 393
Miller, Mark, 429n
Milton, John, 21, 347; *illus.*, 347
Milwaukee Journal, 35
Mister Rogers' Neighborhood, 133
Mobil Oil, 249, 397
Model Railroader, 70
Monaco, James, 202
The Monster, 170
Montana Farmer-Stockman, 67
Morse, Samuel, 5, 25, 97, 149
Morse telegraph, 207
Mortensen, C. David, 17
Mortgage Bankers Association, 257
Mosco, Vincent, 343
Mott, Frank Luther, 425n
Murray, John P., 429n
Murrow, Edward R., 128; *photo*, 129
Mutual Broadcasting System (MBS), 14
Mutual Review, 74
Muybridge, Eadweard, 160
My Little Chickadee, 182
Myers, John G., 259

n

National Aeronautics and Space Administration (NASA), 6
National Association of Broadcasters (NAB), 127, 244, 246, 353, 404; codes, 127–128
National Broadcasting Company (NBC), 14, 126
National Educational Television, 132
National Endowment of the Arts, 136
National News Council, 368
National Observer, 396
National Public Radio (NPR), 106, 136
National Science Foundation, 136
The Navigator, 169
Nebergall, Roger E., 393
Nelson, Ralph, 197
Nelson, Roy Paul, 77, 320
New England Courant, 23
New Orleans Picayune, 33
New Woman, 65
New York Daily Graphic, 150
New York Morning Herald, 27, 33
New York Morning Journal, 37
New York Times, 86, 186, 311, 395, 409
New York Times Company, 49
New York World, 36
New Yorker, 406
Newcomb, Horace, 140
Newman, Paul, 189
Newson, Doug, 260
Newspaper, advertising, 45–46
Newspapers, early America, 22–38; early history, 19; economic indicators, 41–43; England, 21–22; growth, 41; international origins, 21; sectionals, *illus.*, 42; technology, 46–47
Newsweek, 258
Nickelodeon, 162
Nieman, Lucius W., 35
Niepce, Joseph N., 143
A Night at the Opera, 183
9XM, 132
1941, 199
Ninotchka, 183
Nipkow, Paul G., 117
Nixon, Richard M., 368
Nobel, Edward J., 103
Noll, Roger G., 343
No More Ladies, 183
Nyhan, Michael J., 343

o

Oakes, John B., 395
O'Donnell, Karen J., 406, 429n

O'Donnell, William J., 406, 429n
Office of Telecommunications, 335, 336
Office of Telecommunications Policy, 335
Olson, May E., 94
Oppenheimer, Dr. Robert J., 128
Oregonian, 34
Osbon, B. S., 33
Ottaway Newspapers, Inc., 51
Outcault, Richard F., 310

p

Paletz, David L., 343
Paley, William S., *photo*, 104, 320
Palmer, Tony, 232
Paper-making machine, 3
Paper mill, *illus.*, 4
Parton, Dolly, 223
Passion of Joan of Arc, 175–176
Patterson, Joseph Medill, 153
Patton, 195; *illus.*, 196
Paul Pry, 31
Pay cable, 285
Peacock Press, 91
Pearson, Roberta E., 343
Peck, Merton J., 343
Pelton, Joseph W., 298
Pember, Donald, 371
Penguin books, 88
Penn, Arthur, 196
The Pennsylvania Farmer, 68
Pennsylvania Gazette, 23, 24
Penny press, 26–28
People magazine, 59
Pepper, Robert M., 140
Perigee, 290
Person to Person, 129
Peters, Jean, 94
Peterson, James A., 429n
Peterson, Richard A., 232
Peterson, Theodore, 344, 349, 371, 426n
Phantom of the Opera, 170
Phonofilm, 177
Pickett, Calder M., 55, 277
Pickford, Mary, 171
Pictographics, 2
Piepe, Anthony, 393
Pillars of the Sky, 190
Pinocchio, 182
Pittsburgh Dispatch, 32
Playboy, 64, 258, 406
Ploughing press, *illus.*, 81
Poitier, Sidney, 197
Polk, President James, 149
Pollack, Peter, 158
Polycyn, Kenneth, 298

Pool, Ithiel De Sola, 17
Poor Little Rich Girl, 171
Porter, Edwin S., 164
The Poseidon Adventure, 197
Posted bulletins, 19–20; *illus.*, 20
Postindustrial society, 15
Potemkin, 174; *illus.*, 174
Poultry and Egg News, 306
Powell, William, 183
Powers, Ron, 277, 371
Pravda, 351; *illus.*, 350, 351
Presley, Elvis, 221; *photo*, 220
Preston, Ivan L., 260
Primeau, Ronald, 140
Prince Valiant, 309
Printer's Ink, 103
Printing News, 69
Printing press, 4
Professional Woman, 65
Public Broadcasting Act of 1967, 106, 134
Public Broadcasting Service (PBS), 135, 136
Public ledger, 27
Public Relations Wire, 306
Public Service Announcements, 244
*Publick Occurrences, Both Forreign and Domes-
    tick, illus.*, 22
Pudovkin, Vsevlod I., 175
Pulitzer, Joseph, *photo*, 35
Pulitzer prizes, 35
Purdue University, 111

q

QUBE, 280
Quera, Leon, 260
The Quill, 68
Quinlan, Sterling, 320
Quo Vadis, 189

r

Radio Corporation of America (RCA), 101, 102,
    119, 120, 121, 122, 291
Radio/Television News Directors Association
    (RTNDA), 400
Rebecca of Sunnybrook Farm, 171
Red Desert, 195
Reddick, DeWitt, 371
Reid, Whitelaw, 33
Rescued from an Eagle's Nest, 164
Research, market, 235; product, 235
Retirement Living, 409
Reuter, Paul Julius, 300
Reuters, 38
Reuters news reports, 302

Rice, Stanley, 94
Richmond Enquirer, 33
Rivers, William L., 77, 343
The Robe, 188
Roberts, Chalmers, 55
Roberts, Donald, 140, 393
Robin Hood, 171
Robinson, Deanna, 382
Robinson, Deanna Campbell, 428n
Robinson, Edward G., 183
Robinson, Jerry, 320
Robinson, Richard, 231
Robinson, Sol, 116
Rogers, Everett M., 393, 429n
Rogers, Fred, 133
Rogers, Ginger, 183
Roma, 195
Rosemary's Baby, 195
Roshco, Bernard, 415
Ross, Robert D., 260
Royall, Anne, 31
Royle, Joseph, 82
Rubin, Bernard, 277, 393
Ruckelshaus, William, 371
Russell, Charles, 148
Russwurm, John, 28
Rust, Brian, 232
Ryan, R. T., 202

s

St. Hill, Thomas Nast, 320
Sampson, Henry T., 202
San Francisco Examiner, 37
Sanford, Bruce W., 371
Sarnoff, David, 101, 120; *photo*, 102
Satellite, 48; Anik, 291; apogee, 290; COM-
    SAT, 291; Courier 1-B, 288; earth station,
    288; geostationary orbit, 290; INTELSAT,
    290, 291; mobile receiving dish, *photo*, 288;
    NASA tracking, *illus.*, 289; perigee, 290; re-
    lay, 288; repeater, 288; SCORE, 288; Sput-
    nik, 287, synchronous orbit, 290; SYNCOM,
    290; Telstar, 288; Westar, 291; Western
    Union, *illus.*, 289
The Saturday Evening Post, 57, 58; *illus.*,
    60, 91
Savannah Republican, 33
Savary, Louis M., 381
Scheele, Carl W., 142
Schnurman, Ned, 369
Schramm, Wilbur, 109, 344, 350, 371, 393,
    426n
Schreiner, Samuel A., 77
Schultze, Johann H., 142
Schweinfest, George, 219

Schwoebel, Jean, 277
Science Fiction in the Cinema, 188
SCORE satellite, 288
Scott, Alan, 260
Scott, George C., 198
Scott, Harvey, 34
Scripps, E. W., 30, 38
Scripps-Howard, 49
Scripps-MacRae newspapers, 301
Scripps-MacRae Press Association, 301
Scripps, Robert Paine, 40
"See It Now," 128
Seldes, George, 349
Selznick, David O., 185
Semantic noise, 9
Seminole, 190.
Sennett, Mack, 167–169
"Sesame Street," 135; *photo*, 135
Sethi, S. Prakash, 260
Sequoyah, *illus.*, 30
Sevareid, Eric, 427
Seventh Heaven, 173
"The Shadow," 108
Shaft, 197
Shaft Goes to Africa, 197
Shaft's Big Score, 197
Shapiro, Elliot, 232
Shaw, David, 55
Shaw, Donald Lewis, 277, 393
Shaw, George Bernard, 311
"Shazam," 386
Shearer, Norma, 186
Sheba Baby, 197
Shemel, Sidney, 232
Sherif, Carolyn W., 393
Sherif, Muzafer, 393
Sherlock Jr., 169
Shick, F. L., 426n
Shoemaker, F. Floyd, 393, 429n
Shooting Times, 72
Shotland, R. Lance, 393
Siebert, Fred S., 344, 371
Signal Hill, Newfoundland, 97
Silly Symphonies, 181
Silverman, Fred, 126
Simons, Howard, 371
Sinclair, Upton, 349
Sinners in Silk, 170
Sitney, Po Adams, 202
Sjoberg, Gideon, 398, 429n
Skelton, Red, 105
Smight, Jack, 198
Smith, Alfred G., 298, 429n
Smith, Anthony, 55
Smith, Bill, 232
Smith, Robert R., 140
Smithsonian Institution, 136

Snow, Marcellus S., 298
Snow White and the Seven Dwarfs, 181
Society, functional requirements, 3
Society of National Association Publications
   (SNAP), 74
Song of the South, 182
The Sound of Music, 166; *illus.*, 191
The Southern Illustrated News, 146
Space 1999, 199
Spielberg, Steven, 198, 199
Split (wire service), 303
Sports Illustrated, 63
Sprague, Janet, 17
Sputnik, 287
Stambler, Irwin, 232
Standing press, *illus.*, 81
Stanford Daily, 368
Stanford University, Communication Research
   Center, 1
"Star Trek," 89, 90, 91
Star Wars, 198
Stark, Robert, 158
State Times, 362
Station program cooperative (SPC), 317
Steamboat Willie, 180
Stedman, Raymond William, 140
Steiger, Rod, 197
Stein, Aletha, 140
Steinberg, S. H., 94
Stephenson, William, 381, 382, 428
Sterling, Christopher H., 116
Stewart, Jimmy, 183, 190
Stewart, Rod, 223
Stewart, Walt, 360
Stockbridge, Jane, 148, 149
Strickland, Stephen, 393
Stromgren, Richard L., 201
Strong, H. A., 145
Stubblefield, Nathan, 98
Sullivan, Constance, 158
Summer, Donna, 222
Swisshelm, Jane Grey, 32
System of communication, 3
System of defense, 3
System of production, 3

t

Talbot, William H. F., 143
Tarbell, Ida M., *photo*, 31
Tarzan, 183
Taylor, Elizabeth, 189
Tebbel, John, 94
Telegraph, 25; *photo*, 5
Teletext, 49; *illus.*, 50
Telstar, 288

The Temptress, 170
The Ten Commandments, 171
Tess of the Storm Country, 171
Theories of Mass Communication, 378
Thin Man, The, 183
The Thirty-Nine Steps, 185
Thirty Years' War, 20
Thomas, Walter L., 427n
The Three Musketeers, 171
Three Wise Guys, 183
Tiger, 309
Tillie and Gus, 182
Time, 66
Times of London, 26
Times Mirror Company, 49
Titon, Jeff Todd, 232
To Sir with Love, 197
Topping, Malachi, 116
The Towering Inferno, 197
Tracy, Spencer, 183
Trager, Robert, 371
The Tramp, 168, 169
Transportation, 3
Tri-ergon process, 177
Trip to the Moon, 163
Truman, President Harry S., 293
Turner, Ted, 287
Turow, Joseph, 94
Twentieth-Century Fox, 177
2001: A Space Odyssey, 194
Tyler, John, 149

U

Udell, Jon G., 425n
Ullyett, Kenneth, 116
Un Chien Andalou, 175
United Features Syndicate, 308
United Press International (UPI), 38
University of Oregon, 275, 382
University of Tennessee Press, 92
University of Wisconsin, 132; WHA AM,
    TV, 100
Universum Film A. G. (UFA), 173

V

Van Doren, Mamie, 190
Vandercook, John, 39
Very high frequency (VHF) transmission, 279
Victor Talking Machine Company, 214
Vidor, King, 179
Virginia Gazette, 23, 83, 345
Vitascopy, 162

Von Stroheim, Eric, 171
Vyvyan, R. N., 116

W

WABC, 314; TV, 354
Wall Street Journal, 41, 287; Asian Edition, 43
Wallestein, Gerd D., 343
Walters, Richard, 429n
War on the Plains, 171
Warm, Hermann, 175
Warner Brothers, 177
Warner, Daniel S., 260
Washington Post, 311, 369
Waxworks, 174
Wayne, John, 183, 190
WBAA, 111
WBBM-TV, 396
WBZ, 102
WCBS-TV, 369
WDY, 102
WEAF, 102
Weiner, Richard, 260, 320
Weintraub, Neil A., 382
Weintraub, Neil T., 428n
Weissman, Dick, 232
Welling, William, 158
Wendland, Michael F., 277
Wenner, Lawrence, 383, 428n
West, Mae, 182
Western Horseman, 72
Western Union, 291
WGN, 105, 108, 324
WGY, 102
WHA, 100, 106
What Price Glory?, 173
Whipple, Thomas W., 406
Whitcomb, Ian, 232
Whitcover, Jules, 429n
Why Change Your Wife?, 171
Wicker, Tom, 277
Wiio, Osmo, 321, 427n; *model*, 322–324
The Wild Bunch, 196
Will, Thomas, 343
Williams, Herbert Lee, 55
Williams, Paul N., 277
Willis, Donald L., 343
Willwerth, James, 232
Winick, Charles, 393
Winick, Mariann P., 393
WLS, 314
WLW, 105
Wolseley, Ronald E., 77
Wong, Sybil, 415
Wood, Natalie, 199
WOR, 105

WQED-TV, 133
Wright, John S., 260
WTMJ, 125
W2XBS, 119
Wurtzel, Alan, 140
WWJ, 100, 101
WXYZ, 105, 314

y

Yale Daily News, 309
Yellow journalism, 36–38

"Yellow Kid," 37, 310, 311
The Yellow Submarine, 311
Young, Robert, 183

z

Zanuck, Richard, 198
Zenger, John Peter, 24
Zipcode, magazine marketing, 62; *illus.*, 63
Zuckman, Harvey L., 371
Zworykin, Vladimir K., 119